EX·LIBRIS·SUNE·GREGERSEN

Adjectives in Germanic and Romance

Linguistik Aktuell/Linguistics Today (LA)

Linguistik Aktuell/Linguistics Today (LA) provides a platform for original monograph studies into synchronic and diachronic linguistics. Studies in LA confront empirical and theoretical problems as these are currently discussed in syntax, semantics, morphology, phonology, and systematic pragmatics with the aim to establish robust empirical generalizations within a universalistic perspective.

For an overview of all books published in this series, please see
http://benjamins.com/catalog/la

General Editors

Werner Abraham
University of Vienna /
Rijksuniversiteit Groningen

Elly van Gelderen
Arizona State University

Advisory Editorial Board

Josef Bayer
University of Konstanz

Cedric Boeckx
ICREA/UB

Guglielmo Cinque
University of Venice

Liliane Haegeman
University of Ghent

Hubert Haider
University of Salzburg

Terje Lohndal
Norwegian University of Science
and Technology

Christer Platzack
University of Lund

Ian Roberts
Cambridge University

Lisa deMena Travis
McGill University

Sten Vikner
University of Aarhus

C. Jan-Wouter Zwart
University of Groningen

Volume 212

Adjectives in Germanic and Romance
Edited by Petra Sleeman, Freek Van de Velde and Harry Perridon

Adjectives in Germanic and Romance

Edited by

Petra Sleeman
University of Amsterdam

Freek Van de Velde
University of Leuven

Harry Perridon
University of Amsterdam

John Benjamins Publishing Company
Amsterdam / Philadelphia

The paper used in this publication meets the minimum requirements of the American National Standard for Information Sciences – Permanence of Paper for Printed Library Materials, ANSI z39.48-1984.

CIP data is available from the Library of Congress.

Linguistik Aktuell/Linguistics Today, ISSN 0166-0829 ; v. 212
ISBN 978 90 272 5595 2 (Hb ; alk. paper)
ISBN 978 90 272 7068 9 (Eb)

© 2014 – John Benjamins B.V.
No part of this book may be reproduced in any form, by print, photoprint, microfilm, or any other means, without written permission from the publisher.

John Benjamins Publishing Co. · P.O. Box 36224 · 1020 ME Amsterdam · The Netherlands
John Benjamins North America · P.O. Box 27519 · Philadelphia PA 19118-0519 · USA

Table of contents

Foreword	VII
The adjective in Germanic and Romance: Development, differences and similarities *Freek Van de Velde, Petra Sleeman & Harry Perridon*	1

PART I. Change

The adjective-adverb interface in Romance and English *Martin Hummel*	35
The position proper of the adjective in Middle English: A result of language contact *Carola Trips*	73
Strong and weak adjectives in Old Swedish *Ulla Stroh-Wollin & Rico Simke*	95
The resilient nature of adjectival inflection in Dutch *Freek Van de Velde & Fred Weerman*	113

PART II. Variation

On the properties of attributive phrases in Germanic (and beyond) *Volker Struckmeier & Joost Kremers*	149
From participle to adjective in Germanic and Romance *Petra Sleeman*	171
The mixed categorial behavior of *cel* + participle in Romanian *Dana Niculescu*	199
Inside and outside – Before and after: Weak and strong adjectives in Icelandic *Alexander Pfaff*	217
Adjectives in German and Norwegian: Differences in weak and strong inflections *Dorian Roehrs & Marit Julien*	245

Cross-linguistic variation in agreement on Germanic predicate adjectives	263
Erik Schoorlemmer	
Author index	279
Subject index	283

Foreword

Most of the papers in this volume were presented at the two-day conference *Adjectives in Germanic and Romance: variation and change*, which took place in March 2012 at the University of Amsterdam, and which was organized by Harry Perridon, Petra Sleeman, and Freek Van de Velde, in collaboration with the *ACLC* (*Amsterdam Center for Language and Communication*) research group *DP/NP in the Germanic and Romance languages: structure, semantics, acquisition and change*. We gratefully acknowledge the financial support of the ACLC.

A large number of people have assisted us in editing this volume. We would like to thank Kees Vaes of Benjamins Publishers and the editors of the series, Werner Abraham and Elly van Gelderen, for their help in preparing the publication of this volume. We are particularly indebted to the reviewers of the papers: Artemis Alexiadou, Karin Beijering, Elma Blom, Paul Boucher, Patricia Cabredo-Hofherr, Robert Cirillo, Evie Coussé, Marijke De Belder, Ulrike Demske, Hubert Haider, Ans van Kemenade, Olaf Koeneman, Peter Lauwers, Elisabeth van der Linden, Susanne Lohrmann, Mihaela Marchis, Claire Meul, Kristel Van Goethem, Arjen Versloot, Johanna Wood, Hedde Zeijlstra. We are also very grateful to Leston Buell for proofreading the final manuscript of this book.

Amsterdam, August 2013
Petra Sleeman
Freek Van de Velde
Harry Perridon

The adjective in Germanic and Romance
Development, differences and similarities

Freek Van de Velde[1], Petra Sleeman[2] & Harry Perridon[2]
[1]Research Foundation FWO / University of Leuven / [2]ACLC / University of Amsterdam

In this introductory chapter the similarities and differences in the development and the current behavior of the adjective in Germanic and Romance, both within and between the language families, are discussed. A deeper analysis suggests that what seem to be differences may in fact be similarities and vice versa. Topics that are discussed are the emergence of the adjective as a category, the distinction between attributive and predicative adjectives, the position of adjectives within the noun phrase, and adjectival inflection. This introduction forms the basis for the chapters that follow and in which current visions on variation and change with respect to the adjective in Germanic and Romance are presented in more detail.

1. Introduction

In this introductory chapter we discuss recent and more firmly established insights in the historical development and the synchronic analysis of the adjective in Germanic and Romance. This chapter consists of a diachronic part (§2) and a synchronic part in which analyses of the adjective in its current use are discussed (§3–4). Topics discussed are the adjective as a category, the distinction between attributive and predicative adjectives, the position of the adjective within the noun phrase, and adjectival inflection. This discussion leads to a short presentation of the papers contained in this volume at the end of the chapter (§5).

2. Development

2.1 Adjectives in Romance and Germanic

While some scholars maintain, often on theory-dependent grounds, that adjectives constitute a universal category (see e.g. Baker 2003), the surface realization in ancient Indo-European dialects of lexemes that are uncontroversially held to be adjectives in the present-day Romance and Germanic languages suggests that Proto-Indo-European adjectives did not constitute a separate part of speech, a view that goes back at least to Hermann Paul. This does not mean, of course, that speakers of Proto-Indo-European were not able to express properties such as "beautiful", "rich", or "black". They just did not make a morphological distinction between nouns and adjectives (see Prokosch 1939: 259), which suggests they had one part of speech category that covers both categories (Bammesberger 1992: 52; Kurzová 1993: 41; Van de Velde 2009, Chapter 6). Note, in this respect, that the old grammarians saw the adjective as a subtype of nouns (*nomen adjectivum*, see e.g. Törnqvist 1974: 324).

The situation in which there is a single, broader part of speech for what present-day Romance and Germanic languages distribute over two separate parts of speech, namely adjectives and nouns, is cross-linguistically not uncommon. Similar systems have been reported for languages such as Quechua or Turkish (see e.g. Schachter 1985; Hengeveld 1992).

The category of the adjective only emerged in the daughter languages. For Germanic, Bammesberger (1992: 52–53) writes:

> The development of the adjective is perhaps one of the most conspicuous innovations in Germanic morphology. In Germanic the adjective is not only semantically delimitated by generally expressing some "quality" (…), but it is also morphologically clearly definable.

For Romance as well, we can assume an ancestral stage in which the adjective was basically a noun (or more accurately: an undifferentiated nominal) in apposition. The situation lingers on, to some extent, in classical Latin, where declension classes of adjectives match up with nominal classes and where some adjectives do not agree for all genders, resisting full agreement control by its assumed head noun. Latin *felix* "happy" has just one form for all genders and *fortis* "brave" only has a split between neuter and non-neuter. Moreover, many a Latin lexeme is indifferent to the distinction between entity-denoting use ('noun') and property-denoting use ('adjective'), and one has to decide on the basis of the context whether, for instance, a noun like *natus* means "son" ('noun') or "born" ('adjective') (Brugmann & Delbrück 1889: 436–437, 444–448). Moreover, Latin shows cases of what has been termed 'dependency reversal', exemplified in (1), a construction in which the adjective is the controller of a noun in the genitive. This type of construction seems to be favored in languages in which adjectives are underdifferentiated from nouns (or verbs) (see Malchukov 2000: 44).

(1) *extrema*   *agminis*   LATIN
     extreme:NOM/ACC.N.PL battle:GEN.N.SG
     "the extreme battle"   (Kühner & Gerth 1963: 278)

2.2 Inflection

2.2.1 *Germanic*

The specialized adjectival morphology that Germanic developed consists of two sets of endings that are commonly referred to as the strong and weak declensions. An oft-quoted syntactic minimal pair is given in (2)–(3).[1]

(2) *hairdeis   gods*   GOTHIC
    shepherd:NOM.SG good:STRONG.NOM.M.SG
    "the good shepherd"   (John 10:11)

(3) *hairdeis   sa   goda*   GOTHIC
    shepherd:NOM.SG the:NOM.M.SG   good:WEAK.NOM.M.SG
    "the good shepherd"   (John 10:11)

An overview of the formal paradigms can be found in Prokosch (1939: 261–265) or in Ringe (2006: 281–283). The question that immediately arises is: where does this double declension come from? The weak declension draws on the stem-building *n*-suffix in nouns. It is not clear to what extent it was still productively derivational in late Proto-Indo-European, but it seems to trace back to a nominalizing suffix. As can still be seen in Greek (*strabós* "squinting" vs. *strábōn* "squinter") and Latin (*catus* "shrewd" vs. *cato* (stem: *caton*-) "the shrewd one"), the *n*-suffix indicated individual-level properties as opposed to stage-level properties (Brugmann & Delbrück 1889: 131, 424–426, 431, 437; Hirt 1927: 149ff.; Prokosch 1939: 260–161; Ranheimsæter 1945: 13–14; Nielsen 1989: 29–30; Braunmüller 2008; Perridon & Sleeman 2011: 13). These individual-level properties, denoting permanent, distinctive qualities were often used as nicknames, and as such were used in apposition to proper names. Such appositions may have led to the constituency structure in which the first element was analyzed as a dependent of the second (see also Heine & Kuteva 2007: 286–287). The origin of the strong inflection, on the other hand, is the endings in the demonstratives, which rubbed off onto other elements, through an intermediate group of semi-pronouns (Kluge 1913: 209; Prokosch 1939: 261; McFadden 2009). There is some disagreement on what the original function was of strong and weak endings in Proto-Germanic. In an early stage, the weak declension may have retained its Proto-Indo-European nominalizing function while the strong declension had evolved to become the default attributive adjectival ending (see e.g. Van de Velde 2006), but in late Proto-Germanic (Common Germanic 200–500), the system became involved in the marking of definiteness, such that the weak declension

---

1. Gothic examples have been retrieved from: ⟨http://www.wulfila.be⟩

became a marker of definiteness (Harbert 2007: 130–137), although it is not clear whether the system was really clear-cut outside the Scandinavian languages. The strong declension was neutral with regard to definiteness (Quirk & Wrenn 1969: 68; Traugott 1992: 173), but the contrast with the weak declension may have eventually related it to indefiniteness. The semantic and syntactic import of both inflectional types is the subject of several papers in this volume (see Roehrs & Julien; Schoorlemmer; Stroh-Wollin & Simke).

2.2.2 *Romance*

The diachrony of nominal inflection in Romance is largely one of morphological simplification (deflection), with a merger in the formal exponents as well as in a reduction of the functional categories, such as case, gender, and declension classes.[2] The process took place both in nouns and adjectives. In the transition from Latin to modern Romance, nouns and adjectives were reduced from five or six to two cases, from three to two genders and from five to three declension classes, with some subdivisions and relics.[3]

Romance adjectives agree with their head noun in gender, number, and – at least in Latin – in case. In most instances, gender is expressed by different endings on the adjective, except for the adjectives that derive from the third declension class in Latin (e.g. adjectives like *fortis* "brave, strong"). Here, the adjective does not have a gender contrast in Spanish (SG *fuerte*, PL *fuertes*), Italian (SG *forte*, PL *forti*) and Old French (SG *fort*, PL *forz*). In present-day French, these adjectives do distinguish between masculine and feminine, but this is a post-Latin innovation. In Middle French, the third-declension type adjectives analogically converged on adjectives like *sec* "dry", which did differentiate between masculine (Old and Modern French SG *sec*, PL *secs*) and feminine (Old French SG *seche*, PL *seches*, Modern French SG *sèche*, PL *sèches*), by adopting the schwa as a unequivocal marker of the feminine (Alkire & Rosen 2010: 191–192). Ossified relics like *grand-mère* "grand-mother" (instead of *grande-mère*), *pas grand-chose* "nothing much" (instead of *grande-chose*) or the toponym *Rochefort* (instead of *Rocheforte*) still testify to the earlier state (Alkire & Rosen 2010: 192).

---

2. One can call into question whether declension class really is a functional category, with a discernible signifié. We will not pursue the matter, and assume it is (see Carstairs-McCarthy 1994 and Enger 2013 for further discussion).

3. The decision between five or six cases in Latin depends on whether one discerns a separate vocative case.

2.3 Position with regard to the noun

The ancient appositional nature of the relationship between a lexeme referring to an entity (a 'noun') and one denoting a property (an 'adjective') (see Section 2.1) motivates a lack of hard ordering constraints in the ancestral stages of the Germanic and Romance languages. The comparative evidence provided by the old Indo-European dialects indicates that the order of modifiers and heads was flexible, and was probably determined by discourse and pragmatic factors (Fortson 2010: 154). Though there is considerable disagreement among specialists of the early stages of both language families, certain tendencies can be discerned regarding the relative order of adjectives and nouns in Germanic and Romance. In its earliest reconstructable stages, Germanic may have had a preference for adjectives following the noun (see below, Section 2.3.1), but then decidedly developed a default prenominal position for attributive adjectives. In Romance, by contrast, an original adjective–noun word order preference later flipped to a default noun–adjective order (Bauer 2009; Ledgeway 2012: 210–213 and Trips, this volume, for the development in Old French). Still, although these preferences can be perceived in the recorded history of Germanic and Romance, word order remained relatively flexible for quite some time, and both Latin and Gothic display grammatically free word order, though discontinuous structures, which are conspicuously attested in classical Latin, are far less common in Gothic, which may be explained by the time lag.[4] In the course of the early Middle Ages, Germanic and Romance developed so-called configurational word order, with a hierarchical syntactic structure in the noun phrase. The rise of configurationality in Germanic (see Faarlund 2001: 1713, among others) and in Romance (see Ledgeway 2011, 2012 among others) resulted in a designated position for adjectives, which had become inflectionally differentiated from nouns in Germanic (see Section 2.2.1). The crystallization of noun-phrase internal word order transpired gradually over the course of many centuries, and consequently, it is next to impossible to pinpoint more exactly when pragmatically determined word order became syntactically determined.

2.3.1 Germanic

For the oldest stages of Germanic, the data are equivocal. First of all, the ancestral stages of the present-day Germanic languages all could have discontinuous noun phrases (and *noun phrase* may be an anachronism here), with adjectives

---

4. Alternatively, it may simply be due to the restricted size of the Gothic textual corpus. Caution is in order here.

being expressed non-contiguously to the noun. This is attested in all branches of Germanic, but seems to be in rapid recession over time. Modern Swedish still sports this construction, though.

(4) WEST GERMANIC: OLD SAXON (Van der Horst 2008: 305)
huand it an fastaro nis erthu gitimbrid
for it on steady not.is ground built
"for it is not built on steady ground"

(5) EAST GERMANIC: GOTHIC (Behaghel 1932: 241)
dauns sijum woþi
odor we.are sweet
"we are a sweet savour"

(6) NORTH GERMANIC: OLD NORSE (Faarlund 1994: 56)
góðan eigum vér konung
good have we king
"we have a good king"

What about when the adjective is expressed contiguously to the noun? Again, we are not provided with a clear image for the earliest stages. While Hopper (1975) states that adjectives tended to precede the noun in Proto-Germanic, the adjective frequently follows the noun in the oldest Runic inscriptions and in Gothic (Harbert 2007: 127). Some scholars maintain that this was in fact the unmarked position in Gothic (Perridon & Sleeman 2011: 12), and possibly also in other branches of Germanic, especially Ancient Nordic (Faarlund 2002: 730). With regard to the situation in Gothic, however, it is not clear whether the translational interference of the Greek original in the Gothic text has been consistently factored in. The Gothic adjective *fairneis* occurs before as well as after the head noun, see (7) and (8) respectively, but in each case, the Gothic translation consistently copies the Greek word order. Still, there are informative instances of adjectives in postnominal position that are less likely to be due to interference from Greek. In (9), the Greek original has one word, rather than an adjective–noun combination, which we see in Gothic.

(7) ushraineiþ þata fairnjo beist GOTHIC
purge_out:ACT.IMP.2PL that:ACC.N.SG old:ACC.N.SG leaven:ACC.SG
"purge out therefore the old leaven" (Corinthians I 5: 7)
(GREEK: *ekkathárate tèn palaiàn zúmēn*)

(8) in beista fairnjamma GOTHIC
in leaven:DAT.SG old:DAT.N.SG
"with old leaven" (Corinthians I 5: 8)
(GREEK: *en zúmēi palaiāi*)

(9) *naudibandjom eisarneinaim*   GOTHIC
      chain:DAT.PL   iron(ADJ):DAT.PL
      "iron chains"   (Mark 5:3)
      (GREEK: *halúsei*)

One could wonder whether it is appropriate to compare pre- and postnominal position in Germanic as full alternatives: there are reasons to assume that postnominal adjectives are not syntactically integrated in the noun phrase (Harbert 2007: 127; Van de Velde 2009), so that their evidence for N–A word order in the noun phrase is limited. This view is not uncontested, though. Perridon (1996) fails to see any semantic difference between preposed and postposed adjectives in Runic Swedish, and Pfaff (this volume) argues that Modern Icelandic postposed weak adjectives are integrated in the noun phrase, while preposed strong adjectives have a predicative feel.

In sum, it seems safest to assume that Proto-Germanic did not have a 'grammaticalized' template for the position of adjectives, in the sense that left-adjacent position was a syntactic marker of dependency. "Word-position acquiring grammatical significance" (in the words of Jespersen 1993: 111) only happened later (see Van de Velde 2009 for an extensive treatment), especially in West Germanic. The diachrony of the noun phrase in North Germanic is more complex, and is open to different interpretations. Braunmüller (1994) contends that North Germanic is more ambiguous in its typological orientation in its noun phrase, having mixed SVO/SOV characteristics.[5] Indeed, in Old Nordic (7th – 15th century), adjectives could (but need not) follow the noun (see (10)), but in the modern North Germanic languages, the adjective precedes the noun, even in a rather conservative language like Icelandic (Thráinsson 1994: 166, though see Pfaff, this volume,

---

5. Braunmüller operates under the Greenbergian assumption that the relative order between adjective and noun is correlated with the order between verb and object (and subject). This insight has been contested on the basis of large typological surveys (see Dryer 1998). Characterizing languages as belonging to a major linearization type has proven to be difficult. Even among the proponents of a linearization parameter approach, in which languages can be classified as OV vs. VO, there is no consensus on how to deal with noun phrases (see Schoorlemmer, this volume). The prenominal position of attributive adjectives is prima facie evidence for assuming head-final OV organization, yet Haider (2010, Chapter 1) maintains that continental Germanic NPs are head-initial (as opposed to VPs), and draws on PP postmodifiers for making this claim. In Van de Velde (2009, Chapter 3, 2012), on the other hand, it is argued that PP postmodifiers do not qualify as diagnostics for the internal branching for the noun phrase. Compounding the difficult issues in establishing the basic word order in NPs is the fact that some scholars argue that OV vs. VO do not exhaust all the possibilities. Haider (2010, 2013) argues that ancient stages of Germanic and Romance were so-called 'T3 languages', lacking a major branching direction.

for patterns with (weak) adjectives in postposition, like (11)), underscoring the general drift in the Germanic family towards preceding attributive adjectives.

(10) *eldar stórir*   OLD NORSE
    fires great
    "great fires"   (Faarlund 1994: 54)

(11) *kreppan mikla*   ICELANDIC
    crisis great
    "the Great Depression"   (Pfaff, this volume)

In older stages of the Germanic languages, and in Western Scandinavian, see (12) and (13)–(15), respectively, the possessive adjective could follow the noun, rather than precede it. They do not qualify, however, as real adjectives anymore in present-day Germanic, and as such do not detract from the strong A–N tendency.

(12) *sunu min*   OLD ENGLISH
    son my
    "my son"

(13) *bróðir minn*   ICELANDIC
    brother my
    "my brother"

(14) *drongur mín*   FAROESE
    boy my
    "my boy"

(15) *bok-a mi*   NYNORSK
    book-the my
    "my book"

2.3.2 Romance

Latin did not have a fixed position for attributive adjectives. Though certain word order tendencies can be recognized in the relative order of adjective and noun, the position as such did not carry a grammatical meaning, as it does in the present-day Romance languages. So adjectives, including possessives, could either precede or follow the noun, or could even be separated from it in various kinds of discontinuous structures, see (16)–(18).

(16) LATIN   (Ledgeway 2012: 44)
    arbusta   per   alta
    timber.tree:ACC.PL through tall:ACC.N.PL
    "through tall timber trees"

(17) LATIN (Horace, Odes)
vitae summa brevis **spem** *nos vetat*
life:GEN.SG sum:NOM.SG short:GEN.F.SG hope:ACC.SG us:ACC forbids
incohare **longam**
commence:INF long:ACC.F.SG
"Life's brief total forbids us to cling to long-off hope"

(18) LATIN (Perridon & Sleeman 2011:4)
meo *tu epistulam dedisti* **servo**
my:DAT.SG you letter:ACC.SG gave slave:DAT.SG
"to my slave you gave a letter?"

In the transition from Latin to Romance, the noun phrase developed two designated positions for adjectives, one preceding the noun and one following the noun. It has proven notoriously difficult to define the functions of the two positions. It has been suggested that the prenominal position was dedicated to given/non-contrastive adjectives and the postnominal position to new/contrastive readings (see Ledgeway 2012:50). This, interestingly, corresponds to Fischer's (2001) account of the difference between preposed and postposed adjectives in Old English, which she claims to be motived by iconicity. Romance appears to have solidified this iconic difference by grammaticalizing it further, whereas English eventually leveled the iconic difference by discarding postnominal adjectives, after a short-lived increase in Middle English, probably as a grammatical replication from French (Trips, this volume), a certain well-known exception notwithstanding (see Section 3). Eventually this yields a marked difference between Romance, with a default postnominal position for adjectives, and a marked option of preposition, and Germanic, with a default prenominal position for adjectives, and a marked option of postposition. The present situation will be discussed in the next section.

3. The current position of adjectives with respect to the noun

In the modern Germanic languages adjectives generally appear in prenominal position, in modern Romance in postnominal position. Cinque (2010), however, argues that postnominal adjectives (and reduced relative clauses) are underlyingly prenominal. This suggests that, in fact, there is no difference between Germanic and Romance. After comparing the surface position of adjectives in modern Germanic and Romance in §3.1, we discuss Cinque's analysis in §3.2.

3.1 The surface position of adjectives

In modern Germanic, adjectives and participles generally precede the noun, while full relative clauses follow the noun (19–20). In SOV languages such as Dutch and German, adjectives and participles preceded by their complement generally also precede the noun (21):[6]

(19) *lange mensen*   DUTCH
 "tall people"

(20) *mensen die lang zijn*   DUTCH
 people that tall are
 "people who are tall"

(21) *het aan zijn broer verkochte huis*   DUTCH
 the to his brother sold house
 "the house sold to his brother"

In English, some types of adjectives and participles may or must follow the noun. Among these types are adjectives followed by a complement or an adjunct, participles and deverbal adjectives ending in the suffix *-ble* (Bolinger 1967):

(22) parents proud of their children

(23) the stars visible

In Icelandic postnominal adjectives are also accepted (see Pfaff, this volume):

(24) *málfræðingur-inn frægi*   ICELANDIC
 linguist-DEF famous
 "the famous linguist"

Other Germanic languages only marginally allow adjectives or participles in postnominal position. The Dutch example has been taken from Perridon and Sleeman (2011) and the German example from Cinque (1994), who analyze the APs in these examples as predicative attributes:

---

6. For German, see Struckmeier & Kremers (this volume). Dryer (1998) questions the relation between OV/VO and AN/NA (see Footnote 5). Delsing (1992) shows indeed that, although Swedish is an SVO language, adjectives and participles preceded by their complement are also allowed in this language (see also Cabredo Hofherr 2010). He notices, however, that these constructions are literary style in Swedish and that some speakers consider them marginal:

(i) *en över sin insats stolt försvarsadvokat*
 a over his accomplishment proud attorney.for.the.defense
 "a lawyer that is proud of his accomplishment"

(25) *hagelstenen zo groot als tennisballen*   DUTCH
       hailstones as big as tennisballs

(26) *Gewehrkugeln gross wie Taubeneier*   GERMAN
       "bullets big as pigeon eggs"

In Romance, just like full relative clauses, adjectives and participles generally follow the noun:

(27) *la casa que te gustaba*   SPANISH
       the house that you pleased
       "the house that pleased you"

(28) *la falda negra*   SPANISH
       the skirt black
       "the black skirt"

(29) *un libro leído recientemente*   SPANISH
       "a book read recently"

Some types of adjectives and adjectival participles can (or must) precede the noun. According to Bouchard (1998), in French, adjectives occurring in prenominal position modify components internal to the noun (e.g. *futur* "future", *ancien* "ex", *supposé* "alleged"), whereas those occurring in postnominal position modify the components of N as a whole (e.g. *rouge* "red", *intelligent* "intelligent"). Adjectives that can be used in both positions have both functions:

(30) a. *un bon chef*   FRENCH
          "a good chef (= good at cooking)"
    b. *un chef bon*
          "a good chef (= good on a broader scale, as a human being)"

Demonte (2008), on the basis of Spanish, suggests that in Romance prenominal modifiers receive a non-restrictive interpretation, whereas postnominal modifiers receive a restrictive reading:

(31) a. *los pretenciosos amigos de Paloma*   SPANISH
          the pretentious friends of Paloma
          "Paloma's pretentious friends" (= all Paloma's friends are pretentious)
    b. *los amigos pretenciosos de Paloma*
          the friends pretentious of Paloma
          "Paloma's pretentious friends" (= the subset of Paloma's friends who are pretentious)

In situations of language contact between a Germanic and a Romance language, the canonical position of adjectives (prenominal in Germanic vs. postnominal in

Romance) may change. Alber et al. (2012) show that in some cases of German–Italian bilingualism in northern Italy, the postnominal adjectival position seems to have become the non-marked position in the German dialect spoken there:

(32) *Disa is an korpete roat.*   CIMBRIAN OF GIAZZA
this is a sweater red
"This is a red sweater."

Bernstein (1991), on the other hand, shows that in the French dialect Walloon spoken in the southern part of Belgium the canonical position of adjectives, with the exception of ethnic adjectives, is prenominal. This might be due to the vicinity of Flemish, the Belgian variety of Dutch.[7,8]

(33) *dès malâtès bièsses*   WALLOON
"some sick animals"

Despite the opposite canonical positions of the adjective and participle in standard Germanic and Romance (prenominal in Germanic and postnominal in Romance in surface structure), they have been analyzed as underlyingly the same (Cinque 2010). Cinque's seminal work on adjectives and reduced relatives clauses in relation to Germanic and Romance is discussed in §3.2, also because it serves as a basis for the analyses presented in several papers in this volume.

3.2 Cinque's (2010) analysis of adjectives

In Cinque's (2010) analysis, adjectives and (reduced) relative clauses, both in Germanic and Romance, are underlyingly prenominal. Both are merged in the specifiers of functional projections dominating NP. Cinque (2010) makes a distinction between direct and indirect modifiers (cf. Sproat & Shih 1988) and claims that the indirect modifiers are merged in higher functional projections than the direct ones:

---

[7]. The prenominal position might also be a remnant of an earlier stage of the dialect. Boucher (2004) shows that in a late-13th-century translation of a Latin prose text in Old French, 219 modifiers are in pre-N position, whereas 33 are in post-N position in Old French. The analysis of the same text translated into Modern (19th century) French yields 39 modifiers in pre-N position and 254 modifiers in post-N position. However, in our view, another characteristic of Walloon, the schwa suffix on attributive prenominal adjectives might also be an influence of Flemish (contra Bernstein 1991, who analyzes the schwa as the overt realization of a functional head Num^0), see §4.3.

[8]. In this volume two other cases of possible syntactic influence through language contact between Germanic and Romance are discussed: adjectives in postnominal position in English (Trips) and adverbs (Hummel).

(34)

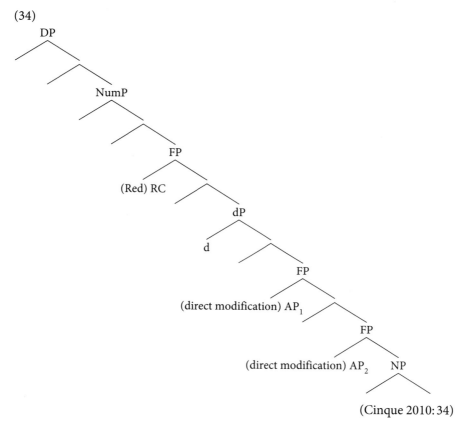

(Cinque 2010: 34)

Following Higginbotham (1985), Larson (1998), and Larson and Marušič (2004), Cinque correlates the distinction between direct and indirect modifiers with a difference in interpretation. Direct modifiers have for instance a non-restrictive, non-intersective, individual-level, and absolute interpretation, while indirect modifiers have a restrictive, intersective, stage-level, and relative reading. The a-sentences of the following examples contain direct modifiers, whereas the b-sentences exemplify indirect modifiers:

(35) a. I do nót appreciate his unsuitable acts (non-restrictive)
 b. Only his unsuitable acts were criticized (restrictive)

(36) a. Olga is a beautiful dancer = dances beautifully (non-intersective)
 b. Olga is a beautiful dancer = a beautiful person (intersective)

(37) a. the visible stars = the stars that are always visible (individual-level)
 b. the visible stars = the stars that are visible now (stage-level)

(38) a. a small mouse = small object (absolute)
 b. a small mouse = small for a mouse (relative)

According to Cinque (2010), direct modifiers only surface in prenominal position in Germanic, whereas indirect modifiers surface both in prenominal and in postnominal position (39). In Romance, indirect modifiers only surface in postnominal position, while direct modifiers surface in both positions (41):

(39) indirect – direct – NP – indirect

(40) the stars visible (stage-level)

(41) direct – NP – direct – indirect

(42) le   noiose   lezioni   di   Ferri (non-restrictive)   ITALIAN
the   boring   lessons   of   Ferri
"Ferri's boring classes"

Cinque's analysis of direct and indirect modifiers is discussed in §3.2.1 and §3.2.2, respectively.

3.2.1 Direct modifiers

Whereas Cinque (1994) proposes that the postnominal position of adjectives in Romance is the result of N-movement, Cinque (2010) proposes that the postnominal position of direct modifiers in Romance is the result of NP movement:

(43) $DP - NumP - d - AP_1 - NP_i - AP_2 - e_i$

Just like Cinque (1994), Cinque (2010) distinguishes several positions for direct modifiers. In Romance, NP obligatorily raises over, e.g. adjectives of nationality (44), optionally over adjectives of color, shape, size, value (45), but not over adjectives such as "former", "future", "alleged" (46–47). This is illustrated by the following Italian examples taken from Cinque (2010):

(44) a. *un cinese vaso
b. un vaso cinese
"a Chinese vase"

(45) a. l'enorme sagoma della cupola
b. la sagoma enorme della cupola
"the enormous outline of the cupola"

(46) a. il futuro presidente
b. *il presidente futuro
"the future president"

(47) il futuro presidente americano
"the future American president"

Cinque's (2010) roll-up/snowballing mechanism can account for the mirror adjective ordering in DPs such as (48)–(49c) (Lamarche 1991). After the NP has moved to the position above AP_2 in (44), it can move to the position dominating AP_1 pied-piping AP_2 (see also Laenzlinger 2005).

(48) a huge Chinese vase

(49) a. un enorme cinese vaso
      b. un enorme vaso$_i$ cinese e$_i$
      c. un [vaso cinese e$_i$]$_j$ enorme e$_j$

As Cinque notices himself, NP movement with direct modifiers is not motivated. Another problem with Cinque's analysis is the relation between direct and indirect modifiers and the interpretations in (35–38). Sproat and Shih's (1988) distinction between direct and indirect adjectives suggests that intersective, restrictive adjectives such as *red* in *a red dress* can be direct modifiers (see also Alexiadou & Wilder 1998). This would mean that direct modifiers can have a restrictive interpretation (see also Pfaff, this volume).

3.2.2 Indirect modifiers

Cinque (2010) claims that the postnominal position of indirect modifiers is the result of attraction of the indirect modifier to a higher position, followed by remnant movement:[9]

(50) a. [the [[recently arrived] nice Greek vases]]
      b. [the [[recently arrived]$_i$ [e$_i$ nice Greek vases]]]
      c. [the [[e$_i$ nice Greek vases]$_j$ [[recently arrived]$_i$ e$_j$]]]

In this analysis, the (remnant) movement of the NP to a position dominating the (reduced) relative clause depends on the prior movement of the relative clause itself. The relative clause only becomes postnominal (after remnant NP movement) if it is moved to a higher position. If it is not moved to a higher position, there is no (remnant) NP movement either, and the relative clause ends up in a prenominal position.

Since the final prenominal or postnominal position of the relative clause depends on its movement to a higher position, Cinque distinguishes prenominal and postnominal relative clauses on the basis of the force with which they are attracted to a higher position. More concretely, Cinque distinguishes three types of relative clauses. For English, he makes a distinction between full relative clauses, participial reduced relatives (*the letters recently sent* or *the letters sent recently*) and

---

9. Cinque calls this 'extraposition', but it is movement to the left (followed by remnant movement), instead of rightward movement as in the case of the traditional type of extraposition.

bare AP reduced relatives, such as *-ble* adjectives or adjectives such as *present*. Full relative clauses are merged in a higher position than participial reduced relatives, which are merged in a higher position than bare AP reduced relatives (which are merged in a higher position than purely adjectival, i.e. direct, modifiers of the noun):

(51)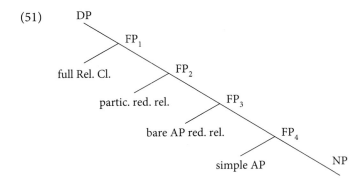

Full relative clauses in English obligatorily occur in postnominal position. This means that in this case the force of attraction is very high (52). Participial reduced relative clauses followed by a complement or adjunct also obligatorily occur in postnominal position, due to a ban on right recursion for phrases found on left branches (Emonds 1976). They are therefore also attracted with great force to a higher position (53). Participial reduced relatives not followed by a complement or adjunct optionally occur in postnominal position. This means that the force of attraction is variably high in this case (54–55). Only bare AP reduced relatives that arguably have an (invisible) right-branching structure, can occur in postnominal position (56). Truly bare AP reduced relatives cannot occur in postnominal position (unless they are stressed), which means that the force of attraction is very low (57):[10]

---

10. Cinque (2010: §6.2) proposes that indirect modifiers can be focused, which means that there is movement to Spec,FocusP, followed by remnant NP movement. This accounts for the fact that a bare adjective such as *industriosi* "industrious" in Italian can follow a DP-internal PP. If *industriosi* is not focalized, it precedes the PP. In Cinque's analysis, only indirect modifiers, but not direct modifiers, can move. On another view, if *industriosi* follows the PP, it might be a normal indirect modifier, whereas it would be a direct modifier if it precedes the PP (see the end of §3.2.1 for an objection against Cinque's distinction between direct and indirect modifiers):

(i) a. [gli [industriósi [greci [di Megara]]]]
　　b. [$_{FocP}$ industriósi$_i$ [i [e$_i$ [greci [di Megara]]]]
　　c. [[i greci di Megara]$_i$ [industriósi t$_i$]]

(52) the letters that I have sent to John
(53) the letters sent to John.
(54) the recently sent letters
(55) the letters recently sent
(56) a star visible
(57) *a colleague angry (just stepped in)

In English there seems therefore to be a relation between the internal structure of the relative clause (full – reduced – bare), i.e. its syntactic complexity (presenting (invisible) right recursion or not), and its position with respect to the noun. In Cinque's analysis, these differences are related to the force with which (reduced) relatives are attracted to the specifier of a functional projection dominating them (followed by remnant movement).

According to Cinque (2010: Chapter 5, Footnote 13), in Romance, all three types of relative clauses obligatorily move to a higher position, followed by remnant NP movement (except for highly formal registers). This means that the force of attraction is equally high for the three types of relative clauses.

Cinque's analysis of indirect modifiers raises several questions. First, why should there be a difference between the internal structure of reduced relatives in prenominal and postnominal position in English (or Germanic in general)? Why should the postnominal reduced relatives in (58) be (invisibly) right-branching, while the prenominal ones in (59) aren't? There is no difference in interpretation that would justify this distinction:

(58) a. the jewels stolen
 b. the letters recently sent
 c. the stars visible

(59) a. the stolen jewels
 b. the recently sent letters
 c. the visible stars

Cinque's assumption that postnominal reduced relatives are invisibly right-branching, might account for the fact that, in Dutch, reduced relatives generally occur in prenominal position. Dutch is an SOV language and thus left-branching. This also holds for German. Cinque (2010: Chapter 5, Footnote 8) observes that, in German, participial reduced relatives cannot occur in postnominal position, which, according to him, is a problem that has yet to be understood:[11]

---

11. Cinque observes, referring to Delsing (1993:9) that in Scandinavian adjectives or participles can occur in postnominal position if they are followed by a complement or an adjunct or are part of a coordinated structure.

(60) a. *Er is ein [sein Studium seit langem hassender] student*
he is a his study for long.time hating student
"He is a student who has been hating his study for a long time."

b. **Er ist ein Student [sein Studium seit langem hassend(er)]*
he is a student his study for long.time hating.INFL

However, in Dutch, reduced relatives can also, marginally, occur in postnominal position. Although in (61) the adjunct follows the bare AP reduced relative, which might account for its postnominal position, in (62) the adjunct precedes the bare AP reduced relative, which is unpredicted under Cinque's analysis of postnominal reduced relatives:

(61) *de mensen aanwezig in dit gebouw*   DUTCH
the people present in this building

(62) *de mensen hier aanwezig*   DUTCH
the people here present
"the people present here"

Second, why are all relative clause types, including the participial and bare AP relative clauses, in Romance obligatorily postnominal? Does this mean that they are always right-branching, even if this is not visible? Does Romance not possess non-right-branching reduced relatives, as the prenominal ones in English?

If attraction does not depend on right branching, we still have to account for the apparent optionality in English, as exemplified in (58–59), or the differences in attraction between English, German, and Romance.

Cinque's unitary analysis of prenominal and postnominal reduced relatives in English is based on the argument that there is no difference in interpretation between the two types of indirect modifiers. The different position is related to the force with which the reduced relative is attracted to a higher position (followed by remnant movement), which might be related to a right-branching structure. Sleeman (2011) argues, however, that there is a difference in interpretation and a difference in internal structure between the prenominal and postnominal participles in (58)–(59), based on an analysis of deverbal modifiers in English and Dutch (see also Struckmeier & Kremers, this volume, for German). Sleeman (this volume) and Niculescu (this volume) show for the Romance languages French and Romanian, respectively, that deverbal modifiers, even if they are postnominal in Romance, can present the same semantic differences as the prenominal and postnominal ones in English. If there is a difference in interpretation, this would imply that Cinque's main argument for a unitary analysis of prenominal and postnominal reduced relatives in English cannot be used anymore.

At the end of §3.1.1 it has been noticed that the relation between source (direct or indirect) and interpretation (35–38) does not always correspond. Restrictive, intersective adjectives such as *red* in *my red dress* might have to be analyzed as direct modifiers with a restrictive interpretation and not as indirect modifiers. As argued by Pfaff (this volume), the reverse holds for indirect modifiers. Pfaff argues that strongly inflected adjectives in the Icelandic DPs are indirect modifiers, in spite of their non-restrictive interpretation. He calls the adjective in (63) an adjectival appositive. It is inherently predicative and may be paraphrased by a non-restrictive relative clause: "the X, which by the way .... ":

(63) Ég   horfði upp í   blá.an   himin-inn
      I   looked up   into blue.STR   sky-DEF
      "I looked up into the sky, which happened to be blue/which BTW was blue (at that moment)"   (Thráinsson 2007: 3)

Pfaff notices that strongly inflected adjectives, i.e. indirect modifiers, can also be used as expressives (*bölvaður* "damn, bloody"). They differ from appositives in not being predicative, therefore they cannot be merged as reduced relative clauses. On the few occasions where a strong and a weak adjective co-occur, the strong one necessarily precedes the weak one:

(64) bölvað.ur   gaml.i   níðingur-inn
      bloody.STR   old.WK   scoundrel-DEF

In Pfaff's view, both appositives and expressives presuppose an already fully established (DP) referent. Interestingly, the same types have been distinguished in Romanian. According to Marchis and Alexiadou (2009), the adjective in the Romanian *cel*-construction is an appositive specificational reduced relative clause (see also Niculescu, this volume). Marchis and Alexiadou adopt De Vries' (2002) analysis of appositive relatives as involving specifying co-ordination. The adjective is generated in the predicative position of the relative clause:

(65) a. băiatul   cel   frumos
          boy.the   cel   beautiful
          "the boy, namely the beautiful one"
      b. [$_{\&:P}$ [$_{DP}$ baiatul]$_i$ &: [$_{DP}$ cel$_i$ [$_{CP}$ [$_{C'}$ [$_{IP}$ Ø$_i$ frumos]]]]

Just like Pfaff (this volume) for Icelandic, Cornilescu and Nicolae (2011) show that in Romanian, emotive adjectives can occur at the left edge of the DP, presupposing the rest of the DP to their right. Since they can precede numerals, they precede NumP in structure (34), cf. (66):

(66) The [$_{NumP}$ three [$_{Ind.mod.}$ recently bought [$_{Dir.mod.}$Chinese [$_{NP}$ vases]]]]

(67) *aceste fenomenale șapte legi*
    these phenomenal seven laws

(68) *acești importanți șapte foști oficiali*
    these important seven former officers

Examples such as (63–65) and (67–68) and their proposed analyses suggest that indirect modifiers might not be restricted to the ones distinguished by Cinque, but come in two flavors.

Cinque's structure (34) contains two determiner/definiteness positions: D(P) and d(P). In the next section we discuss the position of adjectives with respect to determiners and the expression of definiteness.

4. Determiner and adjective

Cinque assumes that there are two DEF-positions within the DP: D and d (see e.g. Julien 2005; Lohrmann 2011; Stroh-Wollin 2011). In this section we discuss the position of the adjective in the case of double definiteness (§4.1), the position of the adjective in the case of single definiteness (§4.2) and the influence of the determiner on adjectival inflection (§4.3).

4.1 Double definiteness

In definite DPs containing an adjective in some Scandinavian languages, viz. in Swedish, Norwegian and Faroese, the suffixal definiteness marker is doubled by a free, pre-adjectival, determiner.[12] In current analyses of double definiteness it is assumed that in a structure such as (34) both D and d are filled (e.g. Julien 2005; Lohrmann 2010, 2011; Stroh-Wollin 2011; Schoorlemmer 2012):

DEF – A – N – DEF
(69) *den lilla flicka-n*   SWEDISH
    DEF little girl.DEF

(70) $[_{DP} [_{D^0} den] [lilla [_{dP} [_d [_N flicka_i [_d n [_{NP} e_i]]]]]]]$
    the   little   girl

---

12. Schoorlemmer (2012) claims that the adjective has to be licensed by a c-commanding D. Since the suffixed definiteness marker on the noun does not c-command the adjective, it does not suffice.

The Romanian *cel*-construction has also been assigned a double definiteness structure as the one in (34) (Cornilescu & Nicolae 2011):[13]

(71)   N – DEF – DEF – A
       băiat-ul cel frumos   ROMANIAN
       boy.DEF cel beautiful
       "the beautiful *cel* boy"

(72)   [$_{DP}$ [$_{dP}$ *băiat-ul*]$_i$ [$_D$ *cel* [$_{AP}$ *frumos* [$_{dP}$ e$_i$]]]]
       boy.def   cel   beautiful
       "the beautiful boy"

The order N–DEF might be the result of movement of N to *d*, as in (70) (e.g. Julien 2005; Lohrmann 2011; Stroh-Wollin 2011) or DEF might be a suffix or the spell-out of a definiteness feature on N, as in (72) (e.g. Perridon 1989; Giusti 1994; Roehrs 2006; Cornilescu & Nicolae 2011).

Cornilescu and Nicolae (2011) claim that in the Romanian *cel*-construction, the suffixed noun moves as dP to Spec,DP. Interestingly, the same word order is attested in Swedish and Norwegian, although it only occurs in verse and in certain fixed expressions. For the Norwegian Example (73), Julien (2003) proposes a structure parallel to (72), viz. one in which the suffixed noun moves as a dP to Spec,DP:

(73)   [$_{DP}$ [$_{dP}$ *skog- en*]   [$_D$ *de-n* [$_{AP}$ *grønn-e* [$_{dP}$ e$_i$]]]]
       forest.DEF.MASC.SG   DEF-SG green-w
       "the green forest"

Lohrmann (2011), partly based on Julien (2005), proposes that, in Scandinavian, D dominates the feature 'discourse', whereas *d* dominates the feature 'specific reference' (in Julien's analysis *d* contains the feature 'inclusiveness'). For French, a distinction has been made between D$_{deixis}$ (referentiality, deixis) and d$_{determination}$ (definiteness, indefiniteness, partitivity) by Ihsane and Puskas (2001) and Laenzlinger (2005). According to Cornilescu and Nicolae (2011), in Romanian, D expresses specificity, whereas the lower *d* expresses genericity.

At the end of the previous section we saw that the adjective in the Romanian *cel*-construction has been analyzed as an appositive, i.e. non-restrictive, indirect, modifier. In structure (34) and in (73) the adjective is in the higher DP and is thus an indirect modifier. Its position in the Swedish structure (70) also suggests that

---

13. These analyses are in line with a split DP-structure as Cinque's structure (34). However, Perridon and Sleeman (2011) analyze both *den* in the Swedish example and *cel* in the Romanian example as an adjectival article in the structures [*den* + A] Ndef (Scandinavian) and Ndef [*cel* + A] (Romanian).

the adjective is an indirect modifier. Being a size adjective, the adjective seems, however, rather to be a direct modifier. This would, however, yield the incorrect order DEF – N – DEF – A.[14]

4.2 Single definiteness

In double definiteness languages, in which the presence of an adjective triggers a preadjectival, free, determiner, definiteness may sometimes also be expressed in one position, as illustrated by the Norwegian Examples (74–75) taken from Julien (2005). According to Julien (2005) and Lohrmann (2011), in (74) prenominal DEF may be left out if the referent is very familiar (recall that in Lorhrmann's analysis D dominates the feature 'discourse', whereas *d* dominates the feature 'specific reference')

(74) (DEF) – A – N – DEF
     Du kan ta (den) ny-e bil-en.   NORWEGIAN
     you can take DEF new-W car-DEF
     "You can take the new car."

In the double definiteness construction (75b), but not in the single definiteness construction (75a), the speaker refers to specific people:

(75)   DEF – A – N – (DEF)
  a. Dei oppfører seg som dei verst-e bøll-ar
     they behave REFL as DEF worst-W brute-PL
     "They behave like the worst brutes"
  b. Dei oppfører seg som dei verst-e bøll-a-ne
     they behave REFL as DEF worst-W brute-PL-DEF
     "They behave like the worst brutes"

Danish and Icelandic do not have double definiteness, but only prenominal DEF and suffixed DEF. Lohrmann (2011) claims that in these languages the features 'discourse' and 'specific reference' are united in one position (either in prenominal DEF, i.e. *D*, or in suffixed DEF, i.e. *d*):[15]

(76)   DEF – A – N
    det stor-e hus   DANISH
    the big.WK house

---

14. In Stroh-Wollin's (2011) analysis, the adjective is in Spec,dP. Although dP is the domain of direct modifiers, Spec,dP is not an adjectival position in structure (34).

15. For the Danish Example (77), Lohrmann argues that there is no feature Disc in the lower *d*.

(77) A – N – DEF
    hel-e   hus-et   DANISH
    whole-WK house-DEF
    "the whole house"

(78) DEF – A – N
    hinn   góð-i   maður   ICELANDIC
    DEF   good-WK man
    "the good man"

(79) A – N – DEF
    gaml-a hús-ið   ICELANDIC
    old.WK   house.DEF
    "the old house"

(80) N – DEF – A (example from Pfaff, this volume)
    Borg-in   eilíf-a   ICELANDIC
    city-DEF eternal.WK
    "~Rome"

The position of the adjective with respect to the suffixed noun suggests that in (79) the adjective is an indirect adjective, whereas it is a direct adjective in (80). For (78) both analyses would be possible. Pfaff (this volume) argues, however, that in all three cases the adjective is a direct adjective.

Next to the *cel*-construction, which has been analyzed as a double definiteness construction (see §4.1), Romanian also has single (suffixed) definiteness constructions.[16,17] If DEF is a suffix, A should be a direct modifier. However, in (82) the adjective can have a restrictive, intersective interpretation:

(81) A – DEF – N
    importante-le legi   ROMANIAN
    important.DEF laws
    "the important laws"

(82) N – DEF – A
    legi-le   importante   ROMANIAN
    laws.DEF important
    "the important laws"

---

16. Since the single (suffixed) definiteness construction exists next to the double definiteness construction, this suggests that there are only definiteness features in *d*, as in the Swedish and Norwegian suffixed construction.

17. In Old Romanian, the order A – N – D existed as well (Cornilescu & Nicolae 2010).

The position and interpretation of the adjective in other Germanic and Romance single definiteness languages have already been discussed in §3. Since there are no corresponding double definiteness constructions in these languages, in Lohrmann's (2011) analysis both definiteness features would be in D (as in the Danish and Icelandic Examples 76 and 78, respectively):

DEF – A – N
(83) the big house   ENGLISH

(84) la   petite maison   FRENCH
      the small   house

DEF – N – A
(85) la   machina rossa   ITALIAN
      the car   red
      "the red car"

4.3 Weak and strong adjectival inflection

In Romance, both attributive and predicative adjectives agree with the noun in gender and number. Whereas in German attributive adjectives may also agree in gender and number in non-definite noun phrases, and whereas in Scandinavian predicative adjectives also agree with the subject in gender and number, in Germanic a distinction is also made between weak and strong inflection. It has been argued in the literature that weak inflection, occurring on attributive adjectives, may depend on the definiteness of the determiner (e.g. Menuzzi 1994; Schoorlemmer 2009, 2012). Predicative adjectives in Northern Germanic only take strong inflection (Schoorlemmer, this volume). In this section we discuss the relation of adjectival inflection to definiteness in Germanic.

Vangsnes (1999) points out that weak adjectival inflection in Norwegian can give the NP a presuppositional reading. In the adjectival Example (86a), where the adjective bears the strong inflectional ending, it is not clear if there is any unripe apple at all, while in (86b), in which the adjective bears the weak ending, there is at least one unripe apple.

(86) a. Legg hvert umoden-t   eple   i   denne kassen.
          put   every unripe-s   apple in   this   box-DEF
          "Put every unripe apple in this box."
      b. Legg hvert umodn-e   eple   i   denne kassen.
          put   every unripe-WK   apple in   this   box-DEF
          "Put each unripe apple in this box".   (Norwegian, Vangsnes 1999)

According to Lohrmann (2010, 2011), the weak adjectival ending individuates the relevant members in the A+N denotation. In her analysis, the weak adjectival ending spells out the feature [Identity] (see also Roehrs and Julien this volume).

(87) [DP2([sref]),([disc][#P [FPAP[F'[ident] [DP1 ([sref]),([disc])[ClassP [ind] NP]]]]]]

According to Roehrs and Julien (this volume), in German the strong/weak endings are a function of the immediate syntactic context, while in Norwegian they are dependent on the general semantic context. Stroh-Wollin and Simke (this volume) show that, in Old Swedish, strong adjectival forms still appeared in semantically definite noun phrases.

Roehrs and Julien propose that the weak ending in German is the result of impoverishment, which applies under certain lexical and structural conditions. This might also hold for the Icelandic Examples (78–80) containing weak adjectival inflection, and which contrast with (63–64) discussed in §3.2.2 containing strong adjectival inflection. While the weakly inflected adjectives in (78–80) are analyzed by Pfaff (this volume) as direct modifiers, those in (63–64) are analyzed as appositive adjectives outside the strict DP, which might account for the strong inflection. Van de Velde and Weerman (this volume) also show that, in Dutch, adjectives bearing weak inflection are closer to the noun than those bearing strong/no inflection.

5. An overview of the contributions to this volume

In the preceding part we have argued that adjectives derive from nouns in Indo-European, and that whereas the weak adjectival inflection in Germanic might trace back to a nominalizing suffix, the origin of strong inflection in Germanic might be demonstratives. The nominal origin of adjectives might be reflected in congruence and agreement, i.e. the expression of gender, number, and case by both nouns and adjectives simultaneously. The nominal. i.e. appositional, nature of adjectives might also explain the non-fixed order of the adjective and the noun in older stages of both Germanic and Romance.

Although historically the adjective might have developed from the noun, which is expressed in both being [+N] categories, adjectives share the feature [+V] with verbs, in a binary feature system such as Chomsky's (1970). Therefore we might expect adjectives to derive from verbs as well.

Historically there was already early a distinction with respect to inflection (the strong vs. weak inflection in Germanic, but not in Romance), but the adjective's position with respect to the noun was not fixed for a long time.

Although a synchronic description should in principle be independent of the historical development of a language (Saussure 1916), diachronic insights might help gain insight into the synchronic analysis of a language. The same holds for a typological analysis. That is why a deeper analysis of a synchronic stage within a language family or between language families might eventually lead to a more similar analysis of apparently different phenomena or to a differentiation of apparently similar phenomena.

In this volume, recent analyses of various aspects of the adjective in Germanic and Romance are presented. We have divided them into two groups (change and variation), although both aspects are sometimes treated in the same paper. The papers are shortly introduced in the following subsections, in the order in which they appear in the volume.

5.1 Change

Martin Hummel discusses the adjective as a category in relation to the adverb. He sets out to challenge the widely-held position that Romance and English make a rigid distinction between adjectives and adverbs with derivational affixes, as opposed to languages like German and Dutch, which use the same lexemes indifferently in both contexts. A careful analysis of the bewildering variation in the languages under scrutiny reveals that the use of suffixes for marking adverbials is to some extent artificial, as it is driven by literacy (and language contact), and that the old system of flexible marking is still alive.

Carola Trips, just like Martin Hummel, who discusses the possible diachronic influence of French on deadjectival adverb formation in English, argues that (Old) French might have influenced Middle English. On the basis of a corpus study, she advances grammatical replication from Old French as a possible explanation for the rise of postposed rhematic adjectives in Middle English.

Ulla Stroh-Wollin and Rico Simke take a closer look at the occurrences of weak and strong adjectival forms in Old Swedish, and arrive at the conclusion that the widespread belief that strong forms are not possible in (formally and/or semantically) definite noun phrases is unfounded: in the oldest periods of post-runic Swedish weak forms are indeed restricted to definite noun phrases, but strong forms may occur in both definite and indefinite contexts. The modern rule, which requires any adjective occurring inside a definite noun phrase to be in the weak form, dates from the latter part of the 15th century.

Freek Van de Velde and Fred Weerman discuss the somewhat erratic nature of Dutch adjectival inflection. In this language adjectives remain uninflected when used predicatively or adverbially, but get an ending *-ə* in prenominal position, unless the noun is singular, indefinite and neuter, in which case it is not inflected. Van de Velde and Weerman argue that there are indications that the schwa-less forms in prenominal position are on their way out of the language. This would result in a situation in which the schwa indicates that the adjective is used attributively, and as such is distinguished from the determiners that precede it within the noun phrase.

5.2 Variation

Volker Struckmeier and Joost Kremers investigate the nature of attributive structures (adjectives, participles, and relative clauses) in German. They propose a common representation for all the attributive structures in this language, viz. a phase-level functional head, which they call CGN-C (Case-Gender-Number-C). A comparison with Dutch, Arabic, and Chinese shows according to Struckmeier and Kremers that similar attributive C heads also exist in other languages.

Petra Sleeman inquires into the participle in Germanic and Romance. In line with her earlier work on English and Dutch, she claims on the basis of her corpus study on the combination of the passive participle with the adverbs *très* "very" and *beaucoup* "much" in French, that participles subsume four subtypes. Apart from a fully adjectival type and a fully verbal type, two intermediate types are to be distinguished: a resultative type, which expresses the result of an event and resorts to the adjectival category, and an eventive property type, which is more verbal in nature, but occurs in prenominal position in Germanic, which is not predicted by Cinque (2010). On the basis of various syntactic tests, Sleeman is able to show that this four-way division runs parallel in both language families.

Dana Niculescu studies the behavior of attributive present participles in Romanian, which are either (a) fully eventive (verbal participle), in which case they do not agree with the noun, or (b) adjectival, agreeing with the noun in case, number, and gender. In the latter case the participle may be preceded by the (adjective-) article *cel*. In her corpus Niculescu found a previously hardly attested construction, viz. *cel* combined with the uninflected verbal participle. The participle in this construction has still a eventive meaning, but less so than without *cel*.

Alexander Pfaff analyzes the adjective's position, interpretation and inflection in Icelandic within the framework of Cinque (2010), just like Petra Sleeman partly arguing against Cinque's analysis. On the basis of Icelandic he argues against a relation between interpretation (restrictive – non-restrictive) and source (indirect – direct). However, he establishes a relation between source and adjectival inflection (strong – weak). Whereas strongly inflected adjectives are merged outside DP in his analysis, weakly inflected adjectives can occur before (after movement) or after the article.

Dorian Roehrs and Marit Julien discuss, just like Alexander Pfaff, the influence of the determiner on adjectival inflection. They claim that adjectival inflection is not necessarily related to the definiteness of a linearly preceding definite determiner in Germanic. While in German weak forms are analyzed as feature-reduced forms that have a specific local relation to certain lexical types of determiner, it is argued that in Scandinavian the weak endings have semantics on their own. Just as in Alexander Pfaff's analysis of Icelandic, the strong endings in German and Norwegian are analyzed as the elsewhere case.

Erik Schoorlemmer analyzes the contrast between the absence of strong adjectival inflection in predicative constructions in Dutch and German as opposed to their presence in Northern Germanic. He discards a purely syntactic difference between the Germanic languages as a possible explanation, and argues that the difference might be either lexical or morpho-syntactic in nature.

References

Alber, Birgit, Stefan Rabanus & Tomaselli, Alessandra. 2012. Contatto linguistico nell'area alpina centro-meridionale. In *La Sensibilità della Ragione. Studi in Omaggio a Franco Piva*, Laura Colombo, Mario Dal Corso, Paolo Frassi, Stefano Genetti, Rosanna Gorris Camos, Pierluigi Ligas & Paola Perazzolo (eds), 1–19. Verona: Edizioni Fiorini.

Alexiadou, Artemis & Wilder, Chris. 1998. Adjectival modification and multiple determiners. In *Possessors, Predicates and Movement in the Determiner Phrase* [Linguistik Aktuell/Linguistics Today 22], Artemis Alexiadou & Chris Wilder (eds), 303–332. Amsterdam: John Benjamins.

Alkire, Ti & Rosen, Carol. 2010. *Romance Languages: A Historical Introduction*. Cambridge: CUP.

Baker, Mark C. 2003. *Lexical Categories: Verbs, Nouns, and Adjectives*. Cambridge: CUP.

Bammesberger, Alfred. 1992. The place of English in Germanic and Indo-European. In *The Cambridge History of the English Language*, Vol. I: *The Beginnings to 1066*, Richard M. Hogg (ed.), 26–66. Cambridge: CUP.

Bauer, Brigitte L.M. 2009. Word order. In *New Perspectives on Historical Latin Syntax*, Vol. 1: *Syntax of the Sentence*, Philip Baldi & Pierluigi Cuzzolin (eds), 241–316. Berlin: Mouton de Gruyter.

Behaghel, Otto. 1932. *Deutsche Syntax: Eine geschichtliche Darstellung*, Band IV: *Worstellung. Periodenbau*. Heidelberg: Winter.

Bernstein, Judy. 1991. DPs in French and Walloon: Evidence for parametric variation in nominal head movement. *Probus* 3(2): 101–126.

Bolinger, Dwight. 1967. Adjectives in English: Attribution and predication. *Lingua* 18: 1–34.

Bouchard, Denis. 1998. The distribution and interpretation of adjectives in French: A consequence of Bare Phrase Structure. *Probus* 10(2): 139–184.

Boucher, Paul. 2004. Perfect adjective positions in French: A diachronic perspective. In *Current Studies in Comparative Romance Linguistics* [Antwerp Papers in Linguistics], Martine Coene, Gretel de Cuyper & Yves D'hulst (eds), 41–61. Antwerp: University of Antwerp.

Braunmüller, Kurt. 1994. Some typological tendencies in the development of the noun phrase in Germanic languages. In *Language Change and Language Structure: Older Germanic Languages in a Comparative Perspective*, Toril Swan & Endre Mørck (eds), 27–50. Berlin: Mouton de Gruyter.

Braunmüller, Kurt. 2008. Observations on the origins of definiteness in ancient Germanic. *Sprachwissenschaft* 33: 351–371.

Brugmann, Karl & Delbrück, Berthold. 1889. *Grundriss der vergleichenden Grammatik der Indogermanischen Sprachen*, Zweiter Band: *Wortbildungslehre* (Stammbildungs- und Flexionslehre). Straßburg: Karl J. Trübner.

Cabredo Hofherr, Patricia. 2010. Adjectives: An introduction. In *Adjectives: Formal Analyses in Syntax and Semantics* [Linguistik Aktuell/Linguistics Today 153], Patricia Cabredo Hofherr & Ora Matushansky (eds), 1–16. Amsterdam: John Benjamins.

Carstairs-McCarthy, Andrew. 1994. Inflection classes, gender, and the principle of contrast. *Language* 70: 737–788.

Chomsky, Noam. 1970. Remarks on nominalization. In *Readings in English Transformational Grammar*, Roderick Jacobs & Peter Rosenbaum (eds), 184–221. Waltham MA: Blaisdell.

Cinque, Guglielmo. 1994. Evidence for partial N-movement in the Romance DP. In *Paths Towards Universal Grammar: Studies in Honor of Richard S. Kayne*, Guglielmo Cinque, Jan Koster, Jean-Yves Pollock, Luigi Rizzi & Raffaella Zanuttini (eds), 85–110. Washington DC: Georgetown University Press.

Cinque, Guglielmo. 2010. *The Syntax of Adjectives. A Comparative Study*. Cambridge MA: The MIT Press.

Cornilescu, Alexandra & Nicolae, Alexandru. 2010. On the syntax of Romanian definite phrases: Changes in the patterns of definiteness checking. In *The Noun Phrase in Romance and Germanic* [Linguistik Aktuell/Linguistics Today 171], Petra Sleeman & Harry Perridon (eds), 193–221. Amsterdam: John Benjamins.

Cornilescu, Alexandra & Nicolae, Alexandru. 2011. Nominal peripheries and phase structure in the Romanian DP. *Revue Roumaine de Linguistique* LVI(1): 35–68.

Delsing, Lars-Olof. 1992. On attributive adjectives in Scandinavian and other languages. In *Papers from the Workshop on the Scandinavian Noun Phrase* [Report 32], Anders Holmberg (ed.), 20–44. Umeå: University of Umeå.

Delsing, Lars-Olof. 1993. *The Internal Structure of Noun Phrases in Scandinavian Languages*. Ph.D. dissertation, University of Lund.

Demonte, Violeta. 2008. Meaning–form correlations and adjective position in Spanish. In *Adjectives and Adverbs*, Luisa McNally & Chris Kennedy (eds), 71–100. Oxford: OUP.

Dryer, Matthew S. 1998. Aspects of word order in the languages of Europe. In *Constituent Order in the Languages of Europe*, Anna Siewierska (ed.), 283–319. Berlin: Mouton de Gruyter.

Emonds, Joe. 1976. *A Transformational Approach to English Syntax: Root, Structure-Preserving and Local Transformations*. New York NY: Academic Press.

Enger, Hans-Olav. 2013. Morphological theory and grammaticalisation: The role of meaning and local generalisations. *Language Sciences* 36: 18–31.

Faarlund, Jan Terje. 1994. Old and Middle Scandinavian. In *The Germanic Languages*, Ekkehard König & Johan van der Auwera (eds), 38–71. London: Routledge.

Faarlund, Jan Terje. 2001. From ancient Germanic to modern Germanic languages. In *Language Typology and Language Universals*, Vol. 2, Martin Haspelmath, Ekkehard König, Wulf Österreicher & Wolfgang Raible (eds), 1706–1719. Berlin: Mouton de Gruyter.

Faarlund, Jan Terje. 2002. Syntactic development from Ancient Nordic to Old Nordic. In *The Nordic Languages: An International Handbook of the History of the North Germanic Languages*, Vol. 1, Oskar Bandle, Kurt Braunmüller, Ernst Håkon Jahr, Allan Karker, Hans-Peter Naumann, Ulf Telemann, Lennart Elmevik & Gun Widmark (eds), 729–732. Berlin: Mouton de Gruyter.

Fischer, Olga. 2001. The position of the adjective in (Old) English from an iconic perspective. In *The Motivated Sign* [Iconicity in Language and Literature 2], Olga Fischer & Max Nänny (eds), 249–276. Amsterdam: John Benjamins.

Fortson, Benjamin W. IV. 2010. *Indo-European Language and Culture: An Introduction*, 2nd edn. Chichester: Wiley-Blackwell.

Giusti, Giuliana. 1994. Enclitic articles and double definiteness: A comparative analysis of nominal structure in Romance and Germanic. *The Linguistic Review* 11: 241–255.
Haider, Hubert. 2010. *The Syntax of German*. Cambridge: CUP.
Haider, Hubert. 2013. *Symmetry Breaking in Syntax*. Cambridge: CUP.
Harbert, Wayne. 2007. *The Germanic Languages*. Cambridge: CUP.
Heine, Bernd & Kuteva, Tania. 2007. *The Genesis of Grammar: A Reconstruction*. Oxford: OUP.
Hengeveld, Kees. 1992. Parts of speech. In *Layered Structure and Reference in a Functional Perspective* [Pragmatics & Beyond New Series 23], Michael Fortescue, Peter Harder & Lars Kristoffersen (eds), 29–55. Amsterdam: John Benjamins.
Higginbotham, James. 1985. On semantics. *Linguistic Inquiry* 16(4): 547–594.
Hirt, Hermann. 1927. *Indogermanische Grammatik*, Teil III: *Das Nomen*. Heidelberg: Carl Winter.
Hopper, Paul J. 1975. *The Syntax of the Simple Sentence in Proto-Germanic*. Den Haag: Mouton.
Ihsane, Tabea & Puskas, Genoveva. 2001. Specific is not definite. *GG@G* 2: 39–54.
Jespersen, Otto. 1993[1894]. *Progress in Language. With Special Reference to English* [Amsterdam Classics in Linguistics, 1800–1925, 9]. Amsterdam: John Benjamins.
Julien, Marit. 2003. Double definiteness in Scandinavian. *Nordlyd* 31(1): 230–244.
Julien, Marit. 2005. *Nominal Phrases from a Scandinavian Perspective* [Linguistik Aktuell/Linguistics Today 87]. Amsterdam: John Benjamins.
Kluge, Friedrich. 1913. *Urgermanisch: Vorgeschichte der altgermanischen Dialekte*. Strassburg: Karl J. Trübner.
Kühner, Raphael & Gerth, Bernhard. 1963. *Ausführliche Grammatik der griechischen Sprache*, Zweiter Teil: *Satzlehre*: Erster Band. Müchen: Max Hueber.
Kurzová, Helena. 1993. *From Indo-European to Latin: The Evolution of a Morphosyntactic Type* [Current Issues in Linguistic Theory 104]. Amsterdam: John Benjamins.
Laenzlinger, Christopher. 2005. French adjective ordering: Perspectives on DP-internal movement types. *Lingua* 115: 645–689.
Lamarche, Jacques. 1991. Problems for N^0 movement to NumP. *Probus* 3: 215–236.
Larson, Richard. 1998. Events and modification in nominals. In *Proceedings from Semantics and Linguistic Theory (SALT) VIII*, Devon Strolovitch & Aaron Lawson (eds), 145–168. Ithaca NY: CLC Publications.
Larson, Richard & Marušič, Franc. 2004. On indefinite pronoun structures with APs: Reply to Kishimoto. *Linguistic Inquiry* 35(2): 268–287.
Ledgeway, Adam. 2011. Syntactic and morphosyntactic typology and change. In *The Cambridge History of the Romance Languages*, Adam Ledgeway, Martin Maiden & John-Charles Smith (eds), 382–471. Cambridge: CUP.
Ledgeway, Adam. 2012. *From Latin to Romance: Morphosyntactic Typology and Change*. Oxford: OUP.
Lohrmann, Susanne. 2010. The Structure of DP and its Reflex in Scandinavian. Ph.D. dissertation, University of Stuttgart.
Lohrmann, Susanne. 2011. A unified structure for Scandinavian DPs. In *The Noun Phrase in Romance and Germanic* [Linguistik Akuell/Linguistics Today 171], Petra Sleeman & Harry Perridon (eds), 111–125. Amsterdam: John Benjamins.
Malchukov, Adrei L. 2000. *Dependency Reversal in Noun–Attributive Constructions: Towards a Typology*. München: Lincom.

Marchis, Mihaela & Alexiadou, Artemis. 2009. On the distribution of adjectives in Romanian: The *cel* construction. In *Romance Languages and Linguistic Theory* 2007 [Romance Languages and Linguistic Theory 1], Enoch Aboh, Elisabeth van der Linden, Josep Quer & Petra Sleeman (eds), 161–178. Amsterdam: John Benjamins.

McFadden, Thomas. 2009. How much of the Germanic strong adjective inflection is pronominal? *Münchener Studien zur Sprachwissenschaft* 63: 53–82.

Menuzzi, Sergio. 1994. Adjectival positions inside DP. In *Linguistics in the Netherlands*, Reineke Bok-Bennema & Crit Cremers (eds), 127–138. Amsterdam: John Benjamins.

Nielsen, Hans F. 1989. *The Germanic Languages: Origins and Early Dialectal Interrelations*. Tuscaloosa AL: University of Alabama Press.

Perridon, Harry. 1989. Reference, Definiteness and the Noun Phrase in Swedish. Ph.D. dissertation, University of Amsterdam.

Perridon, Harry. 1996. Noun phrases in Runic Swedish. In *The Nordic Languages and Modern Linguistics*, Kjartan Ottóson, Ruth Feldt & Arne Torp (eds), 248–261. Oslo: Novus Forlag.

Perridon, Harry & Sleeman, Petra. 2011. The noun phrase in Germanic and Romance. Common developments and differences. In *The Noun Phrase in Romance and Germanic. Structure, Variation, and Change* [Linguistik Aktuell/Linguistics Today 171], Petra Sleeman & Harry Perridon (eds.), 1–21. Amsterdam: John Benjamins.

Prokosch, Eduard. 1939. *A Comparative Germanic Grammar*. Philadelphia PA: Linguistic Society of America.

Quirk, Randolph & Wrenn, Charles L. 1969[1955]. *An Old English Grammar*. London: Methuen & Co.

Ranheimsæter, Harald. 1945. *Flektierte und unflektierte Nominativformen im Deutschen Adjektivsystem*. Oslo: Tanum.

Ringe, Don. 2006. *From Proto-Indo-European to Proto-Germanic*. Oxford: OUP.

Roehrs, Dorian. 2006. The Morpho-syntax of the Germanic Noun Phrase: Determiners Move into the Determiner Phrase. Ph.D. dissertation, Indiana University.

Saussure, Ferdinand de. 1916. *Cours de Linguistique Générale*. Paris: Payot.

Schachter, Paul. 1985. Parts-of-speech systems. In *Language Typology and Syntactic Description*, Vol. 1, Timothy Shopen (ed.), 3–61. Cambridge: CUP.

Schoorlemmer, Erik. 2009. Agreement, Dominance and Doubling: The Morphosyntax of DP. Ph.D. dissertation, Leiden University.

Schoorlemmer, Erik. 2012. Definiteness marking in Germanic: Morphological variations on the same syntactic theme. *Journal of Comparative German Linguistics* 15: 107–156.

Sleeman, Petra. 2011. Verbal and adjectival participles: Internal structure and position. *Lingua* 121(10): 1569–1587.

Sproat, Richard & Shih, Chilin. 1988. Prenominal adjective ordering in English and Mandarin. *NELS* 18: 465–489.

Stroh-Wollin, Ulla. 2011. A semantic approach to noun phrase structure. In *The Noun Phrase in Romance and Germanic* [Linguistik Aktuell/Linguistics Today 171], Petra Sleeman & Harry Perridon (eds), 127–155. Amsterdam: John Benjamins.

Thráinsson, Höskuldur. 1994. Icelandic. In *The Germanic Languages*, Ekkehard König & Johan van der Auwera (eds), 142–189. London: Routledge.

Thráinsson, Höskuldur. 2007. *The Syntax of Icelandic*. Cambridge: CUP.

Törnqvist, Nils. 1974. Zur Geschichte der deutschen Adjektivflexion. *Neuphilologische Mitteilungen* 75: 317–331.

Traugott, Elizabeth C. 1992. Syntax. In *The Cambridge History of the English Language,* Vol. I: *The Beginnings to 1066*, Richard M. Hogg (ed.), 168–289. Cambridge: CUP.

Van der Horst, Joop. 2008. *Geschiedenis van de Nederlandse Syntaxis.* Leuven: Leuven University Press.

Van de Velde, Freek. 2006. Herhaalde exaptatie: Een diachrone analyse van de Germaanse adjectiefflexie. In *Nederlands tussen Duits en Engels*, Matthias Hüning, Arie Verhagen, Ulrike Vogl & Ton van der Wouden (eds), 47–69. Leiden: Stichting Neerlandistiek Leiden.

Van de Velde, Freek. 2009. *De nominale constituent: Structuur en geschiedenis.* Leuven: Leuven University Press.

Van de Velde, Freek. 2012. PP extraction and extraposition in Functional Discourse Grammar. *Language Sciences* 34(4): 433–454.

Vangsnes, Øystein. 1999. The Identification of Functional Architecture. Ph.D. dissertation, University of Bergen.

De Vries, Mark. 2002. The Syntax of Relativization. Ph.D. dissertation, University of Amsterdam.

PART I

Change

The adjective-adverb interface in Romance and English*

Martin Hummel
University of Graz

Hengeveld classifies English as a 'differentiated' language that uses two morphological word-classes for adjective and (manner) adverb. The paper shows that English is instead a language where 'differentiation' coexists and competes with 'flexibility' (one word-class for adjective and adverb). English shares this feature with Romance, whereas it is distinctive with regard to other Germanic languages. The paper therefore aims at investigating the parallels that can be seen between English and Romance in both, synchrony and diachrony. It will be shown that variationist data are crucial for the understanding of this situation. Shared traditions of linguistic standardization in English and Romance explain common features that cannot be reduced to the typological and functional aspects.

1. Introduction

Hengeveld (1992:68–69) classifies English typologically as a "specialized language" ("differentiated" in Hengeveld et al. 2004) because this language has a separate word-class for both adjectives and manner adverbs, English having developed the adverbial suffix *-ly*. This feature distinguishes English from other Germanic languages, where the unmarked (e.g. Dut. *snel*, Ger. *schnell* "fast") or neuter (e.g. Sw. *roligt* "funny") form of the adjective is used for adverbial functions. To put it in the words of Hengeveld (1992:65; cf. Hengeveld & van Lier 2010), Dutch (and other Germanic languages) "combines the functions of adjectives and manner adverbs". They are therefore called "flexible languages". The generalized usage of a suffix for the derivation of English adverbs from adjectives is a striking parallel to Romance, where the successors of Lat. *mente* "spirit, mind, intention" are used. Other word classes are marginally concerned, as Sp. *perramente* (< *perro* "dog"),

---

* I am grateful to Peter Bierbaumer, Jeremy King, Utz Maas, Luca Melchior, Ventura Salazar García, Stefan Schneider and two anonymous referees for their helpful comments.

MexSp. *nuncamente* (< *nunca* "never"). In English *oftenly* and *soonly* are diachronically attested (Nevalainen 1994: 244). In Latin, final *-ē* or *-iter* were used to mark the adverbial function of adjectival stems. Hence, Latin, Romance and English are typologically similar in this domain. Despite the numerous parallels that can be drawn between English and Romance deadjectival adverbs, the semantic origin of Old English *lic* is "body" not "mind" (Guimier 1985). Hence, *-mente* and *-ly* were originally nouns with antonymous meaning, and both passed through the stage of instrumental cases on their way to an adverbial suffix.

The morphological status of Lat. *-iter*, Engl. *-ly* and Romance *-ment(e)* has been controversially discussed (e.g. by Pinkster 1972: 64–70; Haspelmath 1996; Ricca 1998; Dal 2007; Giegerich 2012; Štekauer forthc.). Some argue that they are inflections, others classify them as suffixes, and, finally, adverbs in *-mente* have been analyzed as compounds for historical reasons (this suffix is derived from the ablative case of the feminine Latin noun *mens, mentis* "spirit, mind, intention", which explains why the feminine form of the adjective is still used today: Lat. *sola mente* > Sp. *solamente* "only") and for synchronic features such as separability (e.g. Sp. *Habla tranquila y pausadamente* "s/he speaks calmly and slowly"). I will not tackle this rather dogmatic question here, but will simply classify all adverbs that are morphologically marked for this function as *Type B*, whereas the usage of the unmarked or neuter form of the adjective for adverbial functions will be referred to as *Type A*.

This nice picture of 'differentiated' languages becomes distorted by the fact that English and Romance do not only use Type B adverbs but also Type A. In some cases, Type A is the standard variant (e.g. Engl. *to work hard/*hardly*, Sp. *hablar alto* "to speak loud"/**altamente*), in other cases, Type A belongs to a substandard variety or register (e.g. Engl. *real good* vs. standard *really good*, ChileanSp. *terrible malo* "very bad" vs. standard *terriblemente malo*). Type A is generally neglected, underestimated or restricted to a limited set of exceptions, as the following typical example: "There are only a handful of exceptions [from Type B]" (Diepeveen & Van de Velde 2010: 382). An impressive number of studies reduce manner adverbs to those ending in *-ly* or *-ment(e)* (e.g. Greenbaum 1969; Huang 1975; Buysschaert 1982; Koktova 1986; Ramat & Ricca 1998; Hennemann 2012; Liu 2012, to mention but a few). Diepeveen and Van de Velde (2010: 381) simply stipulate: "English marks the distinction between adjectives and adverbs with an adverbial suffix, whereas Dutch and German allow adjectives to be used adverbially without extra morphology". In particular, sentential adverbs in English and Romance are generally analyzed or illustrated with Type B adverbs. However, Sp. *bueno* "well", *claro* "of course, clearly", *igual* "perphaps, instead", *total* "in sum", *cierto* "sure", etc. are highly frequent uninflected discourse markers that occupy the same functional domain, the main difference being that Type B forms prevail in written texts and

Type A forms in informal oral communication. If we include spoken language, varieties and registers Type A appears to be commonplace. Even more, Type A is the only pan-Romanic type of manner adverb since Romanian, Sardinian and southern Italian dialects recur exclusively or almost exclusively to it as a productive rule. In a certain sense, the same holds for Germanic. In fact, Type A belongs to a common Indo-European background. From this perspective, the generalization of Type B for adverbial functions is more accurately seen as an exception.

This paper intends to show that the perception of English and Romance as "differentiated" languages is one-sided. In fact, these languages are characterized by the systematic coexistence and competition of Type A and Type B in synchrony and throughout their history. It will be argued that their coexistence coincides with traditions of speaking (henceforth *orality*) and traditions of writing (henceforth *literacy*). Since literacy is naturally superimposed on orality, the osmotic relation between Type A and Type B is marked by this process. More concretely, Type B is closely tied to the development of the written standard. The purpose of the present paper is to show that drawing parallels from Romance to English is a valuable heuristic device that allows us to posit good or even better questions about the synchrony and diachrony of the domain under scrutiny. Answers to these questions would require corpus based research that will not be undertaken here, but hopefully stimulated. However, the representative quantitative data on present-day English provided by Biber (1988) and by Opdahl (2000), the diachronic corpus analyses by Donner (1991) and Nevalainen (1994, 1997), as well as the sociolinguistic study on present-day York English by Tagliamonte and Ito (2002) are good points of reference.

First, this paper will give a commented phenomenology of Type A and Type B in English and Romance from the point of view of present-day synchrony (Section 2) and diachronic development (Section 3). Section 4 outlines common features that distinguish English and Romance varieties in the New World from those in Europe. Section 5 discusses the consequences of these observations for linguistic theory. Since this paper starts from previous research on Romance in order to shed new light on English, the sources for the examples in Romance are not always indicated for reasons of space. Detailed information can be found in the publications of the Research Group on "The Interfaces of Adjective and Adverb in Romance" (see http://sites.google.com/site/rsgadjadv).

2. Type A and Type B in present-day English and Romance

In the following, *attribute* will be used as a cover term for modifiers. Section 5 will deal with categorial aspects of units with attributive function.

2.1 Verb-modifying attributes

In Dutch (1) and German (2), the use of the unmarked form of the adjective for adverbial functions is canonical for speaking and writing:

(1) a. een *snelle vrouw*. NP-modifier (+ infl.)
"a fast woman"
b. De vrouw *loopt snel*. VP-modifier (– infl.)
"The woman runs fast."

(2) a. eine *schnelle* Frau. NP-modifier (+ infl.)
"a fast woman"
b. Die Frau läuft *schnell*. VP-modifier (– infl.)
"The woman runs fast."

In English (3) and in Romance (4), Type A is generally tied to informal speaking, except for Romanian and Sardinian, where it is standard:[1]

(3) The men *work hard*.

(4) a. Els homes *treballen dur*. (Catalan)
b. Les hommes *travaillent dur*. (French)
c. Gli uomini *lavorano duro*. (Italian)
d. Os homens *trabalham duro*. (Portuguese)
e. Los hombres *trabajan duro*. (Spanish)
f. Oamenii lucrează *greu*. (Romanian)
g. Sos omine *trabagliana folte*. (Sardinian)

In formal speaking and writing, morphologically marked adverbs are generally preferred, that is, adverbs ending in *-ly* for English (5) and adverbs ending in *-ment(e)* for Romance (5):

(5) *The men work *hardly*.[2] (English)

(6) a. (?) Els homes *treballen durament*. (Catalan)
b. Les hommes *travaillent durement*. (French)
c. Gli uomini *lavorano duramente*. (Italian)
d. Os homens *trabalham duramente*. (Portuguese)
e. Los hombres *trabajan duramente*. (Spanish)

---

1. The sentences in (4) and (6) are equivalent to (3). Engl. *hard* (adv.) < OEngl. *hearde* (adv.), Sp. *duro* "hard" < Lat. *durus, dura,* **durum**, Rom. *greu* < Lat. *gravis, gravis,* **grave** "heavy", Sard. *folte* < Lat. *fortis, fortis,* **forte** "strong". Lexicalization may play a role: Engl. *hard* and Cat. *dur* are standard, but this does not hold for other adjectives.

2. Engl. *hardly* < OEngl. *heardlice* (adv.).

My attempt to find corresponding examples for these languages already provides interesting insights into the relevance of linguistic variation. In the case of Engl. *hard* (adv.), the verb-modifying Type B variant *hardly* (5) is unusual. In fact, *hardly* has become specialized as a quantifier, as shown by many jokes such as *Working hard, or hardly working?*[3] It should be noted, however, that in Romance a few Type B adverbs belong to a popular substandard: e.g. Fr. *malement* "badly", *vitement* "fast", *petitement* "a few", *chichement* "poorly". Hence, adverbs are lexical items that may develop individually (see Hummel & Kröll 2011), but the general tendency is to use Type B in standard or refined style.

The fact that Type A and Type B forms that are based on the same adjective undergo differentiating specialization mirrors the coexistence and competition of both mechanisms. Consequently, Salazar García (2007) convincingly suggests replacing Hengeveld's classificatory approach by (possibly coexisting) "flexible", "differentiated" and "rigid" strategies for attributive (modifying) functions. Type A is named *flexible modifier* (Salazar García 2013). In order to complete the typology, we should add Type C for adverbs with an own underived form (Engl. *well*, Fr. *bien* "well", etc.) and periphrastic solutions (Type D). The latter would be a 'rigid' strategy in languages without adjectives and manner adverbs (cf. Hengeveld 1992:65).

As an additional feature, we may note that Type A tends to be used in attribute-verb-compounds, as in Bolinger's examples from American English (1972:272):

(7) a. He *works* so *hard*. He is so *hard-working*.
    b. Those people *talk loud*. Those people are *loud-talking*.
    c. They *suffer long*. They are *long-suffering*.
    d. The wax *melts* so *readily*. The wax is so *ready-melting*.
    e. This meat *cooks easily*. This meat is *easy-cooking*.

In the last two examples the compound form 'loses' the adverbial suffix. Romance parallels the tendency to lexicalize the unmarked form of the adjective in what might be called *complex verbs*. Complex verbs tend to develop metaphorical meanings (e.g. Fr. *couper court* "to interrupt", *voir grand* "to think big (lit. "to see big")", etc.; see Hummel & Stiegler 2005, with 13,000 attestations). Hence, Romance and English converge again for the building of compounds or complex verbs with the unmarked Type A attribute.

---

3. I do not tackle here the processes of functional and conceptual differentiation of Type A and Type B, as well as their internal development. This domain is highly relevant for the interface of syntax and semantics (e.g. the development of sentential adverbs *naturally* "in a natural way" > "obviously") and the rise of polyfunctionality and polysemy.

2.2 Tertiary attributes (modifiers of adjectives or adverbs)

Use of Type A is not restricted to VP. Their belonging to informal spoken language, and even slang, is particularly evident with tertiary adverbs, that is, modifiers of modifiers (adjectives or adverbs), according to Jespersen's (1992: 96–103) terminology. *Really good* is canonical, but *real good* is used in substandard. The following examples stem from Bolinger (1972) or my own data:

(8) real good, little disposed, dead drunk, mighty weak, right back, precious few, awful good, bitter cold, crazy quick, stark mad, pretty tall, terrible rainy, perfect blue, full glad, less important, wide open, pure white, good deep

According to Bolinger (1972) most of these collocations are more frequent in American English, more frequent in "dialect", and some of them are now perceived as archaic. Present-day speakers' evaluations vary from 'frequent in substandard', to 'never heard' or 'odd', according to the phrase. Hence, the phrases tend to be confined to oral substandard varieties, especially in the New World, and, diachronically, tend to get out of use (with exceptions in colloquial or written standard like *wide open, less important, pretty tall*). *Crazy quick* stems from an Australian speaker. Importantly, *awful quick* and similar phrases are attested in Middle English (Pinsker 1969: 167; cf. Peters 1994). This shows that present-day substandard variants are not innovative 'corruptions', as Bolinger believes, but belong to old traditions of English. According to Bäcklund's (1973) corpus analysis of contemporary English, these groups occur nearly exclusively in conversational data, and many of them are pejorative. Both observations match with the hypothesis that Type A adverbs are closely tied to the oral tradition.

In Romance, most tertiary adverbs of Type A are typical for rural language, slang and elder Romance:

(9) a. Esa película es *terrible mala*. (Spanish, Chile)
"This movie is terribly bad."

b. Ehte es terreno *pobre completo*. (Spanish, Canaries)
"This area is completely poor."

c. *típico sureño* (Spanish, Chile)
"typical(ly) southern"

(10) a. C'était *grave bon*. (French, Quebec)
"It was very good."

b. Elle était *grave belle*. (Parisian slang)
"She was very nice"

Fr. *fort* (adv.), as in *fort important* "very important", is standard. The following examples for French are documented in Hummel & Stiegler 2005:

(11) *ras tondu* "short cut", *fin(e) bonne* "very good", *fin droit* "very straight", *frais levé* "just gotten up", *fraîche cueillie* "freshly picked", *toute bonne* "very good", *grandes ouvertes* "wide open", *clair-voyant* "clairvoyant", *menu serré* "tightly locked", *large baillant* "wide open", *étroit cousu* "closely sewn", *doux coulant* "smoothly gliding", *nouveau venu* "newcomer", *nouveaux mariés* "newly married", *clair-semé* "widely sewn", *raide mort* "dropped dead", etc.

Examples from Italian are *rendere pazzo furioso* "to turn completely crazy" and *innamorato pazzo* "crazy in love".

The inflection of tertiary adverbs is frequent in popular substandard, especially in the rural variants of American Portuguese and Spanish (e.g. Sp. *medios tontos* "half crazy", *de pura tonta* "in a completely crazy way"). In informal oral European Portuguese *muita bom* "very good" combines the feminine form of the quantifier with the masculine of the adjective. In French, a long discussion on the so-called 'illogical' inflection in *toute contente* "so happy" and *fenêtres grandes-ouvertes* "wide open windows" has taken place in grammaticography (cf. variants in (11)), but these alternatives are fully accepted now, as It. *tutta contenta* "so happy" or, to a lesser degree, Pt./Sp. *toda contenta*. In Italian, adverb agreement occurs in standard, and it is very frequent in meridional dialects (Rohlfs 1954: 127; Ledgeway 2000, 2011).

According to Van Goethem (2010), Fr. *nouveau* "new" has undergone grammaticalization as an (inflected or uninflected) prefix with past participles. The productivity of this process in Modern French supports this analysis. As far as diachrony is concerned, Van Goethem points out the shortcomings of the traditional analysis of *nouveau* as a simple adverb. The diachronic process would indeed be more coherently explained within the framework of the Type A system with spontaneous inflection, as it implicitly appears in the following appreciation:

> Dans les adjectifs composés, chaque terme était traité par l'ancienne langue comme un adjectif. De là les formes: *Portes* **grandes** *ouvertes, fleurs* **fraîches** *écloses. Les oreilles* **pures** *françaises* (Montaigne). Le français moderne au contraire tend à considérer le premier terme comme un adverbe et à le laisser invariable: *Une petite fille* **nouveau**-*née,* **court**-*vêtue,* **demi**-*morte.* (Radouant 1922: 145)[4]

---

4. In composed adjectives each member was treated as an adjective by the ancient language. This explains the following forms: *portes grandes ouvertes* "wide open windows", *fleurs fraîches écloses* "flowers just starting to bloom". *Les oreilles pures françaises* "purely French ears" (Montaigne). By contrast, Modern French tends to consider the first member an uninflected adverb: *une petite fille nouveau-née* "a new born girl", *court-vêtue* "wearing short dresses", *demi-morte* "half-dead".

It should be noted that the diachrony of such forms should not be analyzed without taking into account the orality-literacy interface, since the intense debate on the correct orthography of the data in (11) clearly biases Van Goethem's implicit assumption of a simple grammaticalization process on a monolithic vision language.

If we look at the semantics of tertiary attributes, we see that the qualifying function of manner adverbs is overlaid, and in most cases dominated, by quantification or intensification. In (9c), for example, Sp. *típico sureño* is a quality of being "southern *par excellence*", but the phrase simultaneously means "very southern", the same as *typical(ly) German* means "typically and very German". Consequently, tertiary attributes are situated in a continuum that begins with substandard variants such as ChilSp. *terrible mala* "terribly bad" and ends on canonical paradigms for Type A quantifiers:

(12) a.   *molto* "very", *quanto* "how", *tanto* "so", *tutto* "completely" (Italian)
      b.   *tão/tanto, muito, quão/quanto, todo*[5]   (Portuguese)
      c.   *tan/tanto, muy/mucho, cuan/cuanto*   (Spanish)

Interestingly, productive extensions of these paradigms belong to popular substandard (see (9)–(11)). In standard literacy, productivity is ensured by Type B, e.g. Fr. *terriblement grand* "terribly big" which uses the concept 'terrible' as a metaphor for the intensification of an adjective (cf. Engl. *terribly big*). As in individual cases such as Engl. *to work hard* (verb-modification) and Fr. *fort bien* "very well" (adverb-modification), the high degree of implementation of the canonical quantifiers (12) in the old language was the reason why they have resisted the ascension of Type B quantifiers in diachrony. Bolinger was not aware of the fact (noted by Hummel 2010 for Spanish) that most new members of the open list of intensifiers on *-ly* belong to elaborate literacy or elaborate oral rhetoric (e.g. *It should be incandescently clear,* Martin Luther King; example from Bolinger).

2.3 Sentential adverbs and discourse markers

An analogous situation characterizes the domain of sentential adverbs and discourse markers:[6]

(13)   *sure/surely*   (English)

---

5. Pt. *quão* and Sp. *cuan* are archaic.
6. (14) and (15) are equivalent to (13).

(14) a. sûr/sûrement (French)
     b. sicuro/sicuramente (Italian)
     c. seguro/seguramente (Portuguese)
     d. sigur/-- (Romanian)
     e. seguro/seguramente (Spanish)

(15) sigur (Papiamentu creol)

In Romanian Type A is canonical. Therefore, no adverbs ending in -*mente* are used for sentential functions. It is noteworthy, however, that during the standardization of Romanian in the 19th c. according to the model of Romance (especially French and Italian), intellectual promoters of the process tried to introduce the suffix -*mente* as linguistic standard. Similarly to the individual cases of Type A resistance mentioned in 2.1 and 2.2, Type A was too well established in orality for being replaced by learned -*mente* (Chircu 2008: 124–125, 2011: 53–58). Adjective based discourse markers form longer lists in Italian, Portuguese, and Spanish (e.g. Sp. *bueno, claro, cierto, total, fijo, igual,* etc.; see Hummel 2012), but have lower type frequency in French and English. According to Crystal (2003: 347), adjectives are routinely used as adverbs in English-based creoles, as it is also the case in Romance based Papiamentu (15).

Germanic languages like Dutch and German sometimes morphologically mark sentential adverbial functions, as in Dutch *begrijpelijkerwijs* "understandably" and Ger. *begreiflicherweise* (Ramat & Ricca 1998: 204). If we look at informal spoken German, adverbs ending in -*weise* "-wise" (16a) appear to be a simple alternative to Type A (16b) (cf. Dürscheid & Hefti 2006; Giger 2011):

(16) a. Klarerweise/merkwürdigerweise kommt er.
        "Clearly/strangely, he comes."
     b. Klar/merkwürdig, er kommt.

Interestingly, grammars usually introduce the German suffix -*weise* without drawing attention to the current colloquial Type A alternatives (*Duden*: §868; cf. Eisenberg 2002: 70–71).

In English, discourse markers tend to be taken from other word classes than adjectives, Type B adverbs or phrases (Engl. *well,*[7] *obviously, I mean, of course,* etc.). In Greenbaum's (1969: 92) list of "style disjuncts" figure only the following cases: *seriously, in all seriousness, to be serious.* The variant *Serious, do you really*

---

7. It is noteworthy that in English the Type C adverb *well* has developed a similar polyfunctionality to the Spanish adjective *bueno* in the domain of discourse functions (see Lutzky 2012 and Hummel 2012).

mean this? is not indicated (cf. *good, great, excellent*, etc. in Biber et al. 1999: 520). The adjectival alternative is briefly mentioned at the end of Greenbaum's book (1969: 213–215). Tagliamonte and Ito (2002: 248, 253–254) observe that no study was dedicated to Type A sentential adverbs, although *absolute, definite, funny* and *honest* are used for this purpose in their oral York Corpus.

(17)   a.   I was an angel. *Absolute.*
           b.   And she usually baby-sits once a week. *Definite.*
           c.   *Funny enough* we had a telephone call.
           d.   *Honest* they did.

Similarly, Engl. *sure* is a partial alternative to *surely* in the domain of sentential functions, but Downing (2006) only compares Engl. *surely* to Sp. *seguro* and *seguramente*. Pounder (2001: 307) cites an example from the 17th c.: "You will lough sure when I shall tell you".

It is noteworthy that these cases, which were brought to light by systematic corpus analyses, provide evidence for the productive use of Type A attributes with sentential functions. In the same vein, Hummel (2012) finds sentential functions for Sp. *terrible* and *horrible* which may be considered as productive extension of the above mentioned series of lexicalized Type A discourse markers (*bueno, claro*, etc.). The exploration of written corpora would not bring to light the productive usage of Type A sentential attributes. In spoken Romance Type attributes with sentential functions are uninflected (cf. above *bueno, claro, horrible*, etc.). By contrast, written language uses inflected parenthetical adjectives (e.g. Sp. *Cansada, la chica se duerme* "Being tired, the girl falls asleep"). These constructions are almost exclusive for very elaborated, literary style, not only in Romance (Martínez 1994: 230), but also in English (Strang 1978: 140; Biber et al. 1999: 520–521).

The preference of written standard English for the Type B sentential attributes does not hold when the attribute itself is modified. The following example stems from Erdmann's (1997) study on what Quirk et al. (1995: 424–428) call "supplementive adjective clause": "None of these solutions is satisfactory. *More important*, what is going to happen is unpredictable". Erdmann analyzes a sample of written American English texts, where he finds the following units that convey the speaker's evaluation on a predication:

(18)   as bad, better yet, more bizarre, most critical, most crucial, curious, more dangerous, utterly despicable, most essential, least forgivable, more galling, more important, even more important, most important, most impressive, even more intriguing, very likely, more likely, most likely, more ominous, most sad, most scary, more serious, more significant, more telling, even more unsettling, worse, even worse, worse still, worse yet

We obviously could argue that these are adjectives, but the identification of sentential adverbs with the test "*importantly* → *it is important that/I find it important that*" (note: **in an important way* or **it is importantly that*) blurs the edges of the ADJ/ADV distinction. We might even think that the functional basis of using *importantly* is rather weak. As in the case of (16) and (17), single Type B forms such as *importantly* are specifically preferred in written texts and elaborated oral communication, except if the attribute is itself modified (with some dual forms, e.g. *more importantly*). All this shows that Type A is more important than we generally learn and believe it.

2.4   Type A and traditional Type C adverbs (*good* vs. *well*)

In English and Romance, current manner adverbs may have independent forms, as Engl. *well*, Fr. *bien/mal*, etc. (Type C). Interestingly, in Romance and English substandard adjectives may 'replace' Type C adverbs. In fact, *good* can have the same function as its adverbial counterpart *well* (Bolinger 1972; cf. Biber et al. 1999: 543):

(19) a.   a *good deep* breath
      b.   *spank* him *good*
      c.   This ride *shook me up, but good.*
      d.   *good-looking*

Bolinger describes this usage as an American English innovation: "with verbs of a certain class *well* is no longer used in contemporary American English, but gives way to *good*". According to the corpus data analyzed by Biber et al. (1999: 542–543) frequency of adverbial *good* is several times higher in American English, and adverbial *real* (e.g. *real good*) in AmE. conversation is as frequent as *really* in British English. Interestingly, Bolinger suggests the idea of *well* being 'replaced by' *good*, and Biber et al. allude to the 'omission' of *-ly*. While this could be discussed for *real/really*, no one would suggest explaining adverbial *good* as a truncation of *goodly*, *bad* (adv.) from *badly*, or, to take sentential functions, *first* as a marker for discourse organization from *firstly*, not even from a synchronic point of view. This analysis is biased by literacy and corresponds to the way teachers sometimes 'explain' colloquial or dialectal variants as "corruptions" of 'good' (allegedly primary and older) language. In fact, it is far from being evident that, from a diachronic point of view, canonical adverbs like *well* were used before Type A *good*. It is probable that both variants always existed simultaneously. The possibility to alternate *to feel well/good* has been widely discussed for English (for a survey see Martínez Vázquez 1991: 93). Surprisingly, the discussion does not take into account that the antonym *bad* is currently used as adverb: *to sleep bad* (with *badly* being a hypercorrect variant), *bad looking*. Even if *bad* does not have a corresponding adverb with a proper form the same as *well*, it is obvious that the use of *good* and *bad* with adverbial function has to be placed within the same Type A tradition that developed independently from Type B.

Interestingly, Romance provides similar examples where dialects use the adjective 'instead of' canonical Type C adverbs derived from Lat. *bene* and *male* (left column: dialect; right column: standard):

(20) a. *huele feo* vs. *huele mal* "smells bad" (Spanish)
 b. Que te *vaya bonito*! vs.
  ¡Que te *vaya bien*! "it may be well with you"

(21) a. *Ça va moche.* vs. *Ça va mal.* "It's going bad" (French)
 b. Il *fait ça moche.* vs. *Il fait cela mal.* "He is doing it badly"

(22) *Tu sa' lèggiri bonu.* vs. *Sai leggere bene.* "You can read well" (Italian)

2.5 Comparative and superlative

In present-day English, the adverbial suffix *-ly* does not allow for synthetic comparative or superlative forms (e.g. **loudlier*), whereas Type A may be found if analytical alternatives are not preferred (examples from Valera Hernández 1996: 24):

(23) a. So would she mind speaking a *little louder*?
 b. the people *hardest hit* by this suspicion [...]
 c. This newspaper *speaks clearest* of all.

In Latin, the neuter of the adjective was systematically used for adverbial functions (e.g. *melius* "better"). In Romance, the synthetic forms have normally been replaced by the followers of Lat. *plus* (Fr. *plus important* "more important", It. *più importante*) or *magis* (Pt. *mais importante*, Sp. *más importante*) but in lexicalized cases such as Pt. *melhor* and Sp. *mejor* "better", the form is the comparative of both the adjective and the adverb. Consequently, in both English and Romance, Type B did not penetrate the comparative and superlative domain, where Type A was deeply rooted.

3. The diachrony of Type A and Type B in Romance and English

In order to give more space to English, Section 3.1 provides a short synthesis of the development from Latin to Romance. A detailed account can be found in Hummel (2000: 364–481, and 2013b).

3.1 Romance

In Classical Latin, two standard rules were used to transcategorize adjectives into adverbs, the first for the a/o-declension, the second for the i-declension:

(24) *longus, longa, longum* "long" (adj.)   *longē* (adv.)

(25) *fortis, fortis, fortĕ* "strong" (adj.)   →   *fortiter* (adv.)

Both rules provide marked adverbs that can be classified as Type B. The morpheme *-iter* was a suffix, whereas long *-ē* [e:] was an old instrumental case of the adjective, but in Classical Latin it was only productive for adverb formation (Karlsson 1981: 38).

In addition, the neuter nominative-accusative case was used as well:

(26) *longus, longa, longum* (adj.)   →   *longum* (adv.)

(27) *fortis, fortis, fortĕ* (adj.)   →   *fortĕ* (adv.)

The use of the neuter form of the adjective for adverbial functions corresponds to the criteria of Type A. Unlike (24), this rule uses short *-ĕ* [e] for the adverb. Some Type A adverbs are mentioned in manuals, but rather as occasional exceptions composing a heterogeneous list of fossilized units.

On the way to Romance, the canonical rules (24) and (25) were lost, whereas (26) and (27) survived. The first to be lost was *-ē*, since Latin had a tendency to replace canonical *-ē* by *-iter* with adjectives of the a/o-declension (e.g. *humanē* "in a human way" by *humaniter*; see Karlsson 1981: 31; cf. Ramat 2008: 15–16) or to use the ablative case (e.g. *commodō* instead of *commodē* "conveniently"; see Adams 2007: 210–212). In the long run, Type A was reinforced by syncretism with the latter, since instrumental ablatives used as adverbs such as *certō* "certainly", *multō* "very much", etc. phonetically converged with *-um* > *-o*. In Romance, canonical *altē* did not survive, but the followers of *altum* "high", etc. are systematically used as Type A adverbs. The following list shows the continuity of some Type A forms from Latin to Romance:

Latin	Meaning	French	Italian	Portuguese	Spanish
multum	"much"	Ofr. *moult*	*molto*	*muito*	*mucho*
altum	"high/loud"	*haut*	*alto*	*alto*	*alto*
*bassum	"low"	*bas*	*basso*	*baixo*	*bajo*
rapidum	"fast"	(*vite*)	*rapido*	*rápido*	*rápido*
firmum	"firm"	*ferme*	*fermo*	*firme*	*firme*
tranquillum	"calm"	*tranquille*	*tranquillo*	*tranquilo*	*tranquilo*
falsum	"wrong"	*faux*	*falso*	*falso*	*falso*
clarum	"clear"	*clair*	*chiaro*	*claro*	*claro*
paucum	"few"	*peu*	*poco*	*pouco*	*poco*

According to Löfstedt (1967), Type A adverbs prevailed in Late Latin, although *-iter* was still appreciated for writing. Even more, Type A is the only rule that

Latin inherited from Indo-European and transmitted to Romance (Löfstedt 1967:109; Karlsson 1981:5–16; Fortson IV 2004:132–133). Löfstedt goes so far as to shed a doubt on the full productivity of the canonical rules (24) and (25) in times of Classical Latin. If this is true, these rules were essentially used for writing. From this point of view, Type A appears to be an oral tradition that was temporarily submerged by the standardization of literacy known as Classical Latin, and consequently reemerged when the political driving force of standardization, the Roman Empire, collapsed. Interestingly, Old Greek knew a similar situation, since canonical -ως coexisted with Type A adverbs. In Modern Greek, only the latter survived as a productive rule, but -ως can still be fund in erudite words ending in -ης, often as a stylistic alternative to Type A, which (curiously) uses the neuter plural of the adjective (see Dietrich 1995:112; Ruge 1997:50).

Consequently, there is a common Indo-European background of using Type A that Romance shares with the Germanic languages. Type B appears to be a cultural phenomenon that recurrently occurs in socio-historical contexts of standardized literacy. By contrast, Type A is profoundly rooted in the oral tradition(s) and consequently reemerges where the impact of literacy fails or weakens. The most striking case is Romanian. The crucial fact that explains why Romanian only has Type A adverbs is Dacia's split from Rome in the 3rd c. A.D., yet before Latin replaced Greek in Christian liturgy. In contradiction with the general belief that -*mente* is a pan-Romanic suffix, this is only true for those languages that have first developed a 'vulgar' Romance literacy: French, Italian, Portuguese and Spanish (as well as early texts of Catalan). Hence, not the common oral tradition, but instead the shared tradition of literacy in a catholic western context explains the rise of Type B.

The history of –*mente* is complicated and still partially unknown. On the one hand, there is a popular tradition of using grammaticalized forms like *solamente* "only" (8th c.), with variants such as OSpan. -*miente*/-*mientre* that were later readapted to the orthography Lat. -*mente* during the process of standardization, more concretely, by the reintroduction of etymologic spellings according to the model of Classical Latin during the Renaissance. On the other hand, Christian authors used the Latin paraphrase with *mente* for the propagation of religion, where the dialectic of body and mind (*mens*) played a prominent role. As Banniard (1992) convincingly states, the communication of Christian messages obliged its promoters to mediate between the erudite written tradition, where the messages were conserved, and the spoken language of the illiterate addressees. This is probably the reason why -*mente* was more successful than other solutions (e.g. Lat. *in modo* "in a way").

3.2 English

3.2.1 Internal linguistic development in Old and Middle English

As in Romance, the diachrony of manner adverbs runs along two major axes of development. The first one starts from inflected adjectives in Old English (OE; until 1100) and ends with the morphological identity of adjective and adverb in Middle English (ME; until 1500) and Modern English (ModE). This axis will be referred to as *Type A-string*. The second axis begins with the OE suffix *-lice* which developed to *-ly* in ModE (*Type B-string*).

In OE, the bound morpheme *-e* that marked adverbial functions (e.g. *hearde* "hard", *gode* "good", *blinde* "blind") was (identical with) the neuter singular of the instrumental case of the adjective. However, the instrumental case was only marked in the strong declension, whereas in the weak declension *-e* was the nominative-accusative singular neuter (e.g. *blinde*; see Campbell 1977: §656).[8] The comparative followed the patterns of weak declension, whereas the superlative was declined weak or strong (Campbell: §657). OE *-e* is thus in line with the Indo-European features of using a neuter form of the adjective for adverbial functions, with an option to develop the neuter instrumental case, as with OLat. instrumentalis *humanē* (adv.) or ClassLat. *commodō*. With the general loss of declension in ME, final *-e* was lost as well. Consequently, in ME the adjective and the adverb developed into the same form. Thus if it is possibly problematic to consider OE *hearde* simply as a Type A adverb because it was indeed marked for instrumental functions, there can be no doubt that the development to ME reduced the distinctive morphological marks for different functions of the adjective to a single morphological category.

The rise of the modern Type B mark *-ly* for adverbs parallels the decadence of the OE case system. As in Romance, the Type-B-string is more complex and still partially opaque in its development. OEngl. *-lic* was a suffix for adjectives that was added to nouns or adjectives (e.g. *dæglic* "daily", *heofonlic* "heavenly", *tidlic* "temporary"; see Campbell: §642), as in ModE *kingly, knightly, masterly*. While it seems to be natural to use a suffix in order to transcategorize nouns to adjectives, there must have been semantic reasons to add *-lic* to an adjective in order to derive another adjective, as in ModE *sick/sickly*, where the latter weakens the concept. In

---

8. Cf. the Germanic tradition of using this case of the adjective for adverbial functions (Krahe & Meid 1969: 86). For example, the situation in Old High German was similar to OE. For a concise diachronic comparison of English and German and excellent details see Pounder (2001). For this author, their diachronic drift apart is essentially due to efforts of standardization (cf. Maas' (2012) seminal study).

this respect, the OED (*s.v.* *-ly*, suffix¹) observes: "When *-ly* is appended to an adj., the resulting derivative adj. often connotes a quality related to or resembling that expressed by its primary; cf., e.g. Old English *léof* "dear" with *léoflic* "lovely" (or, as it might be rendered, "such as becomes dear")".⁹

According to the standard description in manuals, the OE adjectival suffix *-lic* regularly adopted the morphology *-líce* when it was used as an adverb. In other words, it behaved in exactly the same way as adverbs like OE *hearde*. Hence, *-lic* was an adjectival suffix, with *-líce* being its adverbial extension. The functional change of OE *-lic* from an adjectival suffix to and adjectival and adverbial suffix seems to be a genuine development that starts in OE (OED: *s.v.* *-ly*, suffix²; cf. Jespersen 1974, vol. 6: 408):

> In Old English, however, there are several instances (e.g. *bealdlíce* boldly, *swétlíce* sweetly) in which an adv. in *-líce* has been formed directly from a simple adj. without the intervention of an adj. in *-lic*. In Middle English the number of these direct formations was greatly increased [...].

This means that OE already used *-líce* as an independent suffix to derive adverbs from adjectives. Campbell (§664) specifies more precisely that *-líce* was used as an alternative to regular *-e*:¹⁰

> Since adjs. in *-lič* normally formed advs. in *-liče*, this ending early became regarded as an adverbial suffix, which could be used beside or instead of *-e*, *heardliče, holdliče, hwætliče, lætliče* (beside *hearde, holde, late*), the advs. of *heard, hold, hwæt, læt*.

Uhler (1926: 3) provides substantial evidence for the fact that there was no semantic difference between dual forms such as *gelome/gelomlice* "steadily", *georne/geornlice* "eagerly", *rihte/rihtlice* "rightly", etc. All this shows that *-lice* was not simply the adverbial case of adjectives in *-lic*, but an almost independent adverbial suffix available for all adjectival stems.

According to Strang (1970: 272), *-e* had become unproductive by 1170, in contrast to the high productivity of *-lice*. As indicated in the OED entry for the

---

9. The development of the *adjectival* suffix *-ly* is generally connected with Scandinavian influence (OED: *s.v.* *-ly*, suffix¹). This Scandinavian influence apparently favored a natural tendency of already front spelled OE *-lič* that repeats in the etymology of *I* and *every*. Hence, it operated in the sense of favoring a specific variant. But all this does not explain the functional change of *-ly* from an adjectival to an adverbial suffix. This would presuppose that the equivalent Scandinavian suffixes were specifically adverbial, which is not the case.

10. *Holdlice* "faithfully", *hwætlice* "lively, courageously", *lætlice* "slowly".

adjectival suffix -*ly*, the Germanic etymology of -*lic* is 'having the appearance or form indicated by the first element of the word' (cf. Guimier 1985). This semantic concept suits manner qualities in general. In Modern German attributes such as *affengleich* "like a monkey" apply to adjectival and adverbial functions. In English, an example like **to feel kingly free* is not accepted by usage, but it would be functionally and semantically possible. Hence, the semantics of -*lic* did not intervene selectively with regard to the choice of adjectival or adverbial function, and this is still the case for -*ly* in Modern English, even if the frequency and productivity of the latter as an adverbializing suffix is more salient today. From a semantic point of view, -*lice* did not really need the instrumental ending -*e* when used as a verb modifier (if syntactically identified as such).

3.2.2 *The way to Modern English: External influence and linguistic norm*

Adverbs ending in -*ly* considerably expanded in ME. In Early Middle English, their frequency was already superior to that of Type A (Donner 1991; Nevalainen 1997). Their usage was even fashionable. As a consequence, in the 17th c. adverbial -*ly* was also attached to adjectives ending in -*ly* such as *earlily, godlily, kindlily, livelily, verily*, etc. which are avoided in ModE (cf. Pounder 2001: 339). In French, there was a similar tendency to excessively use -*ment* in the 16th and 17th c., with particular enthusiasm by the *Précieuses* (Hummel 2012: 310–315). According to Onions (1983), the development of English Type B adverbs was consciously encouraged by language policy which followed the French model. This would explain the striking lexical parallels between English and Romance languages in the domain of sentential adverbs, e.g. Fr. *apparemment*, It. *apparentemente*, Pt. *apparentemente*, Sp. *aparentemente*, Engl. *apparently* (Hummel 2012: 257–258). The OED implicitly stresses a French influence in the development of English Type B adverbs in the case of ordinal numbers: "From the early part of the 16th c. the suffix has been added to ordinal numbers to form advs. denoting serial position, as *firstly, secondly, thirdly*, etc. (cf. French *premièrement* "firstly", etc.) (OED: s.v. -*ly*, suffix[2])". The exaggerated usage of Type B adverbs during the 16th and 17th centuries explains why in cases such as Engl. *first/firstly* (Baugh & Cable 1986: 385; Jespersen 1974, vol. 6: 415; cf. also *oftenly, soonly*), Sp. *primero/primeramente* "first/firstly", etc., where Type A is standard, Type B tends to be perceived as hypercorrect, more refined or extremely affected. Their present-day perception traces to the same sociocultural background.

Hence, we can hypothesize that these languages were involved in a common effort to use Type B adverbs for the organization of written discourse. This was already the case in translations from Latin. OE *witudlike* "truly" is twice attested with sentential function in the 8th c. (translation of the Gospel of Matthew 26: 51–52, *apud* Maas 2012: 451–452). This could be a first influence of Latin on English literacy, but there is no direct equivalent in the *Vulgata*. Breivik and Swan (1994) provide a longer list of sentential adverbs in Old English. From the Renaissance onwards, the intellectual efforts concerning language policy belong to the same universe of discourse (cf. Miller 2012: 192–227). English shares with Romance languages the search for linguistic enrichment in the Renaissance, the subsequent desire of linguistic purification in order to eliminate the exaggerations of savage linguistic enrichment (definition of linguistic rules or acknowledgement of the *bon usage*), followed by increasing popularization and liberalization from the 19th c. until today. In the case of sentential adverbs, the parallel development must have been a specific movement of literacy, since studies on discourse markers in informal spoken communication show that informal orality tends to avoid Type B (see Section 1).

French influence in the 16th and 17th c. obviously calls to mind that French could have played a role in the centuries after the Norman Conquest in 1066, when French was the language of the upper class and the educated (together with Latin), at least until the period when the intimate relations with France were cut off (loss of Normandy in 1204, Hundred Years' War (1337–1453), and in administration, law and school until the second half of the 14th c. (Baugh & Cable 1986: 143–152). By this time, French was more and more a language of the educated. In writing, where French paralleled or followed Latin, English replaced the former only during the 15th c. Despite the importance of French until the 15th c., no direct influence on the development of *-ly* can be detected: First, the morphological and functional development of *-ly* is exclusively English-Germanic. Second, if French was used by the elites, there was no policy directed to the English language or cultivation of English (Baugh & Cable 1986: 113, 117). Hence, the French influence on the English grammar was at best likely to occur when English was re-established as the linguistic standard for oral and written communication (cf. Baugh & Cable 1986: 166–167).[11] Now, the development of the adverbial function of OE *-líce* > ME *-lič* > ME > *-ly*, was already accomplished by the end of the 14th c. All French loan adjectives in this period were immediately used as adverbs ending in *-ly*

---

11. Prins (1952) suggests the following examples of French influence in Middle English: Engl. *to cry high* with Fr. *crier (en) haut*; *to cut short: couper court*; *to look hard: regarder durement*; *to stop short: s'arrêter court*; *to take seriously: prendre sérieusement*; *to turn short: tourner court*. Clearly, if there was influencing, it activated rules that already existed in English. Moreover, the examples show that the influence was exerted on both Type A and Type B. The relevant fact seems to be that English authors observed what happened in French. Consequently, they should have been aware of the clear preference for Type B adverbs during the standardization of French. For French influence on sentential adverbs in Middle English see Breivik & Swan (1994: 17–20).

(*ibid.*: 178, Miller 2012: 177). Consequently, the French model was not responsible for the early development of *-ly*. It was rather a grammatical instrument for the integration of foreign elements into the English language.

It appears likely that traditional Type A adverbs like *hard* offered more resistance to *-ly* than new adjectives. Hence, *-ly* could have followed the expansion ('enrichment') of the English vocabulary, especially in literacy. According to Marchand (1969: 364–365), before 1300 "French words were fore [sic] some time felt to be foreign elements and were not 'converted' with the same ease as native stems were". This could in turn have favored the usage of *-ly* for French words. Conversely, Type A was confined to the traditional core lexicon. It is a striking fact that Type A adverbs in present-day Romance (Hummel 2000: 417–481) and English still prototypically belong to the core group of inherited short old items that are current in every day oral communication: ModE. *bright, deep, fair, fast, loud, quick, right, sharp, slow, straight, strong, thick, hard, high, ill, long, wide* (listed by Nilsen 1972: 81; cf. the thorough account by Nevalainen 1994: 246–252). None of these has Latin or French roots. In Jespersen's longer list (1974: 48–51), only *direct, just* and *plain* stem from Latin or Old French. Nevalainen (1997: 168) indicates *just, sure, tender, very*.

In order to understand the competition of Type A and Type B, prescriptive linguistic norm is relevant as well, especially when schooling becomes compulsory (see Pulgram 1968; Pounder 2001). Bolinger (1972: 24) observes that the prestige of Type A quantifiers vanished in the first half of the 19th c.:

> These were once preferred, according to Pegge's *English Language* (1803) [...]: "The best of us, gen. use the adj. for the adv., where there is any degree of comparison to be expressed. *How extreme cold the weather is*". The 1843–1844 edition of the same has the note "Quite out of date now".

Nevalainen (1994: 244) cites Lowth's *A short introduction to English grammar* (1762) as follows: "Adjectives are sometimes employed as adverbs: improperly, and not agreeably to the genius of the English language".

Regardless of this, the 'positive' action of grammars, as I would call it by analogy to *positive law* in legislation, was still more decisive. As Pounder (2001: 336–337) convincingly shows, the critiques directed to Type A were occasional; the systematic fact was that grammars simply ignored it and posited Type B as "the" mechanism of adverb formation. Hummel (2013b) observes a similar situation in Romance.

Schoolmasters actively promoted the replacement of Type A by Type B (Kruisinga 1927: 107–108; cf. Tagliamonte & Ito 2002: 240):

> If the use of the shorter forms is less frequent nowadays than it is in earlier English, it is probably due to the modern schoolmaster. This personage is undoubtedly responsible for the restriction in the use of unchanged adjectives as adjuncts of

degree as in *wide open, clean gone*, etc. It would be quite superfluous to show examples in earlier English, as any reader will be able to find them, not only in familiar writings such as the Verney papers or Pepys, and later in the Diary of Fanny Burney, but also in more dignified writing such as the Spectator and the novels of Jane Austen, and even in Dryden (e.g. *so exceeding vain* [...]).

Kruisinga's remark may appear to be exaggerated, but if we take into account that prescriptive language policy was not always as liberal as today, we can hypothesize that this influence could have been stronger in former times. In light of the preceding paragraphs, we might say that Pegge's turn-around shows that the attempts to purify the English language were being successful. Kruisinga's description mirrors the fact that the schoolmaster's discourse inherited the purist discourse, certainly until today. The normative control acted selectively on adverbial functions to the disadvantage of Type A.

Schoolmasters may have accelerated the marginalization of Type A, but they did not originate it. The corpus data explored by Nevalainen (1994, 1997) show that the decline of Type A is a long term phenomenon, since its proportion with regard to the corresponding Type B forms fell from 21 percent of the adverbs in Early Modern English (1350–1420) to 13 percent in Early Modern English (1640–1710), approaching the oral present-day data of York English (15 percent; Tagliamonte & Ito 2002: 249). These results are not biased by the expansion of Type B at the level of type frequency since Nevalainen observes a given number of alternative forms (e.g. *slow/slowly*). On the other hand, her data do not represent the whole amount of Type A forms. Nevalainen also relates type frequency with the size of the corpora in these epochs, suggesting a rather stable situation of Type A usage, but her data are not entirely clear and biased by the option to only consider dual forms. Importantly, token frequency provides clear evidence for the omnipresence of Type A: In the same period, about 40 percent of the attested adverb tokens belong to Type A (*ibid.:* 172–183). This easily explains how the frequency of Type A may increase under certain conditions (single authors, youth language, trendy usage of single items (e.g. *real*), etc.).

The assumption that the proportion of Type A could have been rather stable is indirectly confirmed by the sociolinguistic research of Tagliamonte and Ito (2002: 238), since the quantitative relation between Type A and Type B "is a stable sociolinguistic marker in the local vernacular", which "can be traced to the earliest stages in the development of variation between *-ly* and zero". Sociolinguistic variation seems to be low and secondary to this tradition, although the frequency of Type A is higher with men with a low level of education. To put it in the authors' words (p.260): "it is not the case that the zero adverb is being used in a new way, but in the same old way". The relevance of the historical impact is corroborated by the fact that Type A is a common feature of substandard in English dialects, Cockney and New World varieties (see survey by Tagliamonte & Ito 2002: 242–243).

The stability and high frequency of Type A corroborate their belonging to the fundamental, essentially Germanic attributes that ensure the necessities of everyday communication (see above). Conversely, the expansion of Type B appears to be the correlate of "Sprachausbau" (cf. Kloss 1967; Maas 2008, 2010; Pountain 2011), with dual forms overlapping the traditional ones (e.g. *fastly, soonly*) and a bulk of new forms with no corresponding Type A adverb, especially for writing. Hence, the striking fact is not so much the decay of Type A, as it is generally assumed, but the "Ausbau" of Type B in literacy and the language of the educated, with secondary osmotic effects on the tradition(s) of speaking (see above *direct, just* and *plain*).

Inferentiality is a major feature in informal oral communication that works on the basis of shared knowledge, whereas literacy tends to be explicit, not only in order to compensate the lack of shared knowledge in written communication between speakers that do not know each other, but also because full explicitness has become a normative imperative of writing, at least in terms of prototypicality. Descriptive linguistic devices such as attributes are crucial for making qualities and circumstances explicit (cf. Drieman 1962; Chafe 1982: 41–42; Biber 1988: 50–51, 104–105, 139–141; Biber et al. 1999: 504–507; Maas 2010: 27, 106). Consequently, the enormous expansion of Type B adverbs is the natural correlate of the increasing importance of literacy (more and more speakers are literate; literacy occupies and creates new domains, etc.). Regardless of this, there are no functional reasons for preferring Type B adverbs to Type A adverbs for the "Ausbau" of literacy since Type A works perfectly in Dutch, German, and Romanian. Consequently, the priority given to Type B in literacy is a cultural phenomenon that requires an historical explanation. Once Type B is preferred by literacy, it naturally follows the expansion of descriptive devices, overrunning Type A at the level of type frequency. As a consequence, Type A progressively appears to be restricted to the small number of frequent adjectives that belong to the basic vocabulary of colloquial orality.[12]

---

12. In both English and Romance, poetry tends to avoid Type B for reasons of stylistic cumbersomeness, suffix repetition (monotony), and rime. Moreover, there is a straight tradition of favoring Type A from Classical Greek and Latin to the Renaissance (Hummel 2013b; Tagliamonte & Ito 2002: 237; Pounder 2001: 337). For OE *-lice* see Uhler (1926: 3). This is a nice micro-scenario of "Sprachausbau" where natural conditions (limited space, rime, expressiveness) and cultural traditions specifically interact. In addition, secondary predication and the power of imagination related with underspecified Type A attributes (e.g. *to think big*) are natural prolongations of Type A at the interface of what is traditionally called 'adjective' and 'adverb'.

Attempts to 'purify' the standards of writing reinforce this cultural process. As far as the impact of cultural traditions for Sprachausbau is concerned, the attempt to clearly separate adjectives from adverbs runs as a common thread through normative efforts (cf. Pounder 2001: 336), especially with authors who prefer *rules* to *usage* in the spirit of Illumination. In *The philosophy of rhetoric* (1776), George Campbell (vol. 1, 374–375) defines as his "first canon" that homographs with different functions should as far as possible be morphologically distinguished. He then illustrates this rule for adjectives and adverbs:

> By the same rule we ought to prefer *scarcely*, as an adverb, to *scarce*, which is an adjective; and *exceedingly*, as an adverb, to *exceeding*, which is a participle.

According to Strang (1970: 139), in the period from 1550 to 1770 "a sense of correctness [...] prescribed that forms with the appearance of adjectives" should not be used as tertiary modifiers such as *pretty, extraordinary, pure, terrible, dreadful, cruel, plaguy,* and *devilish*, was responsible for their replacement by the corresponding adverb in -*ly* and favored *very*, which was rather unusual in the 17th c.[13] *Very* had no adjectival function that could have been criticized. Moreover, the "sense of unease about adverbs homophonous with an adjective [...] has been felt at all periods, and there has been a steady progress from plain to -*ly* forms" (*ibid*.: 273; cf. Nevalainen 1994: 244). Strang does not specify, however, if and by whom (the educated?) unease was felt, if with regard to orality and literacy, or only to the latter.

Similarly, Ger. -*erweise* ("-ly" with sentential adverbs) and Dut. -*erwijs* have colloquial Type A alternatives (see (16)) that are avoided in standard literacy. According to the corpus analyzed by Diepeveen (2012: 165–174), evaluative Dut. -*erwijs* expands from the 17th c. on, with particular acceleration during the 19th c. (cf. Diepeveen & Van de Velde 2010: 394–396). This means that its expansion starts with the standardization of Dutch (cf. Maas 2012: 188).

In the case of English, the important work of Biber clearly documents the result of "Sprachausbau" favoring Type B:

> Conversation and academic prose represent opposite extremes of use: in conversation, over 60% of the common adverbs are simple forms, and only about 20% -*ly* forms; in academic prose, about 55% of the common adverbs are -*ly* forms, and slightly over 30% simple forms.
> (Biber et al. 1999; 540; cf. Pullum & Huddleston 2002: 567)

"Simple forms" refers to all underived adverbs, including *well, soon,* etc.

---

13. According to Nevalainen's (1997: 174) analysis of the Helsinki Corpus, *very* was currently used as early as in the 16th c. The raise of *very* paralleled the decline of adverbial *full* and *right*.

4. The Old-World-New-World gap

In the Portuguese or Spanish speaking parts of America, Type A is the overall standard in informal oral communication, not only in the verb-modifying functions but in all functions listed in Section 2 (see Hummel 2002, 2007, 2008, 2009, 2010, 2012). This is also the case for Lousiana French and Acadian French (Hummel 2000, 2013b). This means that all American varieties of Romance share the feature of prevailing Type A usage in informal oral communication. In Europe, Type A is used where the historical impact of standardization was low (southern Italian dialects, Sardinian) or came late (Romanian). This places the situation in America in line with the traces left by the oral traditions in Europe. In those European languages which introduced standards of writing early on, the impact of using, recommending and teaching Type B surfaces clearly. In spoken European Spanish, Type B correlates with education and formal speaking, being about three times more frequent with educated speakers and formal oral discourse (Kraschl 2008). In French, Type B is most frequent in written standard, whereas frequency of alternative solutions increases in both refined literary style and slang (Kofler 2007). The former diverges from the norms of written standard because literary style is liberal and develops variants ("Sprachausbau"), elegant solutions such as *Il parle les yeux fermés* "He talks with closed eyes", *Il marche le pas lent* "He walks at a slow pace" being very appreciated. The latter uses Type A systematically. In Italian and French, the highest frequency of Type B has been observed in standard texts (newspapers) (Bischoff 1970). Consequently, there is a strong correlation of Type B usage with written standard in those Romance languages where Type B has been implemented. Europe and America converge in literacy, although the osmosis from the oral Type A standard to literacy is naturally more developed in America than in Europe. In orality, however, one could not say that Type A is the informal standard in spoken French, Italian, Portuguese and Spanish, where the impact of education and the attitude to linguistic norms catalyze the usage of Type B, especially in the case of French. As a consequence of this, a considerable gap separates the American oral standard in Romance from oral standards in Europe.

The case of Romance clearly parallels the differences that have been observed between American and British English (see Biber et al. 1999: 542–547; cf. Pullum & Huddleston 2002). The "colonial lag" (Görlach 1991) is a topic in linguistic discussion. American linguists are clearly aware of Type A usage as a distinctive feature from British English (see here in 2.4). This awareness is somehow distorted by two factors. On the one hand, British English is not perceived for its substandard varieties, where Type A plays a major role, but for its standards of writing. On the other hand, Type A is often perceived as a 'corruption' of language, that is, as phenomenon by which the allegedly primary suffix *-ly* is dropped. This means that educated speakers reinterpret Type A as a truncation of Type B. In their excellent study, Tagliamonte & Ito (2002: 238) provide an adequate analysis of this reinterpretation by the educated. The topic is also commonplace in linguistic studies. To give an example, Diepeveen & Van de Velde (2010: 382) argue that in "informal spoken English, *-ly* may be left out" (see also 2.4). The topic of linguistic 'corruption' was a general topic in American English grammars until the 20th c. (and who knows whether or not it survives in the discourse of teachers). Laberge and Sankoff (1979: 424) quote a nice example for the same attitude by a francophone speaker in Montreal: "Le joual, c'est une déformation, comme tu as des patois en France". It comes as no surprise that French linguists have explained Type A adverbs as truncations of 'correct' Type B adverbs, even if this does not morphologically work in cases such as *hautement* > *haute (adv.) (e.g. Moignet 1981, vol. 1: 52). Neither Bolinger nor the French linguists base their impressions on objective linguistic data (Bolinger's data come from Borst 1902 and Kirchner 1955, with data from AmE and BrE). Hence, the source of the peculiar perception has to be located in linguistic education. This discourse systematically confounds normative linguistic standard with the origin of language, as if former generations of dialect speakers had used standard before. As in Romance, the frequency patterns of Type B in written American and British English share significant similarities (Ramat & Ricca 1994: 316–318), displaying a common tradition of writing. This means that the gap does not exist in a significant way at the level of 'correct' standard writing, although the osmotic relation of orality and literacy naturally favors the usage of Type A for writing in America.

To sum up, the diachrony of Type A and Type B has to be situated at the interface of orality and literacy. While this is true for both, America and Europe, a secondary feature appears if we compare the varieties of English and Romance in America with those in Europe: in the former the oral tradition of using Type A is stronger than in the latter. While Type A was stigmatized in British English, as we have seen in 3.2, it was defended by Noah Webster and others in America (see bibliography in Tagliamonte & Ito: 240–241). As in present-day American Portuguese and Spanish, where Type A is standard in the informal communication of all speakers (if they do not personally insist on using a 'better language'), Type A "was constantly heard in the professional and social conversation of cultured people" (Mencken 1961: 389). The attitude of Webster and others clearly parallels the argumentation of their influent contemporary Venezuelan-Chilean colleague, Andrés Bello, and other eminent Hispano-american linguists, who did not accept the European standard in those cases where the American usage was etymologically justified, even if they did not use this argument in favor of Type A. Hence, in spite of sharing the same Western culture with Europe, a secondary process of shared American attitudes began to favor American traditions from North to South. Historically, this process has to be related with the shared struggle for political independence and cultural identity in the second half of the 18th and the first half of the 19th c. In both cases, the immigrants brought to the New World oral traditions where Type A was profoundly anchored. It is obviously not adequate to use the term 'colonial lag' since America simply conserved the genuine tradition, showing more resistance to linguistic models and prescriptive norms.

A final point is (un)productivity. Type A is generally considered as unproductive in English (Nevalainen 1994:243). Manuals of present-day English tend to illustrate manner adverbs with Type B, describing Type A as a limited set, e.g. "of limited application to idioms (Strang 1978:188)". In the same vein, Bolinger characterized Type A adverbs as archaic (see 2.2). As shown in 2.5, a closer look at substandard, and especially at dialects, may uncover the productivity of Type A against the expectation of the educated, whose linguistic education tends to be their 'second nature' (Maas 2012:25). Possibly, Type A in British English gets closer to the idiom-description (Strang), whereas it could be more productive in American substandard. Importantly, the fact that the series of Type A adverbs is rather limited in current corpora does not imply a lack of productivity. The necessity of using descriptive attributes is limited in every day communication. This is probably the reason why Type A has resisted in the core domains of short, old, Germanic adjectives, whereas Type B follows innovation. Consequently, the limited number of Type A adverbs has to be related to the limited necessities of informal every-day communication. Moreover, the productivity of Type B in standard French and standard Spanish is limited as well (cf. Company Company forthc.), whereas more productivity is observed in specialized languages. Roughly speaking, the set of Type A adverbs tends to be adapted to the necessities of informal oral communication, whereas the set of Type B adverbs deserves the imperatives of standard literacy. The former becomes saturated with a small number of attributes, the latter needs a rather huge number, with constant innovation in specialized languages.

5. One or two word-classes?

As we have seen, the traditional separation of the word-classes of adjective and adverb clearly fails to provide an adequate account of the data in English and Romance. In fact, in both cases a 'flexible' word-class (Type A) coexists and competes with 'differentiated' word-classes: Type B (manner adverbs) as opposed to Type A restricted to noun modification (adjectives). The analysis of Type A as a word-class which covers adjectival and adverbial attributes (modifiers) is supported by Hengeveld's (1992) typological approach to part-of-speech systems in a sample of languages of the world. According to Hengeveld, in "flexible" languages one word-class covers the attributive functions of adjective and manner adverb. This analysis is fundamentally correct and adequate for Type A in English and Romance. The only thing I have criticized in the Introduction is the classification of English as a "differentiated language". Even if Hengeveld's typology only refers to "a strong tendency towards one of the types" (1992: 69), from the point of view of language variation there are varieties of English which tend to use Type A for everyday communication (e.g. informal spoken American English), and others which prefer Type B (written standard).[14] The same holds for Romance, at least for Type A, since Type B is not available in all Romance languages and varieties. In sum, the coexistence and competition of Type A and Type B attributes in Romance and English crucially support Evans and Levinson's (2009) claim for considering "language diversity" as starting point for typology. If we abandon the variationist perspective and consider the language as a whole, English and Romance 'hesitate' between the monocategorial and the bicategorial system. Hengeveld's classification is apparently biased by the common vision of standard English as a language that forms adverbs with the suffix -ly. The coexistence of Type A and Type B in English and Romance can be schematized as follows:

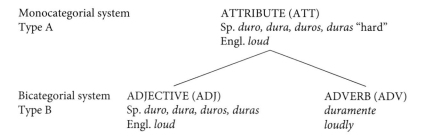

Figure 1. Monocategorial and bicategorial systems of attributive word-classes

---

14. Another problem of word-class separation is the extension of the attributive function of Type B adverbs to the modification of a NP (see discussion of participant-oriented adverbs in Romance -ment(e) and Engl. -ly by Molinier (1985); Guimier (1991); Bartsch (1976: 141–148); Valera Hernández (1998); Broccias (2011). By contrast, Hummel (2000: 111–122) argues that 'adverbial' NP-modification is not based on linguistic function but on contextual inference (except for early stages of grammaticalization, when Lat. *mente* still referred to a mental disposition of the subject).

In contrast to Hengeveld, I do not use *adjective* (ADJ) but *attribute* (ATT) for the monocategorial level. Hengeveld's solution is probably better from the typological and functional point of view of word-class hierarchy, but using *adjective* for the monocategorial level is a permanent source of confusion in studies on Romance, where adjectives are considered to be inflected modifiers of nouns.[15] In other words, I use ATT for simple reasons of understandability. The fact that in the Germanic grammaticographic tradition the term *attribution* is used for syntactic function as opposed to word-class might be a source of confusion, but in this case I argue with Hengeveld that ATT refers to a word-class in the sense of a morphologized function, which is attribution (modification). As pointed out by Hengeveld, this approach implies a division of the traditional category of adverbs since it is restricted to those of manner, adverbs of time and space being excluded. Given the heterogeneity of the word-class of adverbs (see e.g. Guimier 1996: 1; Pullum & Huddlestone 2002: 563; Sonntag 2005), it seems to be legitimate to follow Hengeveld since this approach provides a better description and explanation of the linguistic data. In the case of English, supplementary evidence comes from diachrony since the forerunner of Type A is the instrumental case of the adjective in Old English.

This origin seems to be one reason why Type A adverbs in English do not figure as instances of conversion in older studies on conversion (e.g. Biese 1941) or in historical studies (e.g. Robertson & Cassidy 1954: 134). It is unclear to me why most recent studies on conversion do not mention it either, while most grammars recognize the usage of adjectives as adverbs. This is possibly related to their perception as a limited set of lexicalized exceptions. Amongst those who use the term conversion for Type A adverbs,[16] Nist (1966: 54) goes as far as to misinterpret adjectival *-ly* in *lowly* and *sickly* as adverb→adjective conversion: "from *adjective* to *adverb* in *drive slow, hold tight, think straight*; [...] from *adverb* to *adjective* in *lowly job, sickly child*". He apparently ignores the function of *-ly* as an adjectival suffix.

To be honest, I profoundly share all skepticism about the validity of word-classes and their heuristic value as an explication for linguistic data. A specialist

---

15. In her study on the interfaces of adjectives, Ramaglia (2011) includes all functions that canonically require inflection in Romance, but not the adverbial functions, which instead constitute a major feature of the adjectives' interface with syntax, especially with regard to the discussion on iconicity (pp. 2–6). In the same vein, Teyssier (1968) dedicates its study on the syntax of the English adjective to the noun phrase. The adjective-adverb interface does not exist.

16. E.g. Mustanoja (1960: 648–649); cf. the critical overview by Bauer & Valera (2005). Ježek & Ramat (2009) analyze Type A in terms of "transcategorization".

like Croft (1990: 13) clearly stipulates: "The main problematic categories for cross-linguistic identification are the fundamental grammatical categories: noun, verb and adjective, subject and object, head and modifier [...]". The present paper has provided considerable evidence against the traditional word-classes of adjectives and adverbs. So why should a redefinition of word-classes solve the fundamental problems pointed out by Croft? In the first place, more than word-classes itself, it is the obsession to impose them on all instances we observe in syntax which poses a problem. In German and Dutch the unmarked form of the adjective is used for adverbial functions (see examples in (1)–(2)). Consequently, there are good reasons to argue that the distinction of manner-adverbial and adjectival functions is a matter of syntax, not of word-class. However, grammars of German and Dutch systematically have two chapters on adjectives and adverbs as parts of speech, and school trains students to separate these two classes (Diepeveen 2012: 30–36). We all learned to completely analyze sentences in terms of word-classes. The reason for this is so is our western grammaticographic tradition that follows models elaborated for Latin (see Maas 2012: 165–183, 269–300). The fact that Figure 1 replaces this tradition certainly is a point of progress. In the second place, even if morphologized paradigms are not universals, they have to be considered a possibility. In our case, Type A and Type B clearly display features of morphologicization. The important point is that this does not exclude their coexistence with other strategies, e.g. Type C and Type D (see the excellent synthesis by Salazar García 2013). Historically, languages develop preferences with regard to such strategies, with possible internal differentiations according to their variationist structure. Moreover, the suffix *-mente* has developed from the Latin paraphrases such as *sola mente*. In addition, many Type C adverbs are univerbations of phrases (e.g. Sp. *entonces* > Lat. *in tunc*). All these aspects make Figure 1 an operational point of reference for linguistic analysis.

However, as useful as such a differentiated point of view may be, we have to counterbalance it with the only universal we can rely on, that is, linguistic function. All units we observe in a successful communication have a function. In our case, we may reduce linguistic function to syntactic function. To put it in other words, word-classes may be adapted to series of functions and functions may be realized by series of linguistic solutions. This is the reason why some authors define *conversion* in terms of changed syntactic categories (e.g. Plag forthc.). On the other hand, when a given language displays a tendency to develop attributive word-classes, conversion may be perceived as a strong change. Hence, it seems to be more adequate to consider the data with regard to two extremes: strong paradigmaticization and linguistic function in an utterance.

In the following example, Sp. *bastante* "quite a lot" occupies different syntactic positions and functions:

(29) a. *bastante grande* ADJ modifier (– inflected)
         "quite big"
     b. *bastante bien* ADV modifier (– inflected)
         "quite well"
     c. *habla bastante* VP modifier (– inflected)
         "s/he speaks quite a lot"
     d. *bastantes casas* NP modifier (+ inflected)
         "quite a few houses"

Rather than manifestations of an *invariant* adverb, (29a–c) can be considered as uninflected manifestations of a single word-class. The traditional binary classification of *bastante* in (29a–c) as an adverb and in (29d) as an adjective imposes a dichotomy that does not mirror the fact that (29a-c) show different functions of this word, that is, not a single adverbial function. Belonging to an inflectional category (Type A), *bastante* displays number agreement when modifying a noun (29d). Hence, inflection depends on syntax. To the difference of verb-noun-conversion, where semantic adaptation is necessary (e.g. Engl. *to walk > a walk*), no conceptual difference can be observed in (29) or in cases such as *a loud song/to sing loud*. This is the reason why Quirk et al. (1995: 71) use the term *homomorphs* for *hard* (adj.) and *hard* (adv.) (see the thorough discussion by Valera Hernández 1996). However, this term suggests a rather arbitrary relation between these units, by analogy to the term *homonymy* in semantics. In the same vein, syntactic analyses often use or implicitly apply the notion of *syntactic homonymy* (e.g. Jespersen 1974, vol. 6: 84; Greenbaum 1969: 6). However, it clearly appears that in many cases we must analyze the data in terms of motivated *polyfunctionality* (by analogy to *polysemy*), including simple change of syntactic function, as in (29), and motivated conceptual differentiation, as in Fr. *un homme pauvre* "poor man" vs. *un pauvre homme* "pitiable man" (see details in Hummel 2013a).

Unlike English, the adjective is inflected in Dutch and German. As in Romance, the extension of the domain of inflection is subject to variance and hesitation ('adverbial agreement' in Romance). As Diepeveen and Van de Velde (2010) convincingly show, Dutch and German draw the demarcation line between inflected adnominal attributes, on the one hand, and uninflected predicative attributes and adverbs, on the other, whereas Romance languages conserve the inflection of the latter (copula constructions, secondary predication). The division line in Dutch and German conflicts with the adjective-adverb distinction, since the predicative attributes are usually not considered as adverbs (cf. Eisenberg 2002: 63). Hence, there are some attributes that are not adverbs but still uninflected.

The clear division pointed out by Diepeveen and Van de Velde was probably reinforced by the purifying process of standardization of writing. In the case of

Romance, uninflected predicative attributes can be found in substandard French: Bauche (1951: 93) cites cases such as *Ma femme est jaloux* [sic] "my wife is jealous" in popular French, and similar examples can still be found in Louisiana French, which indicates a common oral tradition (Hummel 2000: 427–433). These cases are often considered 'corruptions', but it seems more plausible to me that standardization has marginalized such spontaneous possibilities. Similarly, Diepeveen and Van de Velde (2010: 385) explain the "proleptic inflection" of Dut. *een hele mooie periode* "a very nice period" as an innovation in Modern Dutch, but the hypothesis that the phenomenon could be a remnant of traditional inflectional liberty or hesitation in spoken language should not be excluded.

Be this as it may, the hypothesis of a Type A system provides an adequate framework for these variationist phenomena. On the one hand, at the level of word-class, Type A attributes are inflectional units in Dutch, German and Romance. On the other hand, inflectional morphemes are activated or not activated only when they enter a syntactic structure, that is, when they are used in utterance. Consequently, the appearance of such morphemes is a spontaneous process. While there is considerable control for this process in writing, informal oral communication lacks systematic planning. Moreover, spontaneous orality possibly tends to use inflection for the marking of the semantic coherence of a phrase (e.g. Sp. *medios tontos* "half crazy", Dut. *een hele mooie periode*), whereas literacy sticks to the dogma that inflection should reflect the modification of a noun, which restricts inflection to so-called adjectives. Interestingly, predicative attributes display two contradictory features with regard to inflection: In *Charles is tall* the attribute belongs to VP but modifies NP. Dutch and German chose the option of uninflected usage, whereas Romance cultivates inflection, underlining the noun-modifying function of the attribute. To sum up, the assumption of a rather general Type A word-class that meets specific syntactic conditions with specific syntactic and semantic conditions for the usage of inflection explains the emergence of the variants we observe in the data.

6. Conclusion

It has been shown that English shares with Romance the fact that synchrony and diachrony are characterized by the coexistence and competition of two systems that cover adjectival and adverbial functions. The first (Type A) covers both domains with a single word class, while the second uses a suffix for the adverbial functions (Type B), restricting Type A to noun modifiers.

Methodologically, the comparison of Romance and English proves to be a heuristic device that brings to light

- the common Indo-European tradition of using Type A
- a shared Western Culture that specifically promotes Type B in standard literacy

Consequently, Type A tends to be conserved where the impact of standardization is lower. This is the reason why the American varieties of English and Romance better conserve the oral tradition of Type A. In Romance, Type B alternatives regularly emerge in the context of literate standardization. This tradition can be traced back to Late Latin (*-iter*), Classical Latin (*-ē, -iter*), and even Old Greek (*–ως*). In Romance, Type A clearly belongs to an old oral tradition that systematically reemerges when literacy decays, lacks or comes late, as in the case of Romanian. By contrast, in English Type A is closely tied to both the oral and written traditions since it was standard in Old English with unbroken tradition through Middle English until today. Consequently, the superimposed nature of *-ly* becomes more salient in English (cf. Robertson & Cassidy 1954:133–134). The fact that Type A has never been standard in the written tradition of Romance (with the exception of Romanian) poses specific methodological problems since Type A scarcely appears in the written sources we can use for diachronic research.

The oral tradition of using Type A is intimately related to the necessities of every-day oral communication. In both English and Romance, the series of Type A adverbs is limited to the domain of words that were inherited via oral tradition from Germanic (English) or Latin (Romance). These words tend to be short and frequent. They do not belong to the fund of learned words, which were systematically integrated into the Type B system. In English, there are some exceptions that can be explained by the historical impact of French (*just, sure,* etc.).

Research could be considerably improved if the interface of oral and written traditions were taken into account. This is generally not the case. The theory of "Sprachbau" provides an adequate framework for this concern. To give a last example, it is simplistic to explain the increase of sentential adverbs in *-ly* with the general expansion of this suffix (Swan 1991), without taking into account the natural (code specific) and cultural conditions and models that intervene in the techniques and traditions of writing.

References

Adams, James N. 2007. *The Regional Diversification of Latin 200 BC – AD 600*. Cambridge: CUP.
Bäcklund, Ulf. 1973. *The Collocation of Adverbs of Degree in English*. Uppsala: Uppsala Reprotryck.
Banniard, Michel. 1992. *Viva Voce. Communication Ecrite et Communication Orale du IVe au IXe Siècle en Occident latin*. Paris: Institut des Études Augustiniennes.
Bartsch, Renate 1976. *The Grammar of Adverbials*. Amsterdam: North Holland.

Bauche, Henri. 1951. *Le Langage Populaire*. Paris: Payot.
Bauer, Laurie & Valera, Salvador. 2005. Conversion or zero-derivation: An introduction. In *Approaches to Conversion/Zero-derivation*, idem (eds), 7–17. Münster: Waxmann.
Baugh, Albert C. & Cable, Thomas. 1986. *A History of the English Language*, 3rd edn. London: Routledge & Kegan.
Biber, Douglas. 1988. *Variation across Speech and Writing*. Cambridge: CUP.
Biber, Douglas, Johansson, Stig, Leech, Geoffrey, Conrad, Susan & Finegan, Edward. 1999. *Longman Grammar of Spoken and Written English*, Harlow: Longman.
Biese, Yrjoe M. 1941. *Origin and Development of Conversions in English*, Helsinki: Annales Academiae Scientiarum Fennicae.
Bischoff, Heinrich. 1970. *Setzung und Transposition des -mente-Adverbs als Ausdruck der Art und Weise im Französischen und Italienischen mit besonderer Berücksichtigung der Transposition in Adjektive*. Zürich: Juris Druck.
Bolinger, Dwight. 1972. *Degree Words*. The Hague: Mouton.
Borst, Eugen. 1902. *Die Gradadverbien im Englischen*. Heidelberg: Carl Winter.
Breivik, Leiv Egil & Swan, Toril. 1994. Initial adverbials and word order in English with special reference to the Early Modern English. In *Studies in Early Modern English*, Dieter Kastovsky (ed.), 11–43. Berlin: de Gruyter.
Broccias, Cristiano. 2011. Motivating the flexibility of oriented -*ly* adverbs. In *Motivation in Grammar and the Lexicon* [Human Cognitive Processing 27], Klaus-Uwe Panther & Günter Radden (eds), 71–87. Amsterdam: John Benjamins.
Buysschaert, Joost. 1982. *Criteria for the Classification of English Adverbials*. Brussels: Paleis der Academiën.
Campbell, Alistair. 1977. *Old English Grammar*. Oxford: Clarendon Press.
Campbell, George. 1776. *The Philosophy of Rhetoric*, 2 Vols. London: Strahan.
Chafe, Wallace L. 1982. Integration and involvement in speaking, writing, and oral literature. In *Spoken and Written Language: Exploring Orality and Literacy*, Deborah Tannen (ed.), 35–53. Norwood NJ: Ablex.
Chircu, Adrian. 2008. *L'adverbe dans les Langues Romanes. Études Étymologique, Lexicale et Morphologique: français, roumain, italien, espagnol, portugais, catalan, provençal*. Cluj-Napoca: Casa Cărţii de Ştiinţă.
Chircu, Adrian. 2011. *Dinamica Adverbului Românesc. Ieri şi azi*. Cluj-Napoca: Casa Cărţii de Ştiinţă.
Company Company, Concepción. Forthcoming. Los adverbios en -*mente*. In *Sintaxis Histórica de la Lengua Española*, 3ª parte, Concepción Company Company (ed.). México: Universidad Autónoma de México, Fondo de Cultura Económica.
Croft, William, 1990. *Typology and Universals*. Cambridge: CUP.
Crystal, David. 2003. *The Cambridge Encyclopedia of the English Language*. Cambridge: CUP.
Dal, Georgette. 2007. Les adverbes de manière en -*ment* du français: Dérivation ou flexion?. In *Morphologie à Toulouse*, Nabil Hathout & Fabio Montermini (eds), 121–147. München: Lincom.
Diepeveen, Ariane. 2012. Modifying Words. Dutch Adverbial Morphology in Contrast. Ph.D. dissertation, FU Berlin.
Diepeveen, Janneke & Van de Velde, Freek. 2010. Adverbial morphology: How Dutch and German are moving away from English. *Journal of Germanic Linguistics* 22(4): 381–402.
Dietrich, Wolf. 1995. *Griechisch und Romanisch. Parallelen und Divergenzen in Entwicklung, Variation und Strukturen*. Münster: Nodus.

Donner, Morton. 1991. Adverb form in Middle English. *English Studies* 72: 1–11.
Downing, Angela. 2006. The English pragmatic marker *surely* and its functional counterparts in Spanish. In *Pragmatic Markers in Contrast*, Karin Aijmer & Anne-Marie Simon-Vandenbergen (eds), 39–58. Amsterdam: Elsevier.
Drieman, G.H.J. 1962. Differences between spoken and written languages: an exploratory study. *Acta Pschologica* 20: 36–57, 78–100.
Duden. Die Grammatik. 2009. Mannheim: Dudenverlag.
Dürscheid, Christa & Hefti, Inga. 2006. Syntaktische Merkmale des Schweizer Standarddeutsch. In *Schweizer Standarddeutsch*, Christa Dürscheid & Martin Businger (eds), 131–161. Tübingen: Narr.
Eisenberg, Peter. 2002. Morphologie und Distribution. Zur Morphosyntax von Adjektiv und Adverb im Deutschen. In *Das Adverb – Zentrum und Peripherie einer Wortklasse*, Frederike Schmöe (ed.), 61–76. Wien: Präsens.
Erdmann, Peter. 1997. Supplementive adjective clauses in English. In *Language History and Linguistic Modelling*, Vol. 2: *Linguistic Modelling*, Raymond Hickey & Stanislaw Puppel (eds), 1433–1451. Berlin: Mouton de Gruyter.
Evans, Nicholas & Levinson, Stephen C. 2009. The myth of language universals: Language diversity and its importance for cognitive science. *Behavioral and Brain Sciences* 32: 429–492.
Fortson IV, Benjamin W. 2004. *Indo-European Language and Culture*. Oxford: Blackwell.
Giegerich, Heinz. 2012. The morphology of *-ly* and the categorial status of 'adverbs' in English. *English Language and Linguistics* 16(3): 341–359.
Giger, Nadio. 2011. *Gut, gibt es einen wie Oliver Kahn*. Zum Phänomen rechtsexponierter Verberstnebensätze im Schweizerhochdeutsch. In *Sprachvergleich und Sprachdidaktik*, Martin Joachim Kümmel, (ed.), 43–65. Hamburg: Kovač.
Görlach, Manfred. 1991. Colonial lag? The alleged conservative character of American English and other 'colonial' varieties. In *Englishes* [Varieties of English Around the World G9], Manfred Görlach (ed.), 90–107. Amsterdam: John Benjamins.
Greenbaum, Sidney. 1969. *Studies in English Adverbial Usage*. London: Longmans.
Guimier, Claude. 1985. On the origin of the suffix *-ly*. In *Historical Semantics. Historical Word-formation*, Jacek Fisiak (ed.), 155–170. Berlin: Mouton de Gruyter.
Guimier, Claude. 1991. Sur l'adverbe orienté vers le sujet. In *Les Etats de l'adverbe, Travaux linguistiques du CERLICO* n⁰ 3, Claude Guimier & Pierre Larcher (eds), 97–114. Rennes: Presses Universitaires.
Guimier, Claude. 1996. *Les Adverbes du Français: Le Cas des Adverbes en -ment*. Paris: Ophrys.
Haspelmath, Martin. 1996. Word-class-changing inflection and morphological theory. In *Yearbook of Morphology 1995*, Geert Booij & Jaap van Marle (eds), 43–66. Dordrecht: Kluwer.
Hengeveld, Kees. 1992. *Non-verbal Predication. Theory, Typology, Diachrony*. Berlin: Mouton de Gruyter.
Hengeveld, Kees, Rijkhoff, Jan & Siewierska, Anna. 2004. Parts-of-speech systems and word order. *Journal of Linguistics* 40(3): 527–570.
Hengeveld, Kees & van Lier, Eva. 2010. An implicational map of parts of speech. *Linguistic Discovery* 8(1): 129–156.
Hennemann, Anja. 2012. The epistemic and evidential use of Spanish modal adverbs and verbs of cognitive attitude. *Folia Linguistica* 46(1): 133–170.
Huang, Shuan-Fan. 1975. *A Study of Adverbs*. The Hague: Mouton.
Hummel, Martin. 2000. *Adverbale und adverbialisierte Adjektive im Spanischen. Konstruktionen des Typs* Los niños duermen tranquilos *und* María corre rápido. Tübingen: Narr.

Hummel, Martin. 2002. Considerações sobre os tipos *Ela fala esquisito* e *Ela chega cansada* no português coloquial e literário do Brasil e de Portugal. *Confluência* 24: 43–70.

Hummel, Martin. 2007. Adjetivos adverbializados y otros atributos directos del verbo en el habla oral informal de Chile. In *Vernetzungen. Bedeutung in Wort, Satz und Text. Festschrift für Gerd Wotjak zum 65. Geburtstag*, Vol. 1, Juan Cuartero Otal & Martina Emsel (eds), 221–233. Frankfurt: Peter Lang.

Hummel, Martin. 2008. La predicación secundaria en el habla oral informal de Chile. *ELUA* 22: 129–149.

Hummel, Martin. 2009. La expansión de las unidades atributivas a las circunstancias de lugar y de tiempo. In *La lingüística como reto epistemológico y como acción social. Estudios dedicados al Profesor Ángel López García con ocasión de su sexagésimo aniversario*, Vol. 1, Montserrat Veyrat Rigat & Enrique Serra Alegre, (eds), 463–480. Madrid: Arco Libros.

Hummel, Martin. 2010. La función atributiva cuantitativa en el habla oral informal de Chile. In *De Arte Grammatica. Festschrift für Eberhard Gärtner zu seinem 65. Geburtstag*, Cornelia Döll, Sybille Große, Christine Hundt & Axel Schönberger (eds), 221–250. Frankfurt: Valentia.

Hummel, Martin. 2012. *Polifuncionalidad, Polisemia y Estrategia Retórica. Los Signos Discursivos con Base Atributiva entre Oralidad y Escritura. Acerca de Esp.* bueno, claro, total, realmente, etc. Berlin: Mouton de Gruyter.

Hummel, Martin. 2013a. Polyfunctionality, polysemy, and rhetorical strategy. The functional, semantic and pragmatic motivation of discourse functions. *Grazer Linguistische Studien* 79.

Hummel, Martin. 2013b. Attribution in Romance: Reconstructing the oral and written tradition. *Folia Linguistica Historica* 34.

Hummel, Martin & Kröll, Andrea. 2011. *Vite* et *vitement*. Une étude de diachronie variationnelle. ⟨http://sites.google.com/site/rsgadjadv/resources/work-of-research-group⟩

Hummel, Martin & Stiegler, Karin. 2005. *Dictionnaire historique de l'adjectif-adverbe*. Database. ⟨http://languageserver.uni-graz.at/dicoadverbe⟩

Jespersen, Otto. 1974. *A Modern English Grammar on Historical Principles*, 7 Vols. London and Copenhagen: Allen & Unwin and Munksgaard (reprint).

Jespersen, Otto. 1992. [1924]. *The Philosophy of Grammar*. Chicago IL: University of Chicago Press.

Ježek, Elisabetta & Ramat, Paolo. 2009. On parts-of-speech transcategorization. *Folia Linguistica* 43(2): 391–416.

Karlsson, Keith E. 1981. *Syntax and Affixation. The Evolution of MENTE in Latin and Romance*. Tübingen: Niemeyer.

Kirchner, Gustav. 1955. *Gradadverbien: Restriktiva und Verwandtes im heutigen Englisch*. Halle: Niemeyer.

Kloss, Heinz. 1967. 'Abstand languages' and 'Ausbau languages'. *Anthropological Linguistics* 9: 29–41.

Kofler, Michaela. 2007. Der Gebrauch der Modaladverbien in drei französischsprachigen Romanen von Andreï Makine, Philippe Djian und Alphonse Boudard. MA thesis, Karl-Franzens-Universität Graz.

Koktova, Eva. 1986. *Sentence Adverbials in a Functional Description* [Pragmatics & Beyond VII:2]. Amsterdam: John Benjamins.

Krahe, Hans & Meid, Wolfgang. 1969. *Germanische Sprachwissenschaft*, Vol. 2. Berlin: Walter de Gruyter.

Kraschl, Carmen Therese. 2008. Adverbien auf -*mente* im gesprochenen Spanisch. Eine Analyse anhand von C-ORAL-ROM. MA thesis, Karl-Franzens-Universität Graz.

Kruisinga, Etsko. 1927. On the history of conversion in English. *English Studies* 9: 103–108.

Laberge, Suzanne & Sankoff, Gillian. 1979. Anything *you* can do. In *Syntax and Semantics*, Vol. 12: *Discourse and Syntax*, Talmy Givón (ed.), 419–440. New York NY: Academic Press.

Ledgeway, Adam. 2000. *A Comparative Syntax of the Dialects of Southern Italy: A Minimalist Approach*. Oxford: Blackwell.

Ledgeway, Adam. 2011. Adverb agreement and split intransitivity: Evidence from Southern Italy. *Archivio Glottologico Italiano* 96: 31–66.

Liu, Mingya. 2012. *Multidimensional Semantics of Evaluative Adverbs*. Leiden: Brill.

Löfstedt, Bengt. 1967. Bemerkungen zum Adverb im Lateinischen. *Indogermanische Forschungen* 72: 79–109.

Lutzky, Ursula. 2012. *Discourse Markers in Early Modern English* [Pragmatics & Beyond New Series 227]. Amsterdam: John Benjamins.

Maas, Utz. 2008. Können Sprachen einfach sein? *Grazer Linguistische Studien* 69: 1–44.

Maas, Utz. 2010. Literat und orat. Grundbegriffe der Analyse geschriebener und gesprochener Sprache. *Grazer Linguistische Studien* 73: 21–150.

Maas, Utz. 2012. *Was ist Deutsch? Die Entwicklung der Sprachlichen Verhältnisse in Deutschland*. München: Fink.

Marchand, Hans. 1969. *The Categories and Types of Present-day English Word-formation*. München: Beck.

Martínez Vázquez, Montserrat. 1991. *Sintaxis Inglesa: La Atribución. Estudio Sintáctico-semántico de las Estructuras Atributivas en Inglés Contemporáneo*. Cáceres: Universidad de Extremadura.

Martínez, José A. 1994. La 'función incidental' y su conexión con otras construcciones del español. In *Cuestiones Marginadas de Gramática Española*, José A. Martínez (ed.), 225–283. Madrid: Istmo.

Mencken, Henry Louis. 1961. *The American Language*, Supplement II. New York NY: Knopf.

Miller, Gary D. 2012. *External Influences on English. From its Beginnings to the Renaissance*. Oxford: OUP.

Moignet, Gérard. 1981. *Systématique de la Langue Française*, 2 vols. Paris: Klincksieck.

Molinier, Christian. 1985. Remarques sur une sous-classe d'adverbes en -*ment* orientés vers le sujet et leurs adjectifs sources. *Linguisticæ Investigationes* 9: 321–341.

Mustanoja, Tauno F. 1960. *A Middle English Syntax*, Vol. 1: *Parts of Speech*. Helsinki: Société Néophilologique.

Nevalainen, Terttu. 1994. Aspects of adverbial change in Early Modern English. In *Studies in Early Modern English*, Dieter Kastovsky (ed.), 243–259. Berlin: de Gruyter.

Nevalainen, Terttu. 1997. The processes of adverb derivation in Late Middle and Early Modern English. In *Grammaticalization at Work*, Matti Rissanen, Merja Kytö & Kirsi Heikkonen (eds), 145–189. Berlin: Mouton de Gruyter.

Nilsen, Don Lee Fred. 1972. *English Adverbials*, The Hague: Mouton.

Nist, John. 1966. *A Structural History of English*. New York NY: St. Martin's Press.

Onions, Charles T. 1983. *The Oxford Dictionary of English Etymology*. Oxford: Clarendon Press.

Opdahl, Lise. 2000. *Ly or Zero Suffix? A Study in Variation of Dual-form Adverbs in Present-day English*, 2 vols. Frankfurt: Peter Lang.

Oxford English Dictionary, 2nd edn, online version June 2012, ⟨http://www.oed.com⟩ (September 2012).

Peters, Hans. 1994. Degree adverbs in Early Modern English. In *Studies in Early Modern English*, Dieter Kastovsky (ed.), 269–288. Berlin: de Gruyter.
Pinkster, Harm. 1972. *On Latin Adverbs*. Amsterdam: North-Holland.
Pinsker, Hans Ernst. 1969. *Historische englische Grammatik*, 3. Auflage. München: Hueber.
Plag, Ingo. Forthcoming. 133. English. In *Word-formation. An International Handbook of the Languages of Europe*, Series *Handbücher zur Sprach- und Kommunikationswissenschaft: HSK*, Peter O. Müller, Ingeborg Ohnheiser, Susan Olsen & Franz Rainer (eds). Berlin: de Gruyter Mouton.
Pounder, Amanda. 2001. Adverb-marking in German and English. System and standardization. *Diachronica* 18(2): 301–358.
Pountain, Christopher J. 2011. Latin and the structure of written Romance. In *The Cambridge History of the Romance Languages*, Vol. 1: *Structures*, Martin Maiden, John Charles Smith & Adam Ledgeway (eds), 606–659. Cambridge: CUP.
Prins, Anton A. 1952. *French Influence in English Phrasing*. Leiden: Universitaire Pers Leiden.
Pulgram, Ernst. 1968. A socio-linguistic view of innovation: *-ly* and *-wise*. *Word* 24: 380–391.
Pullum, Geoffrey K. & Huddleston, Rodney. 2002. Adjectives and adverbs. In *The Cambridge Grammar of the English Language*, Rodney Huddleston & Geoffrey K. Pullum (eds), 525–595. Cambridge: CUP.
Quirk, Randolph, Greenbaum, Sidney, Leech, Geoffrey & Svartvik, Jan. 1995. [1991]. *A Comprehensive Grammar of the English Language*, London: Longman.
Radouant, René. 1922. *Grammaire Française*. Paris: Hachette.
Ramaglia, Francesca. 2011. *Adjectives at the Syntax-Semantics Interface*. München: Lincom.
Ramat, Paolo. 2008. Les adverbes latins du point de vue de l'indo-européen. In *Adverbes et Evolution Linguistique en Latin*, Michèle Fruyt & Sophie Van Laer (eds), 13–24. Paris: L'Harmattan.
Ramat, Paolo & Ricca, Davide. 1994. Prototypical adverbs: On the scalarity/radiality of the notion of *adverb*. *Rivista di Linguistica* 6(2): 289–326.
Ramat, Paulo & Ricca, Davide. 1998. Sentence adverbs in the languages of Europe. In *Adverbial Constructions in the Languages of Europe*, Johan van der Auwera (ed.), 187–275. Berlin: Mouton de Gruyter.
Ricca, Davide. 1998. La morfologia avverbiale tra flessione e derivazione. In *Ars Linguistica*, Giuliano Bernini, Pierluigi Cuzzolin & Piera Molinelli, (eds), 447–466. Roma: Bulzoni.
Robertson, Stuart & Cassidy, Frederic G. 1954. *The Development of Modern English*. Englewood Cliffs NJ: Prentice-Hall.
Rohlfs, Gerhard. 1954. *Historische Grammatik der italienischen Sprache und ihrer Mundarten*, Vol. 3. Bern: Francke.
Ruge, Hans. 1997. *Grammatik des Neugriechischen. Lautlehre, Formenlehre, Syntax*. Köln: Romiosini.
Salazar García, Ventura. 2007. Flexibilidad categorial y adverbios de manera en español: un enfoque funcional. In *Estudios Lingüísticos, Literarios e Históricos. Homenaje a Juan Martínez Marín*, Pedro Barros García, Gonzalo Águila Escobar & Esteban Tomás Montoro del Arco, 309–326. Granada: Universidad de Granada.
Salazar García, Ventura. 2013. Los adjetivos en la lengua izí de Nigeria: Impliaciones para una teoría funcional de las partes de la oración. In *De Lingüística, Traducción y Léxico-fraseología: Homenaje a Juan de Dios Luque Durán*, Antonio Pamies Bertrán (ed.), 51–64. Granada: Comares.

Sonntag, Eric. 2005. *Lexeme, Morpheme und Kategoreme. Die Wortkategorie Adverb und die adverbialen Wortklassen des Französischen und Spanischen.* Aachen: Shaker.
Štekauer, Pavol. Forthcoming. 15. The delimitation of derivation and inflection. In *Wordformation. An International Handbook of the Languages of Europe,* Series *Handbücher zur Sprach- und Kommunikationswissenschaft: HSK,* Peter O. Müller, Ingeborg Ohnheiser, Susan Olsen & Franz Rainer (eds). Berlin: de Gruyter Mouton.
Strang, Barbara M.H. 1970. *A History of English.* London: Methuen.
Strang, Barabara M.H. 1978. *Modern English Structure.* London: Arnold.
Swan, Toril. 1991. Adverbial shifts: evidence from Norwegian and English. In *Historical English Syntax,* Dieter Kastovsky, (ed.), 409–438. Berlin: Mouton de Gruyter.
Tagliamonte, Sali & Ito, Rika. 2002. Think *really different*: Continuity and specialization in the English dual form adverbs. *Journal of Sociolinguistics* 6(2): 236–266.
Teyssier, Jacques. 1968. Notes on the syntax of the adjective in Modern English. *Lingua* 20: 225–249.
Uhler, Karl. 1926. *Die Bedeutungsgleichheit der altenglischen Adjektiva und Adverbia mit und ohne -lic (-lice).* Heidelberg: Winter.
Valera Hernández, Salvador. 1996. *Adjetivos y Adverbios en Inglés: La Relación de Homomorfia.* Granada: Universidad de Granada.
Valera Hernández, Salvador. 1998. On subject-orientation in English *-ly* adverbs. *English Language and Linguistics* 2(2): 263–282.
Van Goethem, Kristel. 2010. The French construction *nouveau* + past participle revisited: Arguments in favour of a prefixoid analysis of *nouveau. Folia Linguistica* 44(1): 163–178.

The position proper of the adjective in Middle English

A result of language contact*

Carola Trips
University of Mannheim

This paper discusses grammatical replication as a possible explanation for the rise of postposed rhematic adjectives in Middle English (ME) times. It will be shown that this phenomenon, which is described by Fischer (2006) as a violation of the Old English pattern, has the potential to have been borrowed from Old French (OF) during the time when language contact between the two languages was most intense. A corpus-based study of OF will confirm that rhematic post-posed adjectives were the marked option and occurred in distinctive and highlighting contexts. This finding will be compared with findings from a corpus-based study of ME. It will reveal that the same pattern suddenly increases between 1250 and 1350, and that the postposition of adjectives correlates with the so-called French plural (marking) in texts which are based on Latin and/or French. Other sources like full texts of direct translations of French texts and mixed texts will be integrated into the study to provide as comprehensive a picture as possible about the contact situation. Although the results cannot be conclusive at present, this investigation shows that grammatical replication cannot be excluded as an explanation of the rise of this (and other) grammatical patterns during ME times.

1. Introduction

Throughout the Middle English period (ME, 1150–1500) adjectives can be found in preposed as well as in postposed position. The examples below from the *Ayenbite of Inwyt* (1340) illustrate this:

(1) a. *vor   he lokeþ / and norissep / alle þe greate **gostliche zennes**.*
       because he looks and nourishes all the great   spiritual sins
       'because he sees and nourishes all the great spiritual sins.'

---

* I would like to thank colleagues, especially Achim Stein, two anonymous reviewers of this paper, and the editors of this volume for valuable comments and suggestions. All remaining errors are of course my own.

> b. *wydoute þise þri* ***þinges gostliche*** */ ne moȝe þe*
> without these three matters spiritual not may the
>
> *ympen of uirtue / ne wexe / ne bere frut.*
> branches of virtue neither grow nor bear fruit
>
> 'without these three spiritual matters the branches of virtues may neither grow nor bear fruit.' (AYENBI, 21.313 and 95.1844)

In the literature, it has been discussed whether the occurrence of post-posed adjectives in early stages of English is related to a number of properties of the grammatical system (see especially Fischer 2000, 2001; 2004, 2006 Haumann 2003 & Lightfoot 1979) or whether it is due to language contact with (Old) French (see e.g. Jespersen 1949; Mossé 1991; Mustanoja 1960; Moskowich 2002). What is clear is that the frequency of postposed adjectives gradually decreased and that examples like

(2) a. *The rugby season **proper** now begins in September.* (BNC, A33 176)
  b. *But **proof positive** they did not have to supply.* (BNC, CAR 1571)
  c. *I suppose because basically I am **the heir apparent** to Michael Jackson.*
  (BNC, ECT 2452)

in Present-Day English (PDE) are remnants of this development. Although Fischer (2006) quite convincingly shows that system-internal factors like for example (in)definiteness of the NP, the nature of the adjective and its information-structural function play a role in the postposition of adjectives, there are aspects that are worth investigating in the light of language contact with French. One rule identified by Fischer is that definite NPs tend to be thematic, and because APs are part of NPs they are thematic too and thus preposed. However, in her study she noted that this rule is violated, i.e. cases of postposed adjectives in definite NPs occur. The question Fischer poses is whether these adjectives are rhematic rather than thematic. One of the tendencies that seem to govern these cases involve French influence:

> Many of the adjectives in definite NPs involve French phrases. Since this is also true for the indefinite counterparts, it shows that the influence of French is a parameter separate from the others, which are all connected with information structure. It is also striking that French influence comes much more to the fore in NPs with only one adjective [...] This is probably due to the fact that most of these phrases are fixed ones, used by English authors, as it were, as a unit.
> (Fischer 2006: 271)

Another tendency discussed by Fischer is contrast. According to her, postposed adjectives in definite NPs occur when they are used contrastively, i.e. with a rhematic function.

Fischer's analysis (that APs in definite NPs are thematic) only holds for NPs without marked intonation as in (3a), where the main accent is on the verb *(talked)*, and *the Dutch professor* must have been introduced before. However, focus structures are compositional. Thus, a definite NP, despite its topichood at sentence level, can still contain a "rhematic" attributive adjective, constituting the focus of the noun phrase. In (3b) the fact 'Sam talked to a professor' is part of the background, whereas *Dutch* bears a pitch accent which introduces the alternatives relevant for focus marking and forces the restrictive interpretation of the adjective (see Blumenthal 1980, 26 for French examples; Umbach 2006 & von Heusinger 1999, and Chapter 5 for a detailed theoretical discussion).

(3) a. Sam talked to [the Dutch professor].
    b. Sam only talked to [the DUTCH professor].

There seem to be parallels between Fischer's observations for ME and the rules that determine the rhematic and thematic function of adjectives in Modern French (ModF). First, postposed adjectives can either have a thematic or rhematic function; second, contrast is expressed by postposition. In his information-structure based syntax of Modern French (ModF) Blumenthal (1980) defines the position of adjectives depending on the degree of informativeness, thus anticipating the focus definition in alternative semantics (Rooth 1985, 1992; Krifka 2007; see also Firbas' 1971 notion of communicative dynamism, and Chafe's 1976 notion of contrastiveness). The following examples illustrate that a postposed adjective can have both a thematic and a rhematic function:

(4) a. *Les gardiens maîtrisèrent le lion furieux.*
       'The zoo keepers got the wild lion under control.'
    b. *Les gardiens maîtrisèrent le lion furIEUX.*
       'It was the wild lion that the zoo keepers got under control.'

In (4a) the property of the lion is inferrable from the context and non-defining because it is not used to distinguish between different lions. Contrast, however, can be evoked by prosody as in (4b). Note that the use of the indefinite article *un* 'a' would not make a difference (which is also what Fischer observed for ME). We will see below that these properties are already part of the Old French (OF, 842–1320)[1] system, the variety of French that came into contact with ME in medieval times.

In this paper, I will discuss the two tendencies proposed by Fischer in the context of the language contact hypothesis. More precisely, I will take a look at

---

1. Old French is used here as a cover term for all varieties of French spoken/written between the 9th and the beginning of 14th century, thus including Anglo-Norman and Anglo-French. Where appropriate, the term Anglo-French will be used to explicitly refer to the variety of OF in England in ME times.

postposed adjectives in definite NPs (i.e. one single adjective in an NP) in OF and ME and compare the information-structural properties of postposed adjectives. Partly in line with Fischer, my assumption is that the violation of the OE rule is likely to be based on French influence. Where I part company with her is in her explanation why these "French phrases" occur. To me it is not entirely satisfying to say that they are probably fixed units because English authors have used them as such. At the present time, it seems to be premature to exclude the possibility that these phrases are an instance of grammatical replication in the sense of Heine and Kuteva (2005, 2008). Recent new insights into the contact situation between OF and ME have shown that the intensity of contact may have been underestimated. This is partly due to the neglect of invaluable material showing code-switching in texts reflecting speech, and the fact that these texts are hard to come by and are not available in corpora. These insights have methodological consequences: only by taking into account different types of sources (i.e. monolingual diachronic corpora, single-text analysis of direct translations, analysis of mixed texts) will we be able to come closer to an adequate description and analysis of a diachronic language contact situation and its analysis. The rise of certain patterns of postposed adjectives in ME can be seen as a good starting point for this enterprise.

The results of the comparison of OF and ME postposed adjectives will be applied to Heine & Kuteva's diagnostics of identifying contact-induced grammatical replication (see Heine & Kuteva 2007; Heine 2009). The authors define grammatical replication as "… a process whereby speakers of a language, called replica language, create a new grammatical structure on the model of some structure of another language, called the model language" (Heine & Kuteva 2008: 59). The definition implies that the new grammatical structure need not be entirely new but can be built on some structure that already existed in the replica language. In the case at hand, the OE NP phrases with only one adjective might have been the basis for a new grammatical structure where rhematic adjectives in postposition in definite NPs became available on the model of OF.

From my point of view, the phenomenon serves well to demonstrate that neither the internal nor the external hypothesis are the sole explanation of language change and that rather multiple causation should be the basis for any study that seeks to account for as complex a phenomenon as language change. As Fischer states "… although postposition often occurs with French adjectives (especially after French nouns), the influence of French cannot be said to govern adjective position *in all circumstances* [emphasis by CT]. In other words, a different or additional explanation for this position is called for" (Fischer 2006: 260). Thus, the task of the historical linguist is to take into account all possible explanations for the complex phenomena under investigation.

The paper is organised as follows: in the next section, the rules and/or tendencies that have been claimed to determine the position of adjectives in OF will be discussed. I will especially concentrate on the pattern identified above for ME (one postposed adjective with rhematic function). The discussion will be based on the (few) recent works on the topic (Wydler 1956; Reiner 1968; Posner 1997 and especially Buridant 1997, 2000), and a small study of some prose works of the MCVF corpus (*Modéliser le changement: les voies du français*, Martineau 2009). The findings gained for OF will be compared with an investigation of the same pattern in *The Penn-Helsinki Parsed Corpus of Middle English 2* (Release 3, Kroch & Taylor 2000) to see whether grammatical replication could be assumed. The methodological aspects mentioned above will also be addressed. In Section 3 new findings from different types of studies and sources will be provided to show that the multilingual situation in ME times can only be fully grasped and understood if direct translations and mixed texts are included in our studies. Some further phenomena found in these text types will be discussed to point to the fact that there was a potential of grammatical replication. Section 4 concludes.

2. Postposition of the adjective in Old French and Middle English

2.1 Old French

The literature on the position of the adjective in OF is sparse. The works cited above in the introduction present the most recent sources of information on the topic. Although a plethora of distinctions is proposed (e.g. *sens indéfini* 'unspecified meaning' and *sens précis* 'specified meaning'; *grande extension* 'non-restricted extension' and *extension réduite* 'restricted extension'), none of the works discuss the differences between preposed and post-posed adjectives in terms of information structure explicitly, i.e. for example the difference between thematic and rhematic adjectives.

Following von den Driesch (1905), Reiner (1968) states that the postposed adjective serves to "logically distinguish" ("logisch zu distinguieren", 238f) between entities which are part of one and the same set by expressing an objective property which can be perceived by everyone. The preposed adjective, on the other hand, serves to express a subjective evaluation of an entity by the speaker. The property is "attributed affectively" ("affektisch attribuiert").

Buridant (1997, 2000) summarises the assumptions made both in synchronic and diachronic works on the topic (see also the literature cited in Buridant 1997). He states that in OF, adjectives anticipate the ModF situation. According to him, their position is mainly determined by semantic and morphophonemic factors. More precisely, the preposition of adjectives is highly frequent, especially with monosyllabic adjectives like e.g. *bon, bel,* etc. Postposition occurs in binomial constructions (Example (5a)), and if the adjective bears emphatic value (see Example (5b)).

(5) a. une tour *grant* et *fort*
      a tower big and strong
    b. S'il   i   muert, c'est domages *grans*
       if he is dying it is damage big (Buridant 2000: 170)

In his 1997 paper, Buridant discusses a study conducted by Attali and Monsonégo (1995) on two prose texts from the 14th and 15th century. They investigated adjectives which they categorised in eight classes (colour, form, temperature, spatial, tactile, gustatory, olfactive, auditive perception) and found that they occurred both in preposition and postposition. Interestingly, these types of adjectives occurred much more often in postposition with a restrictive meaning (in "contextes définitoires"), which generally favours a rhematic function. Since preposed adjectives were much more frequent in OF than they are in ModF, the postposing of adjectives was the marked option in OF. This is the type identified by Fischer as the new type emerging in ME times. Note, however, that the rhematicity of postposed adjectives is not dependent on the presence of a definite determiner. This means that the OF rule is less restricted than the OE one, and that the pattern "definite NP with postposed adjective" is only a subset of NPs with a postposed rhematic adjective in OF.

I conducted a corpus study of postposed adjectives in OF. A query of the MCVF corpus restricted to NPs consisting of definite article, noun and adjective yielded 279 hits for D-N-A and 1069 hits for D-A-N.

The obvious candidates for rhematically marked postposition are adjectives which typically occur in distinctive or highlighting contexts, e.g. *destre/senestre* 'left/right' or *meisme* 'itself'.

(6) et   avoient li archier   les **senestres** bras   garnis   de   manches,
    and had   the archers   the left   arms   equipped with   sleeves,

   et   cil   a pie qui portoient escus   [...] estoient
    and those on foot who wore   coat-of-arms [...] were

   contraint de chaucier chauces de fer   ou trumelieres ou cuissins en
    forced   to put-on   shoes   of iron   or greaves   or cuisses en

   *lor   cuisses **destres***
    their thighs right

                              (*L'art de chevalerie de Jean de Meun*, NCA)

Other examples are adjectives which are normally preposed, but occur in marked (rhematic) postposition:[2]

(7) a. *sire, la aval desoz vostre pales a* **un perron grant**
 sir here upstream above your palace has a stone big
 que j ai veu floter par desus l eve.
 which I have seen float over the water

 b. *se se conmencierent a asambler en* **unes places granz,**
 then REFL started to gather in a place huge
 qui estoient de costentinoble;
 who were from Constantinople

The findings from the study show that in OF postposed adjectives occur in highlighting and contrastive contexts, i.e. they are rhematic. Thus, in OF postposition is a marked option and associated with rhematicity.

2.2 *Middle English*

In the literature, the origin of postposed adjectives in ME has been discussed in some detail, and most of the rather descriptive contributions (e.g. Mustanoja 1960; Mossé 1991; Markus 1997; Moskowich 2002) have argued in favour of the language contact hypothesis. Theoretical contributions like the papers by Fischer and Haumann cited above, as well as Lightfoot (1979, based on Greenberg's 1963 typological observations), have favoured the language internal hypothesis.

In his handbook of Middle English, Mossé (1952, §166, p. 123) discusses three types of postposition, on the model of French:

(8) a. simple post-positive adjective
 of arte magique 'of magic art'
 b. two or more post-positive adjectives
 thise floryns newe and brighte 'these new and bright florins'
 c. pre-positive and post-positive adjective
 with deop dich and dark 'with a deep and dark ditch'

These three types look exactly like the types discussed in Buridant for OF. However, type (8c) also resembles the OE *and*-construction *(halig wær and snotor* 'holy man and wise') elaborately discussed in Fischer (2000, 2001) and Haumann (2003). Thus, the question arises of whether type (8c) (and the other types) were replicated on the model of OF or whether type (8c) is of Germanic origin. I will come back to this issue below.

---

2. Quotations are from the *Nouveau Corpus d'Amsterdam* Stein et al. (2006).

Another analyst in favour of the language-contact hypothesis is Moskowich (2002) who claims that postposed adjectives in PDE are due to French influence and hence the label "French type" can be maintained. In her corpus study on the distribution of adjectives in ME texts she found that although preposition of adjectives is the most frequent order (66.8%), postposition does occur in all of the text types she investigated (6.4%). However, postposed adjectives occur with a higher frequency in text types like documents (15.4%), handbooks (13.2%), fiction (9.4%) and law (9.1%).

To summarise, from a descriptive point of view, many authors have claimed that the occurrence of postposed adjectives in ME times is probably the result of influence of OF on ME during the time when language contact between the two languages was most intense.

Although Fischer and others have argued against French influence as the sole explanandum for the occurrence of postposed adjectives, there are some interesting findings in Fischer's work that show that this factor should not entirely be excluded. In the appendix of her 2006 paper she provides a summary of all her results from the ME corpus she investigated. Among the texts are quite a number which are based on a French original. Most of these texts display APs with postposed adjectives of 50% and more (for example, *The Ayenbite of Inwyt* from the M2 period (1250–1350) has 64%, *The Earliest English Prose Psalter* from the same period has 84%, *Mandeville's Travels* from the M3 period (1350–1420) has 55%, and *The Book of Vices and Virtues* from the M4 period (1420–1500) has 54%. My investigation of the pattern "definite NP with a postposed adjective" in the same corpus[3] confirmed this observation, i.e. most of the texts based on a French original show this pattern (much) more often than those which lack a French basis. Moreover, as Figure 1 illustrates, there is a rise in frequency of the pattern from M1 to M2, with a peak in M3, and a decrease in M4.[4] A closer look at the peak in Figure 1 is based on high frequencies of the pattern in texts like *The Ayenbite of Inwyt*, *The Earliest English Prose Psalter* (M2), *Dan Jon Gaytryge's Sermon*, *Mandeville's Travels* (M3), *The Book of Vices and Virtues* and *The Middle English Sermons* (M4). All of these texts are based on a French and/or Latin original.

---

3. Since I used the PPCME2, Release 3, which was not available at the time when Fischer published her paper, the results are not entirely comparable.

4. The figure is based on the relative frequencies of the pattern found in the texts. Quite a number of them did not exhibit the pattern. The search query included an AP immediately dominated by an NP because postposed adjectives are defined as such in the corpus (see also the comments in Fischer 2006).

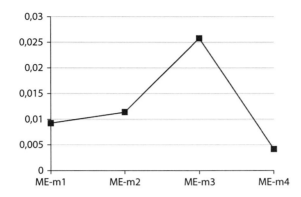

Figure 1. Postposed adjectives in definite NPs in ME (PPCME2)

If this pattern was based on the OE (Germanic) rule the question that would have to be answered is why in ME times the sudden rise illustrated in Figure 1 occurs. One answer or explanation could be that this new pattern is of OF origin and arises in the period of time (between 1250–1420) when contact between OF and ME was most intense. Another explanation could be that the OE rule which allowed the postposing of adjectives was extended to a further pattern, on the model of French.[5] In either case, a new way to mark the rhematic function of an adjective was introduced to OE, which became available for some time. Since OF gradually lost its prominent status in speech and writing (see below), in the fifteenth century less and less evidence for the pattern was available, and it was gradually given up. In any case, both explanations fall under the definition of grammatical replication. From a synchronic point of view, in ME times the status of this pattern would then have to be defined as a (new) grammatical structure rather than fixed phrases stored as such in the lexicon.

Another phenomenon which has been brought in connection with postposed adjectives is plural marking. In his grammar, Jespersen notes that postposed adjectives, which are mainly French, display French plural marking. More precisely, he states,

> Some adjectives clearly borrowed from French take the French plural ending -s as in *places delitables* (Chaucer). It also occurs in French law language as in *heirs males*. (Jespersen 1949: 43f, §2.76)

---

5. For Fischer, the occurrence of definite NPs with a postposed rhematic adjective can be explained by the tendency of these adjectives to be clearly predicative in nature. Still, the question remains how the rise in the ME period can be explained.

In line with Jespersen, Mustanoja (1960) also refers to this phenomenon and attributes it to French influence:

> In works written under strong French influence adjectives borrowed from that language (occasionally even native adjectives) may take -s in the plural. In the majority of these cases the adjective is used attributively and placed after the noun. The plurals of this type are, of course, direct imitations of French usage.
> (Mustanoja 1960, 277)

The occurrence of plural marking on postposed adjectives, i.e. within French phrases, could be taken as proof that these phrases were not borrowed as fixed phrases. Of course, French postposed adjectives with plural marking can be interpreted either way, but hybrid phrases (one part Germanic, one part Romance) would prove that a syntactic property was transferred to ME and replicated. Therefore, I investigated postposed adjectives and the French plural in the ME corpus.[6] The following table presents the data for preposed adjectives (A–N) and postposed adjectives (N–A) only for texts displaying the French plural (FP).

It is evident that the numbers for the FP are small. Nevertheless, two tendencies can be observed: First, the FP predominantly occurs in texts with the highest frequencies of postposed adjectives; second, in all texts in the corpus displaying the FP, the number of postposed adjectives almost doubles the number of texts without the FP (5.92% vs. 3.25%).

Further, from what was shown in the figure above, the texts with the highest frequencies of postposed adjectives are all from the M3 period. The highest frequency of the pattern occurs in Chaucer's *The Tale of Melibee* (23.7%), followed by *The Equatorie of the Planets* (21%) and *A Treatise on the Astrolabe* (20.6%). Whereas there is no doubt that the latter was written by Chaucer, there is some debate whether the former (*The Equatorie of the Planets*) can be attributed to Chaucer as well. These texts are followed by *The Ayenbite of Inwyt* (9.9%) from M2, and *The Mirror of St. Edmund* (*Vernon*) (9%). The only text from the period of M2 displaying both postposed adjectives and the French plural is *The Ayenbite of Inwyt*. In M4, three texts of different text genres and written by different authors display postposed adjectives and the French plural. All of the texts listed in the table are based on either Latin and/or French originals.

Dialect region seems to be a defining factor as well: seven of the thirteen texts listed in the table were written in the East Midlands, a region London was (and still is) part of. From the 13th century onwards London became the centre of trade

---

6. Abbreviations in Table 1: S = Southern, K = Kentish, EM = East Midlands, WM = West Midlands, N = Northern; A–N/N–A = Adjective-Noun/Noun-Adjective orders, FP = French Plural; M1=1150–1250, M2=1250–1350, M3=1350–1420, M4=1420–500.

Table 1. Postposition of adjectives and the French plural in ME (PPCME2)

Text	Date	Dialect	Genre	A-N	N-A	N-A %	FP
The Ayenbite of Inwyt	M2	K	Religious treatise	713	78	9.9	4
Ælred of Rievaulx's De Institutione Inclusarum	M2	WM	Rule	217	5	2.3	1
A Treatise on the Astrolabe	M3	EM	Handbook	108	56	20.6	9
The Mirror of St. Edmund (Thornton Ms.)	M3	N	Religious treatise	182	14	7.1	1
The Mirror of St. Edmund (Vernon Ms.)	M3	WM	Religious treatise	130	13	9.0	3
The Equatorie of the Planets	M3	EM	Handbook	64	17	21.0	8
The Tale of Melibee	M3	EM	Philosophy/fiction	58	18	23.7	2
The Parson's Tale	M3	EM	Religious treatise	530	37	6.5	4
Mandeville's Travels	M3	EM	Travelogue	841	40	4.5	5
John of Trevisa's Polychronicon	M3	S	History	712	12	1.7	2
Malory's Morte Darthur	M4	WM	Romance	615	15	2.4	1
Capgrave's Chronicle	M4	EM	History	900	15	1.6	1
The Book of Vices and Virtues	M4	EM	Religious treatise	95	5	5	1
Total				5165	325	5.92	42
Texts without FP				10315	347	3.25	0

and commerce, at that time it must have been a multilingual place. Therefore, it is not surprising that most of the texts written in that area show foreign influences.

Clearly, three texts attributed to Chaucer display high frequencies for the two phenomena under investigation.[7] *The Tale of Melibee* which is one of

---

7. Chaucer's *The Parson's Tale* which is also part of *The Canterbury Tales* does not show as high a frequency of postposed adjectives as the other texts, but a rather high frequency of the FP (4 cases) in relation to postposed adjectives.

The Canterbury Tales is a translation of the French original (by Reynaud de Louens). Chaucer's treatise on the astrolabe is the oldest known technical manual in English. As Chaucer himself pointed out, it is not at all original but was compiled from a number of different sources (probably Arabic, Latin and French). The Peterhouse manuscript of *The Equatorie of the Planets* has been said to be a companion to the former work and again a translation from French. It is a well-known fact that Chaucer translated Latin and French works and therefore must have had a very good command of these two Romance languages.

If the French plural occurring in these texts was copied as a fixed phrase we would expect the noun and the adjective to be of French (Romance) origin. Below some examples from the three texts are given:

(9) a. *The names of these monthes were clepid somme for her*
      the names of these months were named some for her
      *propirtees and somme by statutes of **lordes Arabiens**, ...*
      properties and some by rules of lords Arabiens
      'Some of these months were named after their properties, some
      of them after the rules of Arabian lords.' (ASTRO, 665.C1.79)

   b. *& set the ffyx point ouer the middel of the bord on which*
      and set the fix point over the middle of the board on which
      *middel shal be nayled a **plate of metal rownd** /*
      middle shall be nailed a plate of metal round
      'and set the fix point over the middle of the board on the middle
      of which shall be nailed a round metal plate.' (EQUATO, 18.13)

   c. *ne ye ne han bretheren, ne **cosyns germayns**, ne*
      nor you neither have brothers nor cousins first nor
      noon oother neigh kynrede, ...
      non other close kinsmen
      'Nor have you either brothers or first cousins or any other close
      kinsmen.' (CTMELI, 228.C2.437)

In (9a) the noun *lordes* is of Germanic origin (OE *hlaford*), and the adjective *Arabiens* of OF origin. Thus, the phrase cannot have been copied as such, rather the French rule of plural marking (and probably the postposing of adjectives) seems to have been applied to a hybrid phrase. In (9b) and (9c), both nouns and adjectives are of OF origin, so these cases could either have been copied as fixed phrases or built according to the French rules (see Example (9a)). If all of the phrases with postposed adjectives (and the French plural) had been copied as fixed phrases we would expect to find a restricted set of these phrases. This assumption is not corroborated by the data, the nouns of both Germanic and Romance origin are combined with a variety of different postposed adjectives of Romance origin. The question remains whether this can also be assumed for (definite) NPs with postposed adjectives only (see the discussion in the following section):

(10) a. *fro   the forseide ring unto the centre of the large hool*
from the aforsaid ring onto the centre of the large hole

*amidde,   is clepid   the south lyne, or ellis **the***
in-the-middle is named the south line   or else the

lyne meridional.
line   meridional
'from the aforementioned ring onto the centre of the large hole in the middle, is called the south line, or else the meridional line.'
(ASTRO, 663.C2.50)

b. *But the **day naturall,** that is to seyn 24 hours, is the*
but the day natural   that is to say   24 hours is the

revolucioun   of the equinoxial...
diurnal-rotation of the equinox
'but 24 hours is the complete rotation of the celestial equator.'
(ASTRO, 672.C1.321)

c. *But I nolde   nat of schrewes, of whiche **the thought crwel***
but I not-wanted not of evil   of which   the thought cruel

woodeth   alwey   into destruccion of gode men, ...
go-out-of-control always into destruction of good men, ...
'but I did not wish for evil of which the cruel thought always leads into the destruction of good men.'
(BOETH, 446.C2.348)

Although we have gained further insights into the nature of postposed adjectives and the French plural, the texts we looked at were probably all written by Chaucer. Therefore, a look at other works displaying the two phenomena is in order. Moreover, since the data in the ME corpus is just a fraction of ME and since only samples are available, I will take a look at some other, full texts. This is especially important for the task at hand, to find proof for the rhematicity of postposed adjectives in context.

One text which is very interesting and suitable in this respect is *The Ayenbite of Inwyt* because it is a direct translation of a French original. Moreover, the authors of both works are known, and the texts are available for research.

3. Language contact and multilingualism in ME

Before we take a closer look at *The Ayenbite of Inwyt* and the French original, *La Somme le roi,* I would like to define the linguistic situation in which these texts were written (translated) and point to recent, new insights into the language contact situation between OF and ME.

Thanks to the invaluable work by Rothwell (e.g. 1968, 1975; 1980, 1993; 2001) today we know that the Norman Conquest of 1066 had a greater effect on the English language than any other political event in the course of its history. As Rothwell points out, the degree of the impact of French on English has been misjudged:

> The sheer size of the debt owed by English to Anglo-Norman French and – just as importantly – the period of time over which this debt was built up are still grossly underestimated by specialists in the history of both the French and English languages. (Rothwell 1993, 310)

Rothwell refers to the period of time during which the language contact situation prevailed, which he dates from 1066 to the 15th century. During that time Anglo-French (cf. also the Anglo-Norman Hub 2001), i.e. OF, at first spoken and written by the new ruling class, gradually gained the role of an official language over Anglo-Latin, whereas (the many varieties of) Middle English, the language of the masses, gradually developed from being a predominantly spoken language to becoming the acknowledged national language, both in spoken and written form in the 15th century. What we find at that time is a multilingual situation which is reflected in many glosses in dictionaries, didactic texts (e.g. Walter of Bibbesworth's *Tretiz*, 13th c., see also Hunt 1991), lexical borrowings especially in Chaucer's works and Langland's Piers *Plowman*, and accounting records (e.g. Trotter 2000; Ingham 2010). Ingham (2009) has found indirect evidence from orthography for French as a spoken language on the island and, connected to it, instances of language mixing in fourteenth-century accounts which reflect bilingualism. He notes that

> ... it is becoming clear that the relationship between French and English in the later medieval period was more a matter of complementarity. The two languages represented not differing communities with opposed interests, but choices available to those who possessed bilingual competence. (Ingham 2009, 80)

This bilingual competence is expressed by a phenomenon Trotter has dubbed "nested code switching" whereby switches occur from OF lexical items to English ones in a matrix Latin text, as illustrated in (11):

(11) lxxiii operibus ad fodum in *la Winyerd*. (1302–3)
 pro *le wyndwou* eiusdem molendini. (1324–5)
 ad ostium *del Poundfold*. (Cuxham, p. 396 (1329–30))
 in emendacione *del bagsadle*. (Durham, II, 518 (1330))
 (Ingham 2009, 87)

In these instances of code-switching, the vernacular content words given in bold are not latinised, and they are preceded by the OF definite articles *le, la* and *del* which function as linkers to the surrounding Latin. As in code-switching contexts today, speakers/writers could use this "device" only because there was a substantial group of people who had a bilingual competence. Hence, if conclusions from investigations of code-switching in language contact situations today (cf. e.g. Poplack 1980; Myers-Scotton 2001, 2005) are applied to the medieval situation, these instances of code-switching indicate bilingualism, i.e. a very good command of two languages.

One expert in this field from a diachronic perspective is Schendl who has elaborately worked on the topic (see e.g. Schendl 1996, 2002; 2012). In a co-authored paper, Schendl and Wright (2011) address the question of whether code-switching in Early English should be seen as a phenomenon of writing only, or whether it reflects multilingual speech. The authors note that although there is no direct and uncontroversial evidence for spoken speech in the texts they investigated, these texts may preserve or even consciously use patterns of speech. Moreover, code-switching was not restricted to formal texts, but is found across a wide range of text types, from formal to informal. They further assume that "[t]he widespread multilingualism in medieval Britain most likely also resulted in spoken code-switching" (Schendl & Wright 2011:28). Unfortunately, at present no comprehensive corpus of these "mixed texts" exist and thus a conclusive answer to this question awaits further research.

However, since we do have attestations of the mixing of French and English in ME texts, i.e. code-switching based on bilingualism, it does not seem unlikely that the situation between 1066 and 1500 had potential for grammatical replication. We have seen above that the pattern identified by Fischer ("definite NP with a postposed adjective") and the French plural discussed in the literature might be instances of this type of replication. In the following, we will investigate these phenomena in further depth in the full text of the *The Ayenbite of Inwyt*[8] ('Remorse of Conscience').

As noted above, this text is a direct translation from *La Somme le roi* by Frere Laurent in 1340. Dan Michel, the author of the English translation, was a monk in the cloister of Saint Augustine's, Canterbury, where he completed the manuscript of the *Ayenbite of Inwyt* on 27th October 1340. The work is unique in providing an example of a ME dialect in an original copy whose date, author and place of writing are exactly known because the author himself directly refers to these pieces of information.

---

8. The analysis is based on the following editions: Morris (1866) and Laurent (2008).

Dan Michel quite strictly followed the OF original in terms of word order. Thus, postposed adjectives occur on the model of the OF text:

(12) ME: *oþer **kuead gostlich**/ase huanne he yherþ/þet zome/þet me hyelde guode men: ys y-blamed/ of zome vice. Ofþelliche þinges/ him gledeþ ine his herte.* (Ayenbite, p. 27)
or sin spiritual as when he hears that some that man held good men is blamed of some vice. of such things him rejoiceth in his heart
OF: *ou **mal esperituel** comme quant il [b]oit que aucuns que l'en tenoit apreudome es blasmez d'aucun vice, de tiex choses s'esjoist il en son cuer.* (Somme, Chapter 33, §35, p. 126)

This example is from the section on the sin of envy. First, sin *(kuead)* as such is addressed, and then the different types of sin are named, one of them being *kuead gostlich* 'spiritual sin'. This is again a distinctive or highlighting context which requires rhematic adjectives in postposition (see Section 2.1 above). The same context is found with examples showing the pattern D-N-A:

(13) ME: *þet is þet bread of þe ilke holy couent. þet bread ofheuene. þet bread of angles. **þet bread lostuol.** þet bread of lyue eurelestinde.* (Ayenbite, p.110)
that is the bread of that same holy covent the bread of heaven the bread of angels the bread delightful that bread of life everlasting
OF: *C'est li pains de celui benoit covent, li pains dou ciel, li pains des anges, li pains **delitables**, li pains de vie pardurable* (Somme, Chapter 51, §209, p. 211)

These examples serve well to demonstrate that rhematic postposed adjectives occur, in indefinite as well as definite NPs, probably on the model of OF.

Coming back to the FP discussed above, in the *Ayenbite of Inwyt* it predominantly occurs with a Germanic noun and a postposed adjective of Romance origin:

(14) a. *þise byeþþe þri **boȝes principales**: þet of þise rote wexeþ.*
these are the three bows principal that of this root grows
(Ayenbite, p. 34)
b. *Ce sont les.III. **branches principaus** qui de ceste racine nessent,* (Somme, Chapter 36, §18, 134)

(15) a. *þanne of þe mouþe/of þe enuious/comeþ out/þri manere **wordes uenimouses**.*
then of the mouth of the envious comes out three manner words venimous (Ayenbite, p. 28)
b. *Dont de la boiche a l'enuieus issent [17].III. **manieres de paroles venimeuses**;* (Somme, Chapter 33, §61, p. 126)

Since the nouns and adjectives combined in these phrases vary, it is hard to see how they could all have been borrowed as fixed phrases. So grammatical replication cannot be excluded as an explanation for the occurrence of these phrases. This also applies to rhematic postposed adjectives without plural marking.

In her investigations of mixed texts, or more precisely on account books from the fourteenth century, Wright found an example which is quite interesting for our discussion:

(16) London, Gilbert Maghfield's Account Book, 1392.
 Itm̃ vij las᷃ de *haryng$_e$ blank$_e$* a vij lī…
 It' il doit pur ij last de *Blanke heryng* xiij lī…
 'And 7 lasts of white herring at 7 pounds sterling … And he owes for 2 lasts of white herring 13 pounds sterling [emphasis added]'
 (Wright 1998: 105)

The text resembles the one given in (11) because it also shows a mixed-language system, incorporating ME into a matrix of Latin and/or OF. In this case, different orderings of noun and adjective occur: in the first line the nominal phrase *haryng(e) blank(e)*, shows the Anglo-Norman adjective *blank(e)* in postposition. This ordering resembles OF and ModF where colour adjectives occur in postposed position in the unmarked case. In the second line, however, that same adjective precedes the noun in line with the positioning of adjectives in Germanic: *Blanke heryng*. According to Wright, there is no doubt that the postposed pattern was borrowed from French.

A further phenomenon that should be discussed in this context is a study of Wright on the distribution of the French articles *le* and *la*. Wright (2010) found that mixed texts of Anglo-French and ME have their own rules of defining the position of articles: *le* signals a following English noun and can also signal a following French noun ((17a) and (17b)), *la* can only signal a French noun (17c). Both *le* and *la* could occur with feminine and masculine French nouns because it did no longer mark grammatical gender:

(17) a. *le keruyng* 'the carving'
 b. *le Belle en chepe* 'the Belle in Cheap' (tenement name)
 c. *p$^{o\sim}$ iij formes en la chapel* 'for 3 forms in the chapel'
   (Merchant Taylors' Company Accounts (1402/08), Wright 2010: 135)

Wright takes the distribution of the French article to mean that at that time, and in these texts, they have acquired a new function in a new, ordered mixed system: the function of the article was reinterpreted as signalling membership of a language system which contains more than one language. This new function could not have arisen, if the texts had not been written in a multilingual context.

The reinterpretation of the function of the French article may be seen as an instance of grammatical replication. According to Heine & Kuteva (e.g. 2005, 2008), determiners are especially susceptible to contact-induced change. In numerous cross-linguistic studies they have found that determiners in one language developed on the model of another language. This also often includes a change in function. A further phenomenon sensitive to language contact is agreement. The emergence of the FP in ME times, i.e, from a synchronic perspective, may thus be seen as a further instance of grammatical replication.

These authors have also proposed a number of diagnostics to identify instances of contact-induced transfer. One of these diagnostics is demographic variables. According to their definition, grammatical replication affects certain social or demographic groups more than others. Accordingly, demographic categories that are more strongly affected by language contact are likely to show more pronounced effects of contact-induced change. In the case at hand, a demographic category clearly affected by language contact with OF are speakers who had some formal educaction, speakers part of the upper class and engaged in the legal profession. From what was said above about mixed texts it is likely that other demographic categories are relevant for the contact situation between ME and OF.

During ME times, the process leading to grammatical replication could have been the following: on the assumption that language contact took place leading to bilingualism, first of all spontaneous replication would have arisen in bilingual interaction. An individual speaker, either consciously or unconsciously, would have propagated novel features in ME (the replica language) that had been influenced by OF. Although, most of the time spontaneous replication will have no effect on the language in question, sometimes some instances catch on. These could have been postposed adjectives, the FP, and the reinterpretation of the definite determiner. Other speakers may have taken it up and use it regularly and integrate it into their speech habits. It may then have spread to other groups of speakers, sometimes even to the entire speech community. Often these pieces of linguistic innovation remain restricted to some specific period of time, which are gradually abandoned by the very same speakers who introduced it in the first place or by the next generation. This must have been the case at the end of the ME period. What remains to be seen is in how far bilingualism in written attestations reflects bilingualism in spoken interaction.

4. Conclusion

In this paper, the possibility of contact-induced grammatical replication during ME times was discussed. More precisely, the pattern identified by Fischer as a violation of the OE pattern ("definite NP with postposed rhe-matic adjective") was investigated under the assumption that it could be an instance of grammatical replication due to language contact with OF. A corpus-based study of OF revealed that adjectives occur in rhematically marked postposition in distinctive or highlighting contexts. A comparison with a corpus-based study of ME showed a steep rise in the frequency of this pattern from 1250 to 1350. A number of texts based on Latin and/or French originals was identified to be the source of this rise. It was further shown that these texts displayed postposed adjectives and the French plural much more frequently than the other texts, and that these two phenomena are correlated. In a full text analysis of a direct translation of an OF text, the findings for these phenomena from the corpus studies were confirmed. Mixed texts displaying similar phenomena (postposed adjectives, the reinterpretation of the definite determiner) were discussed to gain a more comprehensive picture of this contact situation and of the question of whether grammatical replication is likely to have occurred. Although much more work remains to be done, at the moment grammatical replication cannot be excluded as one possible explanation for the occurrence of the phenomena investigated during the ME period.

References

Attali, Arlette & Monsonégo, Simone. 1997. L'emploi des adjectifs dans Le mesnagier de Paris (1394). Les adjectifs de couleur. In *Le Moyen Français: Philologie et linguistique, approches du texte et du discours. Actes du VIIIe Colloque international sur le moyen français. Nancy, 5-6-7 septembre 1994*, Bernard Combettes & Simone Monsonégo (eds), 211–232. Paris: Didier Érudition, 1997.

Blumenthal, Peter. 1980. *La Syntaxe du Message*. Tübingen: Niemeyer.

Buridant, Claude. 1997. La place de l'adjectif épithète en ancien français: Esquisse de bilan et perspectives. *Vox Romanica* 56: 109–145.

Buridant, Claude. 2000. *Grammaire nouvelle de l'ancien français*. Paris: Sedes.

Chafe, Wallace. 1976. Givenness, contrastiveness, definiteness, subjects, topics, and point of view. In *Subject and Topic*, Charles N. Li (ed.), 25–56. New York NY: Academic Press.

Driesch, Johannes von der. 1905. *Die Stellung des attributiven Adjektivs im Altfranzösischen*. Erlangen: Junge.

Firbas, Jan. 1971. On the concept of communicative dynamism in the theory of functional sentence perspective. *Sbornik Praci Filosoficke Fakulty Brnenske University* 19: 135–144.

Fischer, Olga. 2000. The position of the adjective in Old English. In *Generative Theory and Corpus Studies: A Dialogue from 10 ICEHL*, Ricardo Bermúdez-Otero, David Denison, Richard M. Hogg & Chris McCully (eds), 153–181. Berlin: Mouton de Gruyter.

Fischer, Olga. 2001. The position of the adjective in (Old) English from an iconic perspective. In *The Motivated Sign* [Iconicity in Language and Literature 2], Olga Fischer & Max Nanny (eds), 249–276. Amsterdam: John Benjamins.

Fischer, Olga. 2004. Developments in the category adjective from Old to Middle English. *Studies in Medieval Language and Literature* 19: 1–36.

Fischer, Olga. 2006. On the position of adjectives in Middle English. *English Language and Linguistics* 10(2): 253–288.

Greenberg, Joseph. 1963. *Universals of Language*. Cambridge MA: The MIT Press.
Haumann, Dagmar. 2003. The postnominal 'and' adjective construction in Old English. *English Language and Linguistics* 7: 57–83.
Heine, Bernd. 2009. Identifying instances of contact-induced grammatical replication. In *Topics in Descriptive and African Linguistics: Essays in Honor of Distinguished Professor Paul Newman*, Samuel Gyasi Obeng (ed.), 29–56. Munich: Lincom.
Heine, Bernd & Kuteva, Tania (eds). 2005. *Language Contact and Grammatical Change*. Cambridge: CUP.
Heine, Bernd & Kuteva, Tania. 2007. Identifying instances of contact-induced grammatical replication. Paper presented at the symposium "Language Contact and the Dynamics of Language: Theory and Implications". Max Planck Institute for Evolutionary Anthropology, Leipzig, 10–13 May.
Heine, Bernd & Kuteva, Tania. 2008. Constraints on contact-induced linguistic change. *Journal of Language Contact* 2, Thema 2: 57–90.
von Heusinger, Klaus. 1999. Intonation and Information Structure. The Representation of Focus in Phonology and Semantics. Habilitationsschrift, Universität Konstanz.
Hunt, Tony. 1991. *Teaching and Learning Latin in 13th-Century-England*, Vol. 3. Cambridge: D.S. Brewer.
Ingham, Richard. 2009. Mixing language on the manor. *Medium Aevum* 1: 107–124.
Jespersen, Otto. 1949[1927]. *A Modern English Grammar on Historical Principles*, Part II: Syntax, Vol. I. Copenhagen: Munksgaard.
Krifka, Manfred. 2007. Basic notions of Information Structure. In *The Notions of Information Structure*, Caroline Féry, Gisbert Fanselow & Manfred Krifka (eds), 13–55. Potsdam: Universitätsverlag Potsdam.
Kroch, Anthony & Taylor, Ann (eds). 2000. *The Penn-Helsinki Parsed Corpus of Middle English*, 2d edn (PPCME2). Philadelphia PA: University of Pennsylvania.
Laurent, Frère. 2008. *La somme le roi*. Paris-Abbeville: Société des Anciens Textes Français-Paillart.
Lightfoot, David. 1979. *Principles of Diachronic Syntax*. Cambridge: CUP.
Markus, Manfred. 1979. "The men present" vs "the present case": Word-order rules concerning the position of the English adjective. *Anglia* 115: 487–506.
Martineau, France (ed.). 2009. *Le corpus MCVF. Modéliser le changement: Les voies du français*. Ottawa: Université d'Ottawa.
Morris, Richard (ed.). 1866. *Dan Michel's Ayenbite of Inwyt or Remorse of Conscience*, Vol. I [The Early English Text Society 23]. London: N. Trübner and Co.
Moskowich, Isabel. 2002. The adjective in English: The "French type" and its place in the history of the language. *Folia Linguistica Historica* 23(1–2): 59–71.
Mossé, Fernand. 1991[1952]. *Handbook of Middle English*, 10th edn. Baltimore MD: The John Hopkins University Press.
Mustanoja, Tauno F. 1960. *A Middle English Syntax*, Part I. Helsinki: Société Néophilologique.
Myers-Scotton, Carol. 2001. *Contact Linguistics: Bilingual Encounters and Grammatical Outcomes*. Oxford: OUP.
Myers-Scotton, Carol. 2005. *Multiple Voices: An Introduction to Bilingualism*. Oxford: Wiley-Blackwell.
Poplack, Shana. 1980. Sometimes I'll start a sentence in Spanish y termino en español. *Linguistics* 26: 581–618.
Posner, Rebecca. 1997. *Linguistic Change in French*. Oxford: Clarendon Press.

Reiner, Erwin. 1968. *La place de l'adjectif epithète en français*. Vienna: Wilhelm Braumüller.
Rooth, Mats. 1985. Association with Focus. Ph.D. dissertation, University of Massachusetts at Amherst.
Rooth, Mats. 1992. A theory of focus interpretation. *Natural Language Semantics* 1: 75–116.
Rothwell, William. 1968. The teaching of French in Medieval England. *Modern Language Review* 63: 37–46.
Rothwell, William. 1975. The role of French in thirteenth century England. *Bulletin of the John Rylands Library* 58: 445–466.
Rothwell, William. 1980. Lexical borrowing in a medieval context. *Bulletin of the John Rylands Library* 63: 118–143.
Rothwell, William. 1993. The 'Faus franceis d'Angleterre': Later Anglo-Norman. In *Anglo-Norman Anniversary Essays*, Ian Short (ed.), 309–326.
Rothwell, William & Trotter, David (eds). 2001. *Anglo-Norman Dictionary 2*. Online Version. ⟨http://www.anglo-norman.net/⟩
Schendl, Herbert. 1996. Text types and code-switching in Medieval and Early Modern English. VIEWS 5: 50–62.
Schendl, Herbert. 2002. Code-choice and code-switching in some early fifteenth century letters. In *Middle English from Tongue to Text*, Peter J. Lucas & Angela M. Lucas (eds), 247–262. Frankfurt: Peter Lang.
Schendl, Herbert. 2012. Literacy, multilingualism and code-switching in Early English written texts. In *Language Mixing and Code-switching in Writing*, Mark Sebba, Shahrzad Mahootian & Carla Jonsson (eds), 27–44. New York: Routledge.
Schendl, Herbert & Wright, Laura. 2011. Code-switching in Early English: Historical background and methodological and theoretical issues. In *Code-Switching in Early English*, Herbert Schendl & Laura Wright (eds), 15–47. Berlin: Mouton de Gruyter.
Stein, Achim, Kunstmann, Pierre & Gleßgen, Martin-Dietrich. 2007. *Nouveau corpus d'Amsterdam. Corpus informatique de textes français (ca 1150–1350), établi par Antonij Dees (Amsterdam 1987), remanié par Achim Stein, Pierre Kunstmann et Martin-Dietrich Gleßgen*. Stuttgart: Institut für Linguistik/Romanistik.
Trotter, David A. (ed.), 2000. *Multilingualism in Later Medieval Britain*. Cambridge: D.S. Brewer.
Umbach, Carla. 2006. Non-restrictive modification and backgrounding. In *Proceedings of the Ninth Symposium on Logic and Language*, 152–159. Hungarian Academy of Sciences.
Wright, Laura. 2010. A pilot study on the singular definite articles 'le' and 'la' in fifteenth-century London mixed-language business writing. In *The Anglo-Norman Language and its Context*, Richard Ingham (ed.), 130–143. York: York Medieval Press Publication.
Wydler, Karl. 1956. *Zur Stellung des Attributiven Adjektivs vom Latein bis zum Neufranzösischen*. Bern: Francke.

Strong and weak adjectives in Old Swedish*

Ulla Stroh-Wollin & Rico Simke
Department of Scandinavian Languages, Uppsala University, Sweden /
Friedrich-Alexander-Universität Erlangen-Nürnberg, Germany

In modern Swedish, weakly inflected adjectives are obligatory in definite noun phrases. However, strong adjectival forms in definite contexts are still rather common in early mediaeval manuscripts. But this fact has attracted surprisingly little attention by linguists, and the classic handbook on language history rather conveys the idea that strong adjectives in general were restricted to semantically indefinite noun phrases already in the first written records. This article presents empirical evidence that strong adjectival forms appear in semantically definite noun phrases to a considerable – but decreasing – extent in Old Swedish texts. It is also argued that weak adjectives only appear together with formal definiteness markers, which means that strong adjectival forms are not ruled out from semantically definite noun phrases until obligatory definiteness marking is fully established.

1. Introduction

The weak declension of adjectives was a Proto-Germanic innovation by which attributive adjectives did not only agree with the head noun in gender, number and case, but also showed up in two different guises for each combination of gender, number and case: a "strong" form and a "weak" form. Even though there has been a considerable reduction of adjectival forms in most Germanic languages, the strong–weak distinction as such remains in modern Germanic, English being the only exception.

In the modern Mainland Scandinavian languages, adjectives appear in the strong form in indefinite noun phrases and in the weak form in definite noun

---

* The first author of this paper is indebted to The Swedish Research Council for its financial support to her project "The syntax of the early Scandinavian noun phrase" (project number: 421-2010-1272). The second author's contribution to the project was made possible by a student grant from the Swedish Institute.

phrases; see (1a–b).[1] Accordingly, the strong form is sometimes labelled indefinite and the weak form definite.

(1) a. *ett stor-t hus* (Swedish)
a big-STR house
"a big house"

b. *det stor-a hus-et* (Swedish)
DEF big-WK house-DEF
"the big house"

The weak forms seem to have been associated with definiteness very early. However, the origin of the Germanic weak adjectival declension and the original functional distinction between the strong and weak paradigms are not fully transparent (Ringe 2006: 169 f.). Further, weak forms are rare in runic inscriptions and still appear with rather low frequency in early mediaeval manuscripts (13th and 14th century), which shows that the obligatory use of the weak form in semantically definite noun phrases is of a later date.[2]

Surprisingly little attention is paid to this fact in handbooks and, with few exceptions (e.g. Delsing 1994), elsewhere in the literature. In fact, the classic handbook on the history of the Swedish language by Elias Wessén states that, in general, the strong form of adjectives had indefinite meaning and the weak form definite meaning (Wessén 1965: 49).[3]

Obviously, Wessén's statement disregards, for instance, adjectives in noun phrases with possessive attributes. According to Delsing (1994), who focusses on just this kind of noun phrase, the weak form never occurs if the word order is not the modern one: possessive (P) – adjective (A) – noun (N). The earliest Old Swedish manuscripts show other word orders as well (NPA, ANP, APN). But strong forms were for some time also used, alongside with weak forms, in NPs with the modern word order, cf. (2a, b).

---

1. This is also the normal case in Icelandic, but there are exceptions (Naert 1969; Rögnvaldsson 1984).

2. It can also be noted that the distribution of strong and weak forms in modern German is not formally linked to definiteness (even though an adjective following the definite article appears in the weak form). A German adjective takes the weak form when following a determiner with a distinct inflectional morpheme (indicating gender, number and case), whether indefinite (as some forms of the indefinite article: *einen, einem,* etc.) or definite (as some forms of possessives: *meinen, meinem,* etc. "my"). Otherwise it takes the strong form (e.g. after singular masculine/neuter nominatives such as *ein* and *mein*).

3. Nygaard (1966, §42 ff.) on Old Norse is a little more informative. The weak form is, according to Nygaard, chiefly used after the old definite article *hinn* in Old Norse.

(2) a. *hans siuk-t ben*   (*Codex Bureanus, c.*1300)
      his   sick-STR leg
      "his sick leg"

   b. *hans sjuk-a ben*   (Modern Swedish)
      his   sick-WK leg

Recently, the second author of this article has investigated the distribution of strong and weak forms in semantically definite noun phrases of different kinds in Old Swedish (Simke 2012), showing that the use of strongly inflected adjectives in semantically definite noun phrases gradually decreases during the investigated period of time (*c.*1300 to *c.*1450), but the proportion of strong forms is still significant at the end of the 14th century. One aim of this article is to present the global results of Simke (2012).

The regulation of the adjectival form is in itself an interesting and hitherto largely neglected aspect of the language history. But it is also interesting from a wider perspective. The Scandinavian noun phrase is the subject of a complex of morpho-syntactic changes in early historical time, including definiteness marking by means of a suffix on the noun and (in Mainland Scandinavian) a preposed definite article, as in (1b). It is a reasonable hypothesis that the expansion of the weak adjectival form is part of this larger complex and does not evolve just independently of other changes.

This perspective is not focused on in Simke (2012), but is dealt with here in a modest follow-up study.[4] The distribution of noun phrases representing different morpho-syntactic patterns is compared in order to reveal how the constituents of semantically definite noun phrases interrelate.

2. Prerequisites

2.1 The inflection of adjectives in Old Swedish and Modern Swedish

The adjectival forms used in early Old Swedish are presented in Figure 1. Old Swedish is a language with three genders and four cases, and there are a large number of phonetically distinct strong forms. The weak declension, however, shows a highly simplified inflection.

The shaded strong forms with consonantal endings in Figure 1 are clearly distinct from their weak counterparts. The vocalic strong forms also differ from the corresponding weak forms, but the difference is less robust and a levelling takes place during the Old Swedish period. The most prominent change in this development is the spreading of -*a* forms throughout the weak paradigm; see Figure 2.

---

4. The follow-up study has been carried out by the first author of the paper.

Gender:		Masculine		Feminine		Neuter	
Number	Case	Strong	Weak	Strong	Weak	Strong	Weak
Sing.	Nom.	*langer*	*lange*	*lang*	*langa*	*langt*	*langa*
	Gen.	*langs*	*langa*	*langa*	*lango*	*langs*	
	Dat.	*langom*		*lange*		*lango*	
	Acc.	*langan*		*langa*		*langt*	
Plur.	Nom.	*lange (r)*	*lango*	*langa*	*lango*	*lang*	*lango*
	Gen.	*langa*		*langa*		*langa*	
	Dat.	*langom*		*langom*		*langom*	
	Acc.	*langa*		*langa*		*lang*	

Figure 1. The strong and weak inflection of adjectives in early Old Swedish, demonstrated with the adjective *langer* "long"

Gender:		Masculine		Feminine		Neuter	
Number	Case	Earlier forms	Later forms	Earlier forms	Later forms	Earlier forms	Later forms
Sg.	Nom.	*lange*	*lange (-a)*	*langa*	*langa*	*langa*	*langa*
	Obl.	*langa*	*langa*	*lango*	*lango/-a*	*langa*	*langa*
Pl.	Nom	*lango*	*lango/-a/-e*	*lango*	*lango/-a*	*lango*	*lango/-a*
	Obl.		*lango/-a*				

Figure 2. The weak inflection of adjectives in early and later Old Swedish

Since some strong forms also end in *-a* (see Figure 1) it is not always evident, especially during the later Old Swedish period, whether an instance of an adjective appears in its strong or its weak form.

There has been a considerable reduction of adjectival forms in modern Swedish. The reduction is partly due to the loss of case marking. In addition, the former masculine and feminine genders have coalesced into a 'common gender', which, however, still contrasts with the neuter gender. But the scarcity of forms is also due to phonetic levelling.

The resultant paradigm, shown in Figure 3, has three phonetically distinct, singular forms: two strong ones, one for the common gender and one for the neuter, and one weak form (used irrespective of gender).[5] In the plural, on the other hand, the only strong and the only weak form are realized in the same way. Thus, the strong–weak distinction is now retained exclusively by the contrast in the singular.

---

5. There is also a weak *-e* form, normally used if the referent is male. We can ignore it in this context, since the modern variation between *-a* and *-e* forms is purely semantic in nature. Further, weak inflection of superlatives gives *-a* forms for some adjectives and *-e* forms for others.

Number	Gender	Strong form	Weak form
Singular	Common	lång	långa
	Neuter	långt	
Plural	Common + Neuter	långa	långa

Figure 3. The inflection of adjectives in Modern Swedish, demonstrated with the adjective *lång* "long"

2.2 The concept of definiteness

It is possible to speak of definite noun phrases from a structural as well as from a semantic perspective. Structural definiteness concerns definiteness marking by formal definite morphemes, e.g. definite articles, whereas semantic definiteness concerns the meaning and interpretation of the phrase and relates to the hearer's ability to identify the intended referent within the given context.[6]

Of course there is a relation between structural and semantic definiteness; definite morphemes are means to express definite meaning. However, languages exhibit definite morphology to a varying degree, and it is possible to equate structural and semantic definiteness only on the condition that we have in mind a language with access to a definite article and, in generative terms, obligatory determiners in argumental noun phrases, DPs (as proposed in Abney 1987 and normally assumed thereafter).

Semantic definiteness is equally relevant in languages with less abundant definiteness marking, where structurally indefinite (or unmarked) structures may be interpreted as semantically definite. This is of course the case in languages with no definite article, e.g. the Scandinavian language of the Vikings.

Languages developing a definite article use it in a first stage chiefly to avoid misunderstanding in ambiguous contexts, not as soon as a definite interpretation is intended. Leiss (2000, 2007) refers to these languages as hypo-determining, in contrast to hyper-determining languages, such as e.g. the modern Germanic languages, where structural specification of semantic definiteness is obligatory. The language investigated in this article, Old Swedish, is a language on its way from a hypo-determining to the hyper-determining stage.

Below we take noun phrases in Old Swedish manuscripts to be semantically definite if they correspond to structurally definite noun phrases in Modern Swedish, irrespective of their structural appearances in the texts.

---

6. This is a pragmatic 'definition' of (prototypical) semantic definiteness. See Stroh-Wollin 2011 for a more formal view on the meaning of definiteness.

2.3 The structure of definite noun phrases in Modern Swedish[7]

A characteristic grammatical feature of Swedish – and other Scandinavian languages – is the definite inflection of nouns. Thus, nouns appear in an indefinite and a definite form. The definite form is used, for instance, when the noun constitutes the entire noun phrase, as in (3a). In some Scandinavian varieties, Swedish included, it can also be combined with preposed definite article, used when the noun is preceded by an adjectival attribute, as in (3b).

(3) a. *hus-et*
    house-DEF
    "the house"

  b. *det stor-a hus-et*
    DEF big-WK house-DEF
    "the big house"

The combined use of a preposed definite article and a noun in the definite form is sometimes referred to as double definiteness.

Not all Swedish definite noun phrases take the noun in its definite form. The noun always appears in its indefinite form after possessives and various other definite determiners, e.g. *samma* "the same"; see (4a–b).

(4) a. *mitt (stor-a) hus*
    my (big-WK) house.IND
    "my (big) house"

  b. *samma (stor-a) hus*
    the-same (big-WK) house.IND
    "the same (big) house"

If the noun is followed by a restrictive relative clause, it is also possible to combine a definite determiner with a noun in the indefinite form, as in (5a). A more special case is a noun phrase with an absolute superlative, which is semantically quasi-definite and may be given an indefinite paraphrase, as in (5b).

(5) a. *det (stor-a) hus som är till salu*
    "the (big) house that is for sale"

  b. *det utsöktast-e vin*
    DEF most.exquisite-WK wine.IND
    "a very exquisite wine"

Superlatives in noun phrases with a prototypical definite reading precede nouns in the definite form. On the other hand, it is not unusual for the definite article to be left out in such phrases, and that is often the case even in definite noun phrases

---

7. This section concerns standard Swedish and makes no references to regional deviations.

with adjectives pointing out one of two distinct alternatives, e.g. *högra* "right" and *vänstra* "left"; see (6a–b).

(6) a. (*det*) bäst-a vin-et
 (DEF) best-WK wine-DEF
 "the best wine"

 b. (*det*) vänstr-a ben-et
 (DEF) left-WK leg-DEF
 "the left leg"

Ordinary adjectives may also sometimes appear without the preposed article if the context clearly points out two contrasting alternatives. For instance it is possible to talk about *stora huset* "the big house" and *lilla huset* "the little house" in a contextually restricted area with only two houses.

An adjective in a definite noun phrase always appears in its weak form; the strong form would be ungrammatical in all examples above. However, definiteness is not expressed exclusively by a weak adjective, i.e. weak adjectives appear together with either a definite determiner or a noun in the definite form, sometimes in the presence of both. (Here we disregard vocative phrases without a visible determiner, such as e.g. *kära vän* "dear friend", taking the vocative as a special case.)

3. Theoretical presumptions and a hypothesis

As mentioned above, modern Swedish is a hyper-determining language, i.e. a language with obligatory definiteness marking of semantically definite noun phrases. In the following, we take the definiteness marking in hyper-determining languages to be formal in nature. In generative terms this means that some formal feature(s) related to definiteness is (are) checked and valued in the D-head of the DP before spell-out. The formal nature of definiteness may also manifest itself as agreement, e.g. between the article and a following adjective as in modern Swedish.

In hypo-determining languages, on the other hand, definiteness marking is not obligatory, but optional. We also presume it is not (when used) necessarily formal in nature. This means that primitive definite articles (in the normal case former demonstratives) induce a definite interpretation by force of their lexical content, but are not initially associated with any formal features related to definiteness and, thus, are not involved in any agreement relation(s) of this kind with other constituents in the noun phrase. The same holds true for, e.g. possessives and other "definite" attributes in early stages of hypo-determining languages. But, of course, at some time a non-formal article is inevitably transformed into a formal article in a language on the way to hyper-determination. And "definite" attributes may similarly become formal determiners.

When it comes to adjectives, we can take strong forms to be formally indefinite and weak forms to be formally definite in modern Swedish. The strong–weak inflection on adjectives seems above all to be a question of agreement; it is not necessarily the case that the inflectional morphemes carry any meaning.[8]

Now, what conclusion may be drawn from an Old Swedish noun phrase such as the one in (2a), *hans siukt ben* "his sick leg", where a possessive attribute is followed by an adjective in the strong form? The most plausible explanation is that the adjective does not have to agree with the possessive, because this is not used as a formal determiner, i.e. is not associated with any formal definiteness feature.

The underlying hypothesis is that weakly inflected adjectives were formally definite even in Old Swedish, as they only appear in definite noun phrases, but also, just as in modern Swedish, could only be used together with a formally definite determiner or a noun in the definite form. If this hypothesis is correct, then we expect the proportion of the weak adjectival form to increase concurrently with the development towards hyper-determination.

4. The structure of semantically definite noun phrases in Old Swedish – a first glimpse

To get an idea of the structure of semantically definite noun phrases in Old Swedish we can look at the different ways to express "the old laws" in a passage of an Old Swedish text from the beginning of the 14th century (*Pentateukparafrasen*; see Section 5). The passage shows 34 instances of noun phrases corresponding to one and the same double definiteness structure, *de gamla lagarna* "the old laws", in Modern Swedish. Interestingly, these 34 instances are distributed over five different morpho-syntactic patterns. The different patterns are exemplified in (7a–e), in the dative case throughout, since all instances of the three first patterns are in the dative.

(7) a. *gambl-om laghom*
   old-STR laws.IND
   "the old laws"

b. *them gambl-om laghom*
   DEF   old-STR   laws.IND

c. *them gambl-o laghom*
   DEF   old-WK   laws.IND

d. *gambl-o laghom-en*
   old-WK laws-DEF

---

8. Cf. gender inflection, which is formal but has no meaning.

e. *them gambl-o   laghom-en*
    DEF old-WK   laws-DEF

The most frequent pattern is the 'modern' double definiteness construction demonstrated in (7e). It is used 22 times, i.e. in two thirds of the 34 instances. However, one third of the instances still show some other morpho-syntactic pattern that is not used in Modern Swedish.

The pattern demonstrated in (7a) with no formal definiteness marker at all appears in 4 of the 34 instances. In these cases, the semantically definite interpretation is due to the context alone; the same phrase could of course also be used with indefinite meaning, "old laws". There is only one instance of the pattern shown in (7b), which in addition to the combination of strong adjective and indefinite noun in (5a) has a preposed definite article. The patterns illustrated in (7a–b) are very rarely identified in the literature. The b-pattern is hardly recognized at all. The a-pattern is taken by Wessén (1965: 41) to be poetic or archaic, possibly as a relict from a stage before the development of the weak declension of adjectives.

The patterns demonstrated in (7c–e) have, contrary to the ones in (7a–b), the adjective in the weak form, but only (7e) shows double definiteness. In the excerpted passage, 3 instances show the c-pattern and 4 instances show the d-pattern.

Interestingly, the c-pattern is equivalent to the modern Danish construction and the d-pattern to the modern Icelandic construction. Unlike Swedish (and Norwegian and Faroese), Danish and Icelandic do not manifest double definiteness. Danish uses a free-standing definite article before preposed attributes, but does not combine it with the definite form on the noun; cf. (7c). Icelandic, on the other hand, marks definiteness on the noun but can manage without a preposed article; cf. (7d).[9, 10]

5. Sources

The investigations accounted for in the following are based on excerpting Old Swedish prose texts, electronically available at *Fornsvenska textbanken* (see References). The first study is based on the five texts presented below, the second

---

9. Icelandic actually has a definite article, *hinn*, but its use is restricted to formal style. When used, it is not combined with the definite form of the noun.

10. According to Wessén (1965: 45) and Hirvonen (1996), there is (and has been since the earliest Old Swedish manuscripts) a difference in meaning between noun phrases of the d-pattern on the one hand and noun phrases of the c- and e-patterns on the other. Semantically, *gamblo laghomen*, should, according to this view, be related to modern Swedish article dropping, indicating contrast (cf. *stora huset* "the big house" vs. *lilla huset* "the little house", mentioned in Section 2.3), rather than to the Icelandic unmarked phrase.

study only on texts 1–4. None of the texts are preserved in an original manuscript, which means that the electronic files used here are based on editions of later transcripts. Thus, the dating is somewhat uncertain, but the results indicate that the transcripts used mainly reflect the language of the originals. This is also generally confirmed as regards the very late transcript of text 2, which is therefore preferred to an older, but obviously modernized, transcript.

Text 1: *Fornsvenska legendariet* "The Old Swedish Legendary", a free translation from a Latin collection of religious legends, dated as 1276–1307. Only the edition of the oldest transcript, Codex Bureanus, from the middle of the 14th century is used. (*c.*36,000 tokens)

Text 2: *Pentateukparafrasen* "The Pentateuch Paraphrase", including a free version of the Pentateuch with exegetic explications; from the first part of the 14th century. The edition of the transcript from 1525 is used (cf. above), Cod. Holm A 1. (*c.*145,100 tokens)

Text 3: *Birgittas uppenbarelser* (books 1–3) "The Revelations of Saint Bridget", from the late 14th century. An edition of a transcript from the early 15th century is used, Cod. Holm A 33. (*c.*56,000 tokens)

Text 4: *Själens tröst* "Comfort of the Soul", religious legends based on the Low German *Seelentrost*; from the beginning of the 15th century. The edition used is based on a transcript which is only slightly newer than the original, Cod. Holm A 108. (*c.*145,500 tokens) Only p. 1–200 (*c.*69,800 tokens) are excerpted for the first study.

Text 5: *Sagan om Didrik av Bern* "The Saga of Theodoric the Great", a heroic epic based on a Low German original; from the middle of the 15th century. An edition of a transcript from *c.*1500 is used, Cod. Skokloster 115, 116 A. (53,900 tokens) This text is not excerpted for the second study, see above.

Texts 1–2 represent Early Old Swedish (*c.*1225–1375), texts 3–5 represent Late Old Swedish (*c.*1375–1526); see Figure 4 showing the dating of the original manuscripts as well as the edited transcripts.

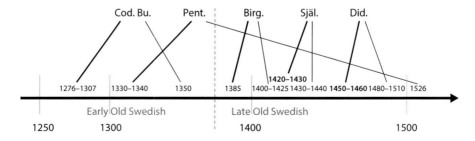

Figure 4. Dating of the texts used in the investigations. Black = original manuscript; Grey = edited transcript

6. Investigation 1

In this section we briefly account for the major result of the empirical investigation, treated extensively in Simke (2012), on the distribution of strong and weak adjectives in semantically definite noun phrases in the Old Swedish texts presented above.

In the study, forty adjectives were chosen for the excerption. In order to make general statements about the syntax, only very common and prototypical adjectives were included in the study, i.e. adjectives for e.g. size, age, value, colour, common personal features and typical religious attributes. The adjectives should also, without doubt, have full sets of strong and weak forms. Only attributive adjectives in the positive form were considered.

Besides the form of the adjective, i.e. strong or weak, the form of the head noun, i.e. indefinite or definite, as well as the case, gender and number were also recorded for each noun phrase. Whether the noun phrases were semantically definite or indefinite was simply determined by comparison with the structure of their modern equivalents (see Section 2.2). Noun phrases are normally definite if the referent is mentioned earlier in the text or when referring to unique referents, such as *the true God*, *the Holy Scripture*, etc. In cases of doubt, no specific definite or indefinite interpretation was forced on the noun phrase. It soon showed that weak forms never appeared in semantically indefinite noun phrases, whereas the adjectives in the definite phrases appeared in both the strong and the weak forms. For these reasons, only the (unambiguously) definite noun phrases were analyzed further.

The primary interest was to investigate if it was possible to capture the development towards obligatory weak adjectives in definite contexts, which clearly turned out to be the case. Figure 5 shows the distribution of strong, weak and uncertain or ambiguous adjectival forms in the five texts investigated, in chronological order.

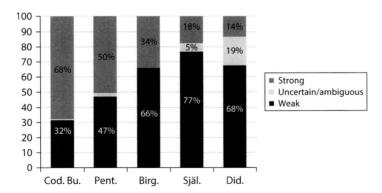

Figure 5. The distribution of strong, weak and uncertain/ambiguous forms of attributive adjectives in the positive in semantically definite noun phrases in the texts investigated, dating from *c.*1300 to *c.*1450

As can be seen from Figure 5, the proportion of strong forms gradually decreases during the 150 years covered by the five texts. Similarly, the proportion of unambiguous weak forms increases until the levelling of strong and weak forms, above all in the plural (cf. Section 2.1 above), raises the proportion of adjectives with ambiguous inflection.

Figure 5 shows the global picture, but it also turned out that the inclination to inflect strongly or weakly depended on various aspects, e.g. number and case. Writers were more apt to use weak forms in the singular than in the plural and, similarly, more inclined to use weak forms in the nominative case than in oblique phrases. Further, it turned out that even lexical aspects could have an impact on the choice of the adjectival form. The adjective *gamall* "old" for instance appeared more often in the weak form (43–100%) than *goþer* "good" (17–59%) and a lot more often than *sander* "true" (0–25%). (For more details, see Simke (2012).)

7. Investigation 2

The investigation in Simke (2012) does not deal with the question of whether the increased use of weak adjectives is related to the development towards formal and obligatory definiteness marking. This question is focussed in this follow-up study. The distribution of noun phrases on different structural patterns is analyzed in order to elucidate how the definite article, adjective and noun interrelate. The investigation also deals with the diachronic development as regards the preferences of the different patterns.

A first analysis is based on the recordings in Simke (2012, p. 98 ff.)[11] and concerns semantically definite noun phrases consisting of only an adjective and a noun. In Section 4, two variants of this kind were presented: strong adjective + indefinite noun (7a: *gamblom laghom*) and weak adjective + definite noun (7d: *gambo laghomen*). There are also a few instances of weak adjective + indefinite noun in the texts, but generally only in certain fixed phrases denoting unique referents, e.g. *milda mø* "the mild maid" or *hælghe thorsdagher* "Holy Thursday" (which actually might have dropped an article). We disregard this pattern as a possibility for normal syntax. The combination of a possibly strong adjective before a definite noun is attested once, but here it is question of an -*a* form in the plural, i.e. presumably an instance of the modernized inflection (cf. Section 2.1).

---

11. A slightly corrected version of the appendix in Simke (2012) is used. The corrections do not affect the global picture presented in the previous section.

In sum, strong adjectives combine with indefinite nouns, weak adjectives with definite nouns, which so far confirms the hypothesis that the use of weak adjectives depends on the presence of a formally definite constituent in the phrase. The latter pattern (weak adjective + definite noun) is not very frequent (see also Note 10) and will not be analyzed further. We concentrate on the former possibility.

The figures in Table 1 show the instances of semantically definite noun phrases that consist exclusively of a strong adjective and an indefinite noun. The table accounts for the total number of this kind of phrase as well as the remaining number when certain instances containing the adjectives *kristen* "Christian" and *sander* "true" are excluded. These adjectives are frequent in the texts and appear mostly in the strong form in fixed religious phrases such as *kristen tro* "the Christian belief" and *sander gudh* "the true god".

Table 1. Semantically definite noun phrases consisting of a strongly inflected adjective and a noun in the indefinite form in text 1–4. Reduced n: set phrases with *kristen* "Christian" and *sander* "true" excluded. (Only the 200 first pages of text 4 are analyzed.)

	Text 1	Text 2	Text 3	Text 4
Tokens	36,000	145,100	56,000	69,800
Total n	82	107	12	17
n per 1000 words	2.28	0.74	0.21	0.24
Reduced n	30	89	2	2
n per 1000 words	0.83	0.61	0.03	0.03

As is seen in Table 1, the two earlier texts reflect a possibility of interpreting noun phrases as semantically definite exclusively from the context, whereas the two later texts imply that this was in practice no longer possible from the late 1300s, if we ignore some set phrases.

In a second analysis, noun phrases containing a string of the definite article, adjectival attribute and noun head (in this order), henceforth DAN phrases, were analyzed. In order to maximize the material, a new search in the electronic files was conducted. The different forms of the definite article were searched for, and any adjective (or perfect participle) with both strong and weak inflection was accepted, including superlatives as well as adjectives in the positive. The recorded phrases were then sorted with regard to the form of the adjective, i.e. strong or weak, as well as the form of the noun, i.e. indefinite or definite.

The number of DAN phrases of different kinds is accounted for in Table 2. The forms of the adjectives are here (as in Delsing 1994) sorted into four categories, taking into consideration the increased confusion of vocalic forms (cf. Section 2.1): I. consonantal forms, II. vocalic forms consistent with strong interpretation, III. vocalic forms consistent with weak interpretation, IV. vocalic forms neither consistent with strong, nor with weak interpretation. Only category I can be considered undoubtedly strong, since category II probably to a large extent reflects the diffusion of *a-* forms into the weak paradigm. The commentaries below focus on phrases with adjectives of category I (unambiguously strong forms) and III (normal weak forms), shaded in Table 2.

Table 2. The distribution of adjectival forms in DAN phrases with indefinite and definite head nouns. I: consonantal forms; II – IV: vocalic forms with originally strong, originally weak and uncertain endings respectively

Form of the noun	Adjectival form	Text 1 (36,000 tokens)	Text 2 (145,100 tokens)	Text 3 (56,000 tokens)	Text 4 (145,500 tokens)	
Indefinite	I	1	13	1	5	cf. (7b)
	II	0	35	0	20	
	III	14	132	31	82	cf. (7c)
	IV	1	13	0	8	
Definite	I	0	0	0	0	–
	II	0	3	1	15	
	III	4	32	24	181	cf. (7e)
	IV	0	5	0	6	

From the first figures in Table 2, we see that there is no strong tendency to use a definite article as the only marker of definiteness in DAN phrases, as in (7b): *them gamblom laghom*. The number of DAN phrases with unambiguously strong adjectives (category I) preceding indefinite head nouns is rather low, and they do not increase as the article-less kind of phrases becomes obsolete.

However, even if the instances are few, it is noteworthy that the presence of the determiner did not necessarily force the adjective to appear in its weak form. By contrast, no instance of a DAN phrase with an unambiguously strong adjective before a noun in the definite form was recorded. The observations speak in favour of an obligatory formal adjectival agreement with nouns in the definite form, whereas the preposed article occasionally appears as a non-formal article, i.e. an article which does not demand adjectival agreement.

Most often noun phrases headed by the definite article take the adjective in the weak form (category III in the first place, probably also to some extent other vocalic forms). The recorded instances are distributed over NPs with indefinite as well as definite nouns; see (7c): *them gamblo laghom* and (7e): *them gamblo laghomen*, respectively.

Table 2 gives the impression of a development from mostly single definiteness (i.e. definite article and indefinite noun) towards a predominance of the double definiteness pattern. But two circumstances obscure the comparison. First, a fair number of the noun phrases contain relative clauses, which, in case they are restrictive, may appear after indefinite nouns even in modern Swedish. Secondly, all texts show a considerable number of religious phrases with the adjective *hælgher* "holy", which seem to have a fixed form with the head noun in the indefinite form, e.g. *thæn hælghe ande* "the Holy Ghost" (which, in modern Swedish, actually still takes the noun in the indefinite form), *thæt hælgha kors* "the holy cross" etc.

Table 3 shows the number of DAN phrases with weak adjectives (of category III) when all instances with relative clauses and the adjective *hælgher* "holy" have been excluded.

Table 3. DAN phrases with weakly inflected adjectives (category III) before head nouns in indefinite and definite form; phrases with relative clauses and the adjective *hælgher* "holy" excluded

Form of the noun	Number/ Frequency	Text 1 (36,000 tokens)	Text 2 (145,100 tokens)	Text 3 (56,000 tokens)	Text 4 (145,500 tokens)	
Indefinite	n	6	24	1	4	cf. (7c)
	n per 1000 words	0.17	0.16	0.02	0.03	
Definite	n	3	29	21	134	cf. (7e)
	n per 1000 words	0.08	0.20	0.38	0.92	

When comparing the figures in Table 3 it seems clear that the single definiteness pattern is practically abandoned in the two later texts, but it is not very frequent in the earlier texts either. On the other hand, the figures for the double definiteness pattern basically confirm the picture from Table 2. The pattern seems well established in the later texts, especially in text 4, but is less attested in the earlier ones.

Of course, one may wonder what semantically definite noun phrases looked like when neither single definiteness, nor double definiteness was very frequent. The answer is found in Table 1. The frequency figures in Table 1 are not absolutely comparable to the ones in Table 3, since they are based on a limited number of adjectives, but they do identify "zero definiteness" as the predominant pattern in the earlier texts.

In sum, this follow-up study shows that two patterns of semantically definite noun phrases, corresponding to the modern Swedish double definiteness constructions, are more frequent than others, namely noun phrases with no definiteness markers at all in the earlier texts and noun phrases following the modern pattern with double definiteness in the later texts.

Furthermore, the investigation confirms that strong and weak adjectives are not randomly distributed. Strong adjectives do not show up in noun phrases with the head noun in the definite form. And weak adjectives are not used unless there is either a head noun in the definite form or a definite article or both.

8. Conclusions and comments

Our investigations clearly show that strongly inflected adjectives were used in semantically definite noun phrases to a high, but decreasing, degree in texts from the 14th century and to some degree even in texts from the 15th century. The clear-cut division in Wessén 1965 (p.49) between strong forms and indefinite meaning on the one hand and weak forms and definite meaning on the other does not hold true.

According to Wessén (1965: 41), it is possible that noun phrases with an indefinite noun preceded by a strongly inflected adjective (and no other attribute), when found, are remnants from a stage before the development of the weak inflection of adjectives. He admits that there are a fair number of instances of this kind of phrase in *Fornsvenska legendariet* (our text 1), but supposes that this is due to the text's peculiar style.

As regards the first assumption, it is of course true that strong adjectives in definite contexts reflect an older stage in the history of the Swedish (Scandinavian) language, but it is not probable that the majority of these adjectives are obsolete remnants from such a stage.

As regards the observation on *Fornsvenska legendariet*, we do not take the high frequency of strong adjective + indefinite noun with definite meaning to be a matter of style. As we see it, the style of *Fornsvenska legendariet* is not remarkable, and Wessén presents no reference to support his characterization of the text. In fact, the kind of phrase in question appears fairly often in *Pentateukparafrasen* (our text 2) too, and all texts in our investigations fall neatly into the pattern of a gradually decreasing use of the strong adjectival form in various definite contexts. So, *Fornsvenska legendariet*, being a very early text, probably just reflects the language of its time of creation on this point.

In this case the shortage of Early Old Swedish texts may partly explain the traditional view. The first provincial laws are very early texts too, but have few instances of attributive adjectives and, thus, provide little evidence on the matter.

What initiated the development of the weak declension of adjectives is unclear, but the weak forms seem to have been associated with definiteness very early. This association is, however, only a question of weak adjectives appearing exclusively in definite contexts. They do not express definite meaning on their own.

Strong adjectival forms, on the other hand, seem to have been formally incongruous with definite nouns as far back as we can see, but in Old Swedish they were not semantically incongruous with a definite interpretation in other contexts. They are gradually excluded from semantically definite noun phrases, but even in the newest of our texts the proportion is not reduced to nil.

The final regulation of the distribution of strong and weak forms of indefinite and definite noun phrases respectively may be due to the development of obligatory definiteness marking. When a primitive definite article and (semantically definite) attributes are transformed into formal determiners, they can only accept adjectival attributes in the weak form.

References

Abney, Steven Paul. 1987. *The English Noun Phrase and Its Sentential Aspect*. Ph.D. dissertation, MIT.
Delsing, Lars-Olof. 1994. Hans sjukt ben – Om starka och svaga adjektiv i fornsvenskan. In *Språkbruk, grammatik och språkförändring: En festskrift till Ulf Teleman 13.1.1994*, 99–108. Lund: Department of Scandinavian Languages, Lund University.
Fornsvenska textbanken ⟨http://project2.sol.lu.se/fornsvenska⟩
Hirvonen, Ilkka. 1996. Konstruktionstyperna *den gamle man, den gamle mannen* och *gamle mannen* i fornsvenskan. In *Studier i Nordisk Filologi* 75 [Skrifter utgivna av Svenska Litteratursällskapet i Finland, nr 603], 7–104.
Leiss, Elisabeth. 2000. *Artikel und Aspekt: Die grammatischen Muster von Definitheit*. Berlin: Mouton de Gruyter.
Leiss, Elisabeth. 2007. Covert patterns of definiteness/indefiniteness and aspectuality in Old Icelandic, Gothic, and Old High German. In *Nominal Determination. Typology, Context Constraints, and Historical Emergence* [Studies in Language Companion Series 89], Elisabeth Stark, Elisabeth Leiss & Werner Abraham (eds), 73–102. Amsterdam: John Benjamins.
Naert, Pierre. 1969. Goður maðurinn. En studie över den syntaktiska kombinationen obestämt–bestämt i isländskan, särskilt den nyare isländskan. *Arkiv för Nordisk Filologi* 84: 115–130.
Nygaard, Marius. 1966. *Norrøn Syntax*. Olso: Aschehoug.
Ringe, Don, 2006. *From Proto-Indo-European to Proto-Germanic*. Oxford: OUP.
Rögnvaldsson, Eiríklur. 1984. Af lýsingaorðsviðurlögum. *Íslenskt mál og almenn málfræiði* 6: 57–80.
Simke, Rico. 2012. Die Entwicklung des schwachen Adjektivs. Studie zur altschwedischen Nominalphrase. MA thesis, Friedrich-Alexander-Universität Erlangen-Nürnberg. ⟨http://www.ricosimke.com/public/simke-2012-adjectives.pdf⟩

Stroh-Wollin, Ulla. 2011. A semantic approach to noun phrase structure and the definite: indefinite distinction in Germanic and Romance. In *The Noun Phrase in Romance and Germanic. Structure, Variation and Change* [Linguistik Aktuell/Linguistics Today 171], Petra Sleeman & Harry Perridon (eds), 127–140. Amsterdam: John Benjamins.

Wessén, Elias. 1965. *Svensk språkhistoria. III Grundlinjer till en historisk syntax.* Stockholm: Almqvist & Wiksell.

The resilient nature of adjectival inflection in Dutch*

Freek Van de Velde[1,2] & Fred Weerman[3]
[1]Research Foundation Flanders FWO / [2]University of Leuven / [3]University of Amsterdam

> The rich Germanic adjectival inflection dramatically eroded in the history of Dutch as part of a general process of deflection. At present, Dutch is left with what appears to be a vestigial structure: an alternation between an inflected form in schwa and an uninflected form, the distribution of which is semantically ill-motivated. As a consequence, one might expect that the inflection is moribund and that Dutch will follow its West Germanic neighbor English in doing away with this dysfunctional piece of morphology. This is not what is happening, though. Dutch adjectival inflection is remarkably resilient. In this article it is argued that this resilience is due to refunctionalization. The inflectional schwa is turning into a transparent marker of attributive adjectives, and comes to function as a watershed between the modification and determination zone in the noun phrase. This account explains many erratic inflectional patterns in non-standard language. The whole reanalysis is a long-term process, which has not yet come to completion, but the existence of the process is supported by a detailed investigation of corpus data.

1. Introduction

Adjectival inflection features prominently in Dutch reference grammars. The ANS (Haeseryn et al. 1997) devotes no less than 13 pages on the system behind the presence or absence of the inflectional schwa (pp. 400–413), although the general rule is fairly easy, at least in comparison to the complicated situation in present-day German. A basic outline is given in (1). This is not to deny that there are numerous exceptions[1] and there is a remarkable degree of geographic and social

---

* We would like to thank Tom Ruette for his support in technical issues concerning MOROCCORP, and Caitlin Meyer for proofreading our non-native English text.
1. Many of the exceptions have to do with the morphophonemics of the adjective, and do not really complicate the syntactic rule under (1), though.

variation, which has led to a steady stream of monographs and articles (see, among others, Blom 1994; Weerman 2003; Weerman et al. 2006; Tummers et al. 2004, 2005; Tummers 2005; Plevoets et al. 2009).

(1) a. predicative use: ADJ-Ø
    (*dat boek is moeilijk* "that book is difficult:UNINFL")
  b. attributive use: ADJ-ə
    (*het moeilijke boek* "the difficult:INFL book")
  c. except: [+sg -def +neutr] NPs: ADJ-Ø
    (*een moeilijk boek* "a difficult:UNINFL book")

The overt inflection in (1b) does not seem to have a special meaning or function, and since adjectives can survive without inflection as well, as (1a, c) and a comparison with for instance modern English may show, it looks as if Dutch could just as well get rid of (1b). In fact, such a step would be entirely in accordance with the loss of inflection that is visible throughout the history of Dutch in all inflectional domains, amongst which adjectival inflection.

Useless as (1b) may look at first sight and notwithstanding the historical trend of deflection, we will argue in this paper that quite the opposite happens. Combining a synchronic and a diachronic perspective by looking at ongoing changes, we will show that (1b) is getting a stronger position in modern Dutch (and that, if anything, (1c) might be in danger). This is due to language learners and users who can be seen to tinker with the available morphology, and take etymologically unwarranted steps, creating pockets of local generalizations (see Joseph 1992). More precisely, we will argue that the available inflectional system is reinterpreted as a way to create order in the set of elements that may precede the noun. Simplifying this, we suggest that a distinction is under construction along the lines of (2), between a more peripheral zone where inflection does not play a role, and a zone that is characterized by the inflectional system illustrated above.

(2) [no inflection] [inflection] Noun
          A   B

Two types of changes are needed to establish this and we will give examples of both. On the one hand, there are elements in zone A that have inflectional features which should be reanalyzed as basically not inflected. On the other hand, the inflectional system of (1) should be introduced on new elements in zone B that were not inflected yet. To some extent, the same may be reached by moving inflected elements to zone B and vice versa. This reorganization and rise of inflection in a language that is generally known to lose it may help us to shed light on the coming into being of inflection in general.

As already noted, language learners and users are the driving force behind the changes just sketched. We will therefore have to consider how they acquire the system in (1). This will be done in Section 3 by reviewing recent work on both L1 and L2 acquisition of Dutch adjectival inflection. In Section 4 and 5 we will see how this helps us to understand the (ongoing) changes. Conclusions will be presented in Section 6. Before we embark, we will first set the scene by presenting some rather basic ideas on the structure of the noun phrase and the history of Dutch adjectival inflection.

2. Preliminaries: The history of the adjectival inflection and the structure of the noun phrase in Dutch

The strange set of rules in (1) is the result of a number of historical changes that have swept through the Dutch language in the course of centuries. The Proto-Germanic adjectival inflection has been mutilated beyond recognition. The exact path the Dutch adjectival inflection followed is notoriously tortuous, and has drawn quite some scholarly attention (see among others Raidt 1968; Van Loon 1988; Van Leuvensteijn & Dekker 1990; Van Marle 1995; Berteloot 2005; Van de Velde 2006). This is not the place to go into the details, but a short historical note may be helpful to see how we ended up with the situation in present-day Dutch.

One of the innovations in the Germanic branch of Indo-European was the emergence of a double adjectival inflection, with a so-called 'weak' declension and a 'strong' declension (see, among others, Ranheimsæter 1945; McFadden 2004; Van de Velde 2006 and Braunmüller 2008).[2] Opinions diverge on what steered the distribution of strong and weak endings in Proto-Germanic. In an early stage, the functions presumably lay closer to the forms' Proto-Indo-European provenance, but in late Proto-Germanic (a period that is sometimes called 'Common Germanic', ca. 200–500), the system became involved in the marking of definiteness, such that the weak declension became a marker of definiteness. The strong declension was neutral with regard to definiteness (Quirk & Wrenn 1969: 68; Traugott 1992: 173), but the contrast with the weak declension may have eventually related it to indefiniteness. In a next step, the declension types did not carry the function of definiteness by themselves anymore, but occurred in combination with

---

2. The double adjectival declension also emerged in Slavic, but the morphology of the system is different in nature. We have a case of cross-linguistic grammatical 'homoplasy' (see Van de Velde & Van der Horst 2013), rather than homology here.

dedicated determiners. This was still the system as it was operational in Old Dutch (Quak & Van der Horst 2002). In Middle Dutch, the distinction was messed up, by mutual influence of the strong and weak inflection upon each other, by influence of the inflection of the preceding determiner and by the confusion between different gender classes and cases (see Raidt (1968) and Van Bree (1987: 247–249) for overviews).

The collapse of the double inflectional paradigm eventually gave rise in Late Modern Dutch to the alternation between schwa and zero, which sometimes is seen as a direct continuation of the weak and strong paradigm respectively (see Royen 1953: 53ff). This is, however, an anachronistic view on the facts. The form in schwa occurs through all genders and cases (as far as Dutch still has them), and is used both in definite and in indefinite contexts, suggesting that the link with the former Germanic double declension is now severed in Dutch, as opposed to German, where the old system still shines through.

The situation in Present-day Dutch is better described as displaying 'junk', 'obsolescent', '(near-) empty', 'remnant' or 'vestigial' morphology.[3] Much like the vermiform appendix in the human digestive system, its structure and remnant function can only be understood in the light of its history.

If the adjectival inflection is in essence a vestigial feature, it may be refunctionalized. This recycling of morphology is common in a complex adaptive system such as language (Lass 1990, 1997; Norde 2002; Heine 2003; Fudeman 2004; Narrog 2007; Booij 2010: 212ff; Simon 2010; Willis 2010; Wischer 2010; Smith 2011), and has been observed in previous stages of the history of the adjectival inflection in particular (Lass 1990; Van de Velde 2006; Braunmüller 2008). The system presented in (2) can be seen as an attempt by language users to make sense of a morphological quirk that is handed down to them through previous generations. In undisturbed intergenerational transmission, quirky morphology can be remarkably stable, but demographic changes by immigration can heavily impact on a non-transparent system like the one in (1). We will come back to this issue in Section 3.

The hypothesis that Dutch adjectival inflection indeed tends to develop in the direction of (2) is related to the question how the noun phrase is syntactically structured. Proposals for the internal syntax of the noun phrase abound (see e.g. Coene & D'hulst 2003 for various suggestions within the generative framework). For Dutch, a detailed treatment is given in De Schutter (1998, 1999). Many of the

---

3. The notion of 'junk' morphology features prominently in the paper by Lass (1990), but other scholars have raised objections to the notion of fully defunct morphology (see Vincent 1995; Giacalone Ramat 1998; Smith 2006; Willis 2010).

extant proposals have a fairly large number of slots or projections (see e.g. the spectacularly elaborate templates in Tucker 1998 or Scott 2002). Partly drawing on earlier structuralist accounts like Van der Lubbe (1958) and Van Roey (1974), a more parsimonious approach is suggested in Van de Velde (2009), which comes close to what is proposed in Payne and Huddleston's chapter in the authoritative English grammar of Huddleston and Pullum (2002). What is generally agreed upon is that noun phrases at least display a major division in two layers, the D-layer for determiners, and the nominal layer for the noun (see also Broekhuis & Keizer 2012).[4] There is ongoing debate on how to accommodate adjectives, but a simple structuralist position would be to assign them to a separate intermediate layer. Ignoring complicating issues in the predeterminer zone (predeterminers, peripheral modifiers), a basic template as in (3) can be put forward.

(3) [NP D   [Adj   [N]]]
    [het/the [mooie/beautiful [meisje/girl]]]

Our claim is that the A-zone and the B-zone in (2) in fact correspond to the D and Adj shell in (3), respectively. It must be stressed that the hypothesis is that the system in (2) and its connection with (3) is *under construction*, as said in Section 1. So far, Dutch has not arrived at a clear division between uninflected Ds versus inflected Adjs: it is well-known that Dutch has several inflecting determiners and uninflected attributive adjectives. However, focusing on micro-variation in several Dutch corpora, we will show in Section 4 and 5 that there are strong indications of an ongoing drift towards a system along the lines of (2).

3. Acquisition

Ongoing changes in the status of adjectival inflection may be a result of the way in which this system is acquired. It may be the case that options that are preferred in L1 acquisition gradually win over forms that are part of the standard language. It is also possible that overgeneralizations that are typical for L2 learners spread over the community or that these strengthen tendencies resulting from L1 acquisition, since we know that in general language contact (that is, different forms of L2 acquisition) may have a disruptive effect on inflection. We therefore need to know more about the way in which the present system in (1), repeated here in (4) for convenience, is acquired by L1 and L2 learners.

---

4. We will not engage in the NP/DP-debate, and use noun phrase (NP) to refer to the whole complex.

(4) a. predicative use: ADJ-Ø
 (*dat boek is moeilijk* "that book is difficult:UNINFL")
 b. attributive use: ADJ-ə
 (*het moeilijke boek* "the difficult:INFL book")
 c. except: [+sg -def +neutr] NPs: ADJ-Ø
 (*een moeilijk boek* "a difficult:UNINFL book")

With respect to (4a) there are no systematic differences between L1 and L2 learners. Using an experiment with elicitation tasks, Weerman, Bisschop and Punt (2006) found that L1 children, L2 children and L2 adults use the uninflected form correctly. In their study, learners hardly make any mistakes, even if their L1 has a system in which the predicative adjective is inflected (like in Romance languages). Similarly, L1 children do not overgeneralize the inflected form of the attributive position to the predicative position.

For both L1 and L2 children the inflected form in (4b) is unproblematic, too, as shown in various studies (Blom, Polišenská & Weerman 2006, 2008; Polišenská 2010). Although children do not (or hardly) overgeneralize uninflected forms in attributive positions, this pattern is very clearly visible in adult L2 acquisition, in particular in early stages (cf. Blom et al. 2006, 2008). The frequency of this pattern is partly dependent on the L1, but as such it is visible in groups with an entirely different language background (for instance, Turkish, Moroccan Arabic, German – cf. Ziemann, Weerman & Ruigendijk 2011).

For all learners the pattern in (4c) is the most problematic one. All learners, young or old, L2 or L1, tend to overgeneralize the form with a schwa to this context. In other words, learners typically use (5a) instead of the target form in (5b).

(5) a. *een moeilijke boek
 b. een moeilijk boek

At first sight, several explanations can be given for this type of overgeneralization. One option is the following. The rule in (4b) contains less information, is a kind of default and is arguably much easier to acquire than the rule in (4c), which is, on the contrary, rather peculiar from a synchronic point of view. Obviously, if at some stage a learner does not have (4c), he or she may automatically apply the default and hence produce (5a) instead of (5b). Blom et al. (2008) argue that this option – (4c) is not available – is the correct interpretation for groups of Moroccan immigrant children acquiring Dutch. In fact, they suggest that this situation may even fossilize so that (5b) never becomes a normal construction for these learners.

Another option to explain the overgeneralizations of (5a) is to reduce it to another effect. It might be the case that learners know the rule in (4c) but that they think it is not applicable since they consider *boek* to be common instead of neuter.

This is a plausible option, too, since it is well-known that learners of Dutch have great difficulty in finding out which nouns are neuter (see for instance Blom et al. 2008). All learners tend to overgeneralize common to neuter. Child L1 learners take at least 7 years to reach the target. As Blom et al. (2008) show, however, they do know rules like (4c) surprisingly early, namely around the age of 3, or possibly even earlier. In other words, they claim that if an L1 child knows that a noun is neuter he or she will correctly use a bare adjective if the phrase is singular and indefinite. What is difficult for L1 children is not the rule, but rather the storage of neuter nouns (gender assignment is largely arbitrary in Dutch). Hence, for the L1 learners, overgeneralizations can be reduced to gender mistakes.

There is some evidence that the difference between child L1 and child L2 is dependent on both age and input. Input plays a role in as far that some immigrant children not only start acquiring Dutch later than L1 children, but that they are also confronted with substantially less and probably also less target-like Dutch. Therefore, they might not acquire the target system before the end of the critical period, and therefore the system without a rule like (4c) may fossilize. Ziemann et al. (2011) show that L2 children with a German background, who are in general far more integrated in the Dutch society, show a development comparable to Dutch L1 children, suggesting that indeed input plays an important role. They also show that adult L2 learners with a German background have persistent problems with (4c), showing that age plays a role as well.

Although the explanation for overgeneralizations like in (5b) may hence differ from group to group, the important observation is that in attributive positions the inflected adjective has a much stronger position than the bare adjective has. Some (L2) learners may not even develop (4c), whereas the inflected form is also for L1 learners the default, both quantitatively as qualitatively. The fact that the inflected adjective has such a strong position in L1 and L2 groups is crucial to understand changes in this domain. It is well-known that language contact plays a central role in the process of deflection (cf. Weerman 2006; Lupyan & Dale 2010; Trudgill 2010 a.o.). If innovations introduced by L2 learners go in the same direction as preferred options in L1 acquisition, we may expect that they can spread easily. As a result, the strong position of the inflected adjective becomes a hallmark for the distinction between zone A and B, as we will now show.

4. The rise of inflection in the adjectival zone

The reanalysis of the inflectional schwa along the lines of (2) boils down to a restoration of a one-to-one relation between form and function, such that the presence of the schwa marks the attributive (non-determiner) function in the NP prefield.

In this section evidence will be mustered for the idea that the schwa has increasingly been associated with the adjectival slot, obscuring the various historical sources from which the present-day schwa morphologically derives. This section deals with extensions of the inflectional schwa to previously unaffected adjectival contexts. In Section 5 we will turn to the ousting of inflection from non-adjectival (determiner) contexts. These two processes jointly produce the reanalysis set out above.

The changes we will discuss are 'from below'. Evidence for this system under construction is therefore not very likely to be found in formal language, but might pop up more frequently the more informal the language is. For this reason we make use of the CONDIV corpus, which represents various levels on a cline of formality (see Grondelaers et al. 2000). We exploited the following sections of the corpus: (i) newspaper texts (NRC and De Standaard), (ii) usenet material, and (iii) internet relay chat (IRC). Since we expect innovations of the sort we are interested in to be visible in particular in Dutch that is influenced by contact, we added internet relay chat from the MOROCCORP corpus (Ruette & Van de Velde 2013). This corpus contains Dutch chats from speakers with a Moroccan immigrant background. The proficiency of the speakers is in general high, which is probably not surprising since they use Dutch in an informal setting. Although precise information on the background of the speakers is not available, it is likely that they, as members of the second or third generation after immigration, were either Child L2 learners or 2L1 learners of Dutch. We will refer to their language as 'Moroccan Dutch' (MD) (see also Boumans 2002).

4.1 Reanalysis of the derivational ending on material adjectives

A first construction in which we see reanalysis of non-adjectival schwa is exemplified in Examples (6)–(7). These examples feature so-called material adjectives, which are excluded from adjectival inflection in Standard Dutch (see Haeseryn et al. 1997: 401).

(6) *een zilveren lepel*   (CONDIV, Newspaper, NRC)
    a   silver   spoon
    "a silver spoon"

(7) *onder de gouden koepel*   (CONDIV, Usenet, n_toer2)
    under the golden dome
    "under the golden dome"

Many material adjectives end in *-en*, historically a derivational suffix (< Proto-Germanic *-īn). This *-en* in material adjectives can be reanalyzed, as the final nasal is routinely dropped in present-day Standard Dutch pronunciation. The result of this reanalysis is that material adjectives look like normal inflected adjectives. Indeed, examples like (8) orthographically acknowledge the reanalysis from the derivational -*en* suffix to an inflectional adjectival schwa. The reanalysis is further supported by the observation that in [+sg -def +neutr] NPs, the -*en* suffix is stripped, as in (9).

(8) *Alleen de goude wereldbeker telt!!!* (CONDIV, Usenet, n_spor12)
only the golden worldcup counts
"Only the golden world cup matters"

(9) *met een goud rantje* (CONDIV, IRC, #caiw_5)
with a gold edge:DIMINUTIVE(NEUTR.SG)
"with a little golden edge"

The reanalysis is not only a present-day Dutch phenomenon, but can be observed in earlier stages of Modern Dutch as well:

(10) *een' goude keeten* (17th century, WNT)
a golden chain
"a golden chain"

(11) *Een groenen rok, die met een goud boordje*
a green skirt that with a gold collar
belegd was (18th century, WNT)
mounted was
"a green skirt that was mounted with a golden collar"

Looking at a number of different registers, it becomes clear that the proportion of reanalyzed forms increases with the informality. Figure 1 presents data from several corpora mentioned above. The internet relay chat from the CONDIV corpus (IRC (NL)) can be compared with Moroccan Dutch data from the MOROCCORP corpus (IRC (MD)).[5]

The absence of the reanalyzed forms in the newspaper material is not surprising in itself. The texts are heavily edited and have a fairly small range of orthographic flexibility, so the black bar on the far left in Figure 1 is in fact a baseline in the counts. More interesting is the comparison of the other three, less edited registers. The more intimate IRC communication has more reanalyzed forms than the Usenet communication, and this tendency is even more outspoken in the MD

---

5. A query was run on *goude(n)* ("golden"), *zilvere(n)* ("silver"), *bronze(n)* ("bronze") and *kopere(n)* ("copper"). The 'bare' form was not included in the counts, as it would be difficult to tell the examples apart from misspelled compounds, as e.g. *een goud vis* (CONDIV, IRC, #holl_7).

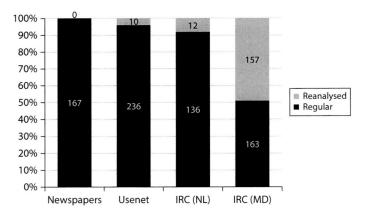

Figure 1. Reanalysis of derivational ending of material adjectives

IRC material. The difference cannot be fully ascribed to the fast-typing production pressure in IRC, as this would leave unexplained why MD IRC communication is so different from NL IRC communication in this respect.[6] The difference between NL and MD is statistically significant (Pearson's Chi-squared test with Yates' continuity correction = 71.81, p < 0.0001), and shows a moderate effect size (Cramér's V = 0.40).[7] Of course, one could argue that MD speakers have more limited orthographic proficiency, but this explanation cannot be upheld: If we look at infinitival *-en*, which similarly suffered from *-n* apocope in spoken Dutch, the difference between IRC-NL and IRC-MD is much less outspoken, see Figures 2 and 3, for two arbitrarily chosen verbs.[8] In other words: MD chatters are only more likely to

---

6. Additional evidence against the idea that the differences between the registers are due to superficial editorial inaccuracy, rather than to grammar-internal factors is provided below.

7. Statistical tests have been carried out with the aid of the open source package R (R Core Team. 2012. *R: A language and environment for statistical computing*. Vienna. http://www.R-project.org). Corpus data extraction and analysis have been done with the Abundantia Verborum software (Speelman 1997). P-values are rendered not as exact values, but in relation to the alpha levels (0.05, 0.01, 0.001 and 0.0001). Effect sizes, measured with Cramér's V, are considered to be weak if the value is between 0 and 0.3, moderate when between 0.3 and 0.5 and strong when between 0.5 and 1. Effect size is only calculated in case of significance.

8. For *zwemme(n)*, the difference between NL and MD is not significant (Pearson's Chi-squared test with Yates' continuity correction = 3.16, p = 0.08); for *drinke(n)*, the difference is significant (Pearson's Chi-squared test with Yates' continuity correction = 12.81, p < 0.001), but the association is the reverse of what is expected: MD chatters are less inclined to drop orthographic *-n*. Cramér's V test for effect size indicates a very weak association: 0.06 for *zwemme(n)* and 0.06 for *drinke(n)*.

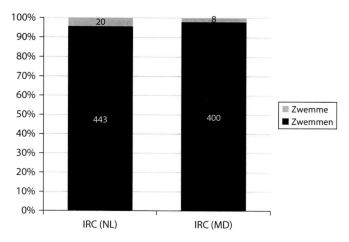

Figure 2. Orthographic *n* in *zwemme(n)*

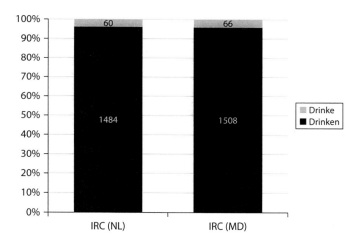

Figure 3. Orthographic *n* in *drinke(n)*

drop the orthographic n than NL chatters when they have a morphological motivation to do so.

The difference between NL and MD IRC in Figure 1 and the fact that this difference is not mirrored in other cases of n-drop, together constitute a strong argument for the idea that the orthographic n-drop in material adjectives is a result of reanalysis along the lines of (2): for reasons outlined in Section 3, regularization of the adjectival inflection is especially advantageous for contact speakers. The orthographic n-drop brings the material adjectives in conformity with the system in (2), which ascribes a transparent function to the adjectival schwa on prefield modifiers in the NP.

4.2 Cooptation of non-adjectival schwa in numerals

A second case of reanalysis of a historically unrelated schwa to adjectival inflectional schwa occurs in numerals, more specifically in higher numerals that derive from nouns, such as *honderd* ("hundred") and *duizend* ("thousand"). In present-day Dutch, these numerals are in most contexts syntactically indistinguishable from everyday numerals like *twee* ("two") or *drie* ("three") or *veel* ("many"), and are used as a dependent of the noun, rather than as a nominal head with a partitive genitive, which was still the common construction in Old Dutch, see (12).

(12) *Ther man ther giuet thusent siluerinero*
the   man that gives thousand silver:GEN.PL

phenningo   (Old Dutch, ca. 1100, Old Dutch Dictionary, s.v. pennink)
penny:GEN.PL

"That man, he gives a thousand silver pennies"

The demise of the morphological genitive led to a reanalysis, by which *honderd* and *duizend* turned into modifiers of one integrated NP, rather than heads in a binominal one.[9] The reanalysis is visible in verbal agreement.

(13) [honderd_Head mensen_Modifier(Partitive Genitive)] > [honderd_Modifier mensen_Head]

(14) *honderd vrouwen kwamen/*kwam naar het feestje*
hundred women came:PL/came:SG to the party
"A hundred women came to the party"

In one particular construction, however, the nominal origin of the numeral is still clearly visible: in (15)–(16), the numerals are used in the plural, and consequently get plural morphology (an *-en* suffix). As modifiers cannot take the plural *-en* suffix, the construction has to be analyzed as a binominal noun phrase with a partitive close apposition.

(15) *Nederland   rekent op de titel, de honderden supporters in de*
the_Netherlands count on the title the hundreds supporters in the

zaal, de miljoenen kijkers in hun huiskamer.   (TwNC)
room the millions viewers in their living_room

"The Netherlands are counting on the title, the hundreds of supporters in the room, the millions of viewers in their living rooms."

---

9. Like other numerals, the precise status of the premodifying *honderd* or *duizend* is ambiguous between determiner and adjective (see also Payne & Huddleston 2002: 355–356 on English numerals). In Section 5.4, it is argued that this ambiguity actually plays a role in the emergence of the system under (2). This is not at issue in this section, however. It suffices to say that the reanalysis assumes that the numerals are in the attributive adjective position in a bare indefinite plural ('zero-article'): [_NP Ø_D honderd(e)_A mensen_N], parallel to structures like *grote mensen* ("tall people"): [_NP Ø_D grote_A mensen_N].

(16) *Duizenden Nederlanders trekken tegenwoordig in vakantietijd met*
thousands Dutchmen go nowadays in vacation_times with
hun racefiets en felgekleurde tenues de
their race_bikes and brightly_colored outfits the
bergen in (TwNC)
mountains in

"Thousands of Dutchmen nowadays go into the maintains with their racebikes and brightly colored outfits during their vacation"

The *n* of the *en*-suffix often remains unpronounced in Standard Dutch (see also Section 4.1), meaning that the plural *-en* is phonologically similar to the schwa. As there is no formal (genitive) marker on the second noun in the partitive appositions in (15)–(16), the patterns can be reanalyzed as an inflected numeral functioning as an attributive modifier of the noun. Interestingly, the construction in (15)–(16) is often misspelled with an *-e* suffix, rather than with an *-en* suffix, which is indicative of precisely the kind of reanalysis envisaged here (see already Van Dijk 1862). While not approved by the official orthography, examples occasionally crop up even in heavily edited texts like newspaper articles. Examples (17) and (18) come from the large-scale Twente News Corpus (TwNC).

(17) *NedCar spreekt vaag over een verlies van 'enkele*
NedCar speaks vaguely about a loss of some
honderde banen' (TwNC)
hundred jobs

"NedCar speaks vaguely about a loss of 'some hundreds of jobs'"

(18) *Radcliffe is een van de duizende kinderen die in Engeland*
Radcliffe is one of the thousand children who in England
auditie deden voor de rol (TwNC)
audition did for the part

"Radcliffe is one of the thousands of children who took an audition in England for the part"

This case of reanalysis is not restricted to present-day Dutch. It has been around since at least the 18th century (see also WNT s.v. honderd (I)), and is very common in the 19th century.

(19) *na honderde overhaalingen,*
after hundred persuasions
broeijingen, meningen (18th century, WNT)
contemplations opinions

"after hundreds of persuasions, contemplations, opinions"

(20) *honderde kleinigheden*   (18th century, WNT)
      hundred trifles
      "hundreds of trifles"

(21) *de   duizende, zoo vreemde, als*
      the thousand   so   foreign   as
      inlandsche woorden   (18th century, WNT)
      indigeneous words
      "the thousands of words, both foreign and indigenous"

(22) *voor duizende beuzelingen*   (18th century, WNT)
      for thousand trifles
      "for thousands of trifles"

An early example could be:

(23) *een groot armade van veele honderde galleyen*   (ca. 1600, WNT)
      a   big   fleet of many hundred galleons
      "a big fleet of many hundreds of galleons"

The reanalysis, is, however, not obsolescent. It can also be found in unmonitored speech, like internet relay chat, see (24)–(25).

(24) *ik wens je   duizende jaren geluk*   (CONDIV, IRC, #nijm_1)
      I wish you thousand years happiness
      "I wish you thousand years of happiness"

(25) *ik heb honderde nummers zelfs uit jou buurt*   (MOROCCORP)
      I have hundred   numbers even from your neighborhood
      "I have hundreds of numbers, even from your neighborhood"

When we look at the different registers represented in the CONDIV and MOROCCORP corpus, we get a clear picture again. In Figure 4, the proportion of reanalyzed forms with orthographic n-drop increases as we move along the cline to the informal registers, and the reanalyzed form is overrepresented in the MD data. The newspaper section of CONDIV, being much smaller than the TwNC corpus, does not feature any reanalyzed forms, but in other registers, they are well-attested. The association between the different registers and the reanalysis is statistically significant (Pearson's Chi-squared test = 147.97, $p < 0.0001$) with a moderate effect size (Cramér's V = 0.33). The difference between NL and MD IRC material is also statistically significant, but the effect size is weak (Pearson's Chi-squared test with Yates' continuity correction = 8.42, $p < 0.01$, Cramér's V = 0.15). In this case as well, we have an argument for the idea that the orthographic n-drop in material adjectives is a result of reanalysis along

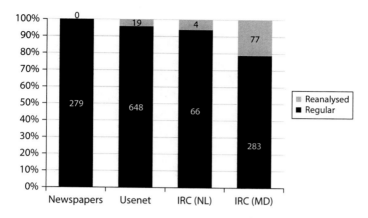

Figure 4. Reanalysis of plural morphology on higher cardinals

the lines of (2): like the material adjectives, an etymologically unrelated schwa has been reanalyzed to make the higher numerals fit the system in (2).

The idea that the differences between the registers is due to grammar-internal factors, and does not simply reduce to more careful editing in formal registers is not only supported by the marked difference between IRC-NL and the IRC-MD data, but also by setting the reanalyzed pattern off against other contexts where orthographic n-drop is possible and is not due to grammatical reanalysis, but where it is phonetically motivated. Figure 5 shows the proportion of misspelled plural *wonderen* and *buizen*.[10] As can be appreciated, n-drop occurs consistently less frequent in comparison to what happens in the higher cardinals. If we test the difference between both contexts (numerals vs. noun plurals) for each of the registers, we obtain statistical significance for the difference in the Usenet data (Fisher's Exact Test $p < 0.05$) and in the IRC-MD data (Pearson's Chi-squared test with Yates' continuity correction = 20.96, $p < 0.0001$). The difference in the IRC-NL data is not significant though (Fisher's Exact Test $p = 0.28$).[11] The most important difference is the one in the Usenet data: as Figure 5 shows, language users are likely to conform to the inflectional norm in this register, but nevertheless occasionally reanalyze the inflection in the higher cardinals.

---

10. The choice for *wonderen* and *buizen* was motivated by their phonological resemblance with the numerals *honderd* and *duizend*. Only nouns have been included in the dataset, excluding the proper noun *Van Wondere(n)*, but including compounds such as *TL-buizen*, *dwangbuizen* etc.

11. The difference in the Newspaper subcorpus was not statistically tested, as the reanalysis occurs in neither condition, which inescapably yields a p value of 1.

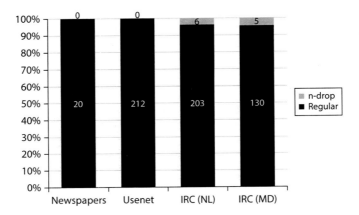

Figure 5. Proportion of n-drop in the nouns *wonderen* and *buizen*

4.3 Proleptic inflection

A third construction in which we see a rise of inflectional schwa on prefield modifiers in the NP, contributing to the two-tier 'zone' system set out in (2), is the structure exemplified in (26), where the adjectival premodifier is accompanied by an adverbial 'submodifier'.

(26) een hele   hoge   boom
     a   very:INFL high:INFL tree
     "a very high tree"

The pattern in (26) deviates from strict normative grammar, as *hele* is not supposed to inflect, because it is used adverbially here and adverbs always remain uninflected. Under a conservative view, the correct way of expressing an NP like (26) would then be *een heel hoge boom*.[12] Patterns like (26) have been called 'proleptic inflection' by Royen (1948: 83–92), as the adverb appears to 'prematurely' copy the adjectival inflection.

(27) van dat ontzettende geile
     of that awful:INFL sexy:INFL

     natte   haar   (CONDIV, IRC, #dutc_6.sml)
     wet:INFL hair
     "this awfully sexy wet hair"

---

12. As a side note, it has to be pointed out that, historically, the non-inflected nature of adverbs is strange in itself, as the schwa used to be one of the derivational strategies for turning adjectives into adverbs (see Diepeveen & Van de Velde 2010 and references cited there).

Proleptic inflection has been attested throughout Modern Dutch, with adverbs such as *erg* ("very"), *echt* ("really"), *geweldig* ("tremendously"), *ontzettend* ("awfully"), *vreselijk* ("terribly"), see Royen (1948: 92). With the degree adverb *heel*, proleptic inflection is so well-integrated that it outnumbers the prescriptive variant (Weerman 2005; Diepeveen & Van de Velde 2010: 385). With other adverbs, proleptic inflection is less frequent. Taking the MOROCCORP data as an indication of innovation, it may be argued that the pattern is on the rise.[13] The difference between NL and MD IRC is statistically significant (Pearson's Chi-squared test with Yates' continuity correction = 4.48, p < 0.05), but with a weak effect size (Cramér's V = 0.14).

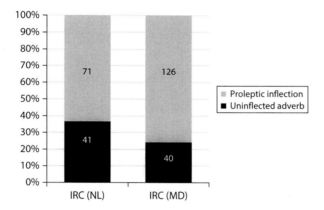

Figure 6. Proleptic inflection

5. The demise of inflection in the determiner zone

The increasingly strong association between the attributive schwa and the adjectival slot in the template in (2) is not only brought about by the extension of the schwa to adjectival slot fillers that historically did not have inflection, but also by the demise of the schwa in determiner slot fillers that historically had inflection.

In present-day Dutch, the most prototypical members of the determiner category – the definite and the indefinite article and the demonstrative pronouns – do not take the inflectional schwa. The singular indefinite article is

---

13. A query was run on the submodifying adverbs *erg(e)*, *vreselijk(e)*, *ontzettend(e)* and *geweldig(e)*, followed by an inflected adjective. Submodifying *heel/hele* was also included, but in order to limit the rather frequent patterns, the query only allowed for four frequent adjectives (*grote, mooie, dikke, zware*) as head of the AP.

indeclinable (*een*),¹⁴ and the definite article and demonstrative pronouns use suppletion (or suppletion-like) morphology to indicate gender and number: *de/het* ("the"), *die/dat* ("that"), *deze/dit* ("this"). The latter examples show that gender information is available in zone A even though it is not inserted via an inflectional rule. The non-schwa-inflecting prototypical determiners function as exemplars on the basis of which the system under (2) crystallizes: language users seize upon the schwa/zero-construction to discriminate adjectives from determiners in the prefield of the NP.

In the following sections, we will show that determiners that undergo schwa inflection (or did undergo it until recently) are all under analogical pressure to conform to the prototypical members of the determiner slot.

5.1 Loss of inflection on possessive pronouns

While they can historically be traced back to genitives of personal pronouns, possessive pronouns were inflected like adjectives in Gothic, Old Dutch and Middle Dutch. With the exception of *ons* ("our"), they have lost their inflection in Present-day Dutch.¹⁵ This is a recent innovation: inflected forms of possessive pronouns and the indefinite article are attested well into the 19th century:

(28) uit reden van zijne
      for reason of   his:INFL

      natuurlijke noodzakelijkheid   (19th century, WNT)
      natural   necessity

      "because of his natural necessity"

---

14. Abstraction is made of the specific indefinite *ene* occuring with proper nouns (*Veertien jaar later (...) arriveerde ene Mansfield, een Britse zakenman* "Fourteen years later there arrived a certain Mansfield, a British business man"), which looks like an inflected indefinite article. Note, however that it has a different vowel: *een* /ən/ vs. *ene* /enə/. Something similar goes for adjectival *ene* (*die ene keer* "that one time").

15. At first sight the existence of two forms for the possessive pronouns of the first person plural (namely *ons* and *onze*) is at odds with our idea that there is no inflection along the lines of (1b–c) in zone A. The form *ons* appears if the NP is singular and neuter, *onze* in all other contexts, which is reminiscent of (1b–c). However, we do not believe that this variation should be considered as productive inflection, but rather as suppletion (comparable to other alternations in D). The main reason is that this variation only exists in present-day Dutch for this possessive pronoun. Note, moreover, that the variation is not exactly the same as in the attributive adjectives since the possessive pronouns are inherently definite (while indefiniteness is crucial for the application of (1c)). We assume that both variants of this possessive pronoun are stored by language learners.

(29) *in mijne   handen*   (19th century, WNT)
In my:INFL hands
"in my hands"

Why did the inflection on these premodifiers disappear? On the basis of syntactic criteria, independent from the morphological criteria under analysis in this section, Van de Velde (2009, 2010) shows that the Dutch possessive pronouns shifted from the adjective slot to the determiner slot, and that the whole process did not reach completion before Late Modern Dutch. This timing is consonant with the hypothesis that the reason for the loss of inflection is the crystallization of the system under (2). The short time lapse between Late Modern Dutch (until 1900) and Present-day Dutch (from 1900 onward) is due to the behavior-before-coding principle (Haspelmath 2010), which states that morphological changes lag behind syntactic changes.

5.2 Reduction of inflection on *zulk*

As argued in Van de Velde (2009, 2010), the Dutch anaphoric pronoun *zulk* undergoes a shift from adjective to determiner slot filler, just like the possessive pronouns, though the process starts later and *zulk* still shows traces of its adjectival provenance in present-day Dutch.

Despite its semantically schizophrenic situation with regard to definiteness (see Duinhoven 1988: 128 and Ghesquière & Van de Velde 2011: 776–780), *zulk* unequivocally behaves like an indefinite element syntactically. As for its inflectional behavior, it then appears to conform to the adjectival inflection: *zulk* is inflected, except in attributive [+sg +neutr] contexts, see (30)–(32).

(30) *Bovendien is de drager van zulke   kleiding   op zijn*
in_addition is the wearer of such:INFL clothing:COMM.SG in his
beurt een wandelende reclamezuil   (TwNC)
turn a   walking   billboard
"In addition, the wearer of such clothes is, in turn, a walking billboard"

(31) *Bij het vervaardigen van zulke   boeken   heeft de*
with the manufacturing of such:INFL book:NEUTR.PL has the
kunstenaar alle touwtjes in handen.   (TwNC)
artist   all strings in hands
"with the conception of such books the artists keeps strict control"

(32) *zulk   onderscheid   is voor Haasses werk*
such:UNINFL distinction:NEUTR.SG is for Haasse's work
niet bruikbaar   (TwNC)
not useful
"such a distinction is not useful for Haasse's work"

If *zulk* is indeed shifting into the determiner class, and if this process lags behind the same shift in the possessive pronouns, we expect that the inflectional schwa would recently have come under pressure. Evidence of such pressure would then be a supporting argument for the hypothesis that Dutch uses the inflectional schwa to discriminate adjectives from determiners, as set out in (2).

This kind of pressure can indeed be seen at work. If we look at the occurrence of the uninflected form in a newspaper corpus (NRC, year 2005, from TwNC), it becomes clear that the inflection is more often 'illegitimately' absent on *zulk* than on the adjectives *blank, wild, vals* and *warm* (chosen to phonologically resemble the VCC coda of *zulk*). In other words: zero-inflection on *zulk* is less often restricted to [+sg -def +neutr] contexts.[16] This is visualized in Figure 7. (Note that the Y-axis does not start at 0, but is truncated.) The difference between the two conditions is significant (Fisher's Exact Test p < 0.05), though with a weak effect size (Cramér's V = 0.14).

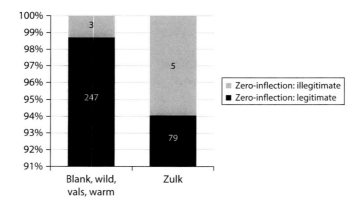

Figure 7. Zero-inflection on adjectives and *zulk*

Figure 8 shows that *zulk* remains uninflected outside [+sg -def +neutr] contexts more often in MD IRC material than in NL IRC material. This further supports the view that the pressure comes from the reanalysis of the prefield NP modifier inflection. The difference is statistically significant (Fisher's Exact Test p < 0.001), with a moderate effect size (Cramér's V = 0.40). Of course, one could argue that the instances of illegitimate zero-inflection in the MD corpus are not

---

16. A reviewer wonders whether the fact that *zulk* can be followed by the indefinite article *een* can be held responsible for the difference, as it increases the chances of zero-inflection in an attempt to avoid a vowel clash. This construction does indeed occur, but as the zero-inflection is here grammatical, it has been counted as legitimate.

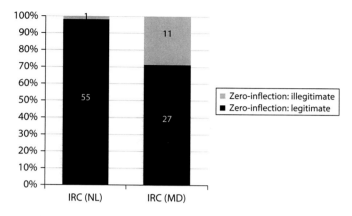

Figure 8. Zero-inflection on *zulk* in NL and MD IRC

really illegitimate, but is due to misattribution of gender (see Section 3 for reference to this argument). The absence of an inflectional schwa is then not due to a pressure to let *zulk* conform to prototypical determiners, but rather the result of the fact that MD speakers mistakenly assume a non-neuter noun to be neuter. This alternative explanation is unlikely for two reasons. First, we would expect the result to be the other way around, as MD speakers tend to overuse the inflected form (see Section 3 and Ruette & Van de Velde 2013).[17] Second, illegitimately uninflected *zulk* occurs in combination with inflected adjectives, as in (33). If the

---

17. To gain more insight in the distribution of illegitimate zero inflection, we ran an additional query in the MD corpus looking for the pattern definite article *de* + uninflected adjective. We took a sample by looking for the adjectives of various syllable length: *mooi* ("beautiful"), *moeilijk* ("difficult") and *belangrijk* ("important"). We retrieved only 7 instances of zero-inflection in total. The proportion of this pattern over the total number of words is not statistically different from what we see in the (northern-)Dutch part of the CONDIV IRC-material (Fisher's Exact Test p = 0.15). Admittedly, absence of significance of association is not the same as significant absence of association, but with the large corpus sizes at hand, we would expect to reach significance fairly easily, if MD chatters would be using zero inflection indiscriminately. The situation is complicated by the existence of a fair number (51 instances of the aforementioned adjectives) of illegitimately uninflected adjectives following the indefinite article, i.e. in combination with non-neuter nouns (e.g. *een mooi vrouw*, "a beautiful-Ø lady"), but these can be explained as a modification of the except-feature in (1c), in the sense that the gender feature has been eliminated, as has been noted before in Weerman et al. 2006. While we have to remain cautious here, especially in the light of the scarce information we have about the background of the MD-chatters, the upshot is that our data indicate that the absence of inflection is not distributed randomly among the adjectives and determiners, but is determined by the reanalysis along the lines of (2) or a motived adjustment of (1c).

absence of inflection on *zulk* were due to gender misattribution, we would expect the adjective to remain uninflected as well here.

(33) met zulk vage uitspraken (MOROCCORP)
with such:UNINFL vague:INFL statements
"with such vague statements"

5.3 Reduction of inflection on determiner-quantifiers *ieder(e)*, *elk(e)* and *sommig(e)*

In this section, it will be shown that quantifiers that syntactically belong to the determiner slot but normally inflect for gender agreement, can recently be observed to jettison their inflection as well, just like *zulk* in the previous section. As such, these quantifiers also approach the morphological behavior of prototypical non-inflecting determiners.

First, let's have a look at the quantifiers *ieder(e)* and *elk(e)*. These quantifiers normally only occur in the uninflected form when they precede [+neutr +sg] nouns. Still, occasional examples can be found in present-day Dutch where they occur in the uninflected form outside this context as well.

(34) Daarom belt zij hem ieder dag op (TwNC)
therefore calls she him every:UNINFL day:COMM.SG PTC
"That's why she calls him every day"

(35) Elk stijging van enige betekenis wordt in de
every:UNINFL rise:COMM.SG of any significance becomes in the
kiem gesmoord (TwNC)
bud nipped
"Every rise of significance is nipped in the bud"

(36) de manier waarop zijn skelet bij ieder aanraking
the way whereon his skeleton with each:UNINFL touch:COMM.SG
aggressief fel oplicht (TwNC)
aggressively brightly lights
"the way in which his skeleton lights up aggressively brightly with each touch"

(37) in elk inleiding esthetica (TwNC)
in each:UNINFL introduction:COMM.SG aesthetics
"in each introduction to aesthetics"

An obvious question is whether the above examples cannot simply be ascribed to editorial negligence with regard to orthography. While the inflected form in a newspaper corpus like TwNC is obviously still by far the most common form, the string *ieder(e) dag* ("every day") occurs without inflection in 0.7% of all instances (total n=3519). In itself, this number is so low that the phenomenon may be dismissed as indicating anything real in the grammar, but if this 0.7% would be due to orthographic omission by an inattentive author, we would expect the same level of absence of schwa with regular adjectives. A case study on adjectives *mooi*, *nieuw*, *bepaald* and *vermoeiend* in combination with the same noun (*dag*) shows that this is not the case: on a total of 630 instances, the inflection never fails to occur, see Figure 9 (Note that the Y-axis does not start at 0, but is truncated).[18] This difference between *ieder* and the other adjectives is statistically significant (Fisher's Exact Test, $p < 0.05$), though obviously, the effect size is very weak (Cramér's $V = 0.03$). In sum, the significance suggests that there is a real effect here, though it is so weak as not to reach perceptible levels in newspaper articles. In itself, this is understandable: newspaper authors are professional writers who arguably polish their grammar,[19] and on top of that, the written products are subjected to final editing (either by a human copy editor or by software).

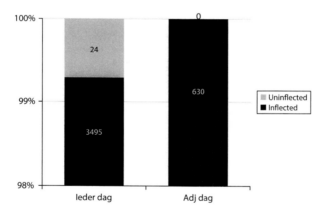

Figure 9. Inflection on adjectives and *ieder*

---

18. By selecting adjectives of variable size (measured in number of syllables), we tried to rule out interference of the factor 'length'. Admittedly, selecting adjectives of variable length introduces a confounding factor, and one could argue that it would be better to stick to equal length adjectives resembling the two-syllable size of *ieder*, but it is difficult to find relatively frequent non-derivationally derived adjectives resembling *ieder* that collocate with *dag*, so we decided to stick to the option of casting our nets a bit wider.

19. Note, to give another example, that double negations of the type *never ... not* are rarely attested in newspapers, though they occur readily in everyday speech.

The quantifier *sommige* ("some") shows a similar tendency. In essence, its inflectional behavior does not differ from that of *ieder* and *elk*. However, *sommige* rarely occurs uninflected, as it almost always precedes plural nouns, unlike *ieder* and *elk*, which can be used with singulars used as distributive plurals. Occasionally, though, *sommige* does precede singular nous, namely when the latter are mass nouns. When these are neuter, they trigger the uninflected form *sommig*:

(38) Sommig   kantoorpersoneel mag niet bij de
     some:UNINFL office_personel may not by the
     ramen   zitten (...)   (TwNC)
     windows sit
     "Some of the office staff may not sit at the windows"

The scarcity of uninflected *sommig* contexts makes it difficult for language users to extend the form to contexts where inflection is the rule: in contrast to *elk* and *ieder*, the average language user is exposed to the target of the reanalysis too little. Still, if we take a look at the attestation of uninflected *sommig* in NL and MD IRC data, we see a clear difference: if MD chatters use uninflected *sommig* they are not restricted to [+sg +neutr] contexts, as opposed to L1 chatters. Though the absolute figures are modest, they are still significant (Fisher's Exact Test, p < 0.01). The mirror image bars in Figure 10 obviously yield a maximum level effect size (Cramér's V = 1).

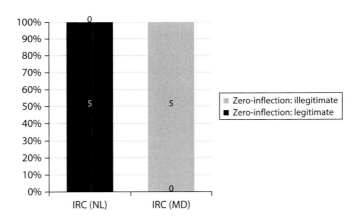

Figure 10. Zero-inflection on *sommig* in NL and MD IRC

5.4 Accommodating inflectional patterns of quantifiers *veel* and *weinig*

The previous section dealt with quantifiers that syntactically behave like determiners: *ieder*, *elk* and *sommig* cannot co-occur with the article (which is a crucial criterion for assigning them determiner status, see Dryer 2007: 161; Van de Velde 2009, 2010, 2011). There are other elements in Dutch that express quantificational meaning, but are not subject to the same constraint, like *veel* and *weinig*. As shown in (39)–(40), these quantifiers can occur both with and without an article.

(39) De weinige mensen die het nog niet hebben gemaakt (TwNC)
the few people that it yet not have made
"The few people that haven't made it yet"

(40) Weinig mensen die zulke plaatjes hebben bewaard (TwNC)
few people that such picture have saved
"few people that have saved such pictures"

At first sight, the quantifiers *veel* and *weinig* seem to inflect like adjectives:[20] before singular neuter nouns in indefinite NPs, the uninflected form is triggered, see (41), and before plural nouns or in definite contexts, we have the inflected form, see (42)–(44).

(41) veel/*vele ongenoegen
much:UNINFL/much:INFL dissatisfaction:NEUTR.SG
"much dissatisfaction"

(42) vele mensen
many:INFL people:PL
"many people"

(43) het vele/*veel ongenoegen
the much:INFL/much:UNINFL dissatisfaction:NEUTR.SG
"much dissatisfaction"

(44) de vele/*veel mensen
the many:INFL/many:UNINFL people:PL
"the many people"

The match is not perfect, however, as the uninflected form also occurs in contexts like (42), see (45), and sometimes even is the only option, see (46). Crucially, however, the uninflected form never occurs after the article, see (47).

---

20. It is not entirely clear where this inflectional schwa comes from: it appears that it does not derive historically from the same source as the adjectival schwa. The quantifier *veel* derives from a noun *felu-* ("large quantity") in Proto-Germanic, and the inflectional schwa is a reduced *u*-vowel. Though it could be used to quantify another noun, this *felu* did not agree, but was indeclinable. In Present-day Dutch, however, the final schwa looks like an adjectival inflection, and it has come (partly) under the influence of the adjectival inflection.

(45) veel   mensen
    many:UNINFL people:PL
    "many people"

(46) veel/*vele   rijst
    much:UNINFL/much:INFL   rice:NON-NEUTR.SG
    "much rice"

(47) *de veel   rijst
    the much:UNINFL rice:NON-NEUTR.SG
    "the much rice"

One could argue that the erratic inflection on the quantifiers *veel* and *weinig* is an impediment to the extension of the system under (2), but on closer inspection, that need not be the case. The inflectional pattern can be interpreted as conforming to the system in (1) and (2). Let's have a closer look. First, when *veel* and *weinig* are preceded by a definite article, they unambiguously occupy the adjectival slot (by the criterion of mutual exclusivity of the article and other determiners – see above), and are inflected. The structure has to be analyzed as in (48)–(49).

(48) [$_{NP}$ de$_D$ vele$_A$ mensen$_N$]

(49) [$_{NP}$ het$_D$ vele$_A$ ongenoegen$_N$]

Indeed, as shown in (43)–(44), absence of inflection is ungrammatical in this context. This seems to be an innovation in Dutch, as uninflected instances are still found in Early Modern Dutch, see (50)–(51), and can thus be seen as conforming to the tendency under (2).

(50) de   veel   schone   thuynen
    the many:UNINFL beautiful gardens

    en   duyvethoornen   (17th century, WNT)
    and dovecotes

    "the many beautiful gardens and dovecotes"

(51) de   veel   andere dingen geheel anders   dan in de
    the many:UNINFL other   things totally differently   than in the

    andere Dieren   gemaakt zijnde   (17th century, WNT)
    other   animals made   being

    "the many other things of a totally different nature than those made in other animals"

Second, when *veel* and *weinig* are not preceded by a definite article, both inflection and absence of inflection are grammatical, see (42) and (45), unless the noun is [+sg], see (41). This is not in conflict, however, with the rule under (1) and (2) (see also Van de Velde 2009: 42). The reason is that a structure like (45) can be interpreted in two ways: either *veel* is in the determiner position, and remains uninflected, or *veel* is in the adjectival position and the determiner slot is not filled (or: has a zero article) as is common in plural indefinite NPs in Dutch (and English, for that matter). In short, the language user can accommodate both the inflected and the uninflected form in the system under (2). This is represented in (52)–(53).

(52) [$_{NP}$ veel$_D$ mensen$_N$]

(53) [$_{NP}$ Ø$_D$ vele$_A$ mensen$_N$]

In [+sg] bare noun phrases (the case of mass nouns), we have the uninflected form. For neuter nouns this is unproblematic, as this is what we expect under condition (1c), and can be accommodated under (2) as well by assuming that *veel* is in the determiner position. For non-neuter nouns, on the other hand, we would expect *veel* to allow inflection, if it is in the adjectival slot. Still, for the language user, this is not an insurmountable problem, as s/he still has the option to parse uninflected *veel* as a determiner. The absence of inflected *veel* in cases like (46) is negative evidence and therefore puts less weight in the deduction of the underlying inflectional system by the language acquirer (recall that *ongenoegen* "dissatisfaction" is neuter and *rijst* "rice" is common).[21]

(54) [$_{NP}$ veel$_D$ ongenoegen$_N$] or [$_{NP}$ Ø$_D$ veel$_A$ ongenoegen$_N$]

(55) [$_{NP}$ veel$_D$ rijst$_N$], but not [$_{NP}$ Ø$_D$ veel$_A$ rijst$_N$]

The unproblematic nature of the deviant inflection of *veel* and *weinig* is supported by NL and MD IRC data: there is no discernable difference between the two groups, see Figure 11 (Fisher's Exact Test, p = 1). In other words, MD speakers are not under pressure to adjust their system.[22]

The difference between Figure 11 (and Figures 2–3) on the one hand and Figures 1, 4, 6, 8 and 10 on the other hand underscores the motivated nature of the MD deviances.

---

21. Alternatively, the pattern in (53) could be obsolescent and the pattern in (52) could be innovative. We do not know of diachronic research into the distribution of *veel* vs. *vele*, but as can be appreciated from Figure 11, the inflected variant is markedly less frequent. If we compare the distribution (29/3) with the chance distribution (16/16), the difference is statistically significant, with a moderate effect size (Pearson's Chi-squared test with Yates' continuity correction = 10.78, p < 0.01, Cramér's V = 0.45).

22. A query was run on *veel* and *vele* followed by a plural noun (*mannen, vrouwen, kinderen, jongens, meisjes, steden, gemeenten, gemeentes*).

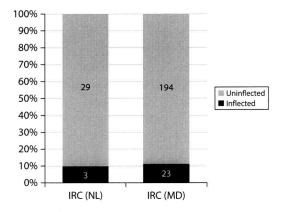

Figure 11. Inflection on *veel* in NL and MD IRC

The double analysis available for interpreting NPs headed by *veel* and *weinig* – one analysis in which the quantifier occupies the determiner slot and another analysis in which the determiner slot is empty ('has zero article') – is also available for cardinal numerals. This means that language users can accommodate both 'uninflected' *honderd* and *duizend* and 'inflected' *honderde* and *duizende* (forms discussed in Section 4.2).

5.5 Reduction of inflection on anaphoric adjectives

A last piece of converging evidence for the idea that Dutch is underway in developing the system under (2) is the inflection on anaphoric adjectives. In Van de Velde (2011), it is argued that Dutch anaphoric adjectives *voornoemd* ("aforementioned"), *gezegd* ("said"), *bedoeld* ("meant"), *vermeld* ("mentioned") etc. diachronically leave the adjective category and come to behave as determiners, as evidenced by their changing syntax. In the course of this process, these elements also start to inflect differently from ordinary adjectives. In short, they remain uninflected in [+def +neutr +sg] contexts, as in (56)–(58). In contexts where they are still unequivocally adjectives, i.e. when they are still supported by a preceding determiner, the absence of inflection is ungrammatical in Standard Dutch, see (59)–(61).

(56) in bedoeld commentaar (TwNC)
in meant comment
"in the intended comment"

(57) in voornoemd artikel (TwNC)
in aforementioned article
"in the aforementioned article"

(58) op vermeld   gironummer   (TwNC)
      on mentioned giro_account
      "on the giro account mentioned"

(59) *in het bedoelde/*bedoeld commentaar*

(60) *in het voornoemde/*voornoemd commentaar*

(61) *op het vermelde/*vermelde gironummer*

These examples show that the anaphoric adjectives are in the middle of a shift towards determiner slot fillers. They have not entirely disposed of their inflection yet, as they still take the schwa ending in the plural or in [−neutr] contexts, but the uninflected form is encroaching on the contexts where inflection is the norm.

6. Conclusion

In its development from Proto-Germanic to present-day Dutch, adjectival inflection has undergone wayward shifts. The constant assaults have not been able to eradicate this inflectional relic in Dutch, even if it is worn down to the most modest of vowels, the schwa. In this article, we have argued that there is no reason to assume that the inflectional schwa will disappear in the near future, as it has in English. Rather, for the time being, the adjectival schwa is here to stay in Dutch, it seems. Its resilience may have to do with the fact that it is currently taking on a new function: extending its present distribution in Dutch, the schwa seems to be increasingly used to discriminate two 'slots' or 'zones' in the NP prefield: a determiner slot, marked by absence of inflection, and an adjectival slot, marked by inflection. The bulk of this paper has been devoted to adducing evidence to corroborate this claim.

The data we have gathered present *circumstantial evidence*. At present, the reanalysis of the adjectival inflection has not reached completion. It has been carried through in sometimes inconspicuous corners of grammar, where it seeps in through small cracks, as it were. Some (frequent) elements still resist the reanalysis (e.g. possessive pronoun *ons*) and there is lexical diffusion in the actualization of the reanalysis. This is in line with observations that language change often proceeds in a 'sneaky' way (see De Smet 2012 and Van de Velde & Van der Horst 2013). This does not mean that the system is stable, and that we cannot uncover the underlying trend in present-day Dutch. By comparing different registers, and unedited language production, and by applying inferential statistics, we have strong indications for an ongoing reanalysis in Dutch. Experimental testing could give further support to our findings, but this requires a different research set-up.

References

Berteloot, Amand. 2005. "... eens wisen subtiils menschen ..." Over de verbuiging van het adjectief in het Middelnederlands. In *Gehugdic Sis Samnungun Thinro. Liber amicorum Willy Pijnenburg*, Aad Quak & Tannke Schoonheim (eds), 23–37. Groningen: Gopher Publishers.

Blom, Alied. 1994. Het ondoorgrondelijk bijvoeglijk naamwoord. *Forum der Letteren* 55: 81–94.

Blom, Elma, Polišenská, Daniela & Weerman, Fred. 2006. Effects of age on the acquisition of agreement inflection. *Morphology* 16: 313–336.

Blom, Elma, Polišenská, Daniela & Weerman, Fred. 2008. Articles, adjectives and age of onset: The acquisition of Dutch grammatical gender. *Second Language Research* 24: 297–331.

Booij, Geert. 2010. *Construction Morphology*. Oxford: OUP.

Boumans, Louis. 2002. Meertaligheid op de Marokkaanse elektronische prikborden. *Levende Talen* 3: 11–21.

Braunmüller, Kurt. 2008. Observations on the origins of definiteness in ancient Germanic. *Sprachwissenschaft* 33: 351–371.

Broekhuis, Hans & Keizer, Evelien. 2012. *Syntax of Dutch*, Vol. I: *Nouns and Noun Phrases*. Amsterdam: Amsterdam University Press.

Coene, Martine & D'hulst, Yves. 2003. Introduction: The syntax and semantics of noun phrases. In *From DP to NP*, Vol I: *The Syntax and Semantics of Noun Phrases* [Linguistik Aktuell/Linguistics Today 56], Martine Coene & Yves D'hulst (eds), 1–46. Amsterdam: John Benjamins.

De Schutter, Georges. 1998. The noun phrase in Dutch. *Leuvense Bijdragen – Leuven Contributions in Linguistics and Philology* 86: 309–356.

De Schutter, Georges. 1999. Het achterveld in de nominale constituent in het Nederlands. *Leuvense Bijdragen – Leuven Contributions in Linguistics and Philology* 88: 323–354.

De Smet, Hendrik. 2012. The course of actualization. *Language* 88(3): 601–633.

Diepeveen, Janneke & Van de Velde, Freek. 2010. Adverbial morphology: How Dutch and German are moving away from English. *Journal of Germanic Linguistics* 22: 381–402.

Dryer, Matthew S. 2007. Noun phrase structure. In *Language Typology and Syntactic Description*, Vol. II: *Complex Constructions*, 2nd edn., Timothy Shopen (ed.), 151–205. Cambridge: CUP.

Duinhoven, Anton M. 1988. *Middelnederlandse Syntaxis, Synchroon en Diachroon*, Deel 1: *De Naamwoordgroep*. Leiden: Nijhoff.

Fudeman, Kirsten. 2004. Adjectival agreement vs. adverbal inflection in Balanta. *Lingua* 114: 105–23.

Ghesquière, Lobke & Van de Velde, Freek. 2011. A corpus-based account of the development of English *such* and Dutch *zulk*: Identification, intensification and (inter)subjectification. *Cognitive Linguistics* 22(4): 765–797.

Giacalone Ramat, Anna. 1998. Testing the boundaries of grammaticalization. In *The Limits of Grammaticalization* [Typological Studies in Language 37], Anna Giacalone Ramat & Paul J. Hopper (eds), 227–270. Amsterdam: John Benjamins.

Grondelaers, Stefan, Deygers, Katrien, Van Aken, Hilde, van den Heede, Vicky & Speelman, Dirk. 2000. Het CONDIV-corpus geschreven Nederlands. *Nederlandse Taalkunde* 5(4): 356–363.

Haeseryn, Walter, Romijn, Kirsten, Geerts, Guido, de Rooij, Jaap & van den Toorn, Maarten C. 1997. *Algemene Nederlandse Spraakkunst*, 2nd edn. Groningen: Martinus Nijhoff.

Haspelmath, Martin. 2010. The behaviour-before-coding principle in syntactic change. In *Mélanges Denis Creissels*, Franck Floricic (ed.), 493–506. Paris: Presses de L'École Normale Supérieure.

Heine, Bernd. 2003. On degrammaticalization. In *Historical Linguistics 2001* [Current Issues in Linguistic Theory 237], Barry J. Blake & Kate Burridge (eds), 163–179, Amsterdam: John Benjamins.

Huddleston, Rodney & Pullum, Geoffrey K. (eds). 2002. *The Cambridge Grammar of the English Language*. Cambridge: CUP.

Joseph, Brian D. 1992. Diachronic explanation: Putting the speaker back into the picture. In *Explanations in Historical Linguistics* [Current Issues in Linguistic Theory 84], Garry W. Davis & Gregory K. Iverson (eds), 123–144. Amsterdam: John Benjamins.

Lass, Roger. 1990. How to do things with junk: Exaptation in language evolution. *Journal of Linguistics* 26: 79–102.

Lass, Roger. 1997. *Historical Linguistics and Language Change*. Cambridge: CUP.

Lupyan, Gary & Dale, Rick. 2010. Language structure is partly determined by social structure. *PLoS ONE* 5(1).

McFadden, Thomas. 2004. How much of the Germanic strong adjective inflection is pronominal? ⟨http://ifla.uni-stuttgart.de/~tom/papers.html⟩

Narrog, Heiko. 2007. Exaptation, grammaticalization, and reanalysis. *California Linguistic Notes* 32(1). ⟨http://hss.fullerton.edu/linguistics/cln/pdf/Exaptation_Narrog.pdf⟩

Norde, Muriel. 2002. The final stages of grammaticalization: Affixhood and beyond. In *New Reflections on Grammaticalization* [Typological Studies in Language 49], Ilse Wischer & Gabriele Diewald (eds), 45–65. Amsterdam: John Benjamins.

Old Dutch dictionary. ⟨http://gtb.inl.nl/⟩

Payne, John & Huddleston, Rodney. 2002. Nouns and noun phrases. In *The Cambridge Grammar of the English Language*, Rodney Huddleston & Geoffrey K. Pullum (eds), 423–523. Cambridge: CUP.

Plevoets, Koen, Speelman, Dirk & Geeraerts, Dirk. 2009. De verspreiding van de -e(n)-uitgang in attributieve positie. *Taal en Tongval* Thematic issue 22: 112–143.

Polišenská, Daniela. 2010. Dutch Children's Acquisition of Verbal and Adjectival Inflection. Ph.D. dissertation, University of Amsterdam.

Quak, Aad & van der Horst, Joop. 2002. *Inleiding Oudnederlands*. Leuven: Leuven University Press.

Quirk, Randolph & Wrenn, Charles L. 1969. [1955]. *An Old English Grammar*. London: Methuen & Co.

Raidt, Edith H. 1968. *Geskiedenis van die Byvoeglike Verbuiging in Nederlands en Afrikaans*. Kaapstad: Nasou Beperk.

Ranheimsæter, Harald. 1945. *Flektierte und unflektierte Nominativformen im Deutschen Adjektivsystem*. Oslo: J.G. Tanum.

Royen, Gerlach. 1948. *Buigingsverschijnselen in het Nederlands*, Vol 2. Amsterdam: Noord-Hollandsche Uitgeversmaatschappij.

Royen, Gerlach. 1953. *Buigingsverschijnselen in het Nederlands*, Vol. 3(2). Amsterdam: Noord-Hollandsche Uitgeversmaatschappij.

Ruette, Tom & Van de Velde, Freek. 2013. MOROCCORP: Tien miljoen woorden uit twee Marokkaans-Nederlandse chatkanalen. *Lexikos* 23: 456–475.

Scott, Gary-John. 2002. Stacked adjectival modification and the structure of nominal phrases. In *Functional Structure in DP and IP. The Cartography of Syntactic Structures*, Vol. 1, Guglielmo Cinque (ed.), 91–120. Oxford: OUP.

Simon, Horst. 2010. "Exaptation" in der Sprachwandeltheorie. Eine Begriffspräzisierung. In *Prozesse sprachlicher Verstärkung. Typen formaler Resegmentierung und semantischer Remotivierung*, Rüdiger Harnisch (ed.), 41–57. Berlin: Mouton de Gruyter.

Smith, John-Charles. 2006. How to do things without junk: the refunctionalization of a pronominal subsystem between Latin and Romance. In *New Perspectives on Romance Linguistics*, Vol. II: *Phonetics, Phonology and Dialectology* [Current Issues in Linguistic Theory 276], Jean-Pierre Y. Montreuil (ed.), 183–205. Amsterdam: John Benjamins.

Smith, John-Charles. 2011. Change and continuity in form-function relationships. In *The Cambridge History of the Romance languages*, Martin Maiden, John-Charles Smith & Adam Ledgeway (eds), 268–317. Cambridge: CUP.

Speelman, Dirk. 1997. Abundantia Verborum. A Corpus-tool for Carrying out Corpus Based Linguistic Case Studies. Ph.D. dissertation, University of Leuven.

Traugott, Elizabeth C. 1992. Syntax. In *The Cambridge History of the English Language*, Vol. I: *The Beginnings to 1066*, Richard M. Hogg (ed.), 168–289. Cambridge: CUP.

Trudgill, Peter. 2010. Contact and sociolinguistic typology. In *The Handbook of Language Contact*, Raymond Hickey (ed.), 299–319. Oxford: Blackwell.

Tucker, Gorden H. 1998. *The Lexicogrammar of Adjectives: A Systemic Functional Approach to Lexis*. London: Cassell.

Tummers, José. 2005. Het Naakt(e) Adjectief: Een Kwantitatief-empirisch Onderzoek naar de Buigingsvariatie bij Neutra in het Nederlands. Ph.D. dissertation, University of Leuven.

Tummers, José, Speelman, Dirk & Geeraerts, Dirk. 2004. Quantifying semantic effects. The impact of lexical collocations on the inflectional variation of Dutch attributive adjectives. In *Le poids des mots*, Gérald Purnelle, Cédrick Fairon & Anne Dister (eds), 1079–1088. Louvain-la-Neuve: Presses Universitaires de Louvain.

Tummers, José, Speelman, Dirk & Geeraerts, Dirk. 2005. Inflectional variation in Belgian and Netherlandic Dutch: A usage-based account of the adjectival inflection. In *Perspectives on Variation. Sociolinguistic, Historical, Comparative*, Nicole Delbecque, Johan van der Auwera & Dirk Geeraerts (eds), 93–110. Berlin: Mouton de Gruyter.

Van Bree, Cor. 1987. *Historische Grammatica van het Nederlands*. Dordrecht: Foris.

Van der Lubbe, Henricus F.A. 1958. *Woordvolgorde in het Nederlands: Een Synchrone Structurele Beschouwing*. Assen: Van Gorcum.

Van de Velde, Freek. 2006. Herhaalde exaptatie. Een diachrone analyse van de Germaanse adjectiefflexie. In *Nederlands tussen Duits en Engels*, Matthias Hüning, Arie Verhagen, Ulrike Vogl & Ton van der Wouden (eds), 47–69. Leiden: Stichting Neerlandistiek Leiden.

Van de Velde, Freek. 2009. *De Nominale Constituent. Structuur en Geschiedenis*. Leuven: Leuven University Press.

Van de Velde, Freek. 2010. The emergence of the determiner in the Dutch NP. *Linguistics* 48(2): 263–299.

Van de Velde, Freek. 2011. Anaphoric adjectives becoming determiners. A corpus-based account. In *The Noun Phrase in Romance and Germanic. Structure, Variation, and Change* [Linguistik Aktuell/Linguistics Today 171], Petra Sleeman & Harry Perridon (eds), 241–256. Amsterdam: John Benjamins.

Van de Velde, Freek & van der Horst, Joop. 2013. Homoplasy in diachronic grammar. *Language Sciences* 36: 66–77.

Van Dijk, Johannes A. 1862. De verbuiging van enkele telwoorden. *De Taalgids* 4: 65–70.

Van Leuvensteijn, Arjan & Dekker, M.C.H. 1990. Adnominale flexie en genusmarkering in 16de-eeuws Brugs. *Leuvense Bijdragen – Leuven Contributions in Linguistics and Philology* 79: 257–278.

Van Loon, Jozef. 1988. Zwakke, sterke en pronominale adjectieflexie in het Oudnederlands. *Naamkunde* 20: 37–41.
Van Marle, Jaap. 1995. On the fate of adjectival declension in overseas Dutch (with some notes on the history of Dutch). In *Historical Linguistics 1993* [Current Issues in Linguistic Theory 124], Hennig Andersen (ed.), 283–294. Amsterdam: John Benjamins.
Van Roey, Jacques. 1974. *A Contrastive Description of English and Dutch Noun Phrases*. Brussel: AIMAV.
Vincent, Nigel. 1995. Exaptation and grammaticalization. In *Historical Linguistics 1993* [Current Issues in Linguistic Theory 124], Hennig Andersen (ed.), 433–445. Amsterdam: John Benjamins.
Weerman, Fred. 2003. Een mooie verhaal. Veranderingen in uitgangen. In *Waar gaat het Nederlands naartoe? Panorama van een Taal*, Jan Stroop (ed.), 249–260. Amsterdam: Bert Bakker.
Weerman, Fred. 2005. Adverbia als adjectiva. In *A.D. 2005. Taalkundige Artikelen voor Ad Welschen*, Els Elffers & Fred Weerman (eds). Amsterdam: Faculteit der Geesteswetenschappen University of Amsterdam.
Weerman, Fred. 2006. It's the economy, stupid! Een vergelijkende blik op men en man. In *Nederlands tussen Duits en Engels*, Matthias Hüning, Arie Verhagen, Ulrike Vogl & Ton van der Wouden (eds), 19–47. Leiden: Stichting Neerlandistiek Leiden.
Weerman, Fred, Bisschop, Jannetje & Punt, Laura. 2006. L1 and L2 acquisition of Dutch adjectival inflexion. *ACLC Working Papers* 1: 5–36.
Willis, David 2010. Degrammaticalization and obsolescent morphology: evidence from Slavonic. In *Grammaticalization: Current Views and Issues* [Studies in Language Companion Series 119], Ekaterini Stathi, Elke Gehweiler & Ekkehard König (eds), 151–178. Amsterdam: John Benjamins.
Wischer, Ilse. 2010. Sekretion und Exaptation als Mechanismen in der Wortbildung und Grammatik. In *Prozesse sprachlicher Verstärkung. Typen formaler Resegmentierung und semantischer Remotivierung*, Rüdiger Harnisch (ed.), 29–40. Berlin: Mouton de Gruyter.
WNT: Woordenboek der Nederlandsche Taal. 2003. 's-Gravenhage: Sdu. Cd-rom version of: Matthias de Vries & Lammert te Winkel (1882–1998). *Woordenboek der Nederlandsche Taal*. 's-Gravenhage: Nijhoff.
Ziemann, Hendrikje, Weerman, Fred & Ruigendijk, Esther. 2011. Nederlands later geleerd: Gebruik van lidwoorden en flexie van bijvoeglijke naamwoorden door Duitstalige kinderen en volwassenen. *Internationale Neerlandistiek* 49(3): 183–207.

Appendix: Corpora

TwNC: Twente News Corpus, see:
⟨http://wwwhome.cs.utwente.nl/~druid/TwNC/TwNC-main.html⟩
CONDIV: see Grondelaers et al. (2000).
MOROCCORP: see Ruette & Van de Velde (Forthcoming).

PART II

Variation

On the properties of attributive phrases in Germanic (and beyond)

Volker Struckmeier[†] & Joost Kremers[‡]
[†]University of Cologne / [‡]University of Göttingen

The syntactic structure of attributive constructions and their (corresponding) semantic integration into nominal projections is the subject of a long-standing debate. In this article, we focus on complex attributes in German, Dutch and Standard Arabic. We argue that adjectival, participial and relative clauses attributes are all essentially predicative structures embedded under a special kind of phase head. Morphophonologically, this head is realized as the (alleged) case, number and gender endings on the adjective/participle and on the relative clause marker. Crucially, we argue that these endings are not agreement suffixes, contrary to common assumptions: rather, they are probing heads whose features identify an argument in the attributive structure. The properties attributed to the head noun are derived from the properties predicated of this argument. This analysis also defines a number of properties along which attributive phase heads can vary, yielding a number of typologically attested types of attributive structures.

1. Introduction

In this article, we propose a common representation for both finite (φ-complete) and infinitival (φ-incomplete) attributive structures in German: a phase-level functional head, called CGN-C (for *case-number-gender*), implements complex attribution in ways we will make precise below. In other languages, a variety of related attributive C heads implement attribution in similar ways, according to their respective feature sets. In this way, a cross-linguistic research program is outlined: given that typological variation should be confined to functional heads (or even just to phase-level functional heads), under current assumptions, what kinds of attributive functional heads do we expect to find? The definition of attributive heads provides a natural locus for the range of attributive constructions of the world's languages and serves as a valuable *tertium comparationis* for comparative research.

The article is structured as follows: in Section 2, a detailed analysis of the morphosyntactic properties found in attributive structures in German is given. This section concludes with the proposal that attributive structures in German – whether adjectival, participial, or clausal – are structures projected from a common functional head, called CGN-C. In Section 3, we demonstrate that attributive heads similar to CGN-C seem to exist in many more languages. However, their respective feature make-ups demonstrably differ from German CGN-C. We discuss possible variations expected to occur and provide examples showing that the expected variants do indeed exist.

2. German

There is a rather wide array of constructions that are considered *attributive* ('Attribute') in German. In this paper, we concentrate on those structures that may be termed 'complex attributes' in that they show projections of complex argument structure and complex inflectional properties. Attributive adjectives and their projections, participial attributes and relative clauses all fall under this heading, while other constructions, such as attributive genitives or PPs, are ignored here for reasons of space (but see Struckmeier 2007 for comments).

2.1 General properties of complex attributes in German

In German, adjectives and participles precede the noun they modify. They obligatorily show suffixes that have traditionally been described as case, gender, and number (henceforth called CGN) agreement with the head noun:[1]

(1) *gut-er   Wein   gut-en   Wein-es*
    good-NOM wine   good-GEN wine-GEN

   gut-em   Wein   gut-en   Wein
   good-DAT wine   good-ACC wine

   "good wine" (*all CGN suffixes are also masculine singular*)

---

[1] Note that there are three paradigms for CGN, depending on the realization of D. In this article, we will only use the so-called 'strong', pronoun-like inflection. The difference, however, is not relevant to the properties we discuss for CGN. Furthermore, although there is some overlap between CGN and inflection on so-called weak nouns, we consider this to be accidental, in much the same way that there is accidental overlap with certain verbal endings (e.g. *-en* on infinitives).

Relative clauses in German follow the noun they modify. The relative pronoun shows an obligatory suffix paradigm nearly identical to the inventory of CGN-forms of adjectives and participles. Note right away, however, that the case of the relative pronoun is determined independently of N. That is to say, the relative pronoun appears to agree with the modified noun in gender and number, but not in case. The CGN suffixes in the following example are all masculine singular, but vary in case:

(2) der Wein
the-NOM wine
"the wine"

    a. d-er gut schmeckt
       REL-NOM good tastes
       "... that tastes good"

    b. dess-en man nie überdrüssig wird
       REL-GEN one never tired becomes
       "... that you never grow tired of"

    c. d-em man reichlich zuspricht
       REL-DAT one lavishly consumes
       "... that you drink a lot"

    d. d-en man mag
       REL-ACC one likes
       "... that you like"

2.2 Differences between attributive structures

Adjectival projections, participial structures, and relative clauses all have a common function: they attribute properties to the referent(s) of the DP that contains them. However, attributes can be differentiated on the basis of morphosyntactic properties that they do *not* share: relative clauses are the only attributes with a φ-complete T, comprising tense and agreement features. Participles show an aspect marking but no tense, and also have CGN. Adjectives form the least complex attributes morphologically, inflecting only for CGN:

(3)
CGN	Tense/Aspect	φ-complete	
yes	yes	yes	= relative clauses
yes	yes	no	= participles
yes	no	no	= adjectives

Insofar as all three types of construction are used to modify noun phrases, the only morphological marking that seems to be relevant for this function is CGN, according to (3). If we assume, then, that CGN is a marking that heads complex attributes, we predict that each attribute will have to include exactly one instance of CGN. This is borne out by the facts, in that more than one instance of CGN (as in (4)) and no instance of CGN (as in (5)) are equally ungrammatical:

(4) der öfter(*-e)   umrührend-e Koch
     the often   stirring-CGN chef
     "the chef who is stirring continuously"

(5) der geschrieben-*(e) Brief
     the written-CGN   letter
     "the written letter"

Participles in German inflect for aspect, in that the present participle denotes an ongoing process, while the past participle in its attributive use designates a completed action:

(6) a. der in   die Station einfahrende Zug
         the into the station in.driving train
         "the train that is pulling into the station"

     b. der in   die Station eingefahrene Zug
         the into the station in.driven   train
         "the train that has pulled into the station"

Given that present and past participles are differentiated by the suffixes -*end* (present participle) and -*t* or -*en* (past participle), these endings will have to be analyzed as aspectual markings: progressive aspect for the present participle, perfective for the attributive past participle.[2]

With all the relevant building blocks in place, the next section derives a detailed morphosyntactic analysis of the various complex attributive structures. As we will see, the functions assigned to the participial suffixes and CGN allow for a unified analysis of all attributive structures in German.

2.3 Attributes in German: The morphosyntactic derivation

The presentation in this section starts out with present participles, since they are the most problematic cases in many ways: while they seem to inflect like adjectives, they clearly behave like verbs in terms of their argument structure and case assignment properties. After the analysis has been shown to work for this particularly

---

2. The same aspectual differences hold for adverbial participles, which use the same suffixes. Also, a modal subtype of the present participle (*das zu lesende Buch* "the book that is to be read") shows a progressive reading and the -*end* suffix. For reasons of space, the reader is referred to Struckmeier (2007) for details on this third attributive participle construction.

troublesome construction in Sections 2.3.1–3, Section 2.3.4 will apply the analysis to the other two (adjectival and relative clause) attributes.

2.3.1   *The structure of participial attributes*
Present participles project transitive argument structures and assign accusative case to their direct objects. In other words, they behave like v^*P level projections (cf. Chomsky 2000):

(7)   der   den   Hund   jagende   Junge
      the.NOM the.ACC dog   chasing   boy.NOM
      "the boy who is chasing the dog"

Note that Burzio's generalization states that "all and only the verbs that can assign theta-role [sic] to the subject can assign (accusative) case to an object" (Burzio 1986: 187). For the time being, we will label the subject argument simply as *subject*. The precise nature of this element will become clear shortly. The v^*P structure projected by a transitive verb, for now, looks like this:

(8) $[_{v^*P}$ *subject* v $[_{VP}$ $[_{DP}$ den Hund$]$ jag$_V$-$]]$

The aspect marker of the present participle is accommodated in the next functional layer:[3]

(9) $[_{T'}$ $[_{v^*P}$ *subject* v $[_{VP}$ $[_{DP}$ den Hund$]$ jag$_V$-$]]$-end-$]$

As for the specifier position of T, Fanselow (1986) already showed that participles and adjectives can have anaphoric object arguments attributively without any overt binder:

(10) die [__   sich   treue] Frau
      the   to.herself   loyal   woman
      "the woman who is loyal to herself"

The anaphor cannot be bound by the modified noun, as this would yield an *i-within-i* configuration:

(11) die $[_i$ ... sich$_i$ treue Frau$_i]$

(12) *$[\gamma$ ... δ...$]$, where γ and δ bear the same index.
                                                           (Chomsky 1986, 212)

---

3. Nothing hinges on the categorization of the aspect marking as T here: while this categorization seems natural enough for German with its heavily intertwined tense and aspect system, the reader may feel free to substitute a category of his or her own choice.

Note that the *i-within-i* filter is doubtlessly operational in German, as e.g. the following example (by Fanselow 1986: 344) shows:

(13) *der Besitzer$_i$ seines$_i$ Bootes
 the owner his.GEN boat.GEN
 "the owner of a boat/his own boat" (unavailable reading)

Note also that, if participles are verbal elements with an obligatory theta projection, the modified noun cannot have moved out of the attributive structure (to, e.g. become the modified noun itself): the arguments of the embedded predicate have been theta-marked in a regular manner and, without stipulation to the contrary, cannot receive an additional theta role from a predicate in the clause that embeds the DP as a whole. Thus, we follow Fanselow (amongst many others) in assuming that there is a covert binder in the attributive construction. For the German constructions, we assume that this element is the covert operator *op*.

Any other analysis is simply not possible: first, PRO is excluded for semantic reasons as the subject of the participle in modern German has to be coreferential with the modified noun – but nothing would force PRO to be interpreted in that way, since in the absence of a controller PRO allows arbitrary reference. Note furthermore that even a stipulation simply requiring PRO to be interpreted as coreferential in configurations such as these (cf. Williams 1980) will not help: in Middle High German, arbitrary reference of the subject of an attribute was possible (Thim-Mabrey 1990):

(14) ein lebendez obez
 a living fruit
 "a fruit that makes X live" not: "a fruit that lives"
 (cf. Thim-Mabrey 1990, p. 374)

Hence, unless the stipulation about the interpretation of PRO were backed up by yet another stipulation to the effect that the attributive structures in Middle High German were wildly different from their modern counterparts, the argument for PRO breaks down. Similarly, *pro* can be excluded as German is simply not a *pro*-drop language. That is, not even φ-complete verbs license *pro* in this language. Any claim that φ-defective participles (and even adjectives) license *pro* would thus be nothing but an unwarranted stipulation.

The remaining choice for the subject then is an empty operator *op*, a solution firmly established in the literature, especially for relative constructions (cf. e.g. Chomsky 1986; Chomsky & Lasnik 1993; Platzack 2000). As will be seen below, this choice also allows prenominal and postnominal attributes to receive an interesting unified analysis. It follows that the attributive construction has to comprise a top-most functional layer that supplies the final (operator) position for *op*:

(15) [op ... [$_{TP}$ *op* [$_{T'}$ [$_{v*P}$ *op* v [$_{VP}$ [$_{DP}$ den Hund] jag$_V$-]]-end-]]...]

At least three questions arise: (a) What is the head of the highest projection? (b) How is case licensed on *op*, if participles are φ-defective? (c) What differences and similarities does the analysis predict for pre- and postnominal attributive structures in German? These questions are addressed in turn in the next subsections.[4]

2.3.2 The head of the C projection

The head of a projection, according to standard assumptions, is the element that determines the principal properties of the projection as a whole. Also, the head of a structure is the element that can never be omitted. This section shows that CGN is exactly this kind of element: every complex attribute has to comprise exactly one instance of CGN. All and only the elements in the DP that receive a CGN suffix are attributes in their own right, while e.g. adverbs, arguments of adjectives and participles, etc. can never receive this ending.

This reinterpretation of the nature of CGN also explains many hitherto mysterious properties of these alleged case, gender, and number suffixes: semantically, it never made much sense to mark adjuncts with case to begin with, if case is taken to be the result of mapping argument (!) roles onto a morphosyntactic realization. One might assume that CGN is merely some 'copied' marking that simply signals which noun the attribute belongs to. However, not only would this analysis not be very illuminating, a real problem is the fact that phonologically, the German CGN suffixes look nothing like the nominal suffixes. This clearly distinguishes German from, say, Latin or Italian, where an attributive suffix can indeed be extremely similar to the corresponding suffix from the nominal paradigm.

Furthermore, separating CGN morphology from the nominal paradigm has another welcome effect: nominal endings in German are becoming more and more obsolete diachronically (the so-called *case loss*, see Gallmann 1996: 287ff). Attributive CGN, on the other hand, is not disappearing. Rather, the paradigm continues to differentiate the relevant distinctions obligatorily – and in a phonologically rather ostentatious manner, too. In other words, what we have been calling (and in spite of these remarks, will continue to call) attributive CGN does not constitute regular case, gender, and number features. Rather, it forms a different morphosyntactic system with its own synchronic and diachronic properties: CGN constitutes the attributive head that implements complex attribution in German.

---

4. Note that we do not wish to make the claim that *all* attribute constructions in *all* languages have an *op* subject, nor that constructions that are (superficially) similar, such as secondary predicates, do. We do not believe that other kinds of elements are excluded as subjects. We simply claim that in German attributive constructions, there must be a subject and it must be *op*.

The element heads a CP-level structure that embeds various types of predicate projections. In the remainder of this paper, we will use the term CGN-C to refer to the features that constitute the attributive ending in German.

If we assume that CGN-C is a C head, it should come equipped with an EPP feature, in order to implement the raising of the empty operator *op* into the Spec,CP position (Chomsky 2000: 13). How might this be implemented? As part of the operation *Internal Merge*, an attracting element needs to identify the goal it attracts (Chomsky 2000: 37ff). It seems to us that CGN-C is uniquely qualified to fulfill this function: we propose that CGN-C does not specify its *own* case, gender, or number. Rather, it identifies an element from the embedded structure, by picking out *this element's* case, gender, and number features. CGN-C, in other words, does not constitute case, gender, or number – rather, it is a feature complex that *identifies* a case, gender, and number feature set.

Compare this to a T head: T identifies the nominative subject by the *subject's* person and number features and assigns nominative case in the process. Yet, it would be clearly nonsensical to claim that T itself is marked for case! Similarly, we argue that CGN-C identifies an argument by the argument's case, gender, and number features without being specified for case, gender, and number itself. CGN-C thus has to attach to predicate projections and attract an operator argument from them. The semantic function of CGN-C is to implement attribution: it states that the properties which are predicated of the raised operator in the embedded structure hold for the referent of the modified DP as well. But can this operator be licensed if CGN-C does not constitute case marking?

2.3.3 *Case-licensing of* op

At first glance there seems to be no way that *op* could have its case-feature licensed within the φ-defective surroundings encountered in adjectival and participial attributes. Note, however, that *op* obligatorily moves to the specifier of CGN-C. If indeed CGN-C is a C head, this means that *op* winds up in the edge of a C phase. Furthermore, *op* can only appear in φ-defective constructions. If we take these properties seriously, a rather innocuous way of implementing case licensing for *op* turns out to be available: if *op* had all the features associated with overt relative operators, there would quite simply be no way to explain why it can never serve in lieu of its overt equivalents (unlike, say, its English counterpart, which can do so in at least some contexts). It thus seems reasonable to assume that *op* is a defective element. In this way, we can easily explain that *op* can only serve as a subject in φ-defective projections: given that *op* lacks features involved in the Agree process with a φ-complete probe, the uninterpretable features of this probe could never be licensed symmetrically, and the derivation is correctly predicted to crash. Recall that participles and adjectives in German do not inflect for [person]. Hence, in order to serve as a subject for predicates of this kind, *op* need not have a [person] feature itself.

If this is correct, it stands to reason that *op*, now a defective category, also yields a defective instance of Agree in cases where its own case licensing in attributive constructions is at stake. Thus, if a case licenser licenses the modified noun's case, it could also license *op*'s case: if *op* is defective, defective Agree between *op* and the case licenser will not affect the case licenser's probing features, under standard assumptions. Thus, if *op* is in an extremely local configuration with a non-defective goal, it could get its case licensed – and the case licenser could, in due turn, check off its features against the feature-complete goal.

Recall now that φ-defective attributive constructions in German have to be in exactly this kind of configuration: they only appear inside the DP, next to the modified noun – i.e. right next to the feature-complete goal. In this way, everything falls into place: the specifier position of CGN-C marks the edge of the CGN-phase. In this position, *op* can license its case defectively against the same probe that licenses the case of the head N, i.e. the noun modified by the CGN-C with *op* in its specifier:[5]

(16)

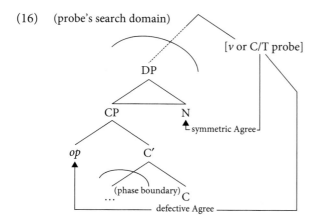

That is, the apparent 'agreement' between CGN-C and the modified noun is explicitly *not* the result of an Agree operation between the noun and CGN-C. Rather, CGN-C identifies the *op* in the attribute phrase. This operator, however, receives its case from the same probe that licenses N's case. CGN-C thus can only identify

---

5. Note that we remain agnostic about the position of the attribute phrase inside the noun phrase it modifies. As far as we can tell, our analysis is in principle compatible with any analysis of noun phrases proposed in the literature. Note also that because the Agree operation between the probe and *op* is defective, there can be more than one such operation. Multiple attributes are therefore handled in the same way as a single attribute.

operators that have the same case as the modified noun – as no other case is available locally. The same of course does not hold for (φ-complete) relative clauses. The defective nature of *op* will thus do double duty as an explanation for the agreement facts in German, as subsection 2.3.4. will show.

For now, we have to double check that *op* indeed behaves like a defective element. As it turns out, German provides a convincing test environment for just this demonstration: some verbs in German specify the case of their arguments lexically – i.e. these verbs assign quirky object cases even when they are passivized:

(17) a. *Ich helfe dem Mann*
      I help the.DAT man
      "I am helping the man"

   b. *Dem/*der Mann wird geholfen.*
      the.DAT/*the.NOM man is helped
      "The man is being helped"

Consequently, these verbs should not appear as attributive participles, where they would have to license their case-assigning features against *op*. Strikingly, this restriction is borne out:

(18) a. **der geholfene Mann*
      the helped man
      "the man that received help" (intended)

   b. **der (vor mir) grauende Mann*
      the (of me) scaring man
      "the man who is scared (of me)" (intended)

Note that present participle formation in German is usually considered to be essentially unrestricted. This gap for present participle formation generally goes unnoticed (but see Haider 1993: 118 for an analysis of similar facts). We would like to submit that the assumption of a feature-defective *op* seems just the right assumption to explain this gap.

As an additional piece of evidence for the relevance of case for the formation of attributive structure, consider the range of arguments that can be used in participial attributes to begin with: without exception, the highest argument of a participle has to raise to Spec,CGN-CP regardless, e.g. of the nature of the predicate or the argument's theta role.

Under the assumption that Spec,CGN-CP is needed to indirectly case-license *op*, it actually follows that only the highest argument (but no other argument or adjunct) can be relativized. If another element were raised to Spec,CGN-CP, blocking the raising of *op* to this position, *op* could not license its case defectively with the probe from the matrix clause: being embedded in TP (Spec,TP at the highest), the argument would be invisible to the probe, for reasons of *phase impenetrability* (see Chomsky 2001: 13): only the edge of the CGN-CP phase (i.e. its specifier and head) is visible for later steps in the derivation, but nothing below this edge. As the following subsection will establish, the case-licensing mechanism explains all the major differences between pre- and postnominal attributes in German.

2.3.4 A unified analysis

Adjectival attributes are easy to implement in a parallel fashion: first of all, note that Fanselow (1986) clearly shows that attributive adjectives are 'sentential' in that they constitute binding domains. Attributive adjectives also use the same CGN-C endings as participial attributes. Hence, if the above is correct, adjectives can extract one of their arguments (invariably the external one, which needs to be case-licensed) from the AP projection and implement coreference for this argument in the same way that CGN-C does in participial structures.

APs in German can also comprise various additional arguments, where these receive lexical case or are spelled out as PPs:

(19) a. seine [$_{AP}$ ihm$_{DAT}$ treue] Frau
         his   to.him   loyal wife
         "his wife, who is loyal to him"

   b. der [[$_{PP}$ auf seinen Vater] stolze] Sohn
       the   of his   father proud   son
       "the son who is proud of his father"

On the other hand, German adjectives do not project obligatory DP objects and are not marked for aspect or tense. Thus, v^* or T projections may not seem necessary at first glance. Note, however, that adjectives allow for various orders of their arguments *vis-à-vis* adverbs. These movements resemble scrambling movements (Struckmeier 2010). Without going into details, it seems reasonable to assume that adjectives project an AP (to host their arguments) and optionally project higher functional layers responsible for these information structure-driven scrambling movements. Adjectival attributes finally embed under the same CGN-C layer that participial attributes use.[6] For the attributes in (19), the structure (which is the simple case without scrambling) looks like (20).

(20) a. [$_{DP}$ seine ... [$_{CGN-CP}$ op [$_{AP}$ op ihm treu]-e] Frau]
     b. [$_{DP}$ der ... [$_{CGN-CP}$ op [$_{AP}$ op [$_{PP}$ auf seinen Vater] stolz]-e] Sohn]

---

6. Note that postnominal adjectives without CGN constitute no counter-evidence against (20), as these (marginal) constructions are invariably simplex, i.e. show no complex argument projection and do not act as binding domains.

One advantage of the analysis of adjectives and participles just outlined is that it links up easily to an analysis of relative clauses with very few adaptations. First of all, there are two relative pronouns in German: *der* and *welcher*. Both implement complex attribution in our understanding of the term, and both show a set of CGN endings. Therefore, if we simply assume that the first parts of these relative pronouns, the parts that do not resemble the CGN-endings, i.e. *d-* and *welch-*, respectively, figure as the operator parts of the relative pronoun, while their suffixes are the actual CGN-C elements, both the similarities and the differences between relative clauses and prenominal attributes become clearly visible: both share the exact same structural layers (*v*P, TP and CGN-CP). On the other hand, the linearization of the CGN-C head and the subject agreement features differ:

(21) **clause (head-initial CGN-C and φ-complete):**
ein Mann, [$_{CP}$ d- er [$_{TP}$ d̶ geht]]
a   man   op CGN   walks
"a man that is walking"

(22) **participle structure (head-final CGN-C, φ-defective):**
ein [$_{CP}$ op [$_{TP}$ o̶p̶ geh-end] -er] Mann
a   op   walk-ing-CGN man
"a walking man"

The derivations work in exactly the same way: CGN-C identifies an argument from the embedded clause (either *op*, *d-* or *welch-*) and raises it into the Spec,CP position where it is interpreted to supply the attributed properties for the modified noun. This allows us to specify exactly what it means formally to be a complex attribute functionally: a complex attribute is a predicate projection embedded within a CGN-CP.

As for differences between different types of complex attributes, note that the operators *d-* and *welch-* obviously differ from *op*. This is in line with the fact that *d-* and *welch-* (i.e. the phonologically overt elements) are case-licensed within the relative clause itself: by finite T when the subject is relativized, by v^* when an object is relativized. This explains why *d-* and *welch-* cannot be used in prenominal attributes: obviously, they can function as goals of probes in symmetric, non-defective Agree processes. Hence, *d-* and *welch-* must be φ-complete elements – unlike *op*, which is φ-defective, as argued above.

Thus, if *d-* and *welch-* were used in prenominal attributes, their case feature could not be licensed inside the defective TP of participial attributes, let alone in the projection of adjectives. This means that their case feature would have to be licensed by the probe that also licenses the case of the modified N. This, however, is impossible, too: *d-* and *welch-* are not defective elements. This is why they cannot 'share' a case-licensing with N like defective *op* can: if the case of *d-/welch-* gets licensed, the case-licensing probe cannot also license N's case. If the probe licenses N's case, *d-/welch-* cannot be taken care of. Thus, there is no way that these φ-complete operators could ever be used in non-finite prenominal attributes.

Recall that in non-finite attributes, only the highest argument, not being case-licensed, can be relativized. In relative clauses, on the other hand, no argument is left without a proper case licensing. We would expect, then, that relative clauses, but not prenominal attributes, can relativize any argument or adjunct, as long as movement to Spec,CP is not barred for independent reasons. This prediction is borne out, as seen in the following table:

Φ-defective attributes	Relativized element	φ-complete relative clauses
der op dicke Mann the fat man "the fat man"	(highest) argument of A	*der Mann, der dick ist* the man that fat is "the man who is fat"
der op laufende Mann the running man "the running man"	(highest) argument of active V	*der Mann, der läuft* the man that runs "the man that is running"
der op geschlagene Junge the beaten boy "the boy that was beaten"	(highest) argument of passive V	*der Junge, der geschlagen wurde* the boy that beaten was "the boy that was beaten"
*der op ich gehende Garten the I walking garden "the garden I walk into" (intended)	locative adjunct	*der Garten, in den ich gehe* the garden into which I walk "the garden I walk into"
*der op ich sehende Mann the I seeing man "the man I see" (intended)	internal argument of active V	*der Mann, den ich sehe* the man that I see "the man I see"

It seems, then, as if the assumption of a CGN-CP (and the auxiliary assumption of a φ-defective operator, *op*) correctly predicts all the major syntactic, morphological and semantic properties of complex attribution in German. Complex attribution is, of course, a phenomenon found in many other languages as well. In the following section, we want to argue that a CGN-like head makes for an interesting proposition for cross-linguistic research, too.

3. Cross-linguistic variations on a theme: Attributive functional heads in other languages

We have established an analysis of German CGN-C that postulates the following features for it:

(23) Pre-nominal, φ-defective CGN-C (for adjectival and participial constructions):
 – EPP feature
 – verbal agreement features on sister T
 – identification features for *op*, namely case, gender, and number

(24) Post-nominal, φ-complete CGN-C (in relative clauses):
 – EPP feature
 – full verbal agreement features on sister T
 – identification features for *d-/welch-*, namely case, gender, and number

With regard to subject agreement features, German already demonstrates that a range of possible scenarios (both subject agreement and no subject agreement) is possible in attributive structures. As for the other two feature sets:

– Can attributive CGN-C variants get by without EPP features? Section 3.1 demonstrates that this case is given by cases of *in-situ* relativization. Proposals by Höhn (2011) and von Prince (2008) seem to us to warrant the idea that even φ-defective structures (showing no subject agreement) can potentially be used without an EPP feature on the attributive head – iff the case licensing of all arguments contained inside the attributive construction can be handled without a φ-complete T and without defective case licensing.
– Can an attributive construction vary with regard to the identification features? Section 3.2.1 demonstrates that attributive C heads can indeed use different identification feature sets. Section 3.2.2 furthermore demonstrates that attribution in Standard Arabic uses identification features so unspecific that ambiguous attributive structures result. Section 3.2.3 goes on to show that even the complete absence of identification features might be attested in languages like Mandarin Chinese.

Variation of these feature sets of attributive heads is not at all harmful to our theory. We explicitly acknowledge that feature variation for attributive heads exists and the feature set of German CGN-C is by no means the only approach to the syntacto-semantic implementation of attribution. Many other possibilities are straightforwardly attested in the world's languages. It is up to future research to identify how these attributive heads function precisely: the following sections only provide a starting point to this worthwhile enterprise, not a list covering all conceivable possibilities.

3.1 EPP-less attribution is *in-situ* attribution

First of all, what if the EPP feature is absent from alternative CGN-Cs? This is no problem at all for φ-complete relative clauses, as it simply leads to (typologically well-attested) cases of *in-situ* relativization, as e.g. in Hindi (see Mahajan 2000: 203) and other languages (see, e.g. Lehmann 1984).

For the φ-defective cases, however, a problem presents itself: if the relativized argument in these structures does not raise to the edge of the attributive phase, the defective case licensing mechanism outlined above will cease to operate. We would thus be forced to assume that the relativized argument receives no case at all and accordingly, the derivation would crash. However, there are two potential ways out of this problem: firstly, the attributive head itself could introduce case-licensing features, such that the nature of the embedded predicate projection becomes irrelevant for case licensing. Alternatively, the attributive head could take a sister that simply does not contain an argument in need of case-licensing. Both of these scenarios have been argued for and are taken up in turn in the following.

Von Prince (2008: 61) assumes that attributive heads themselves could act as case-licensers. In this case, the attributive head itself would license the case of an argument contained in the attributive structure without any need for that argument to raise to the specifier of the attributive element, given the definition of Agree. A derivation containing an attributive head of this kind would thus converge even if the attributive head had no EPP feature. After all, as von Prince points out, the same logic holds for complementizers: English *for*, e.g. embeds a φ-defective clause, whose subject should receive no case. However, if *for* assigns case itself, it is no surprise that *for*-clauses can, as a matter of fact, contain case-marked subjects overtly (e.g. *I want [for [her to go]]*).

Höhn (2011) proposes another solution for attribution without relativization movements. In Basque, the attributive marker *ko-* turns various types of phrases into attributive structures:

(25) [[mahai azpi-∅]-ko]   katu-a
 [[table under$_{locative, sg.}$]-ko] cat-the
 "the cat under the table"

(26) [[ama-ren-tza]-ko]   opari-a
 [[mother$_{genitive, benefactive}$]-ko] present-the
 "the present for the mother"   (both analyses by Höhn 2011: 8)

Höhn (2011:29) explicitly likens *ko-* to German CGN along the lines of Struckmeier (2007). However, in his analysis, the NP and PP predicates project no external argument in need of case-licensing. Accordingly, no such argument raises to the specifier of *ko-* which thus is a head without an EPP feature. Höhn assumes that *ko-* is of the semantic type ⟨et, ⟨et,et⟩⟩. Thus, it links up ⟨e,t⟩ projections such as PPs and the type ⟨e,t⟩ (modified) noun phrase and derives the attributive reading between these two phrases without syntactic movement to the specifier of *ko-* (cf. 2011:32). According to Höhn's analysis, then, the Basque *ko-*structure is an attributive structure whose head contains no verbal φ-features, uses no EPP-feature, and yet still implements the attributive use of predicate projections of various types.

3.2 Variation of the identification features

Case, gender, and number features are used to identify the relativized argument in German attributive structure. The properties that are predicated of these arguments in the attributive structure are the ones that constitute the semantic features attributed to the modified head noun. What other identification feature sets could be used to implement this type of structure?

- Firstly, different languages could differentiate fewer identification features than German. However, in this scenario, the attributive properties are derived in the same way as above: the identified argument's properties are attributed of the modified noun. As Section 3.2.1 shows, attributive heads with different identification feature sets are easily found, even in languages closely related to German.
- Section 3.2.2 shows that these subsets need not be functionally equivalent to their German counterparts: as fewer identification features are used, this may lead to the ambiguous interpretations attested for Standard Arabic attributive constructions.
- We also should not rule out the possibility that languages might opt to use an attributive head that uses no identification features at all. Section 3.2.3 demonstrates that attributive heads of this type may be attested in Chinese.

3.2.1 *Differing identification feature sets in other languages*

Already in many European languages, attributive structures are implemented in essentially comparable ways structurally – but with other identification features in C. Dutch pre-nominal attributive structures, for example, show sentential properties very similar to their German counterparts. Passive participles can be used with PP subject arguments (27a) and active participles allow for their objects to appear inside the attributive structure, too (27b):

(27) a. de door mij gebruikte ingrediënten
          the by   me   used   ingredients
          "the ingredients I have used"
      b. een mij veel overlast bezorgende machine
          a   me   much trouble   getting   machine
          "a machine that causes me a lot of trouble"

(example from Bennis 2004: 100)

We would thus propose that the Dutch structures can be analyzed in a similar way – however, with a twist: the Dutch attributive head only differentiates neuter, singular, definite contexts from all other contexts. Consequently, it makes little sense to adopt the CGN feature specification from German too literally. Rather, a reduced set of identification features (possibly gender and number, but not case) would suffice for Dutch. Compared to Dutch, French uses the opposite feature set: the *que/qui* distinction in French relative clauses differentiates only relativized subject arguments from relativized non-subjects. Thus, *que/qui* identify relativized arguments solely by case (and not by gender or number).

Attributive C heads serve as a locus of these varying feature sets. In this way, these heads constitute a valuable *tertium comparationis* that systematizes differences and similarities between attributive structures both within and across languages: all of these heads derive attributive structures from embedded predication structures. They differ, however, with regard to the identification features for the relativized argument.

3.2.2 *Potentially ambiguous identification features: The case of Standard Arabic*

In Standard Arabic, an attributive marker *alladī* agrees with the modified noun (and not the relativized argument) in case and number. This means that the attributive marker does not always suffice to identify the relativized argument in the same way that German CGN-C would. Sometimes, only features of the arguments themselves (rather than identification features of the attributive head) make clear what the intended reading of a relative clause is:

(28) al-rajul-u   -lladī   raʔaytu-hu   ʔamsi
      the-man-NOM   REL.M.SG   saw.1SG-him   yesterday
      "the man that I saw yesterday"

The relative marker in this example is marked for masculine and singular, as indicated. Inside the relative clause, both the subject *I* and the object *him* are masculine singular arguments. Thus, the relativizing head identifies neither as the relativized argument. It is only the feature make-up of the arguments themselves that disambiguates this structure: the modified noun is a 3rd person element, and the relative clause subject *I* obviously is not. Thus, only the 3rd person object *him* can be construed as the relativized argument. Note that the attributive head itself does not bring about the disambiguation – in case, e.g. the relative marker and the relativized argument do not agree.

With identification features so unspecific, ambiguous attributive structures can easily occur:

(29) al-rajul-u   -lladī   raʔā-hu   ʔamsi
     the-man-NOM REL.M.SG saw.3SG.M-him yesterday
     "the man that he saw yesterday"   or:
     "the man that saw him yesterday"

In this example, both the *pro* subject and the object of the relative clause are 3rd person and could thus be the relativized argument. Consequently, the two readings indicated are both available, since the structure is not disambiguated by any morphological or syntactic means.

3.2.3 No identification at all: Chinese de

Given the variability we have already observed, the question arises whether an attributive C head could get by without any identification features at all. The predictions for the attributive structure headed by such an element would, arguably, be the following:

- The attributive structure contains some sort of predicative projection. However, since the attributive marker does not identify an argument inside this predicative projection, the corresponding restrictions that, e.g. German prenominal attributes show, are not expected. Thus, the set of predicate projections an attributive head without identification features embeds could (at least potentially) be rather unselective.
- Semantically, no argument or adjunct contained in that predicative projection would necessarily have to be interpreted as the relativized argument (since there are no identification features that would pick out the element): all that the attributive head states is that the attributive structure as a whole is an attribute to the modified noun – but no individual element is specifically designated as the relativized argument.

We would like to propose that the marker *de* in Mandarin Chinese is just such an element. With regard to the first prediction, *de* turns surprisingly many types of phrases into attributive constructions (Examples (a–c) by Paul, forthc.; Example (d) by Paul 2005: 774):

(30) a. NP: *Měilì de diànnǎo*
        Mary DE computer
        "Mary's computer"

b. PP: *guānyú tiānwénxué de zhīshi*
about astronomy DE knowledge
"knowledge about astronomy"

c. TP: *nǐ jìlái de xìn*
2SG send DE letter
"the letter you sent"

d. AP: *yi-ge feichang   cingming de haizi*
1-Cl extremely intelligent DE child
"an extremely intelligent child"

With regard to the semantic predictions, *de* essentially conforms to our expectations as well: in many cases, an argument or adjunct contained in these projections can be construed as the relativized argument – but this need not be the case, as the following example demonstrates:

(31) *Liú Xiáobō dé   Nuòbèiěr jiǎng de xiāoxi*
Liu Xiaobo obtain Nobel prize   DE news
"the news that Liu Xiaobo obtained the Nobel prize"

If these examples seem too far-fetched, consider attributive constructions in English: here, too, elements other than C heads appear to be able to embed sentences into DPs as restrictive attributes:

(32) Speaker A: Did you hear the screams?
Speaker B: What screams?
Speaker A: The screams (of the crowd) [as [$_{TP}$ he fell off his bike]]

In the last sentence in this sequence, *as* embeds a full-blown TP structure and turns it into a restrictive attribute. However, there is no relativized argument of any sort: as the possibility of adding *of the crowd* demonstrates, *the screams*, for example, need not be the bike rider's screams. Thus, no element inside this attributive construction (especially not *he*, either) bears any privileged relation to *the screams*. Rather, the whole *as*-construction provides attributive properties that help to identify *the screams*. Suppose now that *as* might semantically bleach and lose the temporal interpretation it has today. In this case, this new *as* element would arguably be analyzed as a functional category – and this functional category would embed a finite clause without having identification features. We consider it plausible that attributive heads of this type can exist in Germanic languages, too.[7]

---

7. Note that that in the English translation of (30) does not qualify: given that only very few nouns accept *that*-clauses inside their extended DP projection, *that*-CPs should be considered (selected) complements.

This concludes our small survey of attributive heads. To sum up, attributive functional heads show differing feature sets. The typologically widespread (and often diachronically robust) appearance of such markers (see also Struckmeier 2007 and von Prince 2008 for more examples) warrants further research, in our opinion: the variable properties of the resulting attributive structures point to the fact that these elements are no simple 'phonological copies' of the modified nouns' paradigms. Rather, they form an integral syntacto-semantic part of the structure of DPs in many of the world's languages. As such, attributive functional heads deserve more attention than they have received to date.

References

Bennis, Hans. 2004. Unergative adjectives and psych verbs. In *The Unaccusativity Puzzle: Explorations of the Syntax-Lexicon Interface*, Artemis Alexiadou, Elena Anagnostopoulou & Martin Everaert (eds), 84–113. Oxford: OUP.

Burzio, Luigi. 1986. *Italian Syntax*. Dordrecht: Reidel.

Chomsky, Noam. 1986. *Barriers* [Linguistic Inquiry Monograph 13]. Cambridge MA: The MIT Press.

Chomsky, Noam. 2000. Minimalist inquiries: The framework. In *Step by Step. Essays on Minimalist Syntax in Honor of Howard Lasnik*, Roger Martin, David Michaels & Juan Uriagereka (eds), 89–115. Cambridge MA: The MIT Press.

Chomsky, Noam. 2001. Derivation by phase. In *Ken Hale: A Life in Language*, Michael Kenstowicz (ed.), 1–52. Cambridge MA: The MIT Press.

Chomsky, Noam & Lasnik, Howard. 1993. The theory of principles and parameters. In *Syntax: An International Handbook of Contemporary Research*, Joachim Jacobs, Arnim von Stechow, Wolfgang Sternefeld & Theo Vennemann (eds), 506–569. Berlin: Mouton de Gruyter.

Fanselow, Gisbert. 1986. On the sentential nature of prenominal adjectives in German. *Folia Linguistica* 20: 341–380.

Gallmann, Peter. 1996. Die Steuerung der Flexion in DP. *Linguistische Berichte* 164: 283–314.

Haider, Hubert. 1993. *Deutsche Syntax – generativ. Vorstudien zur Theorie einer projektiven Grammatik*. Tübingen: Gunter Narr.

Höhn, Georg. 2011. The licensing of adnominal PPs: The case of Basque *ko*. Ms, University of Potsdam.

Lehmann, Christian. 1984. *Der Relativsatz: Typologie seiner Strukturen, Theorie seiner Funktionen, Kompendium seiner Grammatik*. Tübingen: Gunter Narr.

Mahajan, Anoop. 2000. Relative asymmetries and Hindi correlatives. In *The Unaccusativity Puzzle: Explorations of the Syntax-Lexicon Interface*, Artemis Alexiadou, Elena Anagnostopoulou & Martin Everaert (eds), 201–229. Oxford: OUP.

Paul, Waltraud. 2005. Adjectival modification in Mandarin Chinese and related issues. *Linguistics* 43: 757–793.

Paul, Waltraud. Forthcoming. The insubordinate subordinator *de* in Mandarin Chinese: Second take. In *The Attributive Particle in Chinese* [Frontiers in Chinese Linguistics Series], Sze-Wing Tang (ed.). Beijing: Beijing University Press.

Platzack, Christer. 2000. A Complement-of-N⁰ account of restrictive and non-restrictive relatives: The case of Swedish. In *The Syntax of Relative Clauses* [Linguistik Aktuell/Linguistics Today 32], Artemis Alexiadou, Paul Law, André Meinunger & Chris Wilder (eds), 265–308. Amsterdam: John Benjamins.

Struckmeier, Volker. 2007. *Attribute im Deutschen: Zu ihren Eigenschaften und ihrer Position im grammatischen System*. Berlin: Akademie Verlag.

Struckmeier, Volker. 2010. Attributive constructions, scrambling in the AP and referential types. *Lingua* 120: 673–692.

Thim-Mabrey, Christiane. 1990. Attributives Partizip Präsens im Mittelhochdeutschen. *Beiträge zur Geschichte der deutschen Sprache und Literatur* 112: 371–403.

von Prince, Kilu. 2008. Attributive linkers in three languages. Ms, Zentrum für allgemeine Sprachwissenschaft, Berlin.

Williams, Edwin. 1980. Predication. *Linguistic Inquiry* 11: 203–238.

From participle to adjective in Germanic and Romance*

Petra Sleeman
ACLC, University of Amsterdam

Being mixed categories, participles can be fully verbal, fully adjectival, but they can also have a mixed interpretation, viz. as resultatives, which are considered to be a second adjectival type, one that is the result of an event. Parallel to the two types of adjectival participles and the eventive one, a second type of eventive participle has been distinguished, one with an 'eventive property' reading. These four interpretations have been distinguished on the basis of Germanic languages, partly determined by the prenominal or postnominal position of the participle within the noun phrase. In this paper it is argued, based on the combination of the adverbs of degree *très* "very" and *beaucoup* "much" with passive/past participles in French, that participles can also have the four interpretations in Romance.

1. Introduction

Deverbal categories such as nominalizations, nominalized infinitives, gerunds, participles, and forms in "-ble" are so-called mixed categories. They are verbs used as nouns or as adjectives, and they can present properties of their deverbal base and/or of their derived category. Within the framework of the Lexicalist Hypothesis (Chomsky 1970) the discussion focused on the opposite properties and uses of deverbal categories, either verbal or nominal/adjectival (e.g. Chomsky 1970; Wasow 1977; Grimshaw 1990; Levin & Rappaport 1992). More recent research, couched within the framework of Distributed Morphology (Halle & Marantz 1993, 1994; Harley & Noyer 1999), has shifted the attention to the

---

* This paper was presented at the conference *Adjectives in Germanic and Romance, 29–30 March 2012*, University of Amsterdam and at the 14th *Annual Conference of the English Department*, 30 May – 2 June 2012, University of Bucharest. I thank the audiences for discussions and comments. I am also very grateful to the two anonymous reviewers of this paper and Werner Abraham, one of the series editors, for their valuable suggestions and comments.

mixed properties of deverbal categories (e.g. Borsley & Kornfilt 2000; Alexiadou 2001; Embick 2004; Alexiadou et al. 2011; Sleeman 2010). These posed a problem for analyses within the framework of the Lexicalist Hypothesis. This paper is concerned with the deverbal category of passive participles.

Sleeman (2011) claims for English and Dutch that the prenominal or postnominal position of deverbal modifiers, more specifically passive participles (such as *the stolen jewels* vs. *the jewels stolen*), is related to their semantic properties. She distinguishes four types of participles. Besides two types of adjectival participles (statives (*a learnèd scholar*) and resultatives (*the unopened package*)) – which in English are always prenominal – and fully eventive participles – which in English are postnominal – i.e. the three types commonly distinguished in the literature (Kratzer 1994; Embick 2004), she distinguishes a fourth type, viz. eventive property denoting participles, which she claims to be represented by prenominal eventive participles in Germanic. One of the arguments in favor of the eventive nature of prenominal passive participles in English and Dutch is their possible combination with adverbs such as "recently", with agents (in Dutch), or with other complements (in Dutch). She assumes that even bare prenominal participles (in English and Dutch) can have an eventive interpretation (see also Cinque 2010, §5.4). She argues that, due to the prenominal position, normally reserved for adjectives, the prenominal passive participles at the same time express a property.[1]

In Romance, participles generally occur in postnominal position. The question that emerges is then: can these four interpretations also be distinguished for Romance?

It is claimed in this paper that in French, besides a purely verbal and a purely adjectival interpretation, participles can also have intermediary interpretations, just like in Germanic. Niculescu (this volume) argues that in Romanian, (present) participles can also have four interpretations, which suggests that the ambiguity in interpretation of the participle is also a more general Romance phenomenon.

---

1. In the literature, postnominal deverbal modifiers in English have been associated with a stage-level reading, whereas prenominal deverbal modifiers have been claimed to express an individual-level property (e.g. Bolinger 1967):

   (i) the jewels stolen
   (ii) the stolen jewels

This distinction suggests that postnominal participles are eventive, whereas the prenominal ones only express a property. However, in Section 3 it is argued that prenominal participles in Germanic are also eventive, hence the notion 'eventive property'. Cinque (2010) argues that prenominal participles can have exactly the same interpretation as postnominal participles. In this paper, however, I argue against this view.

This paper is organized as follows. In §2, it is shown that mixed categories can be more than two-way ambiguous. It is furthermore shown that in a framework like Distributed Morphology (Halle & Marantz 1993, 1994), compatible with the Generative Grammar model, ambiguities can be accounted for in a syntactic way. In §3, four interpretations of passive participles in Germanic are distinguished. In §4, it is argued that four interpretations can also be distinguished in Romance, which are formally analyzed in §5. The paper ends, in §6, with a conclusion.

2. Mixed categories

Due to their category-shifting nature, mixed categories can present properties both of the original base and of the resulting category. In the Principles and Parameters framework of the Generative model (Chomsky 1981) mixed categories posed a theoretical problem. The X′-structure of phrases made a category switch within syntax theoretically impossible. This is illustrated by nominalized infinitives in Dutch.

Nominalized infinitives are verbs used as nouns, and they can present properties of both categories. In the literature, the more verbal types are generally called verbal infinitives and the nominal types are called nominal infinitives (e.g. Plann 1981; Alexiadou, Iordăchioaia & Schäfer 2011), a distinction that has also been made by Chomsky (1970) for English gerunds. Verbal properties are the combination with a subject, direct complementation, i.e. the combination with direct objects, the combination with auxiliaries, and the combination with adverbs. Nominal properties are the use of a determiner (article, possessive, or demonstrative pronoun), modification by an adjective instead of an adverb, and the combination with genitives instead of a subject or a direct object, gender distinctions, and pluralization. In its most verbal use, the nominalized infinitive is used without a determiner, but occurs in argument position. In its most nominal use, the nominalized infinitive functions in all respects as a noun. Verbal infinitives and nominal infinitives are situated on a scale between these two extremes. The middle of the scale contains nominalized infinitives in which verbal and nominal properties are mixed.

The following examples illustrate the ambiguity of the Dutch nominalized infinitive. In (1), taken from Sleeman (2001), the infinitive is purely verbal: there is no determiner and the direct object precedes the infinitive (Dutch is an SOV language). In (2), also taken from Sleeman (2001), the infinitive is purely nominal:

(1) *Alcohol drinken kan schadelijk zijn.*
alcohol drinking can harmful be
"Drinking alcohol can be harmful."

(2) Heb je   je   drinken al   op?
     have you your drinking already finished
     "Have you already finished your drink?"

Sentences (3)–(5) have been taken from Ackema and Neeleman (2004):

  Deze zanger is   vervolgd   voor…
  This singer has-been prosecuted for…

(3) … dat   stiekem   succesvolle liedjes jatten
       that sneaky.ADV   successful   songs   pinch

(4) … dat   stiekeme   succesvolle liedjes jatten
       that sneaky.ADJ   successful   songs   pinch

(5) … dat   stiekeme   jatten van succesvolle liedjes
       that sneaky.ADJ   pinch   of   successful   songs

In (3), the infinitive is modified by an adverb and is preceded by a direct object. These are verbal properties. Differently from (1), the infinitive in (3) is introduced by a determiner, which is a nominal property. In (4), the infinitive is preceded by its direct object (verbal property), but is introduced by a determiner and is modified by an adjective (nominal properties). In (5), instead of a prenominal direct object, there is a prepositional phrase, which is a nominal property. In these five examples, the nominal infinitive changes thus from purely verbal (1) into purely nominal (2), with three intermediary steps (3)–(5).

In the traditional X′ model, it is difficult to account for these intermediary steps. They show that the infinitive has verbal and nominal properties at the same time. The X′ model does not allow the insertion of a category with verbal properties, i.e. a verb, under, e.g. a nominal head, accounting for the mixed behavior.

The Distributed Morphology model (Halle & Marantz 1993, 1994) and comparable models offered a solution. Category-neutral roots are dominated by, e.g. verbal and nominal functional projections. In this way, the inner verbal behavior (lower verbal functional projections) and the outer nominal behavior (higher nominal functional projections) can be accounted for.

Alexiadou et al. (2011) distinguish between verbal and nominal nominalized infinitives. In the first type, the verbal properties dominate, in the second type it is the nominal properties that dominate.

Many European languages possess nominalized infinitives (and/or other non-derived nominalizations such as the gerund in English and the supine in Romanian). Alexiadou et al. (2011) argue that there is no parametric difference between Germanic and Romance languages with respect to the properties of non-derived nominalizations. The four Germanic and Romance languages that they analyze, viz. English, German, Spanish, and Romanian, possess both verbal and nominal non-derived nominalizations. However, Alexiadou et al. show that there is variation between the non-derived nominalizations with respect to their position on the scale. In some Germanic and Romance languages they can have more verbal or more nominal properties than in others.

On the basis of the presence of the subject of the infinitive in the Spanish Example (6), Alexiadou et al. (2011) analyze the verbal nominalized infinitive in Spanish as the most verbal type. In its structure, it has various verbal functional projections (7).

(6) el   cantar   yo   la   Traviata
    the sing.INF   I.NOM the.ACC Traviata
    "me singing the Traviata"

(7) [DP [TP [Aspect [VoiceP [vP [Root]]]]]]

The verbal nominalized infinitives in languages like German or Dutch do not have a TP in their structure – which Spanish has – because they cannot be combined with a subject.

For nominal non-derived nominalizations a structure as in (8) is proposed by Alexiadou et al.:

(8) [DP [(NumberP) [ClassP [nP [AspP [VoiceP [vP [Root]]]]]]]]

On the basis of the nominal properties of non-derived nominalizations in the four languages under consideration, Alexiadou et al. arrive at the following distinctions for nominal non-derived nominalizations:

(9) a. [DP [ClassP [nP [AspectP [VoiceP [vP …
    b. [DP [ClassP[-count] [nP [VoiceP [vP …
    c. [DP [(NumberP) [ClassP[±count] [nP [VoiceP [vP …

German nominal infinitives have structure (9a): they can be combined with low adverbs such as "constantly", which are assumed to be located in AspectP. Spanish nominal infinitives have structure (9b): they cannot pluralize. English and Romanian nominal non-derived nominalizations have structure (9c): they can pluralize.

In the next sections it will be argued that that there is no parametric difference between Germanic and Romance languages with respect to the types of passive participles and that, furthermore, the distribution on the scale is also identical. The Germanic and Romance languages that will be analyzed, viz. English, Dutch, and French, will be argued to possess both verbal and adjectival passive participles and two mixed steps in between. Although the steps will be claimed to be identical, the argumentation that will be advanced will be different.[2]

In the next section, the ambiguity of the passive participle in Germanic will be discussed.

3. Interpretations of participles in Germanic

In this section the distinction between four types of participles in Germanic, based on their distribution and interpretation is presented. In §3.1 the motivation for a third type of participle, identified alongside the traditionally distinguished verbal and adjectival participles, is presented. In §3.2 a fourth type of participle distinguished for Germanic is introduced.

3.1 Three types of participles

Traditionally, passive participles are divided into two types: verbal passive participles (which can combine with agentive *by*-phrases), as in (10), and adjectival passive participles, which are also called statives (and which can be modified by the adverb *very*), as in (11) (see, e.g. Wasow 1977 and Levin & Rappaport 1992):

(10) The door has been opened by John.

(11) John is very astonished.

Embick (2004), building on Kratzer (1994) for German, distinguishes three sorts of passive participles in English. Besides the two traditionally distinguished passive participles, he distinguishes resultatives, which he classifies as a second type of adjectival passive participle, alongside statives:

(12) a. the door has been opened by John   (verbal passive)
     b. the door opened by John   (verbal passive)

(13) the door remained opened (resultative)

(14) the door is closed (stative)

Embick presents several diagnostics used to distinguish statives and resultatives in English, three of which are mentioned here:

---

2. In Section 5, it is, however, argued that the use of different diagnostics for Germanic and Romance does not mean that they fundamentally differ with respect to the syntactic properties of participles.

I. Unlike pure statives, resultatives allow modification by manner (and other) adverbials (see also Kratzer 1994):

(15) a. The package remained carefully opened.
     b. *The package remained carefully open.

(16) a. the carefully opened package
     b. *the carefully open package

II. Statives, but not resultatives, can occur after verbs of creation, such as *build, create, make*:³

(17) a. This new ruler was built long.
     b. *This new ruler was built lengthened.

III. *Un*-prefixation is fully productive with resultatives, but not with statives (although there are some exceptions such as *unshaven* or *unhappy*):

(18) a. unopened, unshrunk
     b. *unopen, *unshrunken

Embick (2004) also presents several criteria used to differentiate resultatives from eventive, i.e. verbal, passive participles. First, resultatives, but not eventive participles, can be used as a predicate with the copular verb *remain* (19). Second, eventive passive participles can combine with a *by*-phrase, whereas resultatives cannot (20)–(21). Third, with eventive passive participles *un*-prefixation is not productive (22):

(19) The package remained carefully opened.   (resultative)

(20) The door was opened by John.   (eventive)

(21) *The door remained opened by John.   (resultative)

(22) *The door has been unopened (by the children).   (eventive)

3.2 A fourth type of participle

Another criterion that would distinguish resultatives from eventives is their position with respect to the noun. According to Embick (2004, Footnote 1), besides

---

3. Embick observes that with an ambiguous participle like *closed*, only the stative, but not the resultative interpretation is possible:

(i) The door was built closed.

statives, only resultatives, but not eventive passive participles, can be used in prenominal position. *Recently opened* in (23) is analyzed as a resultative:

(23)   the recently opened door   (resultative)

Postnominal participles in English are analyzed as being fully eventive (Bolinger 1967; Fabb 1984; Sadler & Arnold 1994):[4]

(24)   the jewels stolen   (eventive)

(25)   They were only charged for the bottles opened.   (eventive)

(26)   *They were not charged for the bottles unopened. (resultative)

However, Sleeman (2011) argues that participles modified by *recently* simply express an event that took place recently and not the result of an event. One of the arguments is that a participle modified by *recently* cannot be the predicate of a copular verb, such as "be" or "remain", which can only be used with adjectival predicates (cf. 13, 14, and 19):

(27)   the recently opened door   (eventive, ≠ resultative)

(28)   *The door remained recently opened.   (resultative)

(29)   *This document is recently copied.   (resultative)

(30)   *The door was recently unopened.   (resultative)

She claims that the preferred reading of prenominal participles preceded by a manner adverb is not a resultative reading (cf. diagnostic I presented above), but an eventive reading, identical to the reading in the passive sentence in (32):

(31)   the carefully opened package   (eventive or resultative)

(32)   The package was carefully opened by John.   (eventive)

Sleeman (2011) claims that bare prenominal participles, as in (33), can also have an eventive interpretation in addition to a stative or resultative interpretation, just like their sentential counterparts in (34)–(36):

(33)   the closed door   (resultative, stative, or eventive)

(34)   The door remained carefully closed.   (resultative)

(35)   The front patio of the house was built closed.   (stative)

(36)   The door was closed by John.   (eventive)

---

4.   Cinque (Chapter 5, Footnote 8) observes that English is the only Germanic language in which restrictive postnominal bare adjectives are available.

She also advances arguments from Dutch for the analysis of a participle modified by "recently" as eventive. If *pas* "recently" functions as an adverb (37a–b) the participle has an event reading, because *is* in (37b) is an auxiliary expressing tense. If *pas* forms a compound with the participle (37c–d), the participle has a result reading, because *is* in (37d) is a copular verb:

(37)   a.   het pas   getrouwde paar   (eventive)
               the recently married   couple
               "the recently married couple"

        b.   Het paar   is pas   getrouwd.   (eventive)
               the couple   is recently   married
               "The couple recently got married."

        c.   het pasgetrouwde paar   (resultative)
               "the newlywed couple"

        d.   Het paar is pasgetrouwd.   (resultative)
               "The couple is newlywed."

Sleeman (2011) claims that in Dutch, with some manner adverbs with the meaning of "good" or "bad" functioning as an adverb, the participle can have an event reading (38a), or "good" or "bad" can form a compound with the participle, in which case the participle has a result reading (38b):[5]

(38)   a.   *de goed verzorgde tuin*   (resultative or eventive)
               "the well maintained garden"

        b.   *de goedverzorgde tuin*   (resultative)
               "the well-cared-for garden"

Finally, she claims that in Dutch, prenominal passive participles preceded by a *by*-phrase or other arguments are eventive:[6]

(39)   de   door Jan   geopende brief   (eventive)
               the   by   John   opened   letter
               "the letter opened by John"

(40)   de   (*door Jan)   ongeopende brief   (resultative)
               the   by   John   unopened   letter

---

5. Other participles that can have a compound form are *goedgekleed* "well-dressed", *goedgebouwd* "well-built", *goedgevuld* "well-filled", *goedgekozen* "well-chosen", *slechtgeschreven* "ill-written".

6. Whereas in English even bare participles can occur in postnominal position, in Dutch and German the prenominal position is always preferred. In Scandinavian, adjectives or participles can occur in postnominal position if they are followed by a complement or an adjunct or if they are part of a coordination (Delsing 1993:9).

(41) *de   aan hen verkochte producten*   (eventive)
      the to   them sold   products
      "the products sold to them"

(42) *de (*aan hen) onverkochte producten*   (resultative)
      the   to them   unsold   products

Just like the adjectival participles (resultative and stative), Sleeman (2011) distinguishes two types of verbal participles: a fully eventive one (the postnominal participle), and a participle with an eventive property reading (the prenominal one). Because of the prenominal position, Embick claims that prenominal participles are not eventive, i.e. verbal, but adjectival, i.e. stative or resultative. The arguments presented above, however, plead in favor of an eventive interpretation. An analysis of the prenominal participle as expressing an eventive property suggests, just like Embick's analysis of it as a resultative, that the prenominal participle does not have a fully eventive reading, while it does not have a purely adjectival reading either. Furthermore, eventive property participles fill a gap: besides two types of adjectival participles, two types of verbal participles can now be distinguished:

(43) adjectival ← =========================== → verbal
            stative   resultative   eventive   fully
                                      property   eventive

The properties of the four types of participles distinguished in this section are schematized in Table 1:[7]

Table 1. Distinction between four types of participles in Germanic

	Adjectival	Resultative	Eventive property	Fully eventive
with verbs of creation	+	−	−	−
with *remain*	+	+	−	−
productive *un*-prefixation	−	+	−	−
composition with adverbs	−	+	−	−
prenominal position	+	+	+	−
modification by manner adverbs	−	+	+	+
modification by *recently*	−	−	+	+
internal arguments or *by*-phrase	−	−	+ (SOV)	+

---

7. Table 1 has been partially borrowed from Sleeman (2011). Due to space limitations, not all properties have been presented for all categories in the current paper.

In Romance, participles generally occur in postnominal position. The question that arises is if a distinction between two types of verbal participles, a purely eventive participle and a participle expressing an eventive property reading, can also be made for Romance. On the basis of French, I claim in Section 4 that in Romance, just like in Germanic, the four types of interpretation represented in (43) are present, providing support for the distinction of a fourth type of participle, situated on the scale between the purely eventive and the resultative one.

4. Interpretation of participles in Romance

In Romance, participles generally occur in postnominal position. The question arises whether, in Romance, participles also have the four interpretations distinguished in (43). In this section I argue that they do.

4.1 Three types of participles (in French)

Just like for Germanic, the three types of passive participles identified by Kratzer (1994) and Embick (2004) can be distinguished for French (44)–(46). The *by*-phrase in (44) provides the participle with an eventive interpretation. Participles of psych verbs, as in (45), easily get a stative interpretation and can therefore be used after a copula and in combination with the adverb "very" (see, e.g. Brekke 1988). Although the inflected verb in (46) is a copula, the participle is not stative, but expresses the result of an event:

(44) *Le livre a été lu par Paul.* (eventive)
  "The book has been read by Paul."

(45) *La fille semble être très étonnée.* (stative)
  "The girl seems to be very astonished."

(46) *Les rues sont nettoyées.* (resultative)
  the streets are cleaned
  "The streets are clean."

4.2 A fourth type of participle (in French)

In this section it is argued on the basis of French, that besides the three types of participles distinguished in §4.1 a fourth type of participle can be distinguished in

Romance, just as in Germanic. The argument is provided by participles modified by *beaucoup* "much, a lot" and *très* "very".

In the standard case, the adverb of degree *beaucoup* "much, a lot" occurs with verbs and the adverb of degree *très* "very" with adjectives:

(47) *Cela m'étonne beaucoup.*
"That astonishes me a lot."

(48) *Il est très heureux.*
"He is very happy."

Très "very" cannot be used with simple, inflected, verbs, and *beaucoup* does not occur with adjectives:[8]

(49) *Alain travaille *très / beaucoup.*
Alain works   very / a lot
"Alain is working a lot."

(50) *Paul est *beaucoup / très heureux.*
Paul is   a lot   / very happy.

Although *très* generally does not modify verbs, there is an exception: participles can also be modified by *très* "very" (e.g. Doetjes 2008; Abeillé & Godard 2003;

---

8. Gaatone (2007) shows that *très* can be combined with infinitives:

(i) *Dans ces   circonstances-là,   il   faut très s'habiller.*
    in   these circumstances-LOC EXPL must very REFL dress
    "Under these circumstances one must put on warm clothes."

However, a search in the French literary data base Frantext yields only two examples, both with *faire* "make", such as:

(ii) *Ça le fait très rire.*
     that him makes very laugh
     "It makes him laugh out loud."

Besides the Example (i), Gaatone (2007) provides two other examples, both also containing the infinitive *faire*. I suggest that *très* is acceptable with *faire* + infinitive, because in this causative construction the infinitive can be replaced by an adjective: "make jolly". As Gaatone shows, *très* occurs in other contexts in which it modifies a constituent that could semantically be replaced by an adjective: *avoir très peur* lit. "to have very fear" = *être très peureux* = "to be very anxious".

Gaatone 1981, 2007, 2008). This is illustrated by the following examples taken from Gaatone (2007):[9]

(51) On a très apprécié ce discours.
      we have very appreciated that speech
      "We appreciated the speech a lot."

(52) Il s' en est très occupé.
      he REFL of-it is very occupied
      "He has occupied himself a lot with it."

(53) Ce discours a été très apprécié.
      that speech has been very appreciated
      "The speech was appreciated a lot."

According to Gaatone (2007), the use of *très* "very" in these contexts cannot be due to the fact that the contexts in (51)–(53) would express a state, a property, generally related to the class of adjectives. He states that (51)–(53) express activities. He observes that there are also many examples involving *très* with a passive with an agent introduced by "by", which means that they are agentive and express a process, rather than resultative/stative:

(54) Ce comportement est très critiqué par la presse.
      this behavior is very criticized by the press
      "This behavior is much criticized by the press."

In order to know what the choice of the adverb in combination with the participle can tell us about the interpretation of the participle, I counted in the categorized version of the French literary data base Frantext the number of occurrences of *beaucoup* and *très* in combination with eventive participles

---

9. In the English translation *très* has been translated as "much" or "a lot", because it is standardly assumed that *very* only modifies adjectives or adjectival participles (Kennedy & McNally 1999). However, Quirk et al. (1991: 415) observe that there seems to be "increasing acceptance of the co-occurrence of *very* with a *by*-agent phrase containing a personal agent":

   (i)   ?The man was very offended by the policeman.
   (ii) ?I was very influenced by my college professors.

Doetjes (2008) states that *très* might be in the process of changing into an adverb that cannot only be combined with adjectives but also with gradable verbs. The search in Frantext, however, showed that the change is not recent.

(cf. 51–54) and participles with a stative interpretation that are the complement of a copula:[10]

- *avoir* "to have" + participle
- reflexive pronoun + *être* "to be" + participle
- *être* "to be" + participle in passive construction
- copula *être* "to be" + participle

These are the results of the analysis:[11]

Table 2. Percentage of use of *beaucoup/très* with participles

	Beaucoup	Percentage	*très*	Percentage
avoir	2656	99.5%	13	0.5%
reflexive	225	97%	6	3%
passive	33	17%	159	83%
copula + *par*	0	0%	45	100%
copula + adjectival part.	0	0%	(>) 155[12]	100%

Sentence (55) illustrates the use of *beaucoup* with *avoir* + participle, (56) of a reflexive verb with *beaucoup*, and (57) of a passive with *beaucoup*:

(55) *j'ai beaucoup souffert de ma chasteté*
"I have suffered a lot from my chastity"

---

10. The categorized version of Frantext contains 1940 annotated literary works, 127.515.681 words, period 1830–2009.

11. A caveat is in order: occurrences of *beaucoup* "often", *beaucoup* "many/a lot of things" or *beaucoup* + noun (= Quantification at a Distance, QAD) in combination with participles have not been eliminated, especially not from the 2656 sentences containing *avoir* + *beaucoup*. This does not significantly modify the results, however:

(i) *lorsqu'un manuscrit antique a été beaucoup recopié*
"when an old manuscript has often been copied"

(ii) *il a été beaucoup écrit*
"there have been many things written"

(iii) *mon ami a beaucoup perdu d'argent à Aix*
"my friend has lost a lot of money in Aix"

12. In Frantext, adjectival, i.e. stative, participles are partly categorized as participial, and partly as pure adjectives. I have not counted the latter ones. This means that the number of occurrences of a stative participle with *très* must be higher than 155.

(56) je   me   suis beaucoup amusé
     I   REFL   am   much   amused
     "I have had a lot of fun"

(57) Laeta a   été   beaucoup frappée par la mise au tombeau
     Laeta has been   much   struck by   the entombment

Sentence (58) is an example of *très* + *avoir*, (59) of *très* + a reflexive verb, (60) of *très* with a passive. As (61)–(63) show, *très* is, as expected, also used with adjectival participles. In (61), *par* means "because of" and not "by", so that the participle is not verbal. In (62), the participle has a resultative meaning and in (63) it is purely stative.

(58) et   ça   m'   a   très amusé
     and that me   has very amused
     "and that has amused me a lot"

(59) Mars s'   est très rapproché de la Terre en 1877
     Mars REFL   is   very approached of the Earth in 1877
     "Mars closely approached the Earth in 1877"

(60) il   a   été   très frappé par une parole d' Isabelle
     he   has been   very touched by a   word   of Isabelle
     "He has been touched a lot by one word said by Isabelle."

(61) il est midi et   je suis très fatigué par la vie irrégulière que
     it is noon and I am   very tired   by the life irregular   that
     je mène
     I lead
     "it is noon and I am very tired because of the irregular life that I am leading"

(62) Strasbourg vous plaît?   ... Beaucoup. Je suis très séduit.
     Strasbourg you   pleases?   Much.   I   am   very seduced
     "Do you like Strasbourg?   ... Very much. I like it a lot."

(63) ils furent très surpris
     "they were very surprised"

The picture that emerges on the basis of Table 2 and the analysis of the examples presented in (55)–(63) leads me to the interpretation represented in Table 3. *Beaucoup* is used with the fully eventive interpretation of participles, whereas *très* is used with the resultative or stative participle. This is as expected, because in the normal case *beaucoup* combines with verbs, whereas *très* combines with adjectives. Unexpectedly, however, *très* also combines with the eventive interpretation of participles, especially with passives. I take this to mean that *beaucoup* and *très* highlight a different interpretation of the participle. Because of the fact that *très* normally combines with adjectives, it pulls the interpretation of the eventive participle one level down, towards the eventive property interpretation:[13]

Table 3. Interpretation of participles in combination with *beaucoup/très*

	beaucoup	*très*
fully eventive	*avoir/être* + participle reflexive verb passive	
eventive property		*avoir/être* + participle reflexive verb passive
resultative		copula + *par* "because of" resultative participle
stative		stative participle

Just as the Germanic participles related to their position in (43), the French participles related to their combination with *très* or *beaucoup* can be represented on a scale:

(64) adjectival ← =========================== → verbal
                    très   *très*   *très*   *beaucoup*
  cf. Germanic prenominal prenominal prenominal postnominal

4.3 Très + passive participle

In the previous subsection I have shown that, unexpectedly, *très* can be used with verbal participles. This raises at least two questions:

1. Why does *très* only occur with participles, but not with simple verbs?[14]
2. Why does *très* mainly occur with passive participles?

---

13. One of the reviewers wondered whether the differences in interpretation should be attributed to the criteria used (position in Germanic, adverbs in French) or to the interpretational properties of the participles themselves. In line with Coussé (2011) I contend that participles, and mixed categories in general, are ambiguous due to their mixed nature, but that one of the interpretations can be highlighted by, e.g. a syntactic mechanism.

14. It might simply be the case that *très* has to procliticize to another category (Volker Struckmeier, p.c.), which would account for the fact that it cannot occur with simple verbs,

As for the first question, the reason can be sought in the fact that the French passive participle is derived from the Latin perfect passive participle, as in (65), syntactically represented by Steriade (2012) as in (66):

(65) laudatus   sum
     having-been-praised I-am
     "I have been praised"
     lit. "I now exist in a state of having been praised in the past"

(66)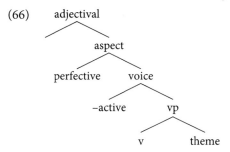

Steriade (2012)

As is well-known, the Latin perfect passive participle developed, on the one hand, into a passive participle (not only expressing perfect aspect), and, on the other hand, into a perfect participle (with active voice). In (67), *habeo* has the meaning of "possess" and *scriptas* is a passive, but in (68), the participle evolved from a passive ("I have (the issue) as an understood one") into a real perfect tense in Late Latin (Perret 2005: 125):

(67) litteras scriptas habeo
     letters written I-have (I have letters in a written state)
     "I wrote letters"

(68) cognitum habeo
     learned I-have
     "I have learned"

However, since both the participle in (67) and the one in (68) have been derived from the Latin participle in (66), all features from the Latin participle might still be inherently present, including the adjectival one. This might explain why, among the verbal forms, *très* can be used with participles.

---

because it would be in postverbal position. However, (i) shows that *très* is not always a proclitic (Gaatone 2007):

(i) Alain est-il intelligent? Très!
    Alain is-he intelligent? Very!
    "Is Alain intelligent? Yes, he is indeed."

The paraphrasing of the verbal participles in the following examples shows that the adjectival feature is latently present in all forms:[15]

(69) *et ça m' a très amusé*
 and that me has very amused
 "and that has amused me a lot" →

(70) *je suis très amusé*
 "I am very amused"

(71) *vous m' avez très intimidé*
 you me have very intimidated
 "you have intimidated me a lot" →

(72) *je suis très intimidé*
 "I am very intimidated"

(73) *qui s' était très atténué depuis*
 which REFL was very softened since
 "which had become softer since then" →

(74) *le son est très atténué*
 the sound is very softened
 "the sound is much softer"

(75) *il est très apprécié par ses élèves*
 he is very appreciated by his pupils
 "his pupils like him very much" →

(76) *un professeur très apprécié*
 a professor very appreciated
 "a well-appreciated professor"

The second question is, why, among the verbal participle types (Table 2), *très* most often modifies passive participles, rather than the active or reflexive ones. Whereas Lieber (1980) proposed that adjectival passive participles are derived from verbal, both perfect and passive, participles, Bresnan (1982) argued that they are only derived from passive participles. Bresnan pointed out that the construction (77) means "the noun was X-ed" but not "the noun has X-ed". This suggests that adjectival participles are closer to passive than to perfect participles (see also Alexiadou 2001; Anagnostopoulou 2003):

(77) the – participle – noun

---

[15]. A second reason for the use of *très* with participles might be that this degree adverb easily modifies psych verbs, present in most of the examples, which, in the present or imperfective tense, have a stative character. According to Doetjes (2008), *très* can be combined with gradable verbs, but not with non-gradable verbs like "walk", which she calls 'eventive'.

I propose the hierarchy (78) of adjectivization, reflexives also sharing some features with passives, e.g. as anticausatives:

(78)　active > reflexive > passive > resultative > stative

The feature [−active] might be the feature that is responsible for the fact that passive participles are closer to adjectival participles than perfect participles are. A thorough discussion of the differences and similarities is beyond the scope of this paper, however.

4.4　Syntactic analysis of the four types of participles

As shown in Section 2, in order to account for the ambiguity of mixed categories syntactic analyses have been put forth, as in, e.g. Alexiadou (2001). Category neutral roots are dominated by verbal and/or nominal or adjectival functional projections, the nature of the functional projections determining the position on the scale going from purely verbal to purely nominal or adjectival. In this section, a syntactic analysis of the four types of participles is proposed. In Doetjes' (1997) analysis, degree quantifiers such as "a lot" are left adjoined to VP. In the same spirit, I propose that in fully eventive participles QP (*beaucoup*) dominates v. For the non-fully eventive participles – participles expressing an eventive property, resultatives, and statives – I propose that the degree quantifier, DegP (*très*), dominates a higher functional projection, viz. AspP. Whereas in resultatives and statives AspP contains the feature stative (with the feature 'become' in vP distinguishing resultatives from statives, see, e.g. Embick 2004), in the eventive property reading Asp is not stative, but perfective or infective. The presence of a perfective or infective AspP accounts for the eventive part of the reading, whereas the dominating DegP highlights the property part of the reading.

- fully eventive: *v* licenses subject or object; QP = quantification over grade or number of events; VoiceP = active, AspP = perfective (79); VoiceP = reflexive, Asp = perfective (80); VoiceP = passive, Asp = perfective/infective (81):

(79)　*Il a beaucoup souffert.*
　　　he has much/often suffered
　　　"He has suffered a lot/frequently."

(80)　*Il s' est beaucoup amusé en mon absence.*
　　　he REFL is much   amused in my absence
　　　"He has amused himself a lot during my absence."

(81)　*Son développement a été beaucoup retardé.*
　　　"His development has been much delayed."

(82)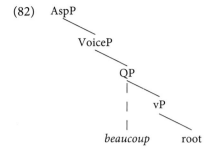

- eventive property reading: *v* licenses subject or object; VoiceP = active, AspP = perfective (83); VoiceP = reflexive, Asp = perfective (84); VoiceP = passive, Asp = perfective/infective (85); DegP = degree:[16]

(83) et m' avait très recommandé au médecin
et me had very recommended to-the doctor
"and he had highly recommended me to the doctor"

(84) Je me suis très enrhumé.
I me am very got-a-cold
"I got a terrible cold."

(85) Il est très fréquenté par les voyageurs marocains
it is very frequented by the travelers Moroccan
"It is visited a lot by the Moroccan travelers."

(86)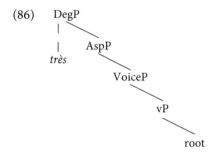

---

16. One of the reviewers points out that, since structures (82) and (86) are essentially the same, nothing in the structure hypothetically prevents QP and DegP from co-occurring:

(i) *Il s' est [très [beaucoup amusé]].
He REFL is very a lot amused

I suggest that degree being expressed on the verb semantically prevents degree to be expressed a second time.

- resultative: v = 'become'; VoiceP = passive; AspP = state; DegP = degree; *be* = copula:[17]

(87) *Est-ce que c'est très détruit, Rostock?*
 is it that it is very destroyed Rostock
 "Is Rostock much damaged?"

(88) *Capus est très frappé par cette mort.*
 Capus is very touched by this death
 "Capus is touched a lot by this death."

(89)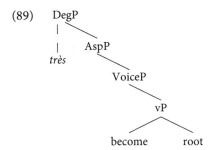

- stative: no v; no VoiceP; Asp = state; DegP = degree; *be* = copula:

(90) *il est très étonné de constater que je suis toujours là*
 "He is very astonished to remark that I am still there."

(91)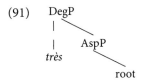

In this section it has been argued that in Romance, just as in Germanic, four types of participles on a scale going from fully verbal to fully adjectival can be distinguished. In §3, it was stated that in Germanic the prenominal and postnominal position of participles within the DP can serve as an argument in favor of the

---

17. Within the class of resultatives, two different types have been distinguished: resultant state and target state participles (Parsons 1990). Anagnostopoulou (2003) argues that, in Greek, resultant state participles have a VoiceP projection, since they can be combined with a *by*-phrase. In her analysis, target state participants are simply VPs. Both types are adjectival: VoiceP and VP are dominated by an adjectival functional projection. The eventive property reading proposed for participles modified by *très* involves even more verbal structure than the resultant state participles in Greek. They contain verbal aspect that is not stative as in resultatives.

distinction between a fully eventive and an eventive property interpretation of participles. Since, in Romance, participles generally occur in postverbal position, the position of the participle could not be used to argue that in Romance a fully eventive and an eventive property interpretation can be distinguished. The argumentation has instead been based on the combinatorial properties of the participle (in French) as part of the predicate of the clause.

The question that arises is whether the four interpretations of the participles in English/Dutch and French are comparable, since different linguistic criteria are used to establish the two eventive categories in Germanic and French (position in the noun phrase in Germanic versus collocation with *beaucoup* and *très* in French).[18] The goal of this paper has been to show that, being a mixed category, just like, e.g. nominalized infinitives, participles can have various interpretations, represented on a scale going from purely verbal to purely nominal and purely adjectival, respectively. After having argued in Sleeman (2011) that in English and Dutch an intermediary step should be distinguished between the fully eventive and the resultative interpretation of the participle, in this paper it has been argued that the same should be done in French. That different criteria have been used is only apparent, as will be argued in the next section.

5. Similarities between Germanic and Romance

Cinque (1994) argues that adjectives in Germanic and Romance are merged within the same positions and in the same order in the DP. They are merged within the specifier position of various functional projections dominating the noun phrase. In Cinque's analysis, the postnominal position of adjectives in the Romance languages results from noun movement to the head of NumP in Romance, exemplified by English in (92) and French in (93):

(92) $[_{DP}$ a $[_{FP}$ beautiful $[_{FP}$ big $[_{NumP}$ $[_{FP}$ red $[_{NP}$ ball]]]]]]

(93) $[_{DP}$ un $[_{FP}$ joli $[_{FP}$ gros $[_{NumP}$ $[_{Num^0}$ $[_{N^0}$ ballon]$_i$ $[_{FP}$ rouge $[_{NP}$ $[_{N^0}$ t$_i$]]]]]]]]

Since the mirror adjective ordering in (94)–(95) seems to provide evidence against the N-raising analysis (Lamarche 1991), Cinque argues that the rightmost adjective in the Italian Example (95) is not an attributive adjective merged in a functional projection dominating NP, as in English, but is a predicate, i.e. a

---

18.   Thanks to one of the reviewers for pointing this out to me.

reduced relative clause, just like the postnominal constituent *just right* in the English Example (96):

(94) a beautiful red car

(95) una macchina$_i$ rossa t$_i$ bellissima

(96) a steak just right

Kayne (1994) also makes a distinction between attributes and predicates and adopts a raising analysis of relative clauses and reduced relative clauses, according to which the 'antecedent' noun raises from inside the (reduced) relative clause to the specifier position of CP, the complement of D^0:

(97) [$_{DP}$ the [$_{CP}$ [$_{NP}$ book]$_i$ t$_i$ sent t$_i$ to John]]

In Cinque's (2010) analysis, eventive participles are merged into the specifier position of functional projections of the NP, just like adjectives in Cinque's (1994) analysis.

Sleeman (2011) adopts Kayne's (1994) analysis for postnominal participles in Germanic and Cinque's (2010) analysis for all prenominal participles, including the eventive ones:

(98) [$_{DP}$ the [$_{CP}$ [$_{NP}$ jewels]$_i$ t$_i$ stolen t$_i$]]

(99) [$_{DP}$ the [$_{FP}$ stolen [$_{NP}$ jewels]]]

This means that two merge positions are adopted for eventive participles: a relative clause position for the fully eventive ones, and a position within the functional projections dominating NP for the participles with an eventive property reading.[19] This holds not only for Germanic, but also for Romance. In Romance, however, the participle in (99) also ends up in a postnominal position, because of noun/NP movement to a higher functional projection, which also accounts for the postnominal position of adjectives in Romance. This means that postnominal participles in Romance should be ambiguous, having all four interpretations

---

19. Neither Cinque (2010) nor Kayne (1994) make a distinction between the merge position of the participle in (98) and (99). For Cinque their merge position is prenominal; for Kayne both participles are reduced relative clauses in his raising analysis. In both analyses, the different surface position of the participle would be the result of noun/NP movement. If the merge position is the same, this suggests that the interpretation is also the same. However, a difference in interpretation between, e.g. manner adjectives and subject-oriented adjectives is a reason for Cinque (1994) to assign them two different merge positions. The goal of this paper is to argue that 'eventiveness' is scalar, and that therefore the same merge position is not justified (cf. Footnote 1).

distinguished in this paper. Example (100) exemplifies a fully eventive participle, whereas the participles in (101)–(103) would have the eventive property reading, according to the analysis presented in this paper. (100) would have a merge structure as in (98), and (101)–(103) one as in (99). This means thus that the surface position being equal to the base-position in Germanic, this can be used as an argument in favor of a difference in interpretation of the participles, whereas in Romance this is not possible. Underlyingly, however, there is also a difference in position in Romance.

(100) *une loi adoptée récemment en France* (fully eventive)
a law adopted recently in France
"a recently adopted law in France"

(101) *la question très débattue par les psychologues* (event. prop)
the question very discussed by the psychologists
"the question discussed a lot by psychologists"

(102) *quelques mots très choisis* (event. prop.)
some words very chosen
"some well chosen words"

(103) *un organisme très débilité* (event. prop.)
an organism very weakened
"a much weakened organism"

Another apparent difference between Germanic and Romance is the use of different adverbs, underlining the different interpretations in the argumentation for French. For French a different argumentation has been used than for English/Dutch, because the position of the participle used in Sleeman (2011) as a diagnostic tool could not be used as an argument. However, the same argumentation could be applied to English. As Doetjes (2008) shows, degree adverbs do not behave the same in different languages. Whereas *trop* "too much" can be used with adjectives, verbs, and nouns in French, *too* in English can only be used with adjectives, whereas with verbs and nouns *too much* has to be used. In standard English, *very* is used with adjectives, whereas (*very*) *much* is used with verbs or nouns. As observed in Footnote 9, however, according to Quirk et al. (1991: 415) there seems to be "increasing acceptance of the co-occurrence of *very* with a *by*-agent phrase containing a personal agent" in English:

(104) ?The man was very offended by the policeman.

(105) ?I was very influenced by my college professors.

This shows that the same criterion, the type of adverb with which the participle occurs, could have been used for English as well.

6. Conclusion

In this paper it has been argued that, not only in Germanic, but also in Romance, participles have various interpretations: fully eventive, an eventive property reading, resultative, and stative. Whereas for Germanic the distinction between a fully eventive and an eventive property reading has been based on the postnominal (English) versus prenominal position, for Romance, on the basis of French, the distinction has been based on the combination with degree adverbs. It has been claimed that fully eventive participles combine generally with *beaucoup* "much, a lot", whereas participles with an eventive property reading, resultatives and statives combine with *très* "very". It has been suggested that the adjectival feature that was present in the Latin perfect passive participle might still be present in the passive participle, and in the resultative and stative participle, which are derived from the passive one, which would account for their combination with *très*. The distinction between a fully eventive and an eventive property reading having been made for Romance as well, it was proposed that, just as in Germanic, this is reflected in a different merge position within the DP.

References

Abeillé, Anne & Godard, Danièle. 2003. The syntactic flexibility of French degree adverbs. *Proceedings of HPSG3 Conference*, East Lansing, 26–46. Stanford CA: CSLI.

Ackema, Peter & Neeleman, Ad. 2004. *Beyond Morphology: Interface Conditions on Word Formation*. Oxford: OUP.

Alexiadou, Artemis, 2001. *Functional Structure in Nominals: Nominalization and Ergativity* [Linguistik Aktuell/Linguistics Today 42]. Amsterdam: John Benjamins.

Alexiadou, Artemis, Iordăchioaia, Gianina & Schäfer, Florian. 2011. Scaling the variation in Romance and Germanic nominalizations. In *The Noun Phrase in Romance and Germanic: Structure, Variation and Change* [Linguistik Aktuell/Linguistics Today 171], Petra Sleeman & Harry Perridon (eds), 25–40. Amsterdam: John Benjamins.

Anagnostopoulou, Elena. 2003. Participles and voice. In *Perfect Explorations*, Artemis Alexiadou, Monika Rathert & Arnim von Stechow (eds), 1–36. Berlin: Mouton de Gruyter.

Bolinger, Dwight. 1967. Adjectives in English: Attribution and predication. *Lingua* 18: 1–34.

Borsley, Robert D. & Kornfilt, Jaklin. 2000. Mixed extended projections. In *The Nature and Function of Syntactic Categories*, Robert D. Borsley (ed.), 101–131. New York NY: Academic Press.

Brekke, Magnar, 1988. The experiencer constraint. *Linguistic Inquiry* 19: 169–180.

Bresnan, Joan. 1982. The passive in lexical theory. In *The Mental Representation of Grammatical Relations,* Joan Bresnan (ed.), 3–86. Cambridge MA: The MIT Press.

Chomsky, Noam. 1970. Remarks on nominalization. In *Readings in English Transformational Grammar*, Roderick Jacobs & Peter Rosenbaum (eds), 184–221. Waltham MA: Blaisdell.

Chomsky, Noam. 1981. *Lectures on Government and Binding*. Dordrecht: Foris.

Cinque, Guglielmo. 1994. Evidence for partial N-movement in the Romance DP. In *Paths Towards Universal Grammar : Studies in Honor of Richard S. Kayne*, Guglielmo Cinque, Jan Koster, Jean-Yves Pollock, Luigi Rizzi & Raffaella Zanuttini (eds), 85–110. Washington DC: Georgetown University Press.

Cinque, Guglielmo. 2010. *The Syntax of Adjectives: A Comparative Study*. Cambridge MA: The MIT Press.

Coussé, Evie. 2011. On ambiguous past participles in Dutch. *Linguistics* 49: 611–634.

Delsing, Lars-Olof. 1993. On attributive adjectives in Scandinavian and other languages. *Studia Linguistica* 47(2): 105–125.

Doetjes, Jenny. 1997. Quantifiers and Selection: On the Distribution of Quantifying Expressions in French. Ph.D. dissertation, Leiden University.

Doetjes, Jenny. 2008. Adjectives and degree modification. In *Adjectives and Adverbs: Syntax, Semantics, Discourse*, Louise McNally & Christopher Kennedy (eds), 123–155. Oxford; OUP.

Embick, David. 2004. On the structure of resultative participles in English. *Linguistic Inquiry* 35(3): 355–392.

Fabb, Nigel. 1984. Syntactic Affixation. Ph.D. dissertation, MIT.

Gaatone, David. 1981. Observations sur l'oppostion *très – beaucoup*. *Revue de Linguistique Romane* 45: 74–95.

Gaatone, David. 2007. Les marqueurs d'intensité et les locutions verbales: Quelques réflexions. *Travaux de Linguistique* 55: 93–105.

Gaatone, David. 2008. Un ensemble hétéroclite: Les adverbes de degré en français. In *Congrès Mondial de Linguistique Française 08*, Jacques Durand, Bruno Habert & Bernard Laks (eds), 2495–2504. Paris: Institut de Linguistique Française.

Grimshaw, Jane. 1990. *Argument Structure*. Cambridge MA: The MIT Press.

Halle, Morris & Marantz, Alec. 1993. Distributed morphology and the pieces of inflection. In *The View from Building 20. Essays in Linguistics in Honor of Sylvain Bromberger*, Ken Hale & Samuel J. Keyser (eds), 111–176. Cambridge MA: The MIT Press.

Halle, Morris & Marantz, Alec. 1994. Some key features of Distributed Morphology. *MIT Working Papers in Linguistics* 21: 275–288.

Harley, Heidi & Noyer, Rolf. 1999. Distributed Morphology. *Glot International* 4(4): 3–9.

Kayne, Richard. 1994. *The Antisymmetry of Syntax*. Cambridge MA: The MIT Press.

Kennedy, Chris & McNally, Louise. 1999. From Event structure to Scale structure: degree modification in deverbal adjectives. In *SALTIX*, Tanya Matthews & Devon Strolovitch (eds), 163–180, Ithaca NY: Cornell University.

Kratzer, Angelika. 1994. The event argument and the semantics of voice. Ms, University of Massachusetts, Amherst.

Lamarche, Jacques. 1991. Problems for N-movement to NumP. *Probus* 3: 215–236.

Levin, Beth & Rappaport, Malka. 1992. The formation of adjectival passives. *Linguistic Inquiry* 17: 623–661.

Lieber, Rochelle. 1980. On the Organization of the Lexicon. Ph.D. dissertation, MIT.

Parsons, Terence. 1990. *Events in the Semantics of English: A Study in Subatomic Semantics*. Cambridge MA: The MIT Press.

Perret, Michèle. 2005. *Introduction à l'Histoire de la Langue Française*. Paris: Armand Colin.

Plann, Susan. 1981. The two *el* + infinitive constructions in Spanish. *Linguistic Analysis* 7: 203–240.

Quirk, Randolph, Greenbaum, Sidney, Leech, Geoffrey & Svartvik, Jan. 1991. *A Comprehensive Grammar of the English Language*. London: Longman.
Sadler, Luisa & Arnold, Douglas. 1994. Prenominal adjectives and the phrasal/lexical distinction. *Linguistics* 30: 187–226.
Sleeman, Petra. 2001. Deverbale procédés in het Nederlands en het Frans. In *Contrastief Onderzoek Nederlands-Frans*, Ludo Beheydt, Pierre Godin, An Neven, Beatrice Lamiroy, William Van Belle, Joop van der Horst & Willy van Langendonck (eds), 195–209. Louvain-la-Neuve: Peeters.
Sleeman, Petra. 2010. The nominalized infinitive in French: Structure and change. *Linguística: Revista de Estudos Linguísticos da Universidade do Porto* 5: 145–173.
Sleeman, Petra. 2011. Verbal and adjectival participles: Internal structure and position. *Lingua* 121: 1569–1587.
Steridade, Donca. 2012. The cycle without containment. Paper presented at the 22nd Colloquium on Generative Grammar. Barcelona, 21–23 March 2012.
Wasow, Thomas. 1977. Transformations and the lexicon. In *Formal Syntax*, Peter Culicover, Thomas Wasow & Adrian Akmajian (eds), 327–360. New York NY: Academic Press.

The mixed categorial behavior of *cel* + participle in Romanian*

Dana Niculescu
University of Amsterdam

The traditional distinction between verbal and adjectival participles has been fine-grained in the last decades. Recently, Sleeman (2011) brought evidence that Germanic languages display two types of verbal participles: the fully eventive and the less fully eventive one. Using evidence from the Romanian present participle in modifier position, this paper argues that these two types of verbal participles also exist in Romance languages. Next to the fully eventive verbal participle, Romanian displays a less fully eventive structure, containing a verbal present participle preceded by the determiner *cel*, which typically selects adjectives. Evidence for the lower eventivity of the *cel*-verbal participle configuration will come from lexical aspect.

1. The adjectivization process

The distinction between verbal and adjectival (past) participles has long been acknowledged in the linguistic tradition. The two types of past participles show a number of syntactic differences, such as postnominal vs. prenominal position when used as modifiers of the noun, the possibility of *un*-prefixation, or the selection of verbal vs. adjectival degree markers (Wasow 1977; Bresnan 1982, among others). Subsequent studies regarding the process of adjectivization in English (Kratzer 1994, 2000; Embick 2004) have brought arguments for a further division inside the category of adjectival past participle, namely between a resultative and a purely stative adjective. While all adjectives are states (Parsons 1990, among others), some of them denote a state which is the result of a previous event, while others simply denote a property of the entity encoded by the head noun, with no event implications. There seems to be evidence that adjectival present participles also have two uses: the purely stative participial adjective, whose diagnostic test

---

* I would like to thank Petra Sleeman for our fruitful discussions and her valuable feedback on previous versions of this paper. I am also grateful to the reviewers for their suggestions.

is represented by the degree modifier *very*, and the participial adjective encoding a progressing situation (instead of an event in progress), which has Progressive Aspect (Sleeman 2011).

Recently, analyzing (past) participles in Germanic languages, Sleeman (2011) brought evidence for the existence of two types of verbal participles in modifier position in the DP, namely the fully eventive verbal participle, placed postnominally (*the letters sent to Mary*), and the less fully eventive one, placed prenominally, and having a more reduced internal structure (*the recently sent letters*). Sleeman shows that the prenominal position of Germanic participles is ambiguous and is not always a proof of their adjectivization. The possibility of combination with temporal adverbials like *recently* in English and Dutch, and the lexicalization of *by*-phrases, as well as of prepositional phrases that encode different thematic roles in Dutch, are tests which prove the verbal character of the prenominal participle. There is morphological and syntactic evidence of their less eventive character: realization of agreement with the head noun (in Dutch) and impossibility of substitution with a full relative clause, as opposed to the postnominal participles (in English and Dutch).

The question which rises is whether Romance languages also show these two different types of verbal participles in modifier position: the fully eventive and the less fully eventive type, which would represent different steps in the gradual process of adjectivization. The difficulty in answering this question resides in the fact that participial modifiers in the Romance DP, be they verbal or adjectival, usually occur in postnominal position, although the prenominal position is also possible (see (1b and c) below). I argue that this distinction exists in Romanian, on the basis of an analysis of the nominal structures containing a present participle in modifier position. I shall look closer at the configuration displaying a verbal participle preceded by the determiner *cel*, which has a mixed categorial behavior: while still verbal in nature, it is the complement of the determiner *cel*, which typically selects adjectives. Since in Romanian word order cannot be brought as an argument for the existence of different uses of verbal participles, I shall use evidence coming from lexical aspect to argue for the existence of an intermediate stage in the adjectivization process between the fully eventive and the adjectival participle.

2. The data: The Romanian present participle in modifier position

2.1 The present participle structures

Romanian displays both verbal and adjectival present participles in modifier position inside the DP (1a–d).

(1) a. *fata   aducând   apă*
    girl.F.THE bringing water
    "the girl bringing water"

   b. *mâna   (cea)   tremurând-ă   (acum de frig)*
     hand.F.THE CEL.F.SG trembling-F.SG now of coldness
     "the hand trembling now with cold"

   c. *(*acum) suferind-a   fată; o ușor   / încă / foarte*
      now   suffering-F.SG.THE girl; a slightly still very
      tremurând-ă   (*de emoție) voce
      trembling-F.SG   of emotion   voice
      "the suffering girl"; "a slightly/still/very trembling voice"

   d. *apa   cea   mirosind a   tămâie*
      water.F.THE CEL.F.SG smelling like incense
      (⟨http://www.poezie.ro⟩)
      "the water smelling like incense"

The participle in (1a) is fully eventive, preserving the morpho-syntactic characteristics of its verbal base, while the postnominal adjective in (1b) displays a number of syntactic characteristics which differentiates it from the verbal participle. The most obvious difference between the participles in (1a) and (1b) is morphological. The adjectival participle agrees in gender, number and case with the head noun (1b). The postnominal adjectival participles can be either lexical or phrasal, and it allows not only an individual, but also an episodic reading, marked by the temporal adverbial *acum* "now". It also allows combination with the adjectival determiner *cel*, a fact which matches with the selectional preferences of this determiner (i.e. it typically takes an adjectival complement). The agreeing present participle can also be placed in prenominal position in the Romanian DP, as in (1c). In this position the participle can only be lexical; it only allows combination with specifiers (modal, aspectual adverbs, degree markers), but not with complements. Moreover, episodic readings are excluded, as one can see from the incompatibility with the adverbial *acum* "now". When it occurs in pre-head position, the adjectival participle is capable to take over the suffixal definite article from the head noun.

Next to these three modifying participles, Romanian has a rarely attested structure, illustrated under (1d). The construction was attested through the analysis of a corpus which consisted of Romanian Internet pages. In this configuration the non-agreeing verbal present participle which modifies the head noun is the complement of the determiner *cel*. It is an unexpected structure, since it seems to be the only verbal constituent selected by *cel*. The *cel*-present participle has not become adjectival, a fact proven by the lack of agreement and by the preservation of the syntactic characteristics of its verbal base. I argue that it is less fully eventive than the verbal participle in (1a), where the adjectival determiner is absent; it follows that the *cel*-participle structure occupies an intermediate place between the fully eventive participle and the postnominal adjectival participle, as in Table 1. I shall also put forth the hypothesis that the realization of the determiner *cel* is possible due to the lower eventivity of the verbal participle in (1d). This means that the determiner *cel* can select verbal complements, but not the most eventive type.

Table 1. The adjectivization of the Romanian present participle

Verbal participle (VP)		Adjectival participle (AP)	
VP →*cel* VP	→	(±*cel*) postnominal AP →	prenominal AP
fully eventive →less eventive	→	adjectival (+episodic) →	adjectival (+individual)

2.2 The syntactic behavior of the participial structures

The verbal present participles in modifier position in structures (1a) and (1d) differ minimally, i.e. through the absence/presence of the adjectival determiner *cel*. I shall show below that the two configurations share the same syntactic characteristics; I shall also show that the two verbal participle configurations differ from the post- and prenominal adjectival participles with respect to most of the characteristics listed in this section. As far as the two structures with adjectival participles are concerned ((1b) and (1c)), they share a number of syntactic features and also show a number of differences which will be discussed here in short. In the case of the postnominal adjectival participle structure, there do not seem to be any syntactic or selectional differences triggered by the absence/presence of the determiner *cel*; the only difference is at the pragmatic/discourse level. For this reason the two adjectival participles, +/– *cel*, will be discussed together below.

(a) The verbal participles obligatorily lexicalize their internal arguments (2a,b), while the adjectival participle does not allow the realization of the direct object of the verbal base (2c).

(2) a. *o femeie   fotografiind   acum un copil*
       a woman.F photographing now a child

   b. *fata   asta cea   mereu fotografiind   copii   sărmani*
       girl.F.THE this CEL.F.SG always photographing children poor
       "this girl who is always photographing poor children"

   c. *natura   (cea)   îmbătând-ă*[1]   (Bolintineanu: 430)
       nature.F.THE CEL.F.SG intoxicating-F.SG
       "the intoxicating nature"

---

1. Bolintineanu, Dimitrie. 1961. *Opere alese*. București: Editura pentru Literatură, p. 430.

(b) The prepositional objects of the verbal participles are also obligatorily realized (3a,b), while they are optional for adjectival participles (3c).

(3) a. *o fată   suferind   *(de anemie)*
      a girl.F suffering (of anemia)
      "a girl suffering from anemia"

  b. *camera   ta   cea   mirosind   *(a   clor)*
      room.F.THE your CEL.F.SG smelling   (like chlorine)
      "your room which smells like chlorine"

  c. *fata   cea   suferind-ă   (de anemie)*
      girl.F.THE CEL.F.SG suffering-F.SG (of anemia)
      "the girl suffering from anemia"

(c) The verbal participles allow the combination with different kinds of adverbials, such as causal, modal and locative (the examples under (4) contain causal adjuncts). The difference between the postnominal and the prenominal adjectival participle is the following: the first one can take any of these three types of adverbials (4c), but the second one only allows combination with modal adverbials expressing intensity, and not with those expressing the manner in which the eventuality is actualized. This is due to its impossibility to receive complements (4d).

(4) a. *mâinile   ei   mereu tremurând **de frig***
      hands.F.THE her always trembling of cold

  b. *mâinile   ei   cele   mereu tremurând **de frig***
      hands.F.THE her CEL.F.PL always trembling of cold

  c. *mâinile   ei   (cele)   mereu tremurând-e   **de frig***
      hands.F.THE her CEL.F.PL always trembling-F.PL of cold
      "her hands always trembling with cold"

  d. *tremurând-ele   (*de frig) mâini*
      trembling-F.PL.THE of cold   hands.F
      "the trembling hands"

(d) The verbal participles can also combine with the temporal adverbial *acum* "now". It has been noticed that modifiers that are preceded by the article *cel* only allow an individual reading (Cornilescu 2006). However, the non-agreeing present participle preceded by the determiner *cel* can also have an episodic reading, although the usual reading is habitual or frequentative. The episodic reading is marked by the combination with the temporal adverbial *acum* "now" (5a,b), and the habitual reading by the adverbial *mereu* "always" (5a–c). One can see that only the postnominal adjectival participle allows combination with the adverbial *acum* (5b); the prenominal adjectival participle can only have an individual reading (5c).

(5) a. *zăpada (cea) căzând acum / mereu peste oraș*
   snow.F.THE CEL.F.SG falling now / always over town
   "the snow falling now/always over the town"

   b. *mâinile (cele) tremurând-e acum / mereu*
   hands.F.THE CEL.F.PL trembling-F.PL now / always
   "the hands now/always trembling"

   c. *o (*acum) / mereu tremurând-ă mână*
   a now always trembling-F.SG hand
   "an always trembling hand"

(e) The two verbal participles display the clausal prefixal negation *ne-* (6a,b). The post- and prenominal adjectival participles marginally allow the constituent negator *ne-* (6c,d).

(6) a. *discursul ei ne-aducând nimic nou*
   speech.F.THE her not-bringing nothing new
   "her speech which brings nothing new"

   b. *camera cea ne-mirosind încă a clor*
   room.F.THE CEL.F.SG not-smelling yet like chlorine
   "the room which does not smell yet like chlorine"

   c. *stele ne-murind-e*[2]
   stars.F un-dying-F.PL
   "the undying stars"

   d. *ne-murind-ele trofee*[3]
   un-dying.F.PL trophies.F
   "the undying trophies"

In Romanian the prefixal negator has two functions: it is a clausal negation for non-finite clauses (the gerund, the participial and the supine clause), and a constituent negation for underived and participial adjectives. Romanian distinguishes between the sentential negator, which is the adverb *nu*, and the clausal negator which attaches to the verb as a prefix. In (6a and b) the prefixal negator takes scope over the whole participial clause; its behavior shows that it functions here as a clausal, and not as a constituent negation. Unlike the English prefixal negation *un-*, which is a diagnostic test for the adjectivization of participles (Wasow 1977; Dowty 1979, among others), the Romanian *ne-* (the equivalent of the English clausal negator *not*) cannot be used as an adjectivization test.

---

2. Asachi, Gheorghe. 1997. *Cântul Cignului. Versuri, Teatru, Nuvele istorice*. Chișinău: Litera, p. 28.

3. Ibid., p. 100.

(f) The verbal participles do not allow the combination with the degree marker *foarte*; combination with degree markers is allowed by adjectival participles (7c,d).

(7) a. *mâinile   (*foarte) tremurând de frig*
       hands.F.THE   very   trembling of cold

   b. *mâinile   cele   (*foarte) tremurând de frig*
       hands.F.THE CEL.F.PL very   trembling of cold
       "the hands trembling with cold"

   c. *fata   (cea)   foarte suferind-ă*
       girl.F.THE   CEL.F.SG very   suffering-F.SG
       "the very suffering girl"

   d. *o foarte suferind-ă   fată*
       a very suffering-F.SG   girl.F
       "a very suffering girl"

(g) The verbal participles cannot occupy the position of complement of the copular verbs *be* and *remain*, while the lexical adjectival participle is allowed in this context.

Be and *remain* have a copular and a predicative use. The two uses can be disambiguated by inserting locative adverbials in the structure, a diagnostic test for predicative verbs. With verbal participles, the insertion of locative adverbials in the sentence is allowed (8a). The possibility of a constituent to occur in predicative position after the copula is also a test of stativization (Kratzer 2000; Embick 2004). As far as adjectival present participles are concerned, they can occur after the copula (8c).

(8) a. *Fata   este / a rămas (în casă) tremurând de frig*
       girl.F.SG   is   remained   in house   trembling of cold
       "The girl is/remained in the house trembling of cold"

   Predicative *fi/rămâne*
   b. **Fata   este / a rămas tremurând de frig*
       girl.F.SG   is   remained   trembling of cold

   Copulative *fi/rămâne*
   c. *Rana   este / a rămas   sângerând-ă*
       wound.F.THE is   remained   bleeding-F.SG
       "The wound is/remained bleeding"

On the basis of this evidence, I conclude that the *cel*-verbal participle shares its syntactic characteristics with the fully eventive participle, which is not preceded by *cel*. On the other hand, a number of its syntactic characteristics set it apart from the post- and prenominal adjectival participle.

3. The determiner *cel* in the present participle structure

Cel is a definite determiner which occurs only in Romanian (among the Romance languages); this determiner has the particular feature of selecting an adjectival/ modifying phrase (for its different uses, see Cornilescu 1992).

The determiner *cel* occurs in configurations with a covert (9a) or an overt head noun (9b) and typically selects an adjectival phrase (which is why it is also sometimes called an *adjectival article*).[4]

(9) a. *cea   frumoasă*
       CEL.F.SG beautiful
       "the beautiful one"

   b. *fata   (cea)   frumoasă*
      girl.F.THE CEL.F.SG   beautiful
      "the beautiful girl"

The configuration in which the adjectival article co-occurs with the head noun is a double definite structure. It is unique among the Romance languages, but is comparable with polydefinite nominal constructions in Greek and Swedish (Campos & Stavrou 2004; Marchiş & Alexiadou 2009). In this structure the head noun has to bear the definite article. *Cel* is the second determiner in the DP, always occurring after the definite noun; its realization is optional.

The range of complements that are selected by the determiner *cel* depends on the overt or covert character of the head noun. The lexicalization of the head noun restricts its complements to those which can occur both attributively ("the beautiful girl"), and in predicative position ("the girl is beautiful"). This means that *cel* has a syntactic role in the configuration: it is a marker of predicative modification (Cornilescu 2006; Marchiş & Alexiadou 2009).

---

4. *Cel* also selects a full relative clause as its complement (i). However, Cornilescu (2006) shows that, even in these contexts, the determiner does not select a verbal, but a nominal category, that is, the relative pronoun. In the absence of the pronoun, the occurrence of *cel* is ruled out (ii).

   (i) *ideea   cea   care   mă obsedează*
        idea.THE CEL.F.SG which   me obsesses
        "the idea that obsesses me"

   (ii) *ideea   (*cea)   că*
        idea.THE CEL.F.SG that

        vom   învinge   (adapted from Cornilescu 2006: 55, (25b))
        (we)shall win
        "the idea that we shall win"

Next to the role it plays in syntax, it has been noticed that *cel* also creates pragmatic/discourse effects. Coene (1999) and Marchiș & Alexiadou (2009) have convincingly shown that *cel* always triggers reference and an anaphoric or deictic interpretation, features which it shares with the demonstrative pronoun. Moreover, at the pragmatic level, the occurrence of the determiner *cel* indicates that the modifier encodes the most salient property of the head noun (Marchiș & Alexiadou 2009; Cornilescu & Nicolae 2011). In (9b), the presence of *cel* adds the pragmatic feature [+salient] to the configuration, which means that this determiner is not really optional.

According to Cornilescu & Nicolae (2011), constituents occurring as complements of the determiner *cel* have to designate a *property*. In order to acquire a property reading, non-finite verb forms must undergo a process of stativization (cf. also Cornilescu 2006). However, one can notice that stativization does not always take place in double definite structures: next to their individual reading, the participles in configurations like (5a) can also have an episodic interpretation. Therefore, the adjectival determiner *cel* does not necessarily impose a property/stative reading upon non-finite verb forms.

In line with the analysis of the complement of *cel* as having a property reading, Cornilescu (2006) and Cornilescu and Nicolae (2011) argue that the modifier preceded by the adjectival determiner is restricted in terms of category, i.e. it should belong to a [–verbal] category. The corpus analysis which I undertook has revealed that the non-agreeing present participle, a verbal category, can be the complement of the determiner *cel* in double definite structures. This configuration is quite rare and was even considered ungrammatical (Cornilescu 2006; Cornilescu & Nicolae 2011). An acceptability test for this structure among native speakers of Romanian showed that it is considered grammatical, and that it is poetic.

4. The *cel*-present participle structure and lexical aspect

In Section 2 I brought arguments that the verbal participle structures in modifier position should be differentiated from the configurations with adjectival participles. In this section I present proof that the *cel*-present participle represents a different type of verbal participle than the one in which the adjectival determiner is absent, and that it is placed between the fully eventive verbal participle and the postnominal adjectival participle on the adjectivization scale.

Verbs belonging to any lexical aspectual class can modify a noun when they are used as present participles, from accomplishments (10a) to states (10b) (Vendler's typology (1967)).

(10) a. *omul   pictând   acum un tablou*
    man.THE painting now a painting
    "the man painting a painting now"

  b. *copii   având   mame   tinere*
    children.THE having mothers young
    "the children having young mothers"

I argue that in double definite structures the predication headed by the verbal present participle cannot belong to the type *accomplishment*. When verbs designating accomplishments occur in the *cel*-verbal participle configuration, they will undergo an aspectual shift, i.e. they will be recategorized into activities. The recategorization of the accomplishment takes place at the level of the predication as a whole (Dowty 1979). Pustejovsky (1995), who follows Verkuyl (1989), argues that the countable/uncountable character of the verb's internal argument, as well as its singular or plural form, are responsible for shifts in the event type denoted by the predication. Specifically, an indefinite plural or a mass noun in direct object position will lead to the reinterpretation of an accomplishment as an activity.

The verb *photograph* in (11) denotes an accomplishment, as its direct object is a countable, singular noun. In the presence of the adjectival determiner *cel*, a countable, quantified noun is illicit in direct object position. On the other hand, an indefinite plural noun is accepted as its internal argument (12). The activity predication usually has a habitual reading (triggered by the adverbial *mereu* "always"); it can also be in progress at reference time (when the temporal adverbial *acum* "now" is lexicalized), although the structure does not seem to be fully acceptable (12). The fact that the activity reading of the *cel*-participle is the only one available is also shown by its incompatibility with *in*-temporal adjuncts, which are allowed by accomplishments (11), and by the possibility to combine with *for*-temporal phrases, which are typical for activities (12). These two eventuality tests were put forth by Dowty (1979).

(11) **fata   cea   fotografiind un copil sărman (acum /*
    girl.THE CEL.F.SG photographing a child poor now /
    într-un minut)
    in a minute
    "the girl photographing a poor child now/in a minute"

(12) *fata   cea   mereu fotografiind   copii   sărmani (ore   în*
    girl.THE CEL.F.SG always photographing children poor hours in
    șir) / fata   cea   fotografiind   (?acum) copii   sărmani
    row girl.THE CEL.F.SG photographing now children poor
    "the girl always photographing poor children for many hours/the girl photographing poor children now"

An anonymous reviewer suggests that a parallel can be drawn between the behavior of the *cel*-participle in modifying position and that of the Romanian supine nominalizations in Noun-Subject (NS) structures, which are discussed by Cornilescu (2001) (*mâncatul*$_{Supine}$ *lui (timp de o oră/*într-o oră) în picioare* "his eating (for an hour/in an hour) while standing"). Both deverbal phrases, one adjectival, the other one nominal, are [–telic], therefore, they denote activities, not accomplishments. In the case of the supine, Cornilescu argues that the supine affix is responsible for the atelic interpretation of the nominalization. In the case of the present participle, I claim that this restriction is contributed by the determiner *cel*.

The other two eventive predication types, activities (13) and achievements (14), can occur in the *cel*-present participle structure. In the case of activities, this is expected, as they are atelic. Achievement predications such as verbs of inherently directed motion (*cădea* "fall") can have two interpretations, telic and atelic (*He fell for ten minutes/All this rain fell in ten minutes*) (Levin & Rappaport Hovav 1995: 172). When such eventualities receive an atelic reading, they are reinterpreted as activities (Ramchand 2008: 81). The *cel*-participle with telic reading is ruled out in (14b), while in (14c), the atelic predication, which is compatible with a *for*-temporal phrase, is grammatical.

(13) *vocile   cele   tremurând de emoție   ale   copiilor*
     voices.F.THE CEL.F.PL trembling   of emotion of   the children
     "children's voices trembling with emotion"

(14) a. *copiii   se joacă prin zăpada   cea   așezată și   prin*
        the children play   in   snow.F.THE CEL.F.SG lain.F and in
        zăpada   cea   căzând încă (⟨http://www.aime.ro⟩)
        snow.F.THE CEL.F.SG falling still
        "the children are playing in the already lain snow and in the still falling snow"

     b. **zăpada cea căzând în două ore*
        "the snow falling in two hours"

     c. *zăpada cea căzând ore în șir în cantități mari*
        "the snow falling for hours on end in great quantities"

The restriction shown by the *cel*-verbal participle on accomplishments and achievements translates as a ban on [+telic] eventualities in general.

Although the present participle of eventive verbs can occur in the double definite structure, stative verbs are by far the most frequent. The corpus analysis has shown, however, that not every type of stative verb can occur in the *cel*-present participle structure. Based on their different syntactic and semantic characteristics,

Maienborn (2005, 2008) makes a division inside the class of statives, between D-states and K-states. Maienborn (2005, 2008) argues that certain states, i.e. the D-states, contain a Davidsonian event argument in their lexical conceptual structure, which means that the state is (A) located in both time and space, and therefore allows combination with locative and temporal adverbials, (B) can be perceived, and (C) can be characterized by the full range of circumstances which characterize an event (therefore allowing the combination with manner, instrumental and commitative adverbials). K-states are pure statives and do not display the three above mentioned characteristics of D-states.

I shall show that D-states are generally accepted in the *cel*-verbal participle configuration, while only a confined sub-group of K-states are allowed. Examples (15a,b) display D-state verbs; under (15c,d), one can see that the two stative verbs pass the eventuality tests proposed by Maienborn.

(15) a. *roua   cea   sclipind   acum   în   soare*
        dew.F.THE   CEL.F.SG   glimmering   now   in   sun
        "the dew glimmering now in the sun"

   b. *camera   cea   mirosind   (acum)   a   clor*
        room.F.THE   CEL.F.SG   smelling   now   like   chlorine
        "the room smelling now like chlorine"

   c. *văd roua sclipind pe frunze*   ("I can see the dew
        glimmering on the leaves") /
        roua cea sclipind frumos pe frunze   ("the dew glimmering nicely
        on the leaves")

   d. *simt camera mirosind a clor într-un colț*   ("I feel the room smelling like
        chlorine in a corner") /
        camera cea mirosind urât   ("the room smelling badly")

Next to D-states, K-states are allowed and are actually the most frequent in the *cel*-verbal participle structure. However, they are severely restricted, i.e. to the sub-group containing the semantic component [+maximal degree]; they denote the fact that a certain property expressed by the prepositional constituent of the structure is present in its maximal degree (16). When this semantic component is absent, such as in (17), the structure is ruled out (compare with the parallel structure (10b), without the adjectival determiner, which is grammatical). I consider that this semantic restriction on stative predications is triggered by *cel*, more precisely by the fact that the adjectival determiner marks salience. This pragmatic feature translates into the selection of both states and events that are perceivable; therefore, the sub-class of K-states that does not contain reference to a perceivable property is ruled out from the *cel*-verbal participle structure. The K-state in (16) is a recategorized achievement.

(16) livada   cea   plesnind de mustul   fructelor
      orchard.F.THE CEL.F.SG   bursting of   juice.THE fruits.THE.GEN
      coapte (*în oraș)   (⟨http://www.confluente.ro⟩)
      ripen   in town
      "the orchard bursting with the juice of ripen fruits = the orchard with
      extremely many ripen fruits"

(17) *copiii   cei   având   mame   tinere   (*în casă)
      children.M.THE CEL.M.PL   having   mothers young   in house
      "the children having young mothers"

One can see that (16) and (17) do not allow combination with a locative adverbial, which is an eventuality test for D-states. They can be complements of a verb of perception (18), however, they pass this eventuality test only seemingly, because what is perceived is not the state, but the property encoded by the PP present in the configuration ("I see my sister's happiness, not the state of radiating").

(18) O văd pe sora mea cea radiind de fericire.
      "I see my sister radiating with happiness = I see the extreme happiness
      of my sister"

As far as grammatical aspect is concerned, the *cel*-verbal participle in modifier position is generally dominated by an imperfective Aspectual head (19), having progressive (19a) or habitual value (19b) (Comrie 1976: 25). The *cel*-participle rarely has perfective aspect value (19c,e). For activity verbs, like *plânge* "cry", it is possible, although not fully acceptable, while for achievements like *cădea* "fall", perfective aspect is ruled out if the eventuality has a telic interpretation (19d) and it becomes possible if it has an atelic interpretation (19e). Ramchand (2008: 81) argues that achievement verbs combined with locative adjuncts are telic; in (19e), the compatibility with a *for*-temporal phrase shows that the predication is [–telic].

(19) a. *zăpada cea căzând încă*
          "the still falling snow"
      b. *stelele cele (mereu) plângând*
          (⟨http://marcelfandarac.wordpress.com⟩)
          "the forever crying stars"
      c. ?*fetele cele plângând ieri toată ziua de durere*
          "the girls that cried of pain all day yesterday"
      d. **zăpada cea căzând recent în București*
          "the snow that has recently fallen in Bucharest"
      e. *zăpada cea căzând recent (ore în șir) în cantități mari*
          "the snow that has recently fallen for hours in great quantities"

Both the progressive and the habitual aspectual values were analyzed as stativization mechanisms for eventive verbs. Parsons (1990: 171) argues that a predication in the progressive no longer has a culmination point, and the event is presented as holding at a certain time interval. Rothmayr (2009: 35–6) mentions the habitual value as a mechanism which is available for turning an event into a state. The *cel*-verbal participle structure makes use of the progressive and of the habitual aspectual values for stativizing the event denoted by the verbal base. This suits the determiner *cel* best, since it prefers adjectival complements, which are stative.

5. The syntactic representation of the four participle structures

This section contains the syntactic analysis of the four present participle structures that were distinguished above. Following Embick (2004) and others, I analyze participial structures as Aspectual Phrases, instead of Tense Phrases, based on their lack of temporal independence with respect to the matrix verb, which translates into their unavailability to express tense oppositions.

My analysis is based on the following theoretical premises: firstly, the difference between verbal and adjectival participles does not originate in their being formed in different modules (syntax vs. lexicon). All participles are formed in syntax and their verbal or adjectival character is given by the type of functional categories which they project (along the lines of Distributed Morphology: Halle & Marantz 1993; Embick 2004; Ramchand 2008). Secondly, I shall assume that the verb's event structure is represented syntactically (Borer 2005; Ramchand 2008).

Within this theoretical framework, I adopt Embick's (2004) analysis of participle structures. I shall discuss the four configurations under (20), (22), (24), (25), which are maximal as far as the number of arguments is concerned and in which the verbal base is agentive.

(20) *fata*   [*aducând o floare*]
    girl.THE   bringing a flower
    "the girl bringing a flower"

(21) [AspP [Asp -ând [vP [v [vP o floare [v √ aduc-]]]]]]

The configuration under (20) contains a verbal present participle in modifier position. As shown in Section 4, the verbal participle which does not display the determiner *cel* can be an accomplishment. Two little v heads are present in the structure. The higher vP, which is the complement of the Aspectual head, is agentive; the lower vP licenses the direct object of the participle (21).

(22) *fata*   [*cea   mereu   fotografiind   copii   sărmani*]
    girl.THE CEL.F.SG   always photographing   children   poor
    "the girl who is always photographing poor children"

(23) [AspP [Asp -ind [vP [v [vP copii$_{[-Quantity]}$ [v √ fotograf-]]]]]]

In (22) the verbal present participle is the complement of the determiner *cel*. This structure contains two little v heads; the higher vP is agentive, while the lower vP licenses the direct object, as in structure (20). The DP in direct object position has a semantic restriction, it is [−quantity], i.e. it does not project a Quantity Phrase (Borer 2005). This gives rise to atelicity, which turns accomplishments into activities in structures like (22) and allows only for an atelic interpretation of achievements (14c). Borer (2005), as well as Ramchand (2008), assume that the verb enters the syntactic derivation without being specified as an accomplishment or an activity. The predication's aspectual class will be determined by the feature [± quantity] carried by the direct object, which Borer represents as a syntactic projection of the noun, the Quantity Phrase (#P). If the noun projects a Quantity Phrase, the predication will belong to the class of accomplishments, while if the #P is not projected, it will be an activity. The feature [+telicity] does not create its own sub-event, according to Ramchand (2008); therefore, there is no difference in event structure between (20), which allows accomplishments, and (22), which rules them out.

(24) *mâna*   [*tremurând-ă*]
     hand.F.THE   trembling-F.SG
     "the trembling hand"

(25) [*tremurând-a*]   *mână*
     trembling-F.SG.THE   hand.F
     "the trembling hand"

(26) [AspP [Asp$_S$ -ând √ tremur-]]]]

In structures (24) and (25) the post- and the prenominal adjectival participles contain a Root which is the complement of the Aspect Phrase, with no verbalizer present in the structure, since these participles are pure adjectives. The participles are headed by an Aspect node, which is stative (Embick 2004). (26) is the syntactic representation of both adjectival present participles in (24) and (25).

6. Conclusions

Four stages can be distinguished in the adjectivization of Romanian present participle structures: the fully eventive verbal participle, the *cel*-verbal participle, the episodic postnominal and the non-episodic prenominal adjectival participle.

The *cel*-verbal participle in modifier position has a mixed categorial behavior; it is the complement of the adjectival article *cel*, while still being a verbal element. The determiner *cel* is responsible for the occurrence of a less fully eventive verbal participle, displaying a number of restrictions in the lexical aspectual classes which can occur in this structure.

This analysis refines the previous analyses regarding the categorial status of *cel*-modifiers in double definite structures. The complement of the adjectival determiner **can** be verbal, but it is aspectually restricted: not the whole range of eventive verbs is licit in this configuration, that is, neither the most eventive type, which are accomplishments, nor [+telic] achievements, are allowed.

References

Borer, Hagit. 2005. *Structuring Sense: The Normal Course of Events*. Oxford: OUP.

Bresnan, Joan. 1982. The passive in lexical theory. In *The Mental Representation of Grammatical Relations*, Joan Bresnan (ed.), 3–86. Cambridge MA: The MIT Press.

Campos, Héctor & Stavrou, Melita. 2004. Polydefinites in Greek and Aromanian. In *Balkan Syntax and Semantics* [Linguistik Aktuell/Linguistics Today 67], Olga Tomic (ed.), 137–173. Amsterdam: John Benjamins.

Coene, Martine. 1999. Definite Null Nominals in Romanian and Spanish. Ph.D. dissertation, University of Antwerp.

Comrie, Bernard. 1976. *Aspect*. Cambridge: CUP.

Cornilescu, Alexandra. 1992. Remarks on the determiner system of Rumanian: The demonstratives *al* and *cel*. *Probus* 4(3): 189–260.

Cornilescu, Alexandra. 2001. Romanian nominalizations: Case and aspectual structure. *Journal of Linguistics* 37(3): 467–501.

Cornilescu, Alexandra. 2006. Modes of semantic combinations: NP/DP. Adjectives and the structure of the Romanian DP. In *Romance Languages and Linguistic Theory 2004* [Current Issues in Linguistic Theory 278], Jenny Doetjes & Paz Gonzales (eds), 43–70. Amsterdam: John Benjamins.

Cornilescu, Alexandra & Nicolae, Alexandru. 2011. Nominal peripheries and phase structure in the Romanian DP. *Revue Roumaine de Linguistique* 1: 35–68.

Dowty, David R. 1979. *Word Meaning and Montague Grammar: The Semantics of Verbs and Times in Generative Semantics and in Montague's PTQ*. Dordrecht: Reidel.

Embick, David. 2004. On the structure of resultative participles in English. *Linguistic Inquiry* 35(3): 355–392.

Halle, Morris & Marantz, Alec. 1993. Distributed Morphology and the pieces of inflection. In *The View from Building 20. Essays in Linguistics in Honor of Sylvain Bromberger*, Kenneth Hale & Samuel J. Keyser (eds), 111–176. Cambridge MA: The MIT Press.

Kratzer, Angelika. 1994. The event argument and the semantics of voice. Ms, University of Massachusetts at Amherst.

Kratzer, Angelika. 2000. Building statives. In *Proceedings of the Twenty-sixth Annual Meeting of the Berkeley Linguistics Society*, Lisa J. Conathan, Jeff Good, Darya Kavitskaya, Alyssa B. Wulf & Alan C. L. Yu (eds), 385–399. Berkeley CA: University of California.

Levin, Beth & Rappaport Hovav, Malka 1995. *Unaccusativity: At the Syntax-Lexical Semantics Interface*. Cambridge MA: The MIT Press.

Maienborn, Claudia. 2005. On the limits of the Davidsonian approach: The case of copula sentences. *Theoretical Linguistics* 31(3): 275–316.
Maienborn, Claudia. 2008. On Davidsonian and Kimian states. In *Existence: Semantics and Syntax*, Ileana Comorovski & Klaus von Heusinger (eds), 107–132. Dordrecht: Kluwer.
Marchiş, Mihaela & Alexiadou, Artemis. 2009. On the distribution of adjectives in Romanian: The *cel* construction. In *Romance Languages and Linguistic Theory* [Romance Languages and Linguistic Theory 1], Enoch Aboh, Elisabeth van der Linden, Josep Quer & Petra Sleeman (eds), 161–178. Amsterdam: John Benjamins.
Parsons, Terence. 1990. *Events in the Semantics of English: A Study in Subatomic Semantics*. Cambridge MA: The MIT Press.
Pustejovsky, James. 1995. The generative lexicon. *Computational Linguistics* 17(4): 409–441.
Ramchand, Gillian C. 2008. *Verb Meaning and the Lexicon. A First-phase Syntax*. Cambridge: CUP.
Rothmayr, Antonia. 2009. *The Structure of Stative Verbs* [Linguistik Aktuell/Linguistics Today 143]. Amsterdam: John Benjamins.
Sleeman, Petra. 2011. Verbal and adjectival participles: Internal structure and position. *Lingua* 121: 1569–1587.
Vendler, Zeno. 1967. *Linguistics in Philosophy*. Ithaca NY: Cornell University Press.
Verkuyl, Henk J. 1989. Aspectual classes and aspectual composition. *Linguistics and Philosophy* 12: 39–94.
Wasow, Thomas. 1977. Transformations and the lexicon. In *Formal Syntax*, Peter Culicover, Thomas Wasow & Adrian Akmajian (eds), 327–360. New York NY: Academic Press.

Inside and outside – Before and after
Weak and strong adjectives in Icelandic*

Alexander Pfaff
University of Tromsø / CASTL

Icelandic has four (definite) ARTICLE – ADJECTIVE – NOUN patterns. In this paper, I present novel data, and put "old" data in a new perspective. I will argue that weakly inflected adjectives (patterns I – III) are merged *inside* the DP below the definite article, whereas strongly inflected adjectives (pattern IV) are merged *outside* DP, at least above the definite article. What distinguishes the weak patterns visibly is whether the adjective/(adjective plus) noun occurs *before* or *after* the article. Some researchers surmise that "non-restrictive adjectives are only direct modifiers and restrictive ones only indirect modifiers" (Cinque 2010: 140). Strong pattern (IV) adjectives are never restrictive, whereas certain weak adjectives may be. Against expectations, I will argue that weak adjectives in Icelandic are direct modifiers, whereas strong adjectives are indirect modifiers. I suggest that the criterion ± RESTRICTIVE as such may not be relevant to properly characterize Icelandic adjectival patterns.

1. Introduction

Icelandic has two definite articles: a prenominal, pre-adjectival freestanding one, and a postnominal suffixed one. In definite DPs, we find four different surface patterns involving the elements ARTICLE – ADJECTIVE – NOUN:[1]

---

* Thanks to: the audience at the conference *Adjectives in Germanic and Romance* (Amsterdam, March 2012) for comments; Gillian Ramchand for discussion and comments; two anonymous reviewers for detailed and insightful comments and constructive criticism; countless Icelandic native speakers for judgments, discussion and participation in my survey. Any misinterpretation and remaining shortcomings are my responsibility.

1. Abbreviations used in this paper: A – adjective; N – noun; ART – freestanding article; DEF – suffixed article; WK – weak adjectival inflection; STR – strong adjectival inflection. I will also use the notation "(I)" instead of *pattern I*, and "(I) adjective" for *adjective occurring in a pattern I DP*, etc. When a pattern is explicitly marked as (I), (II) or (III), and in Section 3, WK will not be marked in the glosses.

(1) a. <u>A.WK – N-DEF</u> (I)
rauð.i bíll-inn
red.WK car-DEF   "the red car"

b. <u>ART – A.WK – N</u> (II)
hinn fræg.i leikari
ART famous.WK actor   "the famous actor"

c. <u>N-DEF – A.WK</u> (III)
kreppa-n mikl.a
crisis-DEF great.WK   "the Great Depression"

d. <u>A.STR – N-DEF</u> (IV)
blá.r himinn-inn
blue.STR sky-DEF   "the blue sky"

In (I)–(III), the adjective is weakly inflected, in (IV) strongly. (I) is the unmarked means of adjectival modification and the most frequently used pattern, whereas (II)–(IV) have a more restricted range of application. In some cases, (I)/(II)/(III) may be semantically equivalent and only stylistic versions of each other, but generally, there are, at times rather subtle, interpretive differences among the four patterns. The main purpose of this paper is to give a brief and non-exhaustive descriptive account of those four patterns, notably with respect to to their semantic and morphosyntactic properties, and the extent to which they are structurally related. A secondary, theoretically oriented purpose of this paper is to view the properties of (I)–(IV) in light of a range of analyses proposed in the literature that assume that adnominal adjectives are derived from two distinct underlying sources, a *direct modification* source, and an *indirect modification* predicative source. The availability of four overtly distinct morpho-syntactic patterns associated with different interpretations of the adjective involved gives rise to the expectation that we may find certain correlations between *source* as used in the literature and *pattern* as used in this paper. To a certain extent, this expectation is borne out. As will be shown, those instances of (IV) adjectives discussed in this paper can be construed as deriving from a *predicative* source, whereas (I)–(III) adjectives can be construed as *direct modifiers*. It is less clear, however, that there is a further distinction among the latter three with respect to their underlying source. NB: As the examples in (1) indicate, I will be exclusively concerned with definite DPs. Claims made in this paper do not (necessarily) apply to indefinite DPs.

The structure of this paper is as follows: in the remainder of this section, I will give an account of the data used in this paper. In Section 2, I will briefly summarize some proposals made in the literature and clarify some theoretical notions. In Section 3, the "weak" patterns (I)–(III) will be characterized and compared. I will show that both readings associated with the direct and the indirect modification source are, *in principle*, available in all three patterns, but also that there is a crucial obstacle to the assumption that those adjectives with an apparent direct modification reading really are direct modifiers. In Section 4, I will discuss the most typical use of (IV) adjectives. I will argue that those adjectives can actually be analyzed as indirect modifiers. Moreover, I will produce evidence suggesting that (IV) adjectives are merged 'outside' DP. Section 5 summarizes the findings of this paper.

Most of the material presented in this paper has not been previously discussed in the literature, so a brief comment is in order. Claims made here and data presented are based on previous research and on the results of field work conducted autumn 2012 in Iceland. This field work involved, in addition to interviews with native speakers, a series of online surveys (more than 600 participants!). Judgments (other than those reported elsewhere) are based on the average score that a respective example obtained in the survey. The tasks given in the survey were highly context-sensitive and meant to elicit appropriateness/felicity rather than grammaticality judgments. Typically, a task consists of three parts:

1. a *context* (which can be a single sentence, a dialogue, or a short narrative)
2. a sentence with a *gap* in a position where a DP is expected (subject/object/complement of P)
3. a set of possible *candidates* to fill in the gaps + a scale of evaluation

In (2), a typical (but simplified) example is given (with fake judgments):

(2) [*For years, a yellow car had been parked in front of my house*]
When I looked out of the window this morning, _____ was gone.

	Fine (3)	Ok (2)	Questionable (1)	Not possible (0)	SCORE
'the yellow car' (I)	X				3.00
'the yellow car' (II)			X		1.00
'the yellow car' (III)		X			2.00
'the yellow car' (IV)				X	0.00

The average score is established on the basis of the arithmetical mean of all scores a particular candidate made. Candidates thus scoring more than 2 are considered good/felicitous; candidates scoring between 2 and 1.5 are considered slightly marked/marginal (?); candidates scoring between 1.5 and 1 are considered strongly marked (??); candidates scoring less than 1 are considered bad (#). Due to limitations of space, I will mostly present the data in terms of those four judgment categories without giving the complete context or score. If the source of an example is not explicitly given, this means that that example was either used in the survey and/or in interviews with native speaker informants.

There is some speaker variation with respect to the use of (I)–(III). Above, it was mentioned that (I) is the unmarked pattern. Also it has often been noted that (II) has "a somewhat literary flavour" (Sigurðsson 1993:180), and indeed, sometimes, the difference between (I) and (II) (and (III), for that matter) can be described in terms of style or register. This can mean, for instance, that a (I) DP is used in spoken language, while the corresponding (II) version is used in written language. It can, however, also be understood the other way round: certain uses of DPs are more common in written language, and therefore there are more proper contexts for (II) in written language than in spoken language (see (16) in Section 3.2). Moreover, there are instances where, apparently for semantic reasons, (II) or (III) has to be used and (I) is bad. This is, at least, the "conservative view". There is, undeniably, a strong tendency in Modern Icelandic to generalize (I) more and more, and many, typically younger speakers accept, or even prefer the (I) version where others only accept (II) and/or (III). Due to the limited scope of this paper, I cannot discuss this variation in any detail. Nonetheless, the scores obtained from the survey, which represent judgments from speakers between 20 and 80 of age, reflect both the conservative view, in so far as the numbers show that (II) or (III) is the unmarked pattern in certain contexts, *and* the increasing acceptance of (I), insofar as many (I) DPs score (sometimes considerably) more than 1.00 (although they are considered bad by "conservative" speakers). For the sake of illustration, let us have a look at an example + judgment by Thráinsson (2007:89):

(3) a. #þekkti leikari-nn Clint Eastwood (I)
        known actor-DEF C. E.

    b. hinn þekkti leikari Clint Eastwood (II)
        ART known actor C. E.

In the survey, I tested (I)–(III) versions of this DP in the context in (4). The scores confirm the judgment on (II), which is clearly the perferred pattern, but not on (I), which is only slightly marginal, but not totally bad. Moreover, (III), which is not mentioned by Thráinsson at all, is fine as well. Compare the average scores:

(4) CONTEXT: _____ showed up at the film festival
    (I)   þekkti leikarinn Clint Eastwood: 1.87
    (II) hinn þekkti leikari Clint Eastwood: 2.87
    (III) leikarinn þekkti Clint Eastwood: 2.48

A characterization of (I)–(III) in absolute terms is beyond the scope of this paper and probably impossible. For the present purpose, the actual use of a certain pattern is only a secondary issue in many cases anyway. What matters most is whether a given pattern/DP can or cannot have a particular reading. For example:

(5) a₁. *þýski   heimspekingur-inn*   (I)
       German philosopher-DEF

 a₂. *hinn þýski   heimspekingur*   (II)
       ART German philosopher

 a₃. *heimspekingur-inn   þýski*   (III)
       philosopher-DEF German

 b₁. *þýski   kanslari-nn*   (I)
       German chancellor-DEF

 b₂. *hinn þýski   kanslari*   (II)
       ART German chancellor

 b₃. *kanslari-nn   þýski*   (III)
       chancellor-DEF German

In (5a), the (I) DP is unmarked, whereas the (II) and (III) versions are stylistically marked. Crucially, however, all three have the same core meaning: the adjective has the (intersective) PROVENANCE reading. This is different in (5b). Only the (I) version can have the (non-intersective) THEMATIC reading 'chancellor of Germany'; (II) and (III) can only have an intersective reading indicating that the chancellor is German (without necessarily implying that s/he is chancellor of Germany).

(I), (II) and (IV) have been discussed in the literature, but except for Pfaff (2007, 2009), (III) – the pattern involving a postnominal adjective – has not been noticed. More generally, postnominal adjectives in Modern Icelandic have been ignored, marginalized or denied to exist altogether.[2] Therefore, it is essential to emphasize that (III) is productively used both in spoken and written language. Some (III) DPs are used as names or name-like designations:

(6) a₁. *Kreppa-n   mikla*   b₁. *Borg-in   eilífa*
       crisis-DEF great   city-DEF eternal
       "The Great Depression"   ~Rome

---

2. Thráinsson (2007:88), for instance, writes: "Although adjectives typically precede the nouns they modify [...] the reverse order is sometimes found in relatively formal or bookish written Icelandic", and Roehrs (2006:95) states that "the noun in the Modern Scandinavian languages **always** [emphasis mine] follows the adjective." Note, however, that Thráinsson's example involves a *strongly* inflected adjective in an *indefinite* DP, while (III) involves a *weakly* inflected adjective in a *definite* DP. The former type is indeed very archaic (frequently used in Old Icelandic Sagas) and hardly used in Modern Icelandic. Obviously, the two cases need to be kept apart, and the rather broad notion 'postnominal adjective' has to be relativized to 'weak adjective following a (noun with a) suffixed article'.

a₂.	*Föstudagur-inn langi*	b₂.	*Eyja-n græna*
	Friday-DEF long		island-DEF green
	"Good Friday"		~Ireland

(III) is not, however, restricted to fixed expressions, but has many other uses. As will be shown, in some of those uses, it is the unmarked or only possibility.

2. Direct and indirect modification

In early generative grammar, prenominal/attributive adjectives (in English) were assumed to derive from underlying postnominal/predicative ones that are generated in reduced relative clauses. Bolinger (1967) shows that this assumption is a gross oversimplification, and that not all prenominal adjectives can plausibly be derived this way.[3] He distinguishes between *reference* modification and *referent* modification. Reference modifiers make a substantial contribution to the NP denotation often denoting properties that are inherent or characteristic with respect to the NP denotation, and they may be intensional. Referent modifiers, on the other hand, predicate a property of a referent that may only hold on a certain occasion; referent modification is purely extensional. In this sense, attributive/prenominal adjectives are reference modifiers, and predicative/postnominal adjectives are referent modifiers – to a large extent. Larson (1998) argues that some prenominal adjectives are, in fact, semantically equivalent to predicative/postnominal ones,[4] in so far as they modify the referent rather than the reference. In those cases, the objections against the reduced relative clause analysis obviously do not apply.

2.1 Two sources

Many linguists nowadays assume that adnominal adjectives are derived from two distinct underlying sources, a predicative source and a non-predicative one (for instance Sproat & Shih 1988, 1991; Sadler & Arnold 1994; Alexiadou 2001, 2012;

---

3. There may be interpretive differences between attributive/prenominal and predicative/postnominal ones: "the visible stars" (= characteristically visible) vs. "the stars visible" (= currently visible), and not all adnominal adjectives can occur in predicative position: "former president" vs. "*the president (who) is former".

4. For instance, "the visible stars" can actually have both readings reported in Footnote 3. Moreover, two instances of the same adjective each associated with a different reading may co-occur, where the leftmost of two prenominal adjectives semantically corresponds to a postnominal one:

(ii)　　the *visible* visible stars ~ the visible stars *visible*　　　　　(Larson 1998: 155)

Alexiadou & Wilder 1998; Ramaglia 2010; Cinque 2010). These two sources have largely been identified with what Sproat and Shih (1988, 1991) label *indirect* modification (IM) and *direct* modification (DM), where indirect modifiers are construed as reduced relative clauses (RRCs). In particular Cinque (2010) elaborates on this distinction and proposes that adnominal adjectives are either generated in a DM-source as specifiers in dedicated functional projections, or in a IM/RRC source as predicates in a reduced relative clause.

Note that the notion *source* actually has two components: a positional/ structural one and a formal one. It can make reference to the *position where* the modifier is merged: direct modifiers are merged closer to the noun, indirect modifiers are merged further away or, in structural terms, they are merged above direct modifiers. But it can also make reference as to *how* the modifier is merged: indirect modifiers are merged *as* (predicates in) reduced relative clauses, direct modifiers are merged *as* specifiers of functional heads. There might be a third component, namely: semantic interpretation (of a modifier) associated with a respective source. Cinque (2010: 5–34) discusses those semantic differences in great detail: direct modifiers are *individual-level, non-restrictive, non-intersective, possibly idiomatic*, etc.; indirect modifiers are *stage-level, restrictive, intersective, only literal*, etc. With reference to Bolinger (1967), he identifies DM with reference modification and IM with referent modification, see above. Thus we can add: direct modifiers are *possibly intensional*, indirect modifiers are *strictly extensional*. Note also that, according to Cinque (2010: 17) all semantic "values necessarily go together", i.e. whenever, for instance, a given adjective is non-intersective it is necessarily also non-restrictive, etc. and vice versa.

For the following discussion, I will distinguish between IM/DM *readings/ properties* (as specified by Cinque), and direct/indirect *modifiers* themselves. Also where relevant, I will distinguish between the two components of *source* mentioned above. Notably this will be the case in Section 4, where I will show that (IV) might be argued to instantiate a third source – but only with respect to position; with respect to form, I will argue that they are indirect modifiers.

2.2 (Non-) restrictivity

As mentioned in the previous subsection, on Cinque's (2010) account, indirect modifiers are restrictive, and direct modifiers are non-restrictive. The way he presents the data (Chapters 2 and 3; pp. 5–34) seems to suggest that he assumes that direct modifiers have a property called *non-restrictivity*. This assumption is problematic as I will show in the following.

Restrictive modifiers are usually thought of as "partitive lexical items that select a subset in the class denoted by the noun they are predicated of" (Eguren 2009: 72);

thus "a modifier M is restrictive if the set of objects denoted by a modified head MH is properly contained in the denotation of the head H alone" (Alexiadou 2012: 1). In other words, a restrictive modifier.

A.) *creates* a proper subset of the set denoted by the noun it modifies, and
B.) *identifies* that subset (= indicates that at least one alternative non-empty subset is accessible)[5]

Even though something more might be said about certain details, it is, in principle clear, what a restrictive modifier is. It is less obvious, however, what exactly a *non-restrictive* modifier is, for we can distinguish several cases of adjectives that are *not* restrictive:

1.) <u>The adjective does *not create a (proper) subset* in the first place</u>. Here, the set theoretic distinction between *subset* and *element* is crucial:

(7) a_1. $x \in \{x, y \ldots\}$ b_1. $\{x\} \in \{\{x\}, \{y\} \ldots\}$ element
       a_2. $\{x\} \subset \{x, y \ldots\}$ b_2. $\{\{x\}\} \subset \{\{x\}, \{y\} \ldots\}$ subset

(8)   a.   The <u>French</u> president talked about the <u>Russian</u> president
       b.   The redhaired <u>French president</u>, not the blond one

A modified N like "French president" seems to denote something that is a part of a set of presidents. But here it is important to note that relational nouns like "president" denote functions from individuals to truth values (sets of ordered pairs), not sets of individuals, and that *thematic* adjectives like "French" do not create a *subset* in a set of presidents. Rather they fill an argument slot, and once that argument slot is filled, a modified NP like "French president" (~ "president of France") has a common noun denotation, i.e. a set of individuals.

There are two different ways to contextualize that set. From a "contemporary" perspective, as in (8a), that set is a singleton since there is, at any given moment, only one French president (and only one Russian president, etc.). Given a set PS of presidents of states, such singleton sets are *elements*, not *subsets* of PS, as in (7b). From a "historical" perspective, the denotation of a modified NP like "French president" is the set F of all French presidents, which, in turn, may have

---

5. Note the importance of the qualifying term 'proper(ly)'. Technically, every set is a (non-proper) subset of itself. Thus, in case the noun denotation is a singleton, there is a (non-empty) subset that could be targeted by a modifier without there being any alternative (non-empty) subset. 'Singleton' must be understood in a contextually relativized sense: NPs like "president (of country X)" have a typical use in which they, at any given moment, denote sets with exactly one member, as in (8a).

all kinds of subsets like the set of those elements of F that are blond, etc., as in (8b). Crucially, it is never the thematic adjective "French" that creates a subset. As a consequence, these adjectives can never be restrictive given the definition above. Something similar may be said about *intensional* adjectives. Somebody who is an alleged thief is not necessarily an actual thief, i.e. they are, at best, a member of a set of *potential* thieves; a former president is *no longer* a member of the set of presidents. These adjectives never create subsets in the N denotation, and thus cannot be restrictive.

2.) The adjective does *not identify a subset*:

(9) Noam Chomsky gave a talk at the conference [...]
    The famous linguist criticized that ...

A modified NP like "famous linguist" as such, obviously, denotes a set of individuals which is a proper subset of the set of all linguists (not all linguists are famous). In this sense, clause A of the definition above applies. Nonetheless, the adjective "famous" in (9) does not single out a particular subset of all linguists that in turn contributes to identifying the DP referent; the referent is already known. Here we see that the referential status of the whole DP may have an impact on the way the adjective is construed in the sense that *not identifying a referent* entails *not identifying a subset in the N denotation*. Note that this entailment does not work the other way round: certain adjectives cannot identify subsets in the N denotation because they do not create subsets in the first place, but they may still make a contribution to determining the DP referent, as in (8a). DPs like 'the famous linguist' in (9) will be discussed in more detail in 3.2.

3.) The adjective predicates a property over an already fully *established* and *identifiable referent*. The "by the way" (BTW) test may be used as a diagnostic for these cases:

(10) John   was watching   the blue sky
     ~John   was watching   the sky, which BTW was blue at that moment

Under the assumption that DPs, rather than smaller projections, denote identifiable referents, it seems reasonable on semantic grounds to assume that such adjectives are merged outside DP. In Section 4, I will show that (IV) adjectives provide morpho-syntactic evidence to corroborate this assumption, at least for Icelandic.

Presumably, there are other instances of adjectives that are not restrictive for similar or different reasons. The upshot of this subsection was merely to show that the concept *non-restrictiveness* is not as strictly defined as *restrictiveness*. Therefore, unless specified more precisely, it is not a very reliable criterion. On the other hand,

I will show that *restrictiveness* (as defined here) is not too useful when it comes to characterizing (I)–(IV) either. In particular, the assumption that restrictive modifiers are indirect modifiers will turn out to be problematic.

3. The "Weak" patterns

Icelandic adjectives come with two sets of inflections, the so-called weak inflection and the strong one (see Section 4). The weak inflection is restricted in its occurrence to definite adnominal contexts; adjectives show up weakly inflected when occurring in definite noun phrases, i.e. when c-commanded by a definite determiner. This section gives a brief characterization and comparison of the "weak" patterns (I)–(III).

3.1 Indirect modifiers – Direct modifiers

Many authors have claimed that a (I) adjective has a restrictive interpretation, whereas (II) adjectives cannot have that interpretation (Vangsnes 1999: Footnote 24; Roehrs 2006: 120–36; Thráinsson 2005: 76/7, 2007: 3/4, 89; Pfaff 2007, 2009). In addition, Pfaff (2007, 2009) argues that a (III) adjective is non-restrictive as well, and claims that the parameter [+/–RESTRICTIVE] is the distinctive feature that sets (I) apart from (II)/(III). Now, given the assumption that "non-restrictive modifiers are only direct modifiers and restrictive ones only indirect modifiers derived from a reduced relative clause source" (Cinque 2010: 140/1), one could conclude from the empirical claims above that a.) (I) adjectives are indirect modifiers, i.e. reduced relative clauses, and b.) adjectives in (II)/(III) DPs are direct modifiers. Cinque himself (ibid.) suggests the former.[6]

It is certainly true that an adjective in a (I) DP can be restrictive as defined in 2.2 (and it may be paraphrased by a restrictive RC). It is also true that (II) and (III) adjectives are typically not restrictive, in so far as they often merely emphasizes a known or implied property of the unique element in the N denotation, for instance:

(11) a. rauði bíll-inn ~ bíll-inn sem er rauð.ur   (I)
       red car-DEF   car-DEF that is red.STR

    b. hin gullna sól   (II)
       ART golden sun

---

6. See also (Alexiadou 2012: 1): "the syntax of restrictive modifiers [...] is tied to the syntax of indirect modification [...] [which] has the syntax of relative clauses."

c. *fjármálaráðherra-nn   umdeildi* (III)
   minister-of-finance-DEF controversial

Also, (II) and/or (III) are the unmarked patterns for a range of inherently non-intersective, intensional (DM) adjectives, where (I) is strongly marked or bad (Example (12) is taken from Pfaff 2007: 47):

(12) a. #*svokallaða afstæðiskenning-in* (I)
        so-called   theory-of-relativity-DEF

 b. <u>*hin svokallaða afstæðiskenning*</u> (II)
    ART so-called theory-of-relativity

 c. <u>*afstæðiskenning-in   svokallaða*</u> (III)
    theory-of-relativity-DEF so-called

(13)[7] a₁. ??*meinti ræningi-nn* (I)
            alleged robber-DEF

 a₂. <u>*hinn meinti ræningi*</u> (II)
     ART alleged robber

 a₃. #*ræningi-nn meinti* (III)
     robber-DEF alleged

 b₁. ??*fyrrverandi forseti-nn* (I)
     former   president-DEF

 b₂. ??*hinn fyrrverandi forseti* (II)
     ART former   president

 b₃. <u>*forseti-nn   fyrrverandi*</u> (III)
     president-DEF former

Thus (11)–(13) seem to confirm conclusions a.) and b.). Upon a closer look, however, the above empirical claims turn out to be somewhat idealizing and do no capture all the data and phenomena. First of all, adjectives in (I) DPs do not necessarily have a restrictive reading:

(14) a. *Hvíta hús-ið* ≠ *húsið sem er hvít.t*
        white house-DEF ≠ 'the house that is white.STR'

 b. *Kalda stríð-ið*
    cold war-DEF

 c. *Franska bylting-in*
    French revolution-DEF

---

7. The unmarked pattern for *meintur* "alleged" is (II), whereas it is (III) in the case of *fyrrverandi* "former". This latter asymmetry is somewhat surprising given that those two adjectives are usually considered to belong to the same group, cf. Heim and Kratzer (1998: 72). I will not address this issue here in any detail.

Many (I) DPs are used as proper names of objects and events. The respective adjective may have a specialized, non-literal meaning ("cold"), it cannot always be used predicatively (on the relevant reading: "French"), and in case it can be used predicatively ("white"), a restrictive relative clause is not an adequate paraphrase. This suggests that the adjective involved is a direct modifier. In light of this conclusion, recall Example (5) where it was shown that the non-intersective (and "non-restrictive") THEMATIC reading is only available in (I), whereas in (II) and (III), we only get the intersective PROVENANCE reading. On a strict interpretation (non-intersective = DM and intersective = IM) as suggested by Cinque (2010), we would have to conclude that (I) is a DM configuration and (II)/(III) are IM configurations, which is the exact opposite of what was suggested in the beginning of this subsection.

All this taken together seems to suggest that all three weak patterns permit both DM and IM readings, and that there is no one-to-one correspondence between what I call *pattern* and *source* in Cinque's sense. Thus the next conclusion seems to be that weak adjectives can be either indirect or direct modifiers. There is, however, a serious problem with the assumption that adjectives with an apparent IM reading really are indirect modifiers: IM adjectives are assumed to be generated as predicates (in a reduced relative clause), but adjectives in predicative position are always strongly inflected (see Section 4), never weakly. As mentioned above, weak inflection is restricted to *adnominal* adjectives in *definite* noun phrases, and never occurs on adjectives in *predicative* position. This is a rather strong empirical argument against the assumption that weak adjectives may be predicates (in reduced relative clauses), and there are two options to approach this problem:

1. weak adjectives with an IM reading can be construed as predicates after all[8]
2. weak – (I)/(II)/(III) – adjectives are categorically direct modifiers, regardless of IM readings

Alexiadou and Wilder (1998: 309) summarizing Sproat and Shih (1988) argue that "[*d*]*irect modification* [...] permits **intersective** [emphasis mine] and non-intersective modifiers". This view, which differs slightly from the one defended by Cinque, suggests that 2. is indeed a viable option and does not express a

---

8. Ramaglia (2010: 168), for instance, considers the possibility that "at least in some languages and/or constructions – adjectival predication can be derived from an underlying structure" containing a covert nominal. Evidence for this claim is provided by languages that do not allow bare adjectival predicates, but require an overt nominal ("this banana is a tasty *thing*" ~ "this banana is tasty", ibid.: 167). This means that, in some cases, apparently *predicative* adjectives can be construed as underlying *adnominal* adjectives. I leave it to further research to examine to what extent this approach allows us to analyze certain weak adjectives as "predicates".

contradiction in the sense that non-intersectivity is not per se a DM property to begin with. Thus I will choose the second option and conclude that weak adjectives are direct modifiers, not RRCs.

3.2 (Non-) referentiality and appositive descriptions

It has been noted that a (II) DP is "not necessarily referential" (Julien 2005: 57). Referentiality is a rather complex notion not easily defined exhaustively, and I do not attempt to discuss it in detail. For the present purpose, I will employ the auxiliary notions DEICTIC and ANAPHORIC properties. A property is thus DEICTIC iff it contributes to *identifying* a referent. A property is ANAPHORIC if it does not contribute to identifying a referent, but is presupposed to hold of the referent. By extension, a DP is DEICTIC iff it, by means of its descriptive/lexical content, identifies its referent. A DP is ANAPHORIC, on the other hand, if it does not identify its referent via its descriptive/lexical content, but presupposes that the referent is already identified/known and has the property denoted by its descriptive content. Given this definition, saying that (II) DPs are not referential amounts to saying that they are not DEICTIC (but they may be ANAPHORIC).

In order to illustrate this, let us have a look at a typical use of (II) which we may call *appositive description* (AD). An AD is a definite A + N description that applies to a specific given/known referent. We can distinguish two instances:

1.) The AD occurs *together with* a proper name (examples/judgments are taken from Thráinsson 2007: 4 and 89, respectively):

(15) a$_1$. *Hin vinsæla hljómsveit 4 x 100 leikur fyrir dansi*
      ART popular band   4 x 100 plays for dance

   a$_2$. #*Vinsæla hljómsveit-in 4 x 100*
      popular band-DEF   4 x 100

   b$_1$. *hinn þekkti leikari Clint Eastwood*
      ART known actor C. E.

   b$_2$. #*þekkti leikari-nn Clint Eastwood*
      known actor-DEF C. E.

2.) The AD *stands for* a known referent. For instance, if a referent has been introduced into the discourse, usually by name, and is uniquely salient, an AD can be used ANAPHORICALLY to "refer" back to it:

(16) [*Noam Chomsky flytti ræðu á ráðstefnunni* ...]
    [N. C. gave a speech at the conference ...]

   Hinn frægi málfræðingur gagnrýndi að ...
   ART famous linguist criticized that

This latter variant is often found in certain kinds of written language, typically, in order to avoid repetition. Crucially, the (II) DP is not DEICTIC, and hence does not actually refer (= *identify* a referent) in the above sense. Rather, the complex A–N property *famous linguist* is presented as a 'known property of the known referent'; it is presupposed (by the speaker) to hold of the uniquely identifiable referent.

The ANAPHORIC and the DEICTIC versions of a DP like 'the famous linguist' differ in terms of presuppositions. I will assume that the standard treatment of definite descriptions as given in Heim and Kratzer (1998:73–85) roughly corresponds to what I call the DEICTIC use. Thus the DEICTIC version, which can only be expressed by the corresponding (I) version, presupposes that, in a given situation, there is exactly one individual who is a famous linguist, and if that is the case, the DP denotes that unique individual. The descriptive content *famous linguist* determines the conditions under which a specific indivdual is picked out, i.e. identified. In the ANAPHORIC version, on the other hand, the same descriptive content does not specify any conditions in order for a referent to be identified; the referent is known and thus already identified. It does, however, introduce a different presupposition, namely that the description *famous linguist* applies to the known referent. In semantic terms: iff Noam Chomsky is a famous linguist, the (II) DP in (16) denotes Noam Chomsky; practically, it means that the speaker assumes that Noam Chomsky is a famous linguist.

Note that (III) DPs are also frequently used as ADs:

(17) a. *málfræðingur-inn frægi*　　　　　　　　　　　　cf. (16)
　　　　linguist-DEF　famous

　　　b. *leikari-nn þekkti Clint Eastwood*　　　　　　　cf. (15b)
　　　　actor-DEF　known　C.　E.

(I) versions of (15)–(17) are considered bad in this use on the conservative view, but it has already been pointed out that many speakers actually consider those acceptable, see in particular the scores in (4). This means that (I) DPs are not categorically banned from the AD use, even though they are, for many speakers, a marked option.

Abstracting away from individual cases, we can say that (II) and (III) adjectives are ANAPHORIC and (I) adjectives may be ANAPHORIC given certain conditions.[9] On the other hand, only (I) adjectives can be DEICTIC. This indicates that it is not,

---

9. Apart from speaker variation, the kind of adjective seems to play a role; nationality adjectives are more natural in (I) than "popular", "known" or "famous", see (15)/(16):

(i)　*bandaríski leikari-nn Clint Eastwood*
　　　American actor-DEF C. E.

strictly speaking, *pattern* as such that receives an interpretation, but more primitive elements that interact in various ways. On a related note, the adjective 'famous' in (16)/(17) is arguably not restrictive, cf. 2.2. Given that the account given above is on the right track, we can see this as a result of the adjective's not being DEICTIC. This, in turn, means that only DEICTIC adjectives can be restrictive. But then, if (I)–(III) can be characterized in terms of DEICTIC/ANAPHORIC properties, it may also be taken to indicate that the notion *restrictiveness* is no longer required.

The discussion so far has focused on DEICTIC/ANAPHORIC adjectives, but note that in (16), the entire description *famous linguist* is an ANAPHORIC property including the property denoted by the noun. Also note, that, when there is no adjective, DEF is obligatorily attached to the noun: *málfræðingur-inn* "linguist-DEF". This DP may be used ANAPHORICALLY, for instance in (16) instead of (II) or (III); the adjective "famous" does not contribute identifying information, i.e. it is not DEICTIC, thus it may be omitted. The same DP may also be used DEICTICALLY, i.e. in order to pick out a certain linguist out of a group of people. Since DEF is used in both (I) and (III), it is a legitimate question to ask whether we find differences, in particular whether the noun can be DEICTIC while the adjective is ANAPHORIC. The following example seems to point in that direction:

(18) a. *hinn fullkomni glæpur* (II)
      ART perfect   crime

  b. *glæpur-inn fullkomni* (III)
      crime-DEF perfect

  c. *fullkomni glæpur-inn* (I)
      perfect   crime-DEF

(18a) illustrates another typical use of (II), namely to express abstract concepts ("platonic ideas"). Like ADs, these DPs are not DEICTIC, but presumably not ANAPHORIC either since they do not denote a referent at all, i.e. they do not make reference to any particular event, e.g. "John has been trying to commit *the perfect crime* – so far, unsuccessfully". (I) and (III) are bad in this case. Note that adjectives like "perfect" and DPs like "the perfect crime" are generally used descriptively rather than DEICTICALLY, not only in Icelandic. But given an appropriate context, we do find other uses. Imagine a context where a crime has taken place, and its

---

Information structure is another likely factor. Some of my native speaker informants seemed to suggest that the less topical/salient the referent is in an example like (16), the more easily the (I) version can be used. If this turns out to be the case, it could be taken to mean "the less salient the referent, the more DEICTIC the DP" and vice versa. However, this assumption needs to be tested more carefully.

planning and execution may be described as *perfect*. Given this background, the (III) DP in (18b) can be used in a sentence like "*the perfect crime* took place at 8:23 p.m." (I) is bad in this context. This is the case described above: the noun contributes a DEICTIC property, the adjective an ANAPHORIC one. Finally, imagine the somewhat artificial scenario where two crimes have taken place, only one of which may be described as perfect. Here only the (I) version in (18c) can be used in the same sentence: '*the perfect crime* took place at 8:23'.

3.3 Structural relations – Sketch of an analysis

So far, (I)–(III) have been presented as separate constructions that may or may not have certain semantic similarities. There are, however, in addition, systematic structural interactions between them. For instance, when a (I) DP like *kalda stríðið* 'The Cold War', see (14b), combines with an adjective like *svokallaður* 'so-called' which is bad in (I), but fine in (II) and (III), as in (12), we get the following mutations:

(19)   a.   #*svokallaða kalda stríð-ið*   (I)
       b.   *hið svokallaða kalda stríð*   (II)
       c.   *kalda stríð-ið svokallaða*   (I) + (III)
           "the so-called Cold War"

(19c) is particularly illuminating in that it shows that the postnominal adjective takes scope over the prenominal one: *so-called [cold war]*, not: *cold [so-called war]*. This is generally the case in (I) + (III) constellations, which suggests that the postnominal adjective is actually merged higher than the prenominal one:

(20)   a.   *franski forseti-nn   fyrrverandi*
              French   president-DEF   former
              former >> French$_{THEMATIC}$
       b.   *þýski   heimspekingur-inn   snjalli*
              German   philosopher-DEF   brilliant
              brilliant >> German$_{PROVENANCE}$
       c.   *guli   bíll-inn   frægi*
              yellow   car-DEF   famous
              famous >> yellow

These facts suggest that (I)–(III) may be derivationally related. Pfaff (2007, 2009) observes that certain inherently non-restrictive adjectives like *svokallaður* "so-called" are fine in (II) and (III), but bad in (I), as in (12) repeated below as (21):

(21)   a.   #<u>*svokallaða*</u> *afstæðiskenning-<u>in</u>*   (I)
       b.   <u>*hin svokallaða*</u> *afstæðiskenning*   (II)
       c.   *afstæðiskenning-in svokallaða*   (III)

Of particular interest is the position of the adjective relative to the article, note the underlining in (21). On Pfaff's (2009: 48) interpretation, this means that.

> whenever an adjective follows the article, regardless of free or suffixed, it has a non-restrictive reading. If an adjective precedes the article, consequently with a noun intervening between the two, it has a restrictive reading.

In other words, the distinction ART vs. DEF is secondary. Based on this observation, Pfaff develops a novel argument in favour of a 'One-Article analysis'.[10] In structural terms, then, the generalization can be rephrased as follows: The underlying base order is ARTICLE – A – N. If the adjective "stays put" below the article, irrespective of NP movement, it receives a non-restrictive interpretation, cf. (22a/b), but a restrictive one if it moves before the article, as in (22c):[11]

(22) a. *Pattern II:* no movement; adjective "stays put":
[DP article [αP AP [α' α⁰ NP]]]   →   ART A N

b. *Pattern III:* NP-movement; adjective "stays put":
[DP NP$_1$ [D' article [αP AP [α' α⁰ t$_1$]]]]   →   <u>N-DEF</u> A

c. *Pattern I:* aP-movement; adjective moves along:
[DP [αP AP [α' α⁰ NP]]$_1$ [D' article t$_1$]]   →   <u>A N</u>-DEF

This analysis accounts for a range of phenomena that previous – both One-Article and Two-Article – analyses (cf. Footnote 10) do not capture, primarily because those do not take into account postnominal adjectives/(III). It gives an account of

---

10. I.e. the idea that ART and DEF are actually identical at some abstract level. The main motivations for this idea are a.) the complementary distribution of ART and DEF, i.e. no "Double Definiteness", b.) identical inflection of the two, c.) the stem of DEF, *-in-*, appears to be a reduced form of ART, *hin-*. In generative accounts (Magnússon 1984; Sigurðsson 1993; Pfaff 2007, 2009), this idea is interpreted as movement with subsequent clitization, as a result of which ART becomes DEF:

(i) hinn rauði bíll   → [rauði bíll]$_i$ (h)inn t$_i$ → *rauði bíll-inn* 'the red car'

A number of authors have discarded this idea assuming that ART and DEF are two genuinely distinct elements, generated in different structural positions or belonging to two different dialects or grammars (for instance Vangsnes 1999; Julien 2002, 2005; Roehrs 2006).

11. Adjective movement means pied-piping along with the NP. The label αP is adopted from Julien (2002, 2005). Note also that I will use the label DP for the projection headed by the article. This is just for convenience's sake and not meant to indicate that I literally assume that the article is generated in D⁰. The only thing that is relevant for the discussion in this and the next section is the position relative to the article regardless of whether the projection is called DP, ArtP, dP, nP or something else.

why (II) and (III) pattern alike, but are both distinct from (I) in many cases. Also it explains why, in a mixed pattern, the postnominal adjective takes scope over the prenominal one (see above): the lower adjective is pied-piped along with the NP and thus *becomes* 'pre-articular', but *remains* prenominal, whereas the higher one 'stays put' in the 'post-articular' position and thus becomes post-nominal. Note also that in all three constellations in (22), the weak inflection can be triggered the same way in so far as the adjective is c-commanded by the article (before movement).

There are, however, some shortcomings. For instance, the analysis does not explain how exactly the difference in meaning is brought about; it merely states that a 'pre-articular' adjective (after αP-movement) receives a different interpretation than an adjective that remains in 'post-articular' position. Notably, this interpretation is categorically considered to be either restrictive or non-restrictive. This could either mean that the adjective is interpreted non-restrictively upon first merge, and reinterpreted restrictively after movement; or it could mean that it is not interpreted at all before all DP-internal movements have taken place. Either way, we have seen that non-restrictiveness is not a straightforward, unambiguous notion, and that many (I) adjectives are not, in fact, restrictive given the set theoretic definition.

Nonetheless, the structural account of this analysis is quite appealing since it does capture some general insights as stated above. What needs to be modified is the account of the distribution of adjectives across (I)–(III). Without going into any detail, I propose some general modifications addressing certain issues discussed above.

Assume that adjectives by default pied-pipe along with the noun to yield (I), the standard pattern. Assume further that there are certain specifications and restrictions on this default rule such as: the higher up in the extended nominal projection the adjective is merged ("brilliant", "famous"), the more easily it can be stranded in post-articular position, and vice versa, the lower it is merged ("yellow", "German"$_{\text{PROVENANCE}}$), the more urgently it has to move along to the pre-articular position, as in (20b/c), (17) and Footnote 11. Adjectives that are merged extremely low, presumably inside NP ("German"$_{\text{THEMATIC}}$), obligatorily pied-pipe along, as in (5b)/(20a). Likewise, adjectives that are merged extremely high ("so-called") systematically resist pied-piping, as in (12) and (19). To a certain extent, this assumption allows us to account for the increasing acceptance of (I) as a consequence of the restrictions on pied-piping being relaxed.

Note that these restrictions are stated in purely syntactic terms without reference to notions such as (*non-*)*restrictiveness*, etc; but there clearly are additional semantic – information-structural and referential – factors that have an impact on whether NP/αP movement can, must, or must not take place. We have seen, for instance, that descriptive information that is presupposed, i.e. ANAPHORIC properties, may remain in the post-articular position → (II)/(III), whereas identifying information, i.e. DEICTIC properties, needs to be fronted to the pre-articular position → (I)/(I) + (III). Also, if the entire A–N description is neither DEICTIC nor ANAPHORIC, cf. (18a), both A and N remain in postnominal position → (II).

Some aspects need to be considered more carefully, for instance the fact that intensional adjectives like "alleged" and "former" strongly resist fronting. To state that both are not DEICTIC properties requires a more precise definition of that notion. Also it may be pointed out that those adjectives do not denote properties in the first place; but the same may, in principle, be said about thematic adjectives. Nonetheless, the Icelandic data show that there is a genuine difference between the two: thematic adjectives can only occur in a pre-articular position, i.e. (I), as in (5b)/(20a), whereas intensional ones strongly prefer a post-articular position, cf. (12)/(13). This may suggest that the notions DEIXIS/ANAPHORA should, to a certain extent, be made sensitive to *intensionality* in order to distinguish between those two kinds of adjectives; after all, a French president really *is* a president, whereas a former president *is no longer* a president, and an alleged thief is *not necessarily* an actual thief.

I leave a more detailed discussion of those problems and a more precise implementation of the analysis sketched above to further research. However, it should have become clear that there is a way to give a unified account of (I)–(III) that takes into account both syntactic and semantic factors without assuming that some weak adjectives are RRCs/indirect modifiers. In particular, the IM reading *restrictiveness* seems to be entirely dispensable since the facts about (I) can be captured in terms of DEICTIC properties + conditions on pied-piping.

4. Strong adjectives in definite noun phrases are outside DP

The strong inflection is the default adjectival inflection occurring on all kinds of predicative adjectives (copular constructions, secondary predicates, etc.) and adnominal adjectives in indefinite noun phrases. Therefore, (IV) is a somewhat unexpected pattern; the adjective is strongly inflected in spite of its co-occurring with a definite noun (N-DEF). Rögnvaldsson (1984) shows that (IV) DPs are indeed constituents, i.e. extended nominal projections, not merely adjacent AP + NP sequences. It has been observed that such strong adjectives cannot receive a restrictive reading (Rögnvaldsson 1984; Delsing 1993: 132; Roehrs 2006: 133–6; Thráinsson 2005: 77, 2007: 3/4; Sigurðsson 2007: Footnote 3; Pfaff 2009: 55/6, 89). Based on the criterion *non-restrictiveness*, Roehrs (2006: 135/6) suggests a semantic correlation between (IV) and (II), the difference being that (II) belongs to a different grammar called 'Literary Icelandic' that has a syntactic derivation different from 'Colloquial Icelandic', and Cinque (2010: 141/1) proposes that the strong inflection is an overt marking of the DM source. These suggestions are problematic for a range of reasons. (II) and (IV) have rather different functions and behave differently semantically. Notably, they instantiate different kinds of *non-restrictiveness*. Those strong (IV) adjectives that are usually referred to in the literature and that will be discussed here are classified as *adjectival appositives* ("lýsingarorðsviðurlög") in traditional Icelandic grammars. They most certainly are not direct modifiers, but I will show that they can be analyzed as indirect modifiers that are generated outside DP.

In 4.1, I will give a brief characterization of (IV) appositives, and point out a range of distinctive properties, and in 4.2, I will discuss a rather peculiar semantic difference between (I) and (IV). 4.3 mentions some open issues and concludes this section.

4.1 Appositive adjectives

Appositive (IV) adjectives are inherently predicative, can only have a literal meaning, and may be paraphrased with a non-restrictive relative clause ('the X, which BTW ...'), as in (23), or sometimes, an adverbial clause, as in (24). Intensional, non-predicative DM adjectives, on the other hand, cannot be used in pattern IV at all, as in (25):

(23) a. Ég horfði upp í blá.an himin-inn
I looked up into blue.STR sky-DEF
"I looked up into the sky, which happened to be blue/
which BTW was blue (at that moment)" (Thráinsson 2007: 3)

b. Æst.ur skríll-inn ruddist inn í húsið
enraged.STR mob-DEF jostled into the house
"The mob, who was in a rage, stormed the house"

c. ... út um opin.n glugga-nn
... out about open.STR window-DEF
"... out through the *currently* open window/the window, which was open BTW"

(24)[12] a. Ósýnileg.ar stjörnur-nar vörpuðu svolitlu ljósi
invisible.STR stars-DEF cast some light

---

12. Thanks to Höskuldur Þráinsson (p.c.) for (24a); Example (24b) is taken from an instruction leaflet, and (24c) is taken from Thráinsson (2001). Translations are mine. To my knowledge, this adverbial connotation has not been noticed before, but all my informants confirmed this intuition. Note also that Sigurðsson (2007: Footnote 3) states that expressions like *rauður bíllinn* "the red car-(IV)", as in (24c), are used "in formal language"; some of my informants even found the example a bit odd. This is rather interesting considering that *blár himinninn* 'the blue sky-(IV)', as in (23a), is relatively natural and informal, which suggests that it is not colour adjectives per se that are "odd" in (IV). Rather it seems to be depending on the

       aftan   á   skýin
       from-behind on   the clouds
       "The stars – *even though* they were invisible at that moment/
       even though we couldn't see them – cast some light on the
       clouds from behind"
    b. Setja skal   smokkinn á   stíf.an   lim-inn
       set   shall the condom on   stiff.STR   penis-DEF
       "... *while/when* it is hard"
    c. Rauð.ur bíll-inn sást   vel á   dökk.u   slitlagi-nu
       red.STR car-DEF   was-seen well on dark.STR   tarmac-DEF
       "The car, which was *red*, could be seen well on the tarmac,
       which was *dark*"
       ~ "*Because* the car was red, it could be seen well ..."

(25) a. #*meint.ur*   *þjófur-inn*   cf. (13a)
        alleged.STR   thief-DEF
     b. #*svokölluð*   *afstæðiskenning-in*   cf. (12)
        so-called.STR   theory-of-relativity-DEF

In many cases, a (IV) adjective may be described as denoting a transitory state where the respective (IV) DP indicates that that state holds of a referent at a certain time, as in (23)/(24). This should not, however, be taken to indicate that (IV) adjectives denote stage level (SL) properties in the strict sense (cf. Carlson 1977), i.e. temporary *properties of a referent*. While it seems, in principle, possible to construe *being slippery* as a temporary property of a floor, it is not possible to construe it as a temporary property of the ice,[13] and yet, (IV) DPs are perfectly fine in both cases:

(26) a. *hann rann   á   hál.u   gólfi-nu*
        he skidded   on   slippery.STR   floor-DEF
     b. *hann rann   á   hál.num   ís-num*
        he skidded   on   slippery.STR   ice-DEF

Moreover, *ósýnilegar stjörnurnar* "the invisible stars" in (24a) does not mean "(only) those stars that are (currently) invisible" (SL), see Larson (1998) and Cinque (2010). It does not, for that matter, mean "the generally invisible stars" (IL), which could, for instance, be said about black holes. Also, remember Cinque's

---

noun: the colour of a car is usually thought of as a stable, characteristic property, whereas the colour of the sky can easily be perceived as an unstable, accidental property.

13. Ice is slippery as long as it is ice; in this sense, *slipperiness* is actually an IL property. Also, (26b) does not express a contrast between two kinds of ice (slippery vs. non-slippery).

(2010: 17) proposal that all semantic values "necessarily go together"; thus, the values STAGE-LEVEL and RESTRICTIVE should go together, both being IM readings. Since appositive adjectives are unambiguously not restrictive, they cannot be analyzed as SL predicates in this sense either.

Rather, the (IV) adjectives discussed here are more properly described as denoting an *accidental* (external or potential) property of the referent such that the corresponding (IV) DP highlights a circumstantial aspect of the referent, which is indicated by the fact that they can be paraphrased by an adverbial clause in many cases. This means that those adjectives do not identify a referent, nor do they denote a known/characteristic property of a known referent.[14] In this respect, strong appositive adjectives are very different from adjectives in the weak patterns. In particular, they cannot be direct modifiers because they are only predicative and non-intensional, only have literal meaning, and do not modify *reference*. Moreover, according to Cinque's (2010) criteria, they cannot be indirect modifiers either because they are clearly not restrictive (which is actually expected if they are appositives). But if they are neither indirect nor direct modifiers, we apparently have to conclude that they are generated/merged in yet another source other than DM/RRC.

Here it is crucial to recall that the notion *source* actually has two components, a positional one and a formal one, see 2.1, and there is reason to believe that, formally, appositive (IV) adjectives are, in fact, indirect modifiers that only differ with respect to position from those discussed by Cinque. Note, for instance, that these adjectives, in contrast to the weak adjectives, fulfill all criteria for "relative clausehood": they are predicative, they can be paraphrased with a (non-restrictive) relative/adverbial clause, and most importantly, they are strongly inflected. Sproat and Shih (1991: 574/5) show that *de*-modifiers in Chinese[15] may "occur either inside or outside specifiers", where 'specifier', in current terminology, means 'determiner' ($\rightarrow$ DP). This 'outside' – 'inside' distinction is overtly marked: in the former case, the *de*-modifier precedes the determiner, in the latter case, it follows it. Those modifiers occurring 'outside' are non-restrictive/appositive, but the ones occurring 'inside' are restrictive. There is an obvious parallelism between the outside modifiers in Chinese and the (IV) appositives in Icelandic: both correspond to (reduced) *non-restrictive* relative clauses.[16] This parallelism strongly suggests that (IV) appositives are also merged 'outside' DP. I therefore propose that appositive (IV) adjectives are merged as RRCs in a position structurally higher than the one

---

14. NB: classificatory (NATIONALITY) adjectives are bad in (IV).

15. NB: *De* modifiers are IM modifiers; moreover, the particle *de* is attached to relative clauses.

16. Likewise, there is a parallelism between the 'inside' modifiers in Chinese and indirect modifiers as characterized by Cinque: both correspond to (reduced) *restrictive* relative clauses.

where restrictive RRCs are merged, namely outside/above DP. In fact, following Sproat and Shih (1991), I suggest that this structural difference is the reason for their being interpreted non-restrictively, as in (10)/Section 2.1.

What remains to be done is to show that (IV) adjectives really are merged outside DP. Strong morpho-syntactic evidence in favour of this assumption is provided by the very fact that (IV) adjectives are strongly inflected. As was mentioned above, adjectives inside a definite DP are weakly inflected, where 'inside' essentially means 'being c-commanded by a definite determiner', as in Section 3. If, on the other hand, the adjective is actually merged outside DP, thus not c-commanded by a definite determiner, obviously, the weak inflection cannot be triggered. From a semantic point of view, the BTW paraphrases, as in (23) indicate that (IV) adjectives say something extra about a referent that is already fully established. If, as already suggested in 2.2, it is DP, rather than a smaller projection, that denotes an identifiable referent, it seems reasonable to assume that (IV) constellations as illustrated above actually consist of an identifiable referent (DP) plus extra information (AP). In the next subsection, it will provide further evidence to substantiate this claim.

4.2 Temporal dependence vs. Temporal independence

Musan (1999) shows that definite/presuppositional noun phrases may be temporally independent, i.e. denote a property that applies to its referent at a time distinct from the time denoted by the tense of the sentence, whereas indefinite/non-presuppositional noun phrases are always temporally dependent. Pfaff (2013) and Rapp (2013) show that this also applies to adnominal participle phrases (in German):

(27) a. *Ein tanzender Mann saß an der Bar*
 a dancing man sat at the bar
 b. *Der tanzende Mann saß an der Bar*
 the dancing man sat at the bar

The indefinite DP in (27a) only has the pragmatically odd reading that some man was simultaneously dancing and sitting at the bar, whereas the definite DP in (27b), when properly contextualized, can easily mean that a certain man was dancing at some time t_1, but sitting at the bar at t_2, viz. in those cases where the property denoted by the participle contributes to identifying the DP referent.

With this in mind, consider the (I) and (IV) versions of the DP 'the drunk boy' in three slightly differing scenarios; the speaker is describing the events at a party:

(28) [... some **boy** was really annoying; I was talking to a friend...]
 a. ... *þegar #full.i / full.ur strákur-inn réðst á mig*
 ... when drunk.#WK/STR boy-DEF attacked me
 [... some **drunk boy** was really annoying ... I was talking to a friend ...]

b. ... þegar full.i / full.ur   strákur-inn réðst á   mig
    ... when drunk.WK/STR boy-DEF   attacked me

The (I) version in (28a) is infelicitous because it tries to identify a "drunk boy", but the discourse domain only contains a "boy". The (IV) version, on the other hand, is basically fine. It does not identify a referent as "drunk boy", but rather describes the circumstances: "the boy was drunk when he attacked me." If the discourse domain does contain a referent that has been introduced as "drunk boy", (28b), both (I) and (IV) are fine given the difference *identification of a referent* vs. *description of the circumstances*. But now see what happens when the boy's being drunk and his attacking the speaker are presented as occurring at different times:

[*continuation of (28b)*: ... two days later I went back there.
    I had hardly entered the house ...]
c. ... þegar full.i/#full.ur strákur-inn réðst aftur á mig
    (þótt hann væri alsgáður núna)
    ... when drunk.WK/#STR boy-DEF attacked me again
    (although he was sober now)

The scenario is similar to the example "the dancing man" in (27b); two different events occurring at two different times. Only the (I) DP is fine in this context. This means, in particular, that the weak adjective is temporally independent in the sense above. The property it denotes may apply to a referent at a time distinct from the time denoted by the tense of the sentence. Therefore "the drunk boy ... was sober" does not express a contradiction. This is expected given the (I) adjective's DEICTIC function to *identify* a (discourse) referent, but also predicted by Musan's account because definite DPs are presuppositional and *weak* adjectives are *inside* the definite DP. The (IV) DP, on the other hand, is infelicitous in this context since it can only mean that the boy's being drunk and his attacking temporally coincide. Thus the temporal anchoring of the state of being drunk denoted by the strong adjective cannot co-vary according to the discourse representation of the referent, which means that it is not temporally independent the same way the weak adjective is. Now if temporal independence is a property of definite noun phrases, which can be shown to also apply to subconstituents like participles and weak adjectives, it follows that strong (IV) adjectives are not a part of that definite noun phrase.

4.3 Expressives and appositives

Note that (IV) adjectives have another use I will only briefly mention here, namely as expressives (*bölvaður* 'damn, bloody'). They differ from appositives in not being predicative, therefore they cannot be merged as RRCs, but they illustrate something else. On the few occasions where a strong and a weak adjective co-occur, the strong one necessarily precedes the weak one:

(29) bölvað.ur   gaml.i   níðingur-inn
     bloody.STR old.WK   scoundrel-DEF

As for semantic commonalities: both appositives and expressives presuppose an already fully established (DP) referent. For a more detailed discussion of this last point, see Potts (2005, 2007).

All the examples given in this section along with their morphological, syntactic and semantic properties provide overwhelming evidence for the assumption that appositive adjectives, or (IV) adjectives more generally, are merged outside DP.

One final comment: I have adopted the term *adjectival appositive* following the Icelandic terminology without indicating to what extent those adjectives correspond to appositive constructions in other languages. But even when looking only at Icelandic, it is crucial to note that there are at least two different kinds of adjectival appositives,[17] the (IV) adjectives discussed above, and adjectives in free apposition. The latter are also plausibly analyzed as some kind of RRCs with the difference that they are "less" reduced than (IV) adjectives because they can have a PP complement, as in (30a), as can adjectives in copular constructions, cf. (30b), whereas (IV) adjectives (actually, adnominal adjectives in general) do not allow PP complements, as in (30c):

(30) a. Maðurinn, stolt.ur   af syni sínum, sagði við   kennarann
        the man,   proud.STR   of son his,   said   to the   teacher ...

     b. Maðurinn er stolt.ur   af syni sínum
        the man   is proud.STR   of son his

     c. *⟨af syni sínum⟩ stolt.ur   ⟨af syni sínum⟩ maður-inn
         ⟨of son his⟩   proud.STR   ⟨of son his⟩   man-DEF

5. Conclusion – Open issues

I have argued that weak adjectives are best analysed as direct modifiers even though they may have interpretations that some authors associate with indirect modification, in particular [+RESTRICTIVE], and that, if there is anything that should be construed as reduced relative clauses, i.e. as indirect modifiers, it is

---

17. In addition to what I called *appositive descriptions* in 3.2. Here it is not the adjective that is outside, rather the entire DP is outside another DP: [the known actor [_DP Clint Eastwood]]

strong (appositive (IV)) adjectives, even though they are [−RESTRICTIVE]. In addition to this formal distinction, I argued for a structural distinction: weak adjectives are merged below the definite article, strong adjectives above. Both conclusions are actually in line with the ordering suggested for instance in Cinque (2010), as diagrammed here:

(31)   A.STR (IM) >> ARTICLE >> A.WK (DM) >> N

I showed that a range of morphological and semantic facts automatically follow from this structure: weak inflection is always triggered when the adjective is c-commanded by the article: (I)–(III). (IV) is not an exception to this rule since the respective adjective is not c-commanded by the article to begin with. (IV) adjectives can never be restrictive because they are merged 'outside' DP, i.e. at a stage where the DP referent has already been established. This, in turn, entails that (IV) adjectives can never contribute to identifying the referent, and thus they cannot be temporally independent in Musan's (1999) sense as certain weak adjectives.

As for the notion *restrictiveness* as understood in the literature, I have argued that, at least for Icelandic, it is not very helpful since it does not distinguish one pattern from another. Some (I) adjectives may be construed as restrictive, but that does not mean that they are RRCs. Other (I) adjectives, (II)/(III) adjectives and (IV) adjectives, on the other hand can be argued to not be restrictive, but as I have shown they are *not restrictive* for different reasons. Also note that I have used *restrictiveness* as a complex notion consisting of two components: *creating* a subset and *identifying* a subset. The former may be construed as genuine adjectival modification depending on the lexical properties of an adjective (and, as a matter of fact, the properties of the noun it combines with): only predicative (intersective and subsective) adjectives create subsets in the N denotation. The latter, on the other hand, is more properly described in terms of information structure or referentiality.

References

Alexiadou, Artemis. 2001. Adjective syntax and noun raising: Word order asymmetries in the DP as the result of adjective distribution. *Studia Linguistica* 55(3): 217–48.
Alexiadou, Artemis. 2012. On the syntactic reality of restrictive adjectival modification. Workshop on Semantic and Pragmatic Properties of (Non-)Restrictivity, University of Stuttgart, March 19/20, 2012.
Alexiadou, Artemis & Wilder, Chris. 1998. Adjectival modification and multiple determiners. In *Possessors, Predicates and Movement in the DP* [Linguistics Aktuell/Linguistics Today 22], Artemis Alexiadou & Chris Wilder (eds), 303–332. Amsterdam: John Benjamins.
Bolinger, Dwight. 1967. Adjectives in English: Attribution and predication. *Lingua* 18: 1–34.

Carlson, Greg. 1977. Reference to Kinds in English. Ph.D. dissertation, University of Massachusetts at Amherst.
Cinque, Guglielmo. 2010. *The Syntax of Adjectives: A Comparative Study.* Cambridge MA: The MIT Press.
Delsing, Lars-Olof. 1993. The Internal Structure of Noun Phrases in the Scandinavian Languages: A Comparative Study. Ph.D. dissertation, Lund University.
Eguren, Luis. 2009. Adjectives and deleted nominals in Spanish. In *Selected Papers from 'Going Romance' 2007.* [Romance Languages and Linguistic Theory 1], Enoch Aboh, Elisabeth van der Linden, Josep Quer & Petra Sleeman (eds), 67–86. Amsterdam: John Benjamins.
Heim, Irene & Kratzer, Angelika. 1998. *Semantics in Generative Grammar.* Oxford: Blackwell.
Julien, Marit. 2002. Determiners and word order in Scandinavian DPs. *Studia Linguistica* 56(3): 265–315.
Julien, Marit. 2005. *Nominal Phrases from a Scandinavian Perspective* [Linguistik Aktuell/Linguistics Today 87]. Amsterdam: John Benjamins.
Larson, Richard. 1998. Events and Modification in Nominals. In *Proceedings from Semantics and Linguistic Theory (SALT) VIII*, Devon Strolovitch & Aaron Lawson (eds), 145–168. Ithaca NY: Cornell University Press.
Magnússon, Friðrík. 1984. Um innri gerð nafnliða í íslensku (On the internal structure of noun phrases in Icelandic). *Íslenskt Mál* 6: 81–111.
Musan, Renate. 1999. Temporal interpretation and information-status of noun phrases. *Linguistics and Philosophy* 22: 621–661.
Pfaff, Alexander. 2007. Eitt eða tvennt? Ákveðinn greinir í íslensku (One or two? The definite article in Icelandic). BA thesis, University of Iceland, Reykjavík.
Pfaff, Alexander. 2009. Structural Relations between Free and Suffixed Articles in Icelandic. MA thesis, University of Tübingen.
Pfaff, Alexander. 2013. On the temporal reference of present participles. In *Situationsargumente im Nominalbereich: Linguistische Arbeiten*, Christian Fortmann, Wilhelm Geuder, Anja Lübbe & Irene Rapp (eds). Berlin: Mouton de Gruyter.
Potts, Christopher. 2005. *The Logic of Conventional Implicatures* [Oxford Studies in Theoretical Linguistics]. Oxford: OUP.
Potts, Christopher. 2007. The expressive dimension. *Theoretical Linguistics* 33: 165–197.
Ramaglia, Francesca. 2010. *Adjectives at the Syntax-Semantics Interface.* [Lincom Studies in Theoretical Linguistics 45]. München: Lincom.
Rapp, Irene. 2013. On the temporal interpretation of present participles in German. *Journal of Semantics.*
Roehrs, Dorian. 2006. The Morpho-Syntax of the Germanic Noun Phrase: Determiners MOVE into the Determiner Phrase. Ph.D. dissertation, Indiana University.
Rögnvaldsson, Eiríkur. 1984. Af lýsingarorðsviðurlögum (On adjectival appositives). *Íslenskt Mál* 6: 57–80.
Sadler, Louisa & Arnold, Douglas. 1994. Prenominal adjectives and the phrasal/lexical distinction. *Journal of Linguistics* 30: 187–226.
Sigurðsson, Halldór Ármann. 1993. The structure of the Icelandic NP. *Studia Linguistica* 47(2): 177–97.
Sigurðsson, Halldór Ármann. 2007. The Icelandic noun phrase: Central traits. *Arkiv för Nordisk Filologi* 121: 193–236.
Sproat, Richard & Shih, Chilin. 1988. Prenominal adjectival ordering in English and Mandarin. *Proceedings of the* 18th *Annual Meeting of the North East Linguistics Society*, 465–489.

Sproat, Richard & Shih, Chilin. 1991. The Cross-linguistic distribution of adjective ordering restrictions. In *Interdisciplinary Approaches to Language: Essays in Honor of S.-Y. Kuroda*, Carol Georgopoulos & Roberta Ishihara (eds), 565–593. Dordrecht: Kluwer.

Thráinsson, Höskuldur. 2001. Íslensk setningafræði (Icelandic syntax). Course manuscript, University of Iceland, autumn 2001. ⟨https://notendur.hi.is//~hoski/islensksetn.html⟩

Thráinsson, Höskuldur. 2005. Setningar: Handbók um setningafræði. *Íslensk Tunga III*. Reykjavík: Almenna bókafélagið.

Thráinsson, Höskuldur. 2007. *The Syntax of Icelandic*. Cambridge: CUP.

Vangsnes, Øystein Alexander. 1999. Identification and the role of morphology in the Scandinavian noun phrase. Ms, University of Bergen.

Adjectives in German and Norwegian
Differences in weak and strong inflections*

Dorian Roehrs & Marit Julien
University of North Texas / Lund University

In this paper, we demonstrate that adjective endings in the Germanic languages do not pattern uniformly. We illustrate this with nine syntactic contexts: possessives involving proper names and pronominals, embedded and unembedded proper names, "disagreeing" pronominal DPs, appositives, definite adjectives, vocatives, and discontinuous noun phrases. We show that German is subject to lexical and structural conditions but Scandinavian is semantic in nature. In German, the weak endings are feature-reduced forms, which always have a specific local relation to a certain type of determiner, which triggers the relevant feature reduction. Adopting Distributed Morphology, this reduction in features is implemented by Impoverishment. In Scandinavian, the weak endings are an agreement reflex of a semantic feature. We follow others in that adjectives are in – what is traditionally called – Spec,AgrP. We propose that the relevant semantic feature is on Agr and the adjective agrees with it. Given the language-specific conditions, the strong endings surface in the remaining contexts in both types of languages as the elsewhere case.

1. Introduction

As is well known, adjectives may vary in their morphological form. In German and in the Scandinavian languages, attributive adjectives alternate between "weak" and "strong" forms. The latter are terms coined by Jacob Grimm (1870: 718–756), where weak endings on adjectives (German: *-n, -e*; Norwegian: *-e*) surface with definite articles. In contrast, strong endings on adjectives appear with indefinite articles and are more diverse; that is, they show more distinctions overtly (German: *-r, -s, -m, -n, -e*; Norwegian: *-t, -Ø, -e*). Consider (1) and (2):

---

* We thank the audience at the conference *Adjectives in Germanic and Romance: Variation and Change* (University of Amsterdam) and our two reviewers for questions and comments.

(1) a. *das große Haus* (German)
    the big(WK) house
    "the big house"

  b. *ein großes Haus*
    a big(ST) house
    "a big house"

(2) a. *det store   hus-et* (Norwegian)
    the big(WK) house-DEF
    "the big house"

  b. *et stort   hus*
    a big(ST) house
    "a big house"

In light of these facts, it might be tempting to relate the weak endings to definiteness and the strong endings to indefiniteness in both German and Norwegian. However, discussing cases like (3), where a weak adjectival form occurs in an indefinite context, Harbert (2007:135) states that German "has lost all association with definiteness" but that continental Scandinavian has brought the weak/strong contrast "fully into line with the definiteness/indefiniteness opposition."

(3) *mit einem alten   Wein* (German)
    with an   old(WK) wine
    "with an old wine"

Restricting their attention to the canonical cases, a number of authors have tried to provide a uniform account for this alternation in Germanic. For instance, Leu (2008) argues that adjectives may, under certain conditions, raise in front of the strong inflection and Schoorlemmer (2009) proposes an Agree-based account. Despite these unifying (i.e. theoretically attractive) analyses, we will argue in this paper that the distribution of strong and weak forms is not regulated by the same principles in German and continental Scandinavian, exemplified here by Norwegian. Considering constructions that are less commonly discussed in this regard, we will confirm Harbert's assessment. We propose that the weak endings are feature-reduced forms in German but that they reflect agreement with definiteness in Norwegian. The strong endings are the elsewhere case in both languages.

Note that at first glance, the last statement is admittedly counterintuitive. However, as we will see, the distribution of the weak adjectival endings has something in common: a specific structure in German and definiteness in Norwegian. In contrast, the distribution of the strong endings is heterogeneous: the relevant structures in German cover a wide range of different syntactic constructions and the semantics in Norwegian involves indefiniteness as well as non-definiteness (i.e. predication).

2. Adjectives in definite contexts

The following sets of data involve overtly definite contexts where German has consistently strong adjectives but Norwegian has weak ones.[1] We begin with Saxon genitives, shown in (4).

(4) a. *Peters großes Auto* (German)
    Peter's big(ST) car
    "Peter's big car"

  b. *Pers store bil* (Norwegian)
    Per's big(WK) car
    "Per's big car"

In pronominal DPs, the pronominal determiner may morphologically "disagree" with the adjective and noun, as in (5), where a morphologically plural pronominal co-occurs with a singular adjective and a singular noun:[2]

(5) a. *Sie dummer Idiot!* (German)
    you stupid(ST) idiot
    "You stupid idiot!"

  b. *De dumme idiot!* (Norwegian)
    you stupid(WK) idiot
    "You stupid idiot!"

Appositives involving third-person pronouns separated from a following adjective and noun by comma intonation show the same pattern, see (6), and so do constructions where proper names involving an adjective are embedded in a definite DP, as in (7).

(6) a. *er, begeisterter Linguist* (German)
    he, enthusiastic(ST) linguist
    "he, enthusiastic linguist"

  b. *han, gamle mann-en* (Norwegian)
    he, old(WK) man-DEF
    "he, that old man"

---

1. All the relevant data points here are in the nominative or accusative. Also, since the adjective ending *-e* in Norwegian is ambiguous in the plural between being weak and strong, we provide the examples in the singular.

2. Just like in German, the Norwegian personal pronoun for 3pl can be used as a polite form for 2sg. Although still possible, this usage is not very common nowadays.

(7) a. *der Indianer Großer Bär* (German)
the Indian big(ST) bear
"the Indian Big Bear"

b. *indianer-en Store Bjørn* (Norwegian)
Indian-DEF big(WK) bear
"the Indian Big Bear"

It is also possible to combine a demonstrative with a possessive pronominal, as in (8). As we see once again, a following adjective is strong in German but weak in Norwegian.

(8) a. *dieses mein großes Glück* (German)
this my great(ST) happiness
"this my great happiness"

b. *denne min store lykke* (Norwegian)
this my great(WK) happiness
"this my great happiness"

On the basis of the data presented above, we propose the following generalization concerning the distribution of the strong and weak endings of attributive adjectives in German and Norwegian: the endings in German are a function of the immediate syntactic context, while the endings in Norwegian are dependent on the general semantic context. In the following, we will give more evidence for this generalization through a closer examination of each language providing a formal account for it.

3. The weak/strong opposition in German

We will start with the empirical observation that the strong adjective endings in German are identical to the endings on the definite determiners, as illustrated in (9ab) with examples in the masculine nominative singular.

(9) a. *großer*
big(ST)
"big"

b. *dieser, der/jener*
this, that/that
"this, that"

Considering the definite items in (9b), we conclude that the strong endings in German cannot be a reflex of indefiniteness. We propose that adjective endings in this language are unmarked in their feature specifications for definiteness. Rather, they are only marked for gender, number, and case.

Adopting Distributed Morphology (Halle & Marantz 1994), we take inflections to involve abstract feature bundles in syntax. For our purposes, the crucial constellation involves an adjective in Spec,AgrP and a determiner in D in a regular DP (for general discussion, see Cinque 2005 & Julien 2005). In other words, the determiner and the adjective stand in a specific, local relation:

(10) a. *das kalte   Bier*
       the cold(WK) beer
       "the cold beer"

b.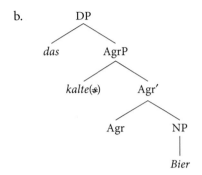

We propose that the weak/strong opposition is a morpho-syntactic phenomenon, and that the weak endings are due to Impoverishment triggered by a determiner in the local domain illustrated in (10) (Roehrs 2009, inspired by Sauerland 1996 & Schlenker 1999).[3] This means that the weak endings are dependent on lexical as well as on structural factors. In fact, they require certain determiners and a very specific, unique structure. On the lexical side, it is important to point out that an indefinite determiner may occur with a weak adjective, (11a) and (3) above, and a definite determiner may be followed by a strong adjective, (11b):[4]

(11) a. *(so) mancher   nette   Student*
       so   some   nice(WK)   student
       "some nice students"

   b. *Wir dumme   Idioten!*
      us stupid(ST) idiots
      "Us stupid idiots!"

---

3. In Roehrs (2009, 2012), this local relation is instantiated by successive cyclic movement of the determiner from a position below the adjective to the DP-level (cf. Schoorlemmer 2012). This explains the fact that "stacked" adjectives may all have a weak ending.

4. The example in (11b) can also have a weak ending (see Roehrs 2009: 166).

We take this to indicate that only certain determiners are marked to trigger Impoverishment. On the structural side, only adjectives in Spec,AgrP in a regular DP, as in (10), undergo Impoverishment. If the above-mentioned lexical and/or structural conditions do not hold, the abstract feature bundles are not reduced and they are spelled out as the strong endings. In that sense, the strong endings in German are the elsewhere case.

We make the following assumptions. First, the ending -*e* is a regular inflection, and masculine/accusative singular is exceptional (cf. Blevins 1995:146 and Eisenberg 1998:173–174). Second, gender and case are not primitives but involve two-category systems. Specifically, gender is represented by the features [N(euter)] and [F(eminine)]. Case consists of the features [O(blique)] and [S(tructural)]. Each of these four features may have negative or positive values (i.e. [–, +]). With this in mind, masculine gender is represented as [–N, –F] and nominative case as [–O, –S].[5]

Employing the value variables α and β for {–, +} and the category variable γ for {N, F}, we can represent the distribution and the feature decomposition of strong and weak adjectival endings in German as in Table 1. We suggest that the weak

---

[5]. A reviewer requests that we motivate this category system. While there are other options (*inter alia*, Müller 2002; Roehrs 2009:173; Sternefeld 2008:72, 80), the system presented in the main text is an attempt, on the one hand, to capture traditional markedness relations where positive values are meant to indicate the marked value (in Roman Jakobson's sense, the presence of a feature) and, on the other, to capture common patterns across the different genders, numbers, and cases where categories of the same value have something in common (cf. Chomsky 1981:48 on lexical categories).

Starting with markedness, Harbert's (1989, 2007:468) Obliqueness/Case Hierarchy states that nominative is the least oblique case and genitive the most: NOM > ACC > DAT > GEN. In our system, this is captured by the nominative having a negative value for both [O] and [S] but genitive has two positive ones. Second, as is commonly assumed, plural is more marked than singular. In our system, all singulars have one negative value but plural has two positive values. In fact, one can take the two positive values for gender to be the "neutralization" of gender in the plural, something Sternefeld (2008:80) calls the "forth gender". This fits well with the well-known fact that gender is not overtly distinguished in the plural in German or Norwegian. Furthermore, Steinmetz (2001) states that the default gender in German is masculine but common gender in the continental Scandinavian languages. In our system, the former is marked by [–N, –F] and the latter by [–N].

Turning to the patterns that the different genders, numbers, and cases have in common, the use of this feature system allows us to state morphological similarities between the different genders and cases but also across different numbers, namely between singular feminine and plural. These commonalities have played an important role in the literature. For instance, Eisenberg (1998:157) points out for German that masculine and neuter pattern together in opposition to feminine and plural. In our system, the former have the feature [–F] and the latter [+F]. Furthermore, nominative and accusative pattern differently from dative and genitive. In the main text, the former share the feature [–O] and the latter [+O].

endings have the same feature specifications as certain strong endings (marked by parentheses). One immediate advantage of the current proposal is that it will allow us to state only eight vocabulary items, rather than the typical nine, as stated in Sternefeld (2008: 81, 83).[6]

Table 1. Strong and weak endings in German

STRONG	[-N, -F]	[+N, -F]	[-N, +F]	[+N, +F]	WEAK	[-γ]	[+N, +F]
[-O, -S]	-r	-s	(-e)	-e	[-O]	(-e)	
[-O, +S]	-n	-s	(-e)	-e			
[+O, -S]	-m	-m	-r	{-n}	[+O]		{-n}
[+O, +S]	-s	-s	-r	-r			

We can now formulate the rules for vocabulary insertion in (12):

(12) a. Exception:
           [-N, -F, -O, +S]   →   -n
      b. Strong (except for feminine -e and plural -n):
           [-N, +F, +O, αS]   →   -r
           [+N, +F, -O, αS]   →   -e
           [αN, αF, αO, αS]   →   -r
           [-F, +O, -S]   →   -m
           [-F, βO, αS]   →   -s
      c. Weak (including strong feminine -e and plural -n):
           [-γ, -O]   →   -e
           []   →   -n

We assume that vocabulary items with the same number of features but a variable in front of a feature are less specific than a corresponding vocabulary item without a variable. Now, with more specific vocabulary items inserted before less specific ones, (12a) is inserted first, followed by (12b), and (12c) in the remaining contexts. More specifically, under the above-mentioned lexical and structural conditions,

---

6. We assume that schwas are inserted before the consonantal endings yielding, for instance, neuter *blau-e-s* 'blue'. Also, as is well known, the endings on the (definite) determiners and strong adjectives are identical in German. There are only two exceptions. First, the feminine/plural nominative/accusative form *die* 'the' is pronounced as [di] (rather than [də]). This unexpected state of affairs may have to do with the fact that the form of this definite article already ends in a vowel and the inflectional schwa is not phonetically realized. Second, in the masculine/neuter genitive, the ending on the adjective is *-n* (rather than *-s*). In view of the overwhelming similarities, we will, for simplicity's sake, abstract away from these minor differences between determiners and adjectives (but see Roehrs 2013 for detailed discussion).

Impoverishment applies deleting [S] on the terminal head of the syntactic tree. Bearing in mind that (12a) is exceptional, this will block the insertion of all items in (12b) under that terminal head. Consequently, the less specific vocabulary items in (12c) can be inserted in these featural contexts.[7]

Note that the traditional terms "strong" and "weak" in (12bc) are used here for expository purposes only. Given our feature system, there is no difference between strong and weak endings other than their feature specification; that is, the strong ones in (12b) are more specified than the endings in (12c) (the former all have at least one feature for [N] or [F]). Note also that (12c) contains both "strong" and "weak" endings – the cases in parentheses in Table 1.

Simplifying somewhat here, our account for the data in Section 2 can now be sketched as follows. Lexically, we submit that the possessive elements in (4a) and (8a) are not marked to trigger Impoverishment. Structurally, the pronominal DP involving feature mismatch in (5a), the appositive in (6a), the embedded proper name in (7a), and the determiner elements themselves in (9b) all involve nominal constellations different from simple, ordinary DPs. Since the relation between the determiner and the adjective is not local as defined above, Impoverishment does not apply. As a result, the (non-reduced) strong endings surface. These lexical and structural ingredients of our proposal for German manifest themselves in other ways.

The significance of the presence of a triggering determiner can also be seen from the examples in (13) and (14). The examples in (13) all have a definite reading (due to (13a) containing an adjective with indexical semantics, (13b) being a name and (13c) being a vocative), but since the adjective is not preceded by a determiner, it shows up, in each case, in the strong form:

(13) a. *folgendes   Beispiel*
following(ST) example
"the following example"

b. *Deutscher   Ritterorden*
German(ST) knight.order
"the Order of the Teutonic Knights"

c. *Dummer   Idiot!*
stupid(ST) idiot
"Stupid idiot!"

---

7. What is interesting to point out is that although Impoverishment brings about the insertion of less specified endings, these inflections must be prevented from appearing in other contexts in German. For instance, one adjectival inflection remains sensitive to number even after Impoverishment has taken place. Specifically, weak *-e* is restricted to singular contexts with adjectives and as such, cannot be identical in features to the homophonous plural ending on nouns (e.g. *Tisch-e* 'tables'). In other words, weak adjectival endings are not featureless in the relevant sense allowing them to occur in any other context.

If a determiner is inserted, as in the examples in (14), the meaning is not changed, but the adjective switches to the weak form:

(14) a. *das folgende*   *Beispiel*
the following(WK) example
"the following example"

b. *der Deutsche*   *Ritterorden*
the German(WK) knight.order
"the Order of the Teutonic Knights"

c. *Der dumme*   *Idiot!*
the stupid(WK) idiot
"Stupid idiot!"

The relevance of the syntactic structure is seen very clearly in split topicalizations involving definite noun phrases, which show different adjectival endings than their unsplit counterparts – see (15):

(15) a. *Ich habe immer dieses billige*   *Bier getrunken.*
I have always this cheap(WK) beer drunk
"I have always drunk only this cheap beer."

b. *Billiges*   *Bier habe ich immer nur dieses getrunken.*
cheap(ST) beer have I always only this drunk
"As for cheap beer, I have always drunk only this."

In (15a) the adjective is located below a determiner which triggers Impoverishment, and as expected, it is spelled out in the weak form. In (15b), however, the adjective has been topicalized away from the determiner (van Riemsdijk 1989) and consequently, the adjective can only be strong.

4. The weak/strong opposition in Norwegian

We claim that the weak/strong opposition in Norwegian is a semantico-syntactic phenomenon. We will note first that while definite determiners in German have endings that are identical to the strong adjective endings, the endings on the definite determiners in Norwegian are mostly identical to the weak adjective endings, as shown in (16ab). One clear exception and a possible one are shown in (16c).

(16) a. *store*
big(WK)
"big"

b. *dette/denne,*   *disse, det* [de]
this(N)/this(M/F), these, that(N)
"this, these, that"

c. *den,* *de* [di]
   that(M/F), those
   "that, those"

Unlike in German, then, adjective endings here are marked for gender, number, and definiteness. However, as we will see below, the weak adjectival endings in Norwegian do not in themselves represent definiteness. Instead, we propose that weak endings have a [-interpretable] feature that has to be checked/valued with a [+interpretable] feature. The latter is located on – what is traditionally called – Agr. Following Lohrmann (2011), we label this feature [Identity].

Due to its definite-like semantics, the [Identity] feature on Agr is only compatible with other definite elements. Furthermore, with adjectives in Spec,AgrP, the presence of an adjective in a nominal structure implies the existence of Agr. Unlike in German, this makes adjective inflection in Norwegian independent of the larger syntactic structure.

The semantics reflected by weak adjectival forms is illustrated by a contrast discussed in Vangsnes (1999: 83). As Vangsnes points out, (17a) is non-presuppositional whereas (17b) is presuppositional, suggesting the existence of unripe apples in the relevant set.

(17) a. *Legg hvert umodent eple i denne kasse-n.*
       put every unripe(ST) apple in this box-DEF
       "Put every unripe apple in this box."

   b. *Legg hvert umodne eple i denne kasse-n.*
      put every unripe(WK) apple in this box-DEF
      "Put each unripe apple in this box."

In other words, while both (17a) and (17b) are semantically definite, there is a visible difference in the form of the adjective that correlates with a subtle effect in interpretation. This does not mean, in our view, that the adjectival form is responsible for the presuppositionality of the phrase as a whole; it only means that the form of the adjective agrees with the feature specification of the containing nominal phrase (i.e. Agr), even in cases where that specification is not overtly reflected on any other constituent of the nominal phrase.

Fleshing out our analysis, we first provide the distribution and the feature decomposition of strong and weak adjectival endings in Norwegian in Table 2.[8]

---

8. Table 2 shows the feature distribution in the three-gender system found in most spoken varieties of Norwegian and also widely used in writing. Instead of that, some speakers have a two-gender system, with masculine and feminine coalesced into the so-called common gender, which contrasts with neuter gender.

Table 2. Strong and weak adjectival endings in Norwegian

	[−N, −F]	[−N, +F]	[+N, −F]	[+N, +F]
STRONG	-Ø	-Ø	-t	-e
WEAK		-e		

The insertion rules for weak and strong adjectival endings follow in (18). Like in German above, α and β are value variables. Crucially, the presence of [Identity] in (18a) blocks the insertion of strong forms, as required.

(18)   a.   [αN, βF; Identity]   →   -e
      b.   [+N, −F]   →   -t
      c.   [−N]   →   -Ø
      d.   []   →   -e

This analysis explains not only the occurrence of the weak adjective in (2a), but also in (4b), (5b), (6b), (7b) and (8b), since definite articles, possessors, personal pronouns, and proper names yield a definite interpretation of the nominal phrase as a whole. Recalling (17), note that [Identity] on Agr is related to presuppositionality, and as such it is compatible with these definite elements.

Interestingly, the examples in (19) demonstrate that in Norwegian, the weak form of the adjective is not dependent on the presence of a prenominal determiner. In (19a), a proper name combines with a non-restrictive adjective, and as we see, the determiner is optional (cf. Julien 2005: 16). In (19b), the determiner is optional in a context of familiarity (although the acceptance of the version without the determiner varies between speakers, see Julien 2005: 32–33, and also Delsing 1993: 118 on Swedish).

(19)   a.   *(Den) vesle   Anna fikk ei dokke.*
         the little(WK) Anna got a doll
         "(The) little Anna got a doll."

     b.   *Du kan ta   (den) nye   bil-en.*
         you can take the   new(WK) car-DEF
         "You can take the new car."

We can observe that the adjective appears in the weak form regardless of whether or not it is preceded by a (definite) determiner. Julien (2005) argues that the optionality of the determiner is a matter of spellout, so that there is a definite D present. In addition, the context will be definite, due to the proper name in (19a) and the suffixed noun in (19b). Hence, these examples show that the weak adjective in Norwegian is sensitive to the general semantic context and crucially not just to a preceding overt definite element.

However, other constructions are more challenging. First, there are cases like (20a), where an adjective in the superlative appears in the weak form, despite the absence of any other markers of definiteness. The question is then what motivates the weak form here. It is striking that (20a) is semantically virtually identical to (20b), where definiteness is overtly marked by the determiner as well as by the suffix on the noun. Hence, (20a) also has a definite interpretation. We suggest that the weak form is triggered by the inclusiveness that the superlative itself suggests (see Roberts 2003; Julien 2005), inclusiveness being one ingredient of definiteness.[9]

(20) a. på beste måte
in best(WK) way
"in the best way"

b. på den beste måte-n
in the best(WK) way-DEF
"in the best way"

Certain proper names in Norwegian present another challenge for the analysis of weak adjectival forms. Just like the phrase in (20a), the company names in (21) both contain weak adjectives, but no other markers of definiteness.[10]

(21) a. Norske Skog
Norwegian(WK) forest
"Norwegian forest (company name)"

b. Oslo Nye Teater
Oslo new(WK) theatre
"Oslo New Theatre"

Note that individual proper names in Norwegian are morphologically fixed, so that there is no alternation of the kind seen in the German proper name shown in (13b) and (14b). On our view, the appearance of weak adjectives in (21) is due to the proper name status of these phrases. By virtue of being names, the phrases involve an [Identity] feature, which leads to the appearance of weak forms.

---

9. The superlative gives its containing nominal phrase an inclusive reading, but in predicative position, it will appear in the strong form:

(i) Denne måt-en er best.
this way-DEF is best(ST)
"This way is best."

Needless to say that there is much more to say about superlatives than we can do here.

10. It should be pointed out here that formally *Oslo* in (21b) is not a possessor.

Vocatives show a syntactically more varied picture. The pattern exemplified in (21) is also found in address vocatives, as in (22) (see Schaden 2010 for a general discussion of vocatives).

(22) Kom hjem nå, unge dame!
 come home now young(WK) lady
 "Young lady, you come home now!"

Again, what we have is a weak adjective followed by an unmarked noun, and moreover, it is not possible to add definiteness markers in this case.

Address vocatives differ from predicational vocatives, which typically involve a weak adjective followed by a definite noun, as in (23), and also from evaluative vocatives, which show considerable variation. The latter can contain a possessive pronoun, in which case there is no definite suffix on the noun—see (24a), or the pronoun may be missing, in which case the definite suffix on the noun is optional, as indicated in (24b) (see also Corver 2008). Strikingly though, if the vocative contains an adjective, the adjective always shows up in the weak form.

(23) Nå er det lenge siden jeg har sett deg. Store jent-a.
 now is it long since I have seen you. Big(WK) girl-DEF
 "It's a long time now since I saw you. You big girl."

(24) a. Se hva du har gjort! Din (dumme) idiot!
 look what you have done your stupid(WK) idiot
 "Look at what you have done! You (stupid) idiot!"
 b. Se hva du har gjort! Dumme idiot(-en)!
 look what you have done stupid(WK) idiot-DEF
 "Look at what you have done! Stupid idiot!"

Following Espinal (2011), we assume that vocatives always have a [Deictic] feature. We take deixis and [Identity] to be related; that is, definiteness is not a primitive but a compositional concept. While we cannot make this intuition more concrete here, we believe that this is the reason for the appearance of weak adjectival forms in Norwegian vocatives.

Finally, predicative adjectives in Norwegian are always strong, even when their subject is definite. Compare (25a) to (25b).

(25) a. et stort hus
 a big(ST) house
 "a big house"
 b. Hus-et er stort.
 house-DEF is big(ST)
 "The house is big."

In other words, predicative adjectives do not agree in definiteness with the subject. Rather, predicate contexts are non-definite. In our proposal, weak adjectival endings are a reflex of an agreement relation with the definite-like semantics on Agr. Since predicative contexts do not involve the presuppositional feature we labeled [Identity], weak endings are not possible here. Instead, predicative adjectives have strong endings, which seem to function as the elsewhere case in Norwegian.

5. Scandinavian more generally

Above, we showed for German that split topicalizations in definite contexts involve a strong adjective. Unfortunately, the inflectional alternation on the adjective cannot be tested in Norwegian. In the constructions that allow a split, the adjective must be preceded by a definite article:

(26) a. *Jeg har hele den gamle serie-n fra før.*
    I have whole the old(WK) series-DEF already
    "I have the entire old series already."
 b. *Den gamle serie-n har jeg hele av fra før.*
    the old(WK) series-DEF have I whole of already
    "As for the old series, I have the entire one already."

While the continental Scandinavian languages pattern uniformly in the eight aforementioned contexts, there is variation with discontinuous noun phrases. Fortunately, Swedish allows us to test the ninth context, where the relevant elements, *hela* 'whole' and *halva* 'half', do not have to be followed by a definite article:[11]

(27) a. *Jag har hela gamla serie-n sen innan.* (Swedish)
    I have whole old(WK) series-DEF already
    "I have the entire old series already."
 b. *Gamla serie-n har jag hela (av) sen innan.*
    old(WK) series-DEF have I whole of already
    "As for the old series, I have the entire one already."

Again, once the appropriate conditions are identified to probe into the issue, the Scandinavian languages differ from German. Similarly to above, this case involves a definite context.

Finally, recall that Harbert described only the continental Scandinavian languages in his statement about the weak/strong opposition in adjective inflections

---

11. There is some variation among speakers as to whether or not they accept the version without an inserted *av*.

(see introduction). In other words, he seems to exclude Icelandic (and Faroese). Interestingly, Icelandic is special in at least two ways. On the one hand, definite noun phrases have, more generally, no free-standing article. Similar to certain cases of continental Scandinavian we discussed above, the adjective is weak, (28a). On the other, this language is special in that it allows strong adjectives to occur in definiteness contexts, (28b). However, if they do, these adjectives must have a non-restrictive interpretation (see Delsing 1993: 132, Footnote 25; Thráinsson 2007: 3, 89).

(28) a. *guli   bíllinn*   (Icelandic)
       yellow(WK) car-DEF
       "the yellow car"
   b. *gulur   bíllinn*
       yellow(ST) car-DEF
       "the car, which is yellow"

Jonathan Bobaljik (p.c.) made the intriguing suggestion that the strong adjective in (28b) might actually be syntactically predicative assuming there is some hidden structure. Although we have not investigated this in detail, if he is right, our proposal might also extend to Icelandic (and Faroese).

6. Conclusions

In this paper, we documented that German and Norwegian attributive adjectives differ. As an empirical basis, we presented eight sets of data: possessives involving proper names and pronominals, embedded and unembedded proper names, "disagreeing" pronominal DPs, appositives, definite adjectives, and vocatives. Extending the discussion to Swedish, discontinuous noun phrases supplied a ninth set. In each of these definite contexts, German showed a strong adjective and Norwegian or, more generally, continental Scandinavian used a weak one. *Pace* Leu (2008) and Schoorlemmer (2009), we argued with Harbert (2007) that the weak/strong contrast of adjectives is regulated by different factors in these languages.

In order to find a plausible account for this difference, we pointed out that there are a number of cases where Norwegian employs a weak adjective although there is no free-standing definite article (cf. also Icelandic) or not even a definite suffix. In fact, there are cases where only the weak/strong contrast in the adjective inflection indicates a difference with regard to presuppositionality.

Observing that weak endings only occur inside DPs, we proposed that German has feature-reduced endings and Norwegian has definite endings, or rather endings reflecting an agreement relation with the feature [Identity] on Agr. Feature reduction in German was implemented by Impoverishment. Moreover, in both languages strong endings seem to be the elsewhere case. In German, they appear when the conditions for Impoverishment do not apply, and in Norwegian, they appear in contexts that do not involve definiteness of any kind (e.g. adjectives in predicative, DP-external contexts).

We also documented that Icelandic allows a strong adjective in a definite context and that German allows a weak adjective in an indefinite context (cf. (3) and (11a) above). Making the plausible and desirable assumption that Icelandic is basically like the other Scandinavian languages, we tentatively suggested that this case is special and involves hidden structure. As to the German case, these instances follow from our proposal that certain indefinite elements are marked to trigger Impoverishment.

Summing up, although the weak/strong distinction in adjective endings has the same origin in German as in Scandinavian, and the distribution of weak and strong forms in the canonical cases appears to be similar, we have shown that the principles regulating the distribution are different after all. Hence, adjectival morphology in German and Scandinavian is an interesting case of closely related languages developing different grammars over time.

References

Blevins, James P. 1995. Syncretism and paradigmatic opposition. *Linguistics and Philosophy* 18(2): 113–152.
Chomsky, Noam. 1981. *Lectures on Government and Binding*. Dordrecht: Foris.
Cinque, Guglielmo. 2005. Deriving Greenberg's Universal 20 and its exceptions. *Linguistic Inquiry* 36(2): 315–332.
Corver, Norbert. 2008. Uniformity and diversity in the syntax of evaluative vocatives. *Journal of Comparative Germanic Linguistics* 11(1): 43–93.
Delsing, Lars-Olof. 1993. The Internal Structure of Noun Phrases in the Scandinavian Languages: A Comparative Study. Ph.D. dissertation, Lund University.
Eisenberg, Peter. 1998. *Grundriß der deutschen Grammatik*, Band 1: *Das Wort*. Stuttgart: Metzler.
Espinal, M. Teresa. 2011. On the structure of vocatives. Ms, Free University of Barcelona.
Grimm, Jacob. 1870. *Deutsche Grammatik*, Vol 1, 2nd edn. Berlin.
Halle, Morris & Marantz, Alec. 1994. Some key features of Distributed Morphology. *MIT Working Papers in Linguistics* 21: 275–288.
Harbert, Wayne. 1989. Case attraction and the hierarchization of case. *Proceedings of the Eastern States Conference on Linguistics* 6: 138–149.
Harbert, Wayne. 2007. *The Germanic Languages*. Cambridge: CUP.
Julien, Marit. 2005. *Nominal Phrases from a Scandinavian Perspective* [Linguistik Aktuell/Linguistics Today 87]. Amsterdam: John Benjamins.
Leu, Thomas. 2008. The Internal Syntax of Determiners. Ph.D. dissertation, New York University.
Lohrmann, Susanne. 2011. A unified structure for Scandinavian DPs. In *The Noun Phrase in Romance and Germanic: Structure, Variation, and Change* [Linguistik Aktuell/Linguistics Today 171], Petra Sleeman & Harry Perridon (eds), 111–125. Amsterdam: John Benjamins.

Müller, Gereon. 2002. Remarks on nominal inflection in German. In *More than Words. A Festschrift for Dieter Wunderlich*, Ingrid Kaufmann & Barbara Stiebels (eds), 113–145. Berlin: Akademie Verlag.

Riemsdijk, Henk van. 1989. Movement and regeneration. In *Dialect Variation and the Theory of Grammar*, Paola Benincà (ed.), 105–136. Dordrecht: Foris.

Roberts, Craige. 2003. Uniqueness in definite noun phrases. *Linguistics and Philosophy* 26: 287–350.

Roehrs, Dorian. 2009. *Demonstratives and Definite Articles as Nominal Auxiliaries* [Linguistik Aktuell/Linguistics Today 140]. Amsterdam: John Benjamins.

Roehrs, Dorian. 2012. Semantically vacuous elements: Adjectival inflections and the article *ein* in German. Ms, University of North Texas.

Roehrs, Dorian. 2013. The inner make up of definite determiners: The case of Germanic. *Journal of Germanic Linguistics* 25(4): 295–411.

Sauerland, Uli. 1996. The late insertion of Germanic inflection. Ms, MIT.

Schaden, Gerhard. 2010. Vocatives: A note on addressee-management. *University of Pennsylvania Working Papers in Linguistics* 16(1): 176–185.

Schlenker, Philippe. 1999. La flexion de l'adjectif en allemand: La morphologie de haut en bas. In *Recherches Linguistiques de Vincennes* 28: 115–132. ⟨http://rlv.revues.org/document1216.html⟩

Schoorlemmer, Erik. 2009. *Agreement, Dominance and Doubling: The Morphosyntax of DP*. Utrecht: LOT Publications.

Schoorlemmer, Erik. 2012. Definiteness marking in Germanic: Morphological variations on the same syntactic theme. *The Journal of Comparative Germanic Linguistics* 15(2): 107–156.

Steinmetz, Donald. 2001. The Great Gender Shift and the attrition of neuter nouns in West Germanic: The example of German. In *New Insights in Germanic II*, Irmengard Rauch & Gerald F. Carr (eds.), 201–224. Frankfurt: Peter Lang.

Sternefeld, Wolfgang. 2008. *Syntax. Eine morphologisch motivierte generative Beschreibung des Deutschen*, Vol I. Tübingen: Stauffenberg.

Thráinsson, Höskuldur. 2007. *The Syntax of Icelandic*. Cambridge: CUP.

Vangsnes, Øystein Alexander. 1999. The Identification of Functional Architecture. Ph.D. dissertation, University of Bergen.

Cross-linguistic variation in agreement on Germanic predicate adjectives*

Erik Schoorlemmer
MIT / Leiden University

The Germanic languages display cross-linguistic variation with respect to whether predicative adjectives agree. This paper attempts to determine which component of the grammar is responsible for this variation. In order to do so, it examines three different options: the variation has a lexical source, a syntactic source, or is due to an interaction between syntax and morphology. The conclusion the paper reaches is that the variation is either situated in the lexicon or has a morphosyntactic source. A purely syntactic source will, however, be excluded.

1. Introduction

Adjectives used predicatively display agreement in some Germanic languages, but not in others. Predicative adjectives do not agree in Dutch and German, as shown in (1).

(1) a. [Het huis/ de man] is **oud**. (Dutch)
    the.NTR.SG house the.CMN.SG man is old
 b. [Das Haus/ der Mann] ist **alt**. (German)
    the.NTR.SG house the.MASC.SG man is old
    "The house/the man is old."

In Northern Germanic, Swedish, Norwegian and Danish, predicative adjectives, however, agree with their subject in gender and number, as illustrated in (2)

---

* I would like to thank Jenny Doetjes, Marjo van Koppen, David Pesetsky, Johan Rooryck and Tanja Temmerman, two anonymous reviewers, as well as audiences at BCGL 6, the Amsterdam workshop on adjectives, and CGSW 27 for insightful comments and/or judgments. The research reported here has been supported by a Rubicon grant of the Netherlands Organization for Scientific Research (NWO).

(see among others Delsing 1993:83–84 for Swedish). In Faroese and Icelandic, they also agree in case, in addition to gender and number.[1]

(2) a. *Hus-et   är   **gammal-t**.*   (Swedish)
       house-the is old-SG.NTR
       "The house is old."

   b. *Mann-en är   **gammal-Ø***
       man-the is old-SG.CMN
       "The man is old."

At first, it is not clear to which component of the grammar this cross-linguistic variation should be attributed. It might be the case that Dutch and German adjectives are not lexically specified for agreement, contrary to their Northern Germanic counterparts. This would put the variation in the lexicon. A second possibility is that the variation has a syntactic source. The syntactic licensing of agreement could be blocked for some reason in Dutch and German, but not in Northern Germanic. This is the approach taken in Vikner (2001, 2005, 2006). Finally, the variation might also be due to an interaction between the syntax and morphology. It might be the case that agreement is lexically and syntactically licensed on predicative adjectives in all Germanic languages, but fails to be spelled out by the morphological component in Dutch and German. This paper aims to explore which of these options should be held responsible for the variation illustrated in (1)–(2).

2. A lexical approach

One way to approach the cross-linguistic variation illustrated by (1)–(2) is to claim that it originates in the lexical specification of predicative adjectives. Under such an approach, the lexical entries of Dutch and German predicative adjectives lack the necessary features to trigger agreement. As a consequence, agreement is not licensed. Predicative adjectives in the Northern Germanic languages would be specified for the features that trigger agreement, yielding agreeing predicative adjectives.

---

1. In (1)–(2), the adjectives constitute the main predicate and are combined with the copular verb BE. In this paper, I will focus exclusively on this use of predicative adjectives. The agreement facts are similar if adjectives are used as secondary predicates (see e.g. Dürscheid 2002 for German & Levinson 2010:146 for Norwegian) or when another copular verb than BE is used.

The main appeal of such an approach is its simplicity. At closer inspection, however, things are more complicated than might appear at first. More specifically, this lexical approach requires separate lexical entries, at least in Dutch and German, for the attributive and predicative uses of a given adjective (cf. Siegel 1976 for Russian). The reason for this is that attributively used adjectives in Dutch and German do agree, as shown in (3) and (4), contrary to predicatively used adjectives, as in (1).

(3) a. een **oud-Ø**   huis
           a   old-SG.NTR house
          "an old house"

      b. een **oud-e**   man
           a   old-SG.CMN man
          "an old man"   (Dutch)

(4) a. ein **alt-es**   Haus
           a   old-SG.NTR.NOM house
          "an old house"   (German)

      b. ein **alt-er**   Mann
           a   old-SG.MASC.NOM man
          "an old man"

This shows that attributive adjectives in Dutch and German are lexically specified for features that trigger agreement, contrary to their predicative counterparts. The Dutch adjective *oud* "old" would thus need to have an entry in the lexicon with agreement features for its attributive use and another one without these features for its predicative use.[2] One might object that this is an unwanted complication of the lexicon, and that, ideally, there should only be one single entry per adjective. However, if one assumes only one lexical entry per adjective, the differences between the attributive and predicative uses of adjectives, including those concerning agreement, must be attributed to other components of the grammar. If this turns out to be impossible, the greater complexity of the lexicon created by having separate entries for predicative and attributive uses of adjectives might be justified. In order to determine whether the lexical approach to cross-linguistic variation in agreement on predicative adjectives is on the right track, we therefore must investigate whether this variation could also be attributed to other components of the grammar. I will do so in the following sections.

---

2. Alternatively, there might be a lexical rule that maps attributive adjectives onto predicative adjectives or vice versa.

3. Syntactic approaches

Agreement needs to be licensed syntactically. This licensing only occurs in certain syntactic configurations and only when particular conditions are met (see, e.g. Chomsky 2000). It might therefore be possible that the distribution of agreement on predicative adjectives has a purely syntactic source. Predicative adjectives would then be lexically equipped with agreement-triggering features in all Germanic languages. These languages, however, would differ with respect to whether the syntactic conditions on agreement are met. In Northern Germanic, these conditions are met on predicative adjectives. In Dutch and German, this is not the case and agreement fails to be syntactically licensed.

An approach along these lines can only be successful if one succeeds in determining the reason for which the syntactic licensing fails in Dutch and German. In this section, I will first briefly discuss a proposal by Vikner (2001, 2005, 2006). Under Vikner's proposal, agreement fails to be licensed in Dutch and German since he takes APs to be head-final in these languages. I argue that this claim lacks empirical support. Finally, I argue that any proposal that proposes that the lack of agreement on predicative adjectives in Dutch and German is due to a failure in the syntactic licensing of agreement is on the wrong track.

3.1 Vikner's (2001, 2005, 2006) syntactic approach

According to Vikner (2001, 2005, 2006), the absence of agreement of predicative adjectives in Dutch and German is the result of a failure of the syntactic licensing of agreement. He claims that this failure is connected to the basic word order of Dutch and German. These languages are both (underlying) OV, as illustrated in (5).

(5)   ... dat Jan het boek **kocht.**   (Dutch)
           that Jan the book bought
           "... that Jan bought the book."

The languages that have agreeing predicative adjectives, i.e. the Northern Germanic languages, on the other hand are all VO-languages, as shown for Swedish in (6), taken from Holmberg and Platzack (1995:73).

(6)   ... att Ulf (inte) **köpte** bok-en.   (Swedish)
           that Ulf (not) bought book-the
           "...that Ulf bought/didn't buy the book."

There thus seems to be a correlation between VO word order and agreeing predicate adjectives on the one hand, and OV word order and non-agreeing predicate adjectives, on the other.[3] According to Vikner, this correlation is not accidental. Instead, he claims that the distribution of agreement on predicative adjectives is causally linked to the basic word order, i.e. VO vs. OV. He assumes that the OV–VO difference corresponds to a difference in the headedness of VP. VP is head-final in OV-languages, while it is head-initial in VO-languages. He then proposes that the headedness of VP determines that of AP. In the OV-languages Dutch and German, AP is therefore head-final, just like VP. According to Vikner, a head-final AP is the reason why agreement is not syntactically licensed on Dutch and German predicative adjectives.

I will first discuss how Vikner accounts for Northern Germanic. Given the correspondence in headedness between AP and VP, AP is head-initial in these VO-languages. According to Vikner, head-initial APs do not block the syntactic licensing of agreement. He proposes that in most cases the subject of predicative adjectives is directly inserted in the specifier of AP, before moving to other positions in the clause. While in spec AP, the subject triggers spec–head agreement, (7).

(7)   A-INITIAL LANGUAGES: SPEC–HEAD AGREEMENT

       ... [$_{AP}$ Subject [$_{A'}$ A^0 (Compl)]]

       SPEC–HEAD AGR   (Vikner 2001, 2005, 2006)

This spec–head agreement syntactically licenses the agreement on predicative adjectives.

Vikner offers two different accounts of how the head-final character of AP blocks the syntactic licensing of agreement in the OV-languages Dutch and German. In Vikner (2001, 2005), he claims that the head-finality of AP allows the subject to be inserted as an adjunct to AP. The adjoined position in which the adjectival subject is inserted is higher than spec AP. As a consequence, the adjective will never move to spec AP and no spec–head agreement between the adjective and its subject can be established, as in (8). This lack of spec–head agreement explains the absence of adjectival agreement on predicative adjectives in languages with a head-final AP.

(8)   A-FINAL LANGUAGES: ADJUNCTION TO AP

       ... [$_{AP}$ Subject [$_{AP}$ Spec [$_{A'}$ (Compl) A^0]]]

       SPEC–HEAD AGR   (Vikner 2001, 2005)

Vikner (2006) replaces this account with a newer version. Given that adjunction is optional, the adjunction account only explains why adjectives *can* appear without agreement in OV-languages, but not why they *must*. Vikner (2006) therefore

---

3. But see Footnote 10.

no longer assumes any difference between head-final and head-initial APs with respect to the position in which the adjectival subject is inserted. Instead, he assumes that, in both types of languages, the subject enters the derivation in the majority of cases directly in spec AP. According to Vikner (2006), the difference between the two types of languages concerns the need for licensing the specifier of AP.

He claims that specifiers to the left are exceptional in head-initial projections and require additional licensing. This is based on the idea that heads in such projections only license positions to their right. Given that it is not directly licensed by A^0, the specifier of a head-initial AP needs some other mechanism in order to be licensed. This mechanism is spec–head agreement. The adjectival subject is, according to Vikner, always in spec AP at some stage of the derivation. Hence, spec–head agreement always takes place in head-initial APs. As described above, this spec–head agreement syntactically licenses the agreement on the adjective (see (7) above).

In OV-languages, Vikner (2006) claims that the head-final character of AP directly licenses a specifier without the need for spec–head agreement. According to Vikner, this is the case because heads in head-final projections freely license positions to their left. The subject, although present in spec AP at some stage of the derivation, therefore doesn't participate in spec–head agreement with A, (9).

(9) A-FINAL LANGUAGES: NO SPEC–HEAD AGREEMENT
    … [$_{AP}$ Subject [$_{A'}$ A^0 (Compl) A^0]]

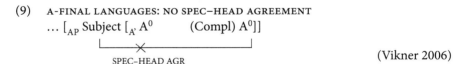
SPEC–HEAD AGR   (Vikner 2006)

Due to this absence of spec–head agreement, no agreement morphology is licensed on predicative adjectives in Dutch and German.

3.2 A problem for Vikner's analysis

The claim that AP is head-final in Dutch and German and head-initial in Northern Germanic constitutes the backbone of Vikner's analysis. Unfortunately, there is no empirical support for it.

First, there is no clear indication that AP is head-final in Dutch and German. Adjectival complements can both precede and follow the adjective. Predicate adjectives typically precede their complements, as shown in (10).[4]

---

4. In marked contexts, complements can also precede predicative adjectives. There is therefore no decisive evidence in favor of a head-final or head-initial AP, even if one only considers predicative adjectives.

(10)　…　dat ik **trots**　[op mijn kinderen] ben.　　　(Dutch)
　　　　　that I proud　[of my children] am
　　　　　"… that I am proud of my children."

On their attributive use, Dutch and German adjectives, however, follow their complements, as shown in (11).

(11)　de　[op zijn kinderen]　**trotse**　vader.　　　(Dutch)
　　　　the　[of his children]　proud　father
　　　　"the father who is proud of his children"

Since complements can thus both precede and follow adjectives, there is no empirical ground for claiming that APs are head-final in Dutch and German.

Secondly, there is also no support for proposing a difference in headedness of AP between Northern Germanic, on the one hand, and Dutch and German on the other. If such a difference existed, we would expect to find different orderings between adjectives and their complements in the two groups of languages. This is, however, not the case. Like in Dutch and German, predicative adjectives in Northern Germanic are followed by their complements, while attributive adjectives are preceded by them, as shown in (12) and (13) (data taken from Cabredo Hofherr 2010: 15).

(12)　Mamma-n　är　**stolt**　[över sin dotter].　　　(Swedish)
　　　mother-the　is　proud　of　her daughter
　　　"The mother is proud of her daughter."

(13)　den　[över sin dotter]　**stolta**　mamma-n.　　　(Swedish)
　　　the　of her daughter　proud　mother-the
　　　'the mother who is proud of her daughter'.

These data shows that there is no empirical support for the claim that APs are headed differently in Northern Germanic than in Dutch and German. Together with the lack of support for a head-final AP in Dutch and German, this observation casts serious doubt on the foundations of Vikner's analysis.

3.3 Problems for any syntactic approach

Under Vikner's proposal, the absence of agreement on German and Dutch predicative adjectives is due to this agreement not being syntactically licensed. In order to determine whether such an approach is on the right track, one must ask the question whether the German and Dutch facts correspond to cases where we know that agreement fails to be syntactically licensed. Preminger (2011) has studied such cases in a number of different languages. He concludes that such a failure results in the occurrence of default agreement morphology. As shown in (1), Dutch and German predicative adjectives simply lack an agreement ending. If this were due to the failure of the syntactic licensing of agreement, this would mean that the Dutch and German adjectival default agreement morpheme is zero (-∅).

Dutch and German adjectives, however, have non-zero default agreement morphemes. These default morphemes are -*e* in Dutch and -*en* in German, (14). These endings are part of the group of so-called weak endings, which show up on attributive adjectives in Dutch and German when the determiner is uninflected (Roehrs 2009; Schoorlemmer 2009).

(14) a. *de oud-e man* (Dutch)
the.COMMON.GENDER old-DEFAULT man

b. *dem alt-en Mann* (German)
the.DAT.SG.MASC old-DEFAULT man
"the old man"

The Dutch -*e* ending shows up in the weak paradigm on adjectives modifying nouns with any gender and number specification. It is therefore not specified for gender and number. In addition, it also shows up in the plural of the strong paradigm and can therefore not be specified as weak. It must therefore be a default morpheme. The German -*en* ending occurs on German attributive adjectives in both weak and strong contexts with nouns whose gender, number, and case distinctions do not constitute a natural class. It therefore must be a default morpheme (cf. also Zwicky 1986).[5,6]

Given that Dutch -*e* and German -*en* express default adjectival agreement, −∅ cannot also express default adjectival agreement. This conclusion casts serious doubts not only on Vikner's proposal, but also on any approach that tries to explain the lack of agreement on German and Dutch predicative adjectives by invoking a

---

5. There is a possibility that Dutch -*e* and German -*en* are not (absolute) defaults. They could encode a [+attributive]-feature, or, as suggested by a reviewer, a [+D] feature licensed via agreement with D. This, however, is unlikely. If [±attributive] or [±D] were features encoded by the agreement endings in Germanic, we would expect different sets of endings for predicative and attributive adjectives in those Germanic languages that have agreeing predicative adjectives. This is not the case. These languages use the same set of endings with predicative adjectives as with their (strong) attributive counterparts.

6. A reviewer observes that the analysis of German adjectival -*en* ending as a default morpheme entails that all other adjectival agreement suffixes mark "something that is describable in terms of a combination of features". I think that this is indeed the case. Since I cannot discuss this here in detail because of space limitations, I refer the interested reader to Chapter 5 of Schoorlemmer (2009).

failure of the syntactic licensing of agreement. It is therefore highly unlikely that the variation in agreement on predicative adjectives should be blamed on such a failure.

4. A morphosyntactic account

I will now investigate whether the variation in agreement on predicative adjectives might, at least in part, have a morphosyntactic cause. In particular, I will do so by developing an account that attributes the absence of an agreement ending in Dutch and German to a morphological deletion operation that is triggered to repair the violation of a morphological well-formedness condition.

Dutch and German adjectives do get agreement endings when they are used attributively (see (3) and (4) above). There is thus no absolute morphological constraint in Dutch and German that prohibits the combination of an adjective with an agreement ending. For this reason, the account that I will present below is not entirely morphological. Instead, I will propose that the syntactic derivation in Dutch and German results in a morphological representation that is ill-formed. The proposal will retain Vikner's (2001, 2005, 2006) original insight that the absence of predicative adjectives is somehow linked to the OV word order in Dutch and German. However, the rest of the proposal will be completely different. Before discussing the actual proposal, I will first introduce how agreement on predicative adjectives in the Northern Germanic languages can be derived.

4.1 Agreement on predicative adjectives in Northern Germanic

I assume that adjectival agreement, like any other type of agreement, is syntactically licensed via the operation Agree (Chomsky 2000). Agree is established between a Probe, the syntactic representation of the element displaying the agreement, and a Goal, the syntactic representation of the element whose features determine the agreement. The Probe starts out the derivation with unvalued features, while the Goal has matching valued features. Agree between the Probe and the Goal is established if the Probe c-commands the Goal and there is no other potential Goal that is closer to the Probe. When established, Agree results in the valuation of the features on the Probe with the values of the matching features on the Goal.

In the case of predicative adjectives, the Goal is the subject of the adjectival predicate. I assume that the adjectival Probe is a functional head that will be morphologically realized as the agreement ending. For convenience, I label this head AgrA. In order for Agree to be established, AgrA must c-command the adjectival subject (see above). I assume that the subject enters the derivation in the specifier of an aP-projection (cf. vP in the verbal domain). Hence, AgrA must dominate aP, as in (15). Agree then results in the valuation of the unvalued features on AgrA, as in (16).

(15)   [$_{AgrAP}$ AgrA$_{[\phi:\_]}$ ... [$_{aP}$ Subject$_{[\phi:x]}$ [$_{a'}$ a [$_{AP}$ A]]]]

(16)   [$_{AgrAP}$ AgrA$_{[\phi:x]}$ ... [$_{aP}$ Subject$_{[\phi:x]}$ [$_{a'}$ a [$_{AP}$ A]]]]
                       AGREE

The next step is the merger of the copular V-head and the functional material associated with it, including T. Finally, the adjectival subject moves to spec TP for EPP-reasons. In the case of VO-languages, these operations result in the structure in (17).

(17)   [$_{TP}$ Subj$_{[\phi:x]}$ T ... [$_{VP}$ V$_{BE}$ [$_{AgrAP}$ AgrA$_{[\phi:x]}$ [$_{aP}$ t$_{subj}$ a [$_{AP}$ A]]]]]

This structure is handed over to the post-syntactic morphological component. In line with Distributed Morphology (Halle & Marantz 1993), vocabulary items are inserted in this component. Some operations that combine affixes with roots and that invert their respective ordering also take place in this component, like Lowering and Local Dislocation (see Embick & Noyer 2001). I assume that the adjectival agreement ending is combined with the adjective at this level of the grammar by one of these operations, yielding the following string.

(18)   Subject BE A-AgrA

4.2 The absence of agreement on Dutch and German predicative adjectives

I assume that the syntactic derivation of copular sentences containing predicative adjectives in Dutch and German is for the most part similar to that in Northern Germanic: AgrA c-commands the subject in spec aP, as in (15) above, and Agree is established between AgrA and this subject, as in (16). The syntactic derivation only starts to diverge after merge of the copular V-head, because of the OV-character of Dutch and German.

German and Dutch are OV-languages since the object precedes the finite verb in embedded clauses (as in (5)). Zwart (1993) claims that this word order is not base-generated. Instead, he argues that it is derived from an underlying (S)VO word order by moving the object over the verb, (19).

(19)   ... V O   →   ... O V t$_O$

Like objects, adjectival predicates precede the finite (copular) verb in Dutch and German embedded clauses, as shown in (20).

(20) ... dat het huis **groot** is. (Dutch)
      that the house big is
      "... that the house is big."

If OV word order is indeed the result of movement of the object over the verb, then the facts concerning adjectival predicates must most probably be analyzed in a similar fashion. Put differently, predicative adjectives, like objects, probably move over V, as in (21).

(21) ... V$_{BE}$ A → ... A V$_{BE}$ t$_A$

A further question arises with respect to the amount of structure that is targeted by this movement. Is it only A° that moves or does more structure (AP, aP, etc.) move along with it? There are reasons to believe that the latter is the case. Adjectival complements can occur to the left of the copula, see (10) above, repeated here in (22).[7] Given that complements can move along with the adjective, I conclude that the entire AP can move over (copular) V, (23).

(22) ... dat ik **trots** [op mijn kinderen] ben. (Dutch)
      that I proud [of my children] am
      "... that I am proud of my children."

(23) ... V$_{BE}$ [$_{AP}$ A PP$_{compl}$] → ... [$_{AP}$ A PP$_{compl}$] V$_{BE}$ t$_{AP}$

Can the constituent that moves over the copula be bigger than AP? The answer to this question is negative. I assumed above (as in (15)) that AP is dominated by aP and that the subject is first inserted in spec aP. I assume that in copular clauses, the subject has to move to spec TP in order to check T^0's EPP-feature. If the movement over the copula targets aP, the subject would need to be extracted out of a moved constituent in a specifier position, (24).

(24) ... V$_{BE}$ [$_{aP}$ DP$_{subj}$ A] → ... [[$_{aP}$ DP$_{subj}$ A PP$_{compl}$] V$_{BE}$ t$_{aP}$]

      → DP$_{subj}$ ... [[$_{aP}$ t$_{subj}$ A PP$_{compl}$] V$_{BE}$ t$_{aP}$]

This extraction would constitute a violation of whatever condition blocks Left Branch Extraction in Dutch and German. I therefore conclude that aP, contrary to AP, cannot be moved over the copula. Above, I argued that AgrA dominates

---

7. Although adjectival complements can occur to the left of the finite copula as in (22), this is not obligatory. Adjectival complements can also be "extraposed" to the right of the copular verb, e.g. *dat ik trots ben [op mijn kinderen]*.

aP. If aP does not move over the copula, AgrA will also not move. Instead only AP moves, stranding both AgrA and aP, (25). Abstracting away from V2, the final relevant step of the syntactic derivation is movement of the subject from spec aP to spec TP, cf. (26).

(25)   [AP... [$_{VP}$ V$_{BE}$ [$_{AgAP}$ AgrA$_{[\phi:x]}$ ... [$_{aP}$ Subject$_{[\phi:x]}$ [$_{a'}$ a t$_{AP}$]]]]]

(26)   [$_{TP}$ Sub$_{[\phi:x]}$ T... AP... [$_{VP}$ V [$_{AgrAP}$ AgrA$_{[\phi:x]}$ ... [$_{aP}$ t$_{sub}$ a t$_{AP}$]]]]

The structure in (26) is submitted to the morphological component. In this component, the terminal nodes receive a morpho-phonological realization. The A-head is realized as an adjective, and AgrA as an agreement marker. This marker is a suffix. It therefore needs to combine with an adjective. Unlike in VO-languages, this is impossible. As shown in (26), the copular V-head separates AgrA from A. This blocks all morphological operations that potentially could combine the suffix with the adjective. First, Local Dislocation and other forms of rebracketing operations are blocked. The reason for this is that they only operate on string adjacent elements. The copula, however, causes the adjective and the ending to be non-adjacent. Lowering is blocked both by the intervening copular head, as well by the fact that one cannot lower out of a specifier. Finally, Head Movement, if one believes it to be morphological, is blocked as a result of intervention by the V-head. This leaves the agreement ending stranded without a suitable adjectival host. This violates morphologically well-formedness. A suffix cannot remain unbound. In order to rescue the derivation, the morphological component carries out a rescue operation: it deletes the agreement ending.[8] This explains the absence of agreement on Dutch and German predicative adjectives.

4.2 Additional support for the analysis

Under this proposal, Dutch and German predicative adjectives occur without agreement, because syntactic movement separates the agreement ending from the adjective. If this is on the right track, one would expect attributive adjectives also to be able to loose their endings via movement. Dutch and German attributive

---

8. One might wonder why the morphological component doesn't insert a support element akin to English *do*-support. There is, however, a crucial difference between the present case and *do*-support. Besides uninterpretable agreement features, *Do* in *do*-support spells out an interpretable tense feature. I would like to suggest that a prerequisite for using a support element is having a stranded interpretable feature. Given that in the present case only uninterpretable agreement features are stranded, this prerequisite is not met.

adjectives normally do not move, due to the ban on Left Branch Extraction. However, there seems to be one exception: German *solch* 'such'. Demske (2005) shows that *solch* behaves like an adjective. First, it follows the indefinite article just like an adjective, (27). Secondly, it displays adjectival-type agreement, taking the same endings and displaying the strong-weak distinction, cf. (27a–b) vs. (27a'–b').

(27) a. ein solch-er   Sturm   (German)
         a   such- STRONG.NOM.SG.MASC storm
     b. ein-em solch-en   Sturm
         a-DAT such-WEAK storm
         "such a storm"
     a'. ein heftig-er   Sturm
         a   violent-STRONG.NOM.SG.MASC storm
     b'. einem heftig-en   Sturm
         a-DAT violent-WEAK storm
         "a violent storm"   (Demske 2005: 56)

Solch can also precede the indefinite article. In that case, it lacks an agreement ending, as in (28b) (Duden 2001).

(28) a. ein solch-es   Buch   (German)
         a   such-AGR book
     b. solch ein Buch
         such a   book
         "such a book"   (Leu 2008: 142)

Leu (2008) suggests that (28b) might be derived via movement of *solch* over the indefinite article. The lack of agreement on *solch* in (28b) can then be explained in the same way as that with German and Dutch predicative adjectives. The movement of *solch* strands the agreement suffix, as in (29).

(29)   [solch [ein t_solch -es Buch]]

The stranded agreement suffix gets deleted in the morphological component, in order to ensure morphological well-formedness.[9] In this way, the otherwise mysterious invariable pre-determiner *solch* receives the same analysis as German and Dutch predicative adjectives. This constitutes additional support for the proposal.

---

9. (Leu 2008) briefly mentions this option, but he does not explore it.

4.4 A challenge for the analysis

The proposed morphosyntactic account seems promising in that it offers a unified account for the absence of agreement on Dutch and German predicative adjectives and German *solch*. It, however, also faces a serious empirical challenge. Like Vikner's (2001, 2005, 2006) syntactic approach, the current morphosyntactic approach links the lack of agreement on Dutch and German predicative adjectives to OV-word order. We therefore expect to find non-agreeing predicative adjectives in any language with an OV-word order that is derived in the same way as in Dutch and German. The Southern Swiss German dialects constitute a real challenge in this respect. These dialects are SOV, like German and Dutch. Yet, predicative adjectives display agreement in these dialects, as in the example from Giffers Swiss German in (30).

(30) [*Wieso ziehst du den Schuh aus?*] *Wül er nass-a isch.*
 why take you the shoe off? because he wet-MASC.SG is
 "Why do you take off the shoe? Because it is wet'
 (Bucheli Berger & Glaser 2004: 195)

The only way to maintain the current morphosyntactic account would be to claim that the SOV word order in these dialects is derived differently, i.e. not via movement of the object over the verb. This, however, seems highly unlikely. There is no evidence to support such a claim. The OV word order in the relevant Swiss German dialects seems to have exactly the same distribution as in standard German. I therefore conclude that the morphosyntactic account presented here is probably not on the right track.[10]

5. Conclusion

The aim of this paper was to determine the component of the grammar that is most likely to be responsible for the variation with respect to agreement on Germanic predicative adjectives: the lexicon, syntax or an interplay between syntax and morphology.

Of these three options, I discarded the syntactic one. If the variation were to have a purely syntactic source, the lack of agreement on Dutch and German predicative adjectives must be due to a failure in the syntactic licensing of agreement. Such an approach is, however, problematic. If syntactic licensing of agreement

---

10. Note that the Southern Swiss German dialects are also problematic for Vikner's (2001, 2005, 2006) account.

fails, one would expect to find non-zero default agreement on Dutch and German predicative adjectives, contrary to fact.

At first sight, ascribing the variation to a particular interplay between the syntactic and morphological components seemed to be more promising. This approach was based on the idea that agreement on predicative adjectives is syntactically licensed in all Germanic languages. I then developed an account in which the absence of agreement in Dutch and German is the result of repairing an ill-formed morphological representation. I proposed that this morphological ill-formedness is the consequence of the movement associated with the German and Dutch OV word order. However, this part of this proposal turned out to be untenable. There are Germanic varieties that are OV and have agreeing predicate adjectives. This forms persuasive evidence against any link between OV word order and the absence of agreement, and therefore against the particular proposal I made. This, however, does not invalidate every possible morphosyntactic account.

Finally, the third option I considered is that the lexicon is responsible for the variation in agreement on Germanic predicative adjectives. This could be implemented by proposing that predicative adjectives carry agreement features in some languages but not in others. The only drawback of such an approach would be that it requires separate entries for predicative and attributive adjectives. That is, however, not a conclusive argument against it.

Given these considerations, I conclude that the variation in agreement on Germanic predicative adjectives should either be attributed to the lexicon or to an interaction between syntax and morphology (although not along the lines sketched above). I will leave it to future research to narrow this further down.

References

Bucheli Berger, Claudia & Glaser, Elvira. 2004. Zur Morphologie des (ko)prädikativen Adjektivs und Partizips II im Alemannischen und Bairischen. In *Morphologie und Syntax deutscher Dialekte und Historische Dialektologie des Deutschen*, Franz Patocka & Peter Wiesinger (eds), 189–226. Vienna: Edition Praesens.

Cabredo Hofherr, Patricia 2010. Adjectives: An introduction. In *Adjectives: Formal Analyses and Semantics* [Linguistik Aktuell/Linguistics Today 153], Patricia Cabredo Hofherr & Ora Matushansky (eds), 1–26. Amsterdam: John Benjamins.

Chomsky, Noam. 2000. Minimalist Inquiries: The framework. In *Step by Step. Essays in Minimalist Theory in Honor of Howard Lasnik*, Roger Martin, David Michaels & Juan Uriagereka (eds), 89–155. Cambridge MA: The MIT Press.

Demske, Ulrike. 2005. Weshalb Demonstrativpromina nicht immer Determinantien sind. In *Deutsche Syntax: Empirie und Theorie*, Franz-Josef d'Avis (ed.), 53–80. Göteborg: Acta Universitatis Gothoburgensis.

Delsing, Lars-Olof. 1993. The Internal Structure of Noun Phrases in Scandinavian Languages: A Comparative Study. Ph.D. dissertation, Lund University.

Duden. 2001. *Die deutsche Rechtschreibung*, Dudenredaktion (eds). Mannheim: Bibliographisches Institut.

Dürscheid, Christa. 2002. "Polemik satt und Wahlkampf pur": das postnominale Adjektiv im Deutschen. *Zeitschrift für Sprachwissenschaft* 21(1): 57–81.

Embick, David & Noyer, Rolf. 2001. Movement operations after syntax. *Linguistic Inquiry* 32(4): 555–595.

Halle, Morris & Marantz, Alec. 1993. Distributed Morphology and the pieces of inflection. In *The View from Building 20. Essays in Linguistics in Honor of Sylvain Bromberger*, Kenneth Hale & Samuel Jay Keyser (eds), 111–176. Cambridge MA: The MIT Press.

Holmberg Anders & Platzack, Christer. 1995. *The Role of Inflection in Scandinavian Syntax*. Oxford: OUP.

Leu, Thomas. 2008. The Internal Syntax of Determiners. Ph.D. dissertation, New York University.

Levinson, Lisa. 2010. Arguments for pseudo-resultative predicates. *Natural Language & Linguistic Theory* 20(1): 135–182.

Preminger, Omer. 2011. Agreement as a Fallible Operation. Ph.D. dissertation, MIT.

Roehrs, Dorian. 2009. *Demonstratives and Definite Articles as Nominal Auxiliaries* [Linguistik Aktuell/Linguistics Today 140]. Amsterdam: John Benjamins.

Siegel, Muffy. 1976. Capturing the Russian adjective. In *Montague Grammar*, Barbara Partee (ed.), 293–309. New York NY: Academic Press.

Schoorlemmer, Erik. 2009. *Agreement, Dominance and Doubling: The Morphosyntax of DP*. Utrecht: LOT.

Vikner, Sten. 2001. Predicative adjective agreement: where German may be "easy". In *Sprachkontakt, Sprachvergleich, Sprachvariation: Festschrift für Gottfried Kolde zum 65. Geburtstag*, Kirsten Adamzik & Helen Christen (eds), 399–414. Tübingen: Max Niemeyer.

Vikner, Sten. 2005. Predicative adjective agreement and Optimality Theory. Paper presented at Copenhagen Business School, June 17, 2005.

Vikner, Sten. 2006. SOV/SVO and predicative adjective agreement. Paper presented at DGfS/GLOW Summer School: Micro- & Macrovariation, August 14–September 2, 2006, University of Stuttgart.

Zwart, Jan-Wouter. 1993. Dutch Syntax a Minimalist Approach. Ph.D. dissertation, University of Groningen.

Zwicky, Arnold M. 1986. German adjective agreement in GPSG. *Linguistics* 24: 957–990.

Author index

A
Abeillé, Anne 182
Abney, Steven Paul 99
Ackema, Peter 174
Adams, James N. 47
Alber, Birgit 12
Alexiadou, Artemis vii, 15, 19, 172–175, 188–189, 206–207, 222–224, 226, 228
Alkire, Ti 4
Anagnostopoulou, Elena 188, 191

B
Bäcklund, Ulf 40
Baker, Mark 1
Bammesberger, Alfred 2
Banniard, Michel 48
Bartsch, Renate 60
Bauche, Henri 64
Bauer, Brigitte L.M 5
Bauer, Laurie 61
Baugh, Albert C. 51–52
Behaghel, Otto 6
Bennis, Hans 165
Bernstein, Judy 12
Berteloot, Amand 115
Biber, Douglas 37, 44–45, 55–57
Biese, Yrjö M. 61
Bischoff, Heinrich 57
Bisschop, Jannetje 118
Blevins, James P. 250
Blom, Alied 114
Blom, Elma vii, 118
Blumenthal, Peter 75
Bolinger, Dwight 10, 39–40, 42, 45, 53, 58–59, 172, 178, 222–223
Booij, Geert 116
Borer, Hagit 212–213
Borsley, Robert D. 172
Borst, Eugen 58
Bouchard, Denis 11
Boucher, Paul vii, 12
Boumans, Louis 120
Braunmüller, Kurt 3, 7, 115–116

Breivik, Leiv Egil 52
Brekke, Magnar 181
Bresnan, Joan 188, 199
Broccias, Cristiano 60
Broekhuis, Hans 117
Brugmann, Karl 2–3
Bucheli Berger, Claudia 276
Buridant, Claude 77–79
Burzio, Luigi 153
Buyssechaert, Joost 36

C
Cable, Thomas 51–52
Cabredo Hofherr, Patricia 10, 269
Campbell, Alistair 49–50
Campbell, George 56
Campos, Hector 206
Carlson, Greg 237
Carstairs-McCarthy, Andrew 4
Cassidy, Frederic G. 61, 65
Chafe, Wallace L. 55, 75
Chircu, Adrian 43
Chomsky, Noam 25, 153–154, 156, 159, 171, 173, 225, 229–230, 250, 266, 271
Cinque, Guglielmo 9–10, 12–18, 20–21, 27, 172, 178, 192–193, 217, 223, 226, 228, 235, 237–238, 242, 249
Coene, Martine 116, 207
Company Company, Concepción 59
Comrie, Bernard 211
Cornilescu, Alexandra 19, 21, 23, 203, 206–207, 209
Corver, Norbert 257
Coussé, Evie vii, 186
Croft, William 62
Crystal, David 43

D
Dal, Georgette 36
Dale, Rick 119
De Schutter, Georges 116

De Smet, Hendrik 141
Dekker, M.C.H. 115
Delbrück, Berthold 2–3
Delsing, Lars-Olof 10, 17, 96, 107, 179, 235, 255, 259, 264
Demonte, Violeta 11
Demske, Ulrike vii, 275
D'hulst, Yves 116
Diepeveen, Janneke 36, 56, 58, 62–64, 128–129
Dietrich, Wolf 48
Doetjes, Jenny 182–183, 188–189, 194, 263
Donner, Morton 37, 51
Downing, Angela 44
Dowty, David R 204, 208
Drieman, G.H.J. 55
Dryer, Matthew S. 7, 10, 137
Duinhoven, Anton M. 131
Dürscheid, Christa 43, 264

E
Eguren, Luis 223
Eisenberg, Peter 43, 63, 250
Embick, David 172, 176–177, 180–181, 189, 199, 205, 212–213, 272
Emonds, Joe 16
Enger, Hans-Olav 4
Erdmann, Peter 44
Espinal, M. Teresa 257
Evans, Nicholas 60

F
Faarlund, Jan Terje 5–6, 8
Fabb, Nigel 178
Fanselow, Gisbert 153–154, 159
Firbas, Jan 75
Fischer, Olga 9, 73–76, 78–81, 87, 90
Fortson, Benjamin W. 5, 48
Fudeman, Kirsten 116

G
Gaatone, David 182–183, 187
Gallmann, Peter 155

Gerth, Bernhard 2
Ghesquière, Lobke 131
Giacalone Ramat, Anna 116
Giegerich, Heinz 36
Giger, Nadio 43
Giusti, Giuliana 21
Glaser, Elvira 276
Godard, Danièle 182
Görlach, Manfred 57
Greenbaum, Sidney 36, 43–44, 63
Greenberg, Joseph 79
Grimm, Jacob 245
Grimshaw, Jane 171
Grondelaers, Stefan 120
Guimier, Claude 36, 51, 60–61

H
Haeseryn, Walter 113, 120
Haider, Hubert VII, 7, 158
Halle, Morris 171, 173–174, 212, 249, 272
Harbert, Wayne 4, 6–7, 246, 250, 258–259
Harley, Heidi 171
Haspelmath, Martin 36, 131
Haumann, Dagmar 74, 79
Hefti, Inga 43
Heim, Irene 227, 230
Heine, Bernd 3, 76, 90, 116
Hengeveld, Kees 2, 35, 39, 60–61
Hennemann, Anja 36
Higginbotham, James 13
Hirt, Hermann 3
Hirvonen, Ilkka 103
Höhn, Georg 162–164
Holmberg, Anders 266
Hopper, Paul J. 6
Huang, Shuan-Fan 36
Huddleston, Rodney 56–57, 117, 124
Hummel, Martin 12, 26, 35, 39–40, 42–44, 46, 51, 53, 55, 57, 60, 63–64
Hunt, Tony 86

I
Ihsane, Tabea 21
Ingham, Richard 86
Iordăchioaia, Gianina 173
Ito, Rika 37, 44, 53–55, 58

J
Jespersen, Otto 7, 40, 50–51, 53, 63, 74, 81–82
Ježek, Elisabetta 61
Joseph, Brian D. 114
Julien, Marit 4, 20–22, 24–25, 27, 229, 233, 245, 249, 255–256

K
Karlsson, Keith E. 47–48
Kayne, Richard 193
Keizer, Evelien 117
Kennedy, Chris 183
Kirchner, Gustav 58
Kloss, Heinz 55
Kluge, Friedrich 3
Kofler, Michaela 57
Koktova, Eva 36
Kornfilt, Jaklin 172
Krahe, Hans 49
Kraschl, Carmen Therese 57
Kratzer, Angelika 172, 176–177, 181, 199, 205, 227, 230
Krifka, Manfred 75
Kroch, Anthony 77
Kröll, Andrea 39
Kruisinga, Etsko 53–54
Kühner, Raphael 2
Kurzová, Helena 2
Kuteva, Tania 3, 76, 90

L
Laberge, Suzanne 58
Laenzlinger, Christopher 15, 21
Lamarche, Jacques 14, 192
Larson, Richard 13, 222, 237
Lasnik, Howard 154
Lass, Roger 116
Laurent, Frère 87
Ledgeway, Adam 5, 8–9, 41
Lehmann, Christian 163
Leiss, Elisabeth 99
Leu, Thomas 246, 259, 275
Levin, Beth 171, 176, 209
Levinson, Lisa 264
Levinson, Stephen C. 60
Lieber, Rochelle 188
Lightfoot, David 74, 79
Liu, Mingya 36, 167
Löfstedt, Bengt 47–48
Lohrmann, Susanne VII, 20–22, 24, 254

Lupyan, Gary 119
Lutzky, Ursula 43

M
Maas, Utz 35, 49, 51, 55–56, 59, 62
Magnússon, Friðrík 233
Mahajan, Anoop 163
Maienborn, Claudia 210
Malchukov, Adrei L. 2
Marantz, Alec 171, 173–174, 212, 249, 272
Marchand, Hans 53
Marchis, Mihaela VII, 19
Markus, Manfred 79
Martineau, France 77
Martínez Vázquez, Montserrat 45
Martínez, José A. 44–45
Marušič, Franc 13
McFadden, Thomas 3, 115
McNally, Louise 183
Meid, Wolfgang 49
Mencken, Henry Louis 58
Menuzzi, Sergio 24
Miller, Gary D. 52–53
Moignet, Gérard 58
Molinier, Christian 60
Morris, Richard 87
Moskowich, Isabel 74, 79–80
Mossé, Fernand 74, 79
Müller, Gereon 250
Musan, Renate 239–240, 242
Mustanoja, Tauno F. 61, 74, 79, 82
Myers-Scotton, Carol 87

N
Naert, Pierre 96
Narrog, Heiko 116
Neeleman, Ad 174
Nevalainen, Terttu 36–37, 51, 53–54, 56, 59
Nicolae, Alexandru 19, 21, 23, 207
Nielsen, Hans Frode 3
Nilsen, Don Lee Fred 53
Nist, John 61
Norde, Muriel 116
Noyer, Rolf 171, 272
Nygaard, Marius 96

Author index

O
Onions, Charles T. 51
Opdahl, Lise 37

P
Parsons, Terence 191, 199, 212
Payne, John 117, 124
Perridon, Harry VII, 3, 6–7, 9–10, 21
Peters, Hans 40, 247
Pfaff, Alexander 7–8, 10, 15, 19, 23, 25, 27, 217, 221, 226–227, 232–233, 235, 239
Pinkster, Harm 36
Pinsker, Hans Ernst 40
Plag, Ingo 62
Plann, Susan 173
Platzack, Christer 154, 266
Plevoets, Koen 114
Polišenská, Daniela 118
Poplack, Shana 87
Posner, Rebecca 77
Potts, Christopher 241
Pounder, Amanda 44, 49, 51, 53, 55–56
Pountain, Christopher J. 55
Preminger, Omer 269
Prins, Anton A. 52
Prokosch, Eduard 2–3
Pulgram, Ernst 53
Pullum, Geoffrey K. 56–57, 61, 117
Punt, Laura 118
Puskas, Genoveva 21
Pustejovsky, James 208

Q
Quak, Aad 116
Quirk, Randolph 4, 44, 63, 115–116, 183, 194

R
Radouant, René 41
Raidt, Edith H. 115–116
Ramaglia, Francesca 61, 223, 228
Ramat, Paulo 36, 43, 47, 58, 61
Ramchand, Gillian C. 209, 211–213, 217
Ranheimsæter, Harald 3, 115
Rapp, Irene 239
Rappaport, Malka 171, 176, 209

Reiner, Erwin 77
Ricca, Davide 36, 43, 58
Riemsdijk, Henk van 253
Ringe, Don 3, 96
Roberts, Craige 256
Robertson, Stuart 61, 65
Roehrs, Dorian 4, 21, 24–25, 27, 221, 226, 233, 235, 245, 249–251, 270
Rögnvaldsson, Eiríklur 96, 235
Rohlfs, Gerhard 41
Rooth, Mats 75
Rosen, Carol 4
Rothmayr, Antonia 212
Rothwell, William 86
Royen, Gerlach 116, 128–129
Ruette, Tom 113, 120, 133
Ruge, Hans 48
Ruigendijk, Esther 118

S
Sadler, Luisa 178, 222
Salazar García, Ventura 35, 39, 62
Sankoff, Gillian 58
Sauerland, Uli 249
Saussure, Ferdinand DE 25
Schachter, Paul 2
Schaden, Gerhard 257
Schäfer Florian 173
Schendl, Herbert 87
Schlenker, Philippe 249
Schoorlemmer, Erik 4, 7, 20, 24, 28, 246, 249, 259, 263, 270
Scott, Gary-John 117
Shih, Chilin 12, 15, 222–223, 228, 238–239
Siegel, Muffy 265
Sigurðsson, Halldór Ármann 220, 233, 235–236
Simke, Rico 4, 25–26, 95, 97, 105–106
Simon, Horst 116
Sleeman, Petra VII, 3, 6, 9–10, 18, 21, 27, 171–173, 178–180, 192–194, 199–200
Smith, John-Charles 116
Sonntag, Eric 61
Speelman, Dirk 122
Sproat, Richard 12, 15, 222–223, 228, 238–239
Stavrou, Melita 206

Stein, Achim 73, 79
Steinmetz, Donald 250
Štekauer, Pavol 36
Steriade, Donca 187
Sternefeld, Wolfgang 250–251
Stiegler, Karin 39–40
Strang, Barbara M.H. 44, 50, 56, 59
Stroh-Wollin, Ulla 4, 20–22, 25–26, 95, 99
Struckmeier, Volker 10, 18, 27, 149–150, 152, 159, 164, 168, 186
Swan, Toril 52, 65

T
Tagliamonte, Sali 37, 44, 53–55, 58
Taylor, Ann 77
Teyssier, Jacques 61
Thim-Mabrey, Christiane 154
Thráinsson, Höskuldur 7, 19, 220–221, 226, 229, 235–236, 259
Törnqvist, Nils 2
Traugott, Elizabeth C. 4, 115
Trotter, David 86
Trudgill, Peter 119
Tucker, Gorden H. 117
Tummers, José 114

U
Uhler, Karl 50, 55
Umbach, Carla 75

V
Valera Hernández, Salvador 46, 60–61, 63
Van Bree, Cor 116
Van de Velde, Freek VII, 2–3, 7, 25–26, 36, 56, 58, 63–64, 115–117, 120, 128–129, 131, 133, 137, 139–141
Van der Horst, Joop 6, 115–116, 141
Van der Lubbe, Henricus F.A. 117
Van Dijk, Johannes A. 125
Van Goethem, Kristel VII, 41–42
Van Leuvensteijn, Arjan 115
van Lier, Eva 35

Van Loon, Jozef 115
Van Marle, Jaap 115
Van Roey, Jacques 117
Vangsnes, Øystein 24, 226, 233, 254
Vendler, Zeno 207
Verkuyl, Henk J. 208
Vikner, Sten 264, 266–271, 276
Vincent, Nigel 116
von Heusinger, Klaus 75

von Prince, Kilu 162–163, 168
Vries, Mark de 19

W
Wasow, Thomas 171, 176, 199, 204
Weerman, Fred 25–26, 114, 118–119, 129, 133
Wessén, Elias 96, 103, 110
Wilder, Chris 15, 223, 228
Williams, Edwin 154

Willis, David 116
Wischer, Ilse 116
Wrenn, Charles L. 4, 115
Wright, Laura 89
Wydler, Karl 77

Z
Ziemann, Hendrikje 118–119
Zwart, Jan-Wouter 272
Zwicky, Arnold M. 270

Subject index

A
accomplishments *see* event types
accusative *see* case
achievements *see* event types
activities *see* event types
adjectival inflection 1, 20, 24–28, 113–117, 120, 123, 128, 131, 137, 141, 217, 235, 252
  inflected adjectives 19, 25, 27, 49, 95, 97, 102, 107, 109–110, 119, 121, 129, 133, 217, 221
  strong adjectives 3–4, 7, 19, 24–27, 49, 95–98, 101–103, 106–108, 110, 115, 217, 221, 228, 235, 238–240, 242, 245–253, 255–256, 258–260
  uninflected adjectives 26–27, 36, 41, 44, 63–64, 113, 117–118, 128, 132–134, 136–141, 270
  weak adjectives 3, 7, 19, 24–27, 49, 95–98, 101–103, 105–111, 115–116, 217, 221, 226, 228–229, 234–235, 238–242, 245–246, 248–260, 270
adjective position
  postnominal 6–7, 9–12, 14–18, 154–155, 159, 171–172, 178–181, 186, 191–193, 195, 199–203, 207, 213, 217, 221–222, 232–235
  prenominal 5, 7, 9, 11–12, 14–15, 17–18, 22, 26–27, 154, 160–161, 166, 171–172, 174, 178–180, 186, 191, 193, 195, 199–205, 213, 217, 222, 232, 234, 255

adjectives *passim*
  anaphoric adjectives 140–141, 231
  appositive adjectives 19, 21, 25, 229, 236, 238, 240–242
  attributive adjectives 1, 3, 5, 7–8, 12, 24, 26, 75, 82, 95, 105, 111, 113–114, 118–119, 124–125, 129–131, 150, 159, 192, 206, 222, 245, 248, 259, 265, 269–271, 274, 277
  bare adjectives 16, 119, 178
  expressive adjectives 19, 240–241
  intensional adjectives 222–223, 225, 227, 235–236
  intersective adjectives 13, 19, 221, 223, 227–228, 242
  material adjectives 120–123, 126–127
  non-restrictive adjectives 217, 232, 255
  parenthetical adjectives 44
  participial adjectives 199–200
  predicative adjectives 1, 7, 10, 19, 24, 28, 63–64, 81, 114, 118, 149, 166, 205–206, 218, 222, 228, 235–236, 238, 240, 242, 256–260, 263–277
  restrictive adjectives 15, 217, 232, 255
adverb form
  Type A 36–49, 51–65
  Type B 36–37, 39, 42–49, 51–60, 62, 64–65
  Type C 39, 43, 45–46, 62
adverbs 12, 26–27, 35–65, 128–129, 155, 159, 171, 173–183, 186, 194–195, 200–201, 203–205, 208, 211

degree adverbs 54, 129, 171, 182, 188–191, 194–195, 200–201, 205
manner adverbs 35–37, 39, 42, 45, 49, 59–60, 178–180
sentential adverbs 36, 39, 42, 44–45, 51–52, 56, 65
agreement 2, 25, 41, 63, 90, 101–102, 108, 124, 134, 149–151, 157–158, 160, 162, 200–201, 245–246, 258–259, 263–272, 274–277
Anglo-French 75, 86, 89
Anglo-Norman 75, 86, 89
appositives 19, 236, 238, 240–241, 245, 247, 259
atelic(ity) 209, 211, 213

C
case 4, 25, 27, 36, 47, 49–50, 95–98, 102, 105–106, 116, 149–153, 155–166, 201, 248, 250, 270
  accusative 47, 49, 153, 247, 250–251
  dative 102, 250
  genitive 2, 124–125, 250–251
    Saxon genitives 247
  instrumental 36, 47, 49, 51, 61
  nominative 47, 49, 96, 106, 156, 247, 250–251
case marking 98, 156
cel 19, 21, 23, 27, 199–214
checked/valued 254
code-switching 76, 86, 87
colonial lag 57, 59
comparative 5, 46, 49, 149
complex verbs 39
contrast(ive) 4, 9, 25, 28, 74–75, 79, 98, 103, 115, 254, 259
conversion 61–63

copula 63, 177–179, 181, 184, 186, 191, 205, 264, 273–274
copular verb *see* copula

D
Danish 22–24, 103, 263
dative *see* case
definiteness 3–4, 20–24, 27, 74, 95–97, 99–103, 106, 108–111, 115, 131, 233, 246, 248, 254, 256–260
   double definiteness 20–24, 100, 102–103, 109–110, 206–209, 214, 233
   definite article 78, 86, 96–97, 99–101, 103, 106–111, 130, 133, 138, 201, 206, 217, 242, 245, 251, 255, 258–259
   definite determiner 27, 78, 90–91, 100–102, 206, 226, 239, 248–249, 253
   definite inflection 100
   definite noun phrases 24–26, 95–97, 99–102, 105–107, 109–111, 226, 228, 235, 240, 253, 259
   definite suffix 257, 259
deflection 4, 113–114, 119
determiner 20, 22, 24, 27, 78, 90–91, 96, 100–102, 108, 116, 119–120, 124, 129–132, 134, 137, 139–141, 173–174, 199–203, 206–210, 212–214, 226, 238–239, 245, 247, 249, 252–253, 255–256, 270, 275
   determiner position 139
direct modification 218–219, 223
discourse markers 36, 42–44, 52
distributed morphology 171, 173–174, 212, 245, 249, 272
Dutch 10–12, 17–18, 25–28, 35–36, 38, 43, 55–56, 62–64, 75, 113–122, 124–125, 129–134, 137–141, 149, 164–165, 172–173, 175, 179, 192, 194, 200, 263–277
   Moroccan Dutch 118, 120–121

E
-*e* 49–51, 98, 125, 152, 159, 245, 247, 251–252, 255
-*en* 120–122, 124–125, 150, 152, 257
English 8–10, 12, 15–18, 24, 26–27, 35–40, 42–46, 49–61, 63–65, 73–74, 76–77, 79–80, 84, 86–87, 89, 95, 113–114, 117, 124, 139, 141, 156, 163, 167, 171–176, 178–179, 183, 192–195, 199–200, 204, 222, 274
   Middle English 9, 26, 40, 49–52, 65, 73–91
   Old English 8–9, 36, 49–50, 52, 65
   Present-Day English 74, 80
episodic reading 201–203, 207, 213
event types
   accomplishments 10, 207–209, 212–214
   activities 183, 208–209, 211, 213
   achievements 209–211, 213–214
   states 199, 207, 210–211
eventive property reading 27, 171–172, 180–181, 186, 189–195

F
Faroese 8, 20, 103, 259, 264
feminine *see* gender
French 4–5, 9, 11–12, 18, 21, 24, 26–27, 38, 40–41, 43, 46–48, 51–53, 57–59, 64–65, 73–77, 79–87, 89–91, 165, 171–172, 175, 181–183, 186–187, 192, 194–195, 224–225, 227–228, 232, 235
   Old French 4–5, 12, 26, 53, 73, 75–81, 84–86, 88–91
French influence 51–52, 74, 76, 80, 82

G
gender 4, 24–25, 27, 89, 95–96, 98, 102, 105, 116, 119, 130, 133–134, 149–151, 155–156, 162, 164–165, 173, 201, 248, 250, 254, 263–264, 270
   common gender 98, 250, 254
   feminine 4, 36, 41, 89, 98, 250–251, 254
   masculine 4, 89, 96, 98, 150–151, 165, 248, 250–251, 254
   neuter 2, 26, 35–36, 46–49, 96, 98, 118–119, 130, 133, 136–137, 139, 165, 250–251, 254
   non-neuter 2, 133, 139
genitive *see* case
German 10–12, 17–18, 24–28, 36, 38, 42–43, 49, 51, 55, 62–64, 96, 104, 113, 116, 118–119, 149–162, 164–166, 175–176, 179, 221, 232, 234, 239, 245–248, 250–256, 258–260, 263–277

H
hypo-determining 99, 101
hyper-determining 99, 101

I
Icelandic 7–8, 10, 19, 22–25, 27, 96, 103, 217, 220–221, 225–226, 231, 235–236, 238, 241–242, 259–260, 264
[identity] 24, 254–259
impoverishment 25, 245, 249–250, 252–253, 259–260
inclusiveness 21, 256
indefiniteness 4, 21, 115, 130, 246, 248
   indefinite article 75, 96, 129–130, 132–133, 245, 275
   indefinite noun phrases 95, 105, 235
indexical semantics 252
indirect modification 218–219, 222–223, 226, 241

Subject index

individual level 3, 13, 172, 203, 207, 223
infinitive 173–175, 182
inflection 1, 3–4, 20, 24–28, 41, 61, 63–64, 97–100, 102, 106–107, 110, 113–117, 119–120, 123, 127–141, 150, 217, 226, 228, 233–235, 239, 242, 246, 250, 252, 254, 259
Italian 4, 12, 14, 16, 24, 37–38, 41–43, 46–48, 57, 155, 192
language acquisition 115, 117–119
language change 76, 141
  contact-induced 76, 90

L
language contact 11–12, 26, 73–76, 79–80, 85–87, 90–91, 117, 119
Latin 2–5, 8–9, 12, 36, 46–48, 51–53, 55, 62, 65, 73, 80, 82, 84, 86–87, 89, 91, 104, 155, 187, 195
-*lice* 49–50, 52, 55
-*ly* 35–36, 38, 42, 45–46, 49–54, 56, 58, 60–61, 65
literacy 26, 37, 42, 45, 48, 52–53, 55–59, 64–65

M
masculine *see* gender
-*mente* 36, 43, 48
mixed categories 171, 173, 186, 189
modifiers *passim*
multilingual 77, 83, 86–87, 89

N
name 89, 221, 229, 252, 255–256
ne- 204
neuter *see* gender
nominalized infinitive 173, 175
nominative *see* case
Norwegian 20–25, 27, 103, 245–248, 250, 253–260, 263–264
number 4, 24–25, 27, 63, 95–96, 105–106, 130, 149–151, 155–156, 162, 164–165, 201, 248, 250, 252, 254, 263–264, 270
plural 48, 73, 81–85, 87, 89, 91, 98, 106, 124–125, 127, 130, 136–137, 139, 141, 208, 247, 250–252, 270
French plural 73, 81–85, 87, 91
singular 26, 49, 96, 98, 106, 119, 130, 136, 150, 165, 208, 247–248, 250

O
Old Norse 6–8, 96
orality 37, 42–43, 52, 55–58, 64

P
participle
  eventive participle 27, 171–172, 177–181, 183, 185–186, 188–195, 199–202, 205, 207, 209, 212–214
  passive participle 27, 176, 186–187, 195
  past participle 41, 152, 171, 199
  present participle 27, 152–153, 158, 199–203, 205–209, 212–213
  resultative participle 27, 170, 172, 176–181, 183, 185–186
  stative participle 172, 176–178, 180–181, 183–186, 188–189, 191, 195, 199, 207, 209–210, 212–213
  verbal participle 27, 180–181, 186, 188, 199–205, 207–213
plural *see* number
Portuguese 38, 41–43, 47–48, 57–58
possessive 8, 96, 100–102, 130–132, 141, 173, 245, 248, 252, 257, 259
possessive pronoun 130–132, 141, 248, 257
postnominal position *see* adjective position
postposition *see* adjective position

prenominal position *see* adjective position
preposed adjectives *see* adjective position
preposed article 101, 103, 108
prescriptive linguistic norm 53
presuppositional 24, 239–240, 254, 258
proleptic inflection 64, 128–129
proper names 3, 228, 245, 247, 255–256, 259
property reading 180–181, 189–191, 193–195, 207
Proto-Germanic 3, 6–7, 95, 115, 120, 137, 141
Proto-Indo-European 2, 3, 115

Q
quantifiers 39, 41–42, 53, 134, 136–138, 140, 189
quasi-definite 100

R
reanalysis 113, 119–127, 132–133, 136, 141
  reanalyzed forms 121, 126
recycling of morphology 116
referentiality 21, 229, 242
relative clause 9–12, 15–19, 27, 100, 109, 149–151, 153, 158, 160–163, 165–166, 193, 200, 206, 222–223, 226, 228, 238, 241
  reduced relative clause 19, 193, 222–223, 226, 228
  restrictive relative clause 19, 100, 228, 236
restrictiveness 223, 225–226, 231, 234–236, 242
rhematic 26, 73–79, 81, 88–89
Romanian 18–19, 21, 23, 27, 37–38, 43, 48, 55, 57, 65, 172, 174–175, 199–202, 204, 206–207, 209, 213

S
schwa 4, 12, 26, 113, 116, 118–121, 123–125, 127–130, 132–133, 135, 137, 141, 251
semantically definite 25, 95–97, 99, 101–103, 105–107, 109–111, 254

sentential adverbs *see* adverbs
singular *see* number
spoken language 37, 40, 48, 64, 86, 220
stage-level reading 3, 13–14, 172, 223, 238
states *see* event types
stative *see* participle
strong adjectives *see* adjectival inflection
suffixed article 217, 221
superlatives 46, 49, 98, 100, 107, 256
   absolute superlative 100
supine 174, 204, 209
Swedish 6–7, 10, 20–21, 23, 25–26, 95–105, 109–111, 206, 255, 258–259, 263–264, 266, 269
Old Swedish 25–26, 95–99, 102–105, 110–111

T
telic(ity) 209, 211, 213–214
thematic 74–75, 77, 200, 221, 224–225, 228, 234–235
topicalization 253, 258
   split topicalizations 253, 258

U
unique(ness) 87, 105–106, 206, 226, 230, 249

V
vocabulary insertion 251
vocative 4, 101, 245, 252, 257, 259

W
weak adjectives *see* adjectival inflection
written language 44, 220–221, 230

Z
zulk 131–134